MEASUREMENT AND EVALUATION IN HEALTH EDUCATION AND HEALTH PROMOTION

MEASUREMENT AND EVALUATION IN HEALTH EDUCATION AND HEALTH PROMOTION

LAWRENCE W. GREEN
University of Texas
Health Science Center at Houston

FRANCES MARCUS LEWIS
University of Washington
Department of Community Health Care Systems

With Chapter 7 on qualitative methods
by Patricia D. Mullen and Donald C. Iverson

Mayfield Publishing Company
Palo Alto, California

Library of Congress Catalog Card Number: 85-061759
International Standard Book Number: 0-87484-481-0

Manufactured in the United States of America
10 9 8 7 6 5 4

Mayfield Publishing Company
1240 Villa Street
Mountain View, Ca. 94041

Sponsoring editor: James Bull

Manuscript editor: Linda Purrington

Managing editor: Pat Herbst

Designer: Cheryl Carrington

Cover designer: Cynthia Bassett

Illustrator: Cindy Clark-Huegel

Production manager: Cathy Willkie

Compositor: Publisher's Typography

Printer and binder: Malloy Lithographing

CREDITS

Portions of Chapter 2 are adapted from L. W. Green, What is quality in patient education and how can we assess it? in W. D. Squyres (Ed.), *Patient Education: An Inquiry into the State of the Art* (New York: Springer, 1980), pp. 137–156. Copyright © 1980 by Springer Publishing Company, Inc., New York. Used by permission. Portions are adapted from L. W. Green and P. Brooks-Bertram, Peer review and quality control in health education, *Health Values* 2(4):191–197, 1978, by permission of Slack Incorporated, Thoroughfare, N.J.

Chapter 7 is by Patricia Dolan Mullen, Dr.P.H., and Donald C. Iverson, Ph.D., and is based on their presentations to the Committee on Health Services Research/Qualitative Methods Study Group and the Public Health Education Section, American Public Health Association Annual Meeting, October 19 and October 21, 1980, Detroit. It is a revised version of their article in *Health Education* 13(3), May–June 1982, adapted with permission of the authors and of the publisher, the Association for the Advancement of Health Education. The authors gratefully acknowledge the helpful comments and suggestions of Lawrence W. Green, Frances Marcus Lewis, Jane G. Zapka, and Richard A. McCuan.

Portions of Chapter 9 are adapted from L. W. Green, Research methods translatable to the practice setting: From rigor to reality and back, in S. J. Cohen (Ed.), *New Directions in Patient Compliance* (Lexington, Mass.: Lexington Books, D. C. Heath and Company, 1979), pp. 141–151, with permission of the publisher; copyright 1979 by D. C. Heath and Company. Portions are adapted from L. W.

(*continued after the Index*)

DEDICATION

Judith, Beth, and Jennifer
John, Steven, David, and Deloris

Contents

Preface

Our title, *Measurement and Evaluation in Health Education and Health Promotion,* reflects two subjects and two objects. The word *measurement* refers to the procedures applied systematically in the objective quantification of needs, processes, and outcomes. It applies both to the diagnostic phases and to the evaluation phases of professional practice and programs. The word *evaluation* refers to the additional procedures required to draw valid conclusions about the value or effects of practices or programs. The term *health education* describes any combination of learning experiences designed to predispose, enable, and reinforce voluntary adaptations of behavior conducive to well-being. *Health promotion* refers to any combination of health education and related organizational, economic, and environmental supports for behavior conducive to well-being.

INTENDED AUDIENCE

The impulse for this book was the conviction that professional practice in health education and health promotion will improve if it is measured and evaluated. Some aspects of professional practice can be measured and evaluated independently by managers, auditors, or research scientists. The evaluation of health education, however, usually requires the informed participation and cooperation—if not the initiative—of the practitioners whose programs or activities are to be judged. All the health professions are engaged in health education and, together with other professionals, contribute to health promotion. This book, then, is as much for practitioners and students in health and related professions as for health education specialists, administrators, and behavioral scientists.

You may need more or less than this book offers, depending on the scope of your responsibilities and on how much accountability your constituents, peers, and supervisors expect. In some organizations, health education specialists or program evaluation specialists who can share their expertise with other professionals will be available. We have written this book with the hope that access to such educational consultation will become the norm rather than the exception, but we expect for the near future that most health professionals will need to take the initiative in measuring the educational needs of their patients, clients, or communities, and in evaluating their own educational efforts. This book, therefore, seeks a middle ground between the depths of understanding expected of the health education specialist and the essential skills that all health professionals require to assess their health education and health promotion practices and programs.

Clinicians obviously need to know more about the measurement of health than this book offers. Educational specialists will need additional preparation in psychometrics, statistics, and behavioral research methods. The student in health education or related health fields will find that this book integrates theoretical issues in health education with methodological and practical know-how. Both advanced undergraduate students and graduate students in the health fields will derive rigor as well as practicality from the text. For all groups, this book carries a message and an orientation not found in most other textbooks on measurement and evaluation. This message—the rock supporting our middle ground—is that no amount of theoretical sophistication and statistical wizardry can fully compensate for a misunderstanding of the purposes, processes, and circumstances of professional practice in health education or health promotion. Planners and evaluators need the experience of practitioners. For this reason we are committed more to the concept of the evaluating practitioner than to the practice of intruding evaluators.

This book introduces the concepts and methods of measurement and evaluation in a way that should have particular meaning to health professionals and students whose primary business is not research. Our experience is that the first exposure of most professionals to statistical and other research concepts has been abstract and numerical, leaving them unconvinced of the utility and practical significance of these concepts and methods in their work. By presenting the meaning and application of these concepts in the health education and health promotion context, we hope that the generalist will find immediate applications in everyday practice, that the specialist will be encouraged to go beyond these pages to more advanced measurement and evaluation, and that the student will aspire to be an "experimenting practitioner."

SCOPE AND OBJECTIVES

We could presume to address measurement, evaluation, health education, and health promotion in this book only by acknowledging that about each of them there is much to be said that we do not address. Whole textbooks are now available on each topic. The need we have sought to fill is for an introduction to the highly specialized region in which these four topics overlap. The scope of this book is therefore limited to the aspects of measurement and evaluation that pertain to health education and health promotion. Within the broader realm of health promotion, we have concentrated on the educational component. Within the broader range of philosophical, theoretical, political, and practical concerns in health education, we have limited our focus to concerns that are subject to measurement and evaluation. Our first objective for this book, therefore, is to increase the usability and the use of measurement and evaluation by the people who practice health education, and to gain thereby the most immediate benefits for recipients of their programs through innovation and experimentation.

Beyond the immediate application of measurement and evaluation by health practitioners, there is the longer-range need to build the cumulative scientific base from which the theories and policies that guide the practice of health education and the training of health professionals are derived and tested. Large-scale programs and policies cannot afford a trial-and-error approach; they must be based on the cumulative experience of past successes and must avoid repeating past failures. To provide for these expanded uses of evaluation, we also advocate a more systematic, rigorous, documented, and disseminated form of evaluation than can be expected from the everyday practice of health education. A second objective of this book is to bridge the numerous levels of measurement and evaluation required and to encourage the experimenting practitioner to aspire—with appropriate restraint—to these broader goals of measurement and evaluation. We do so by suggesting steps or hierarchies of increasing rigor while maintaining a clear focus on the limitations, demands, and priorities of service delivery settings.

ORGANIZATION OF THE TEXT

We have cast the twelve chapters in four parts. In Part One we attempt to place measurement and evaluation in a practical as well as a scientific perspective for health education and health promotion. We seek to answer the question "What needs to be measured or evaluated?" In Chapter 1 we review the perception versus the reality of health education as an inherently unscientific, undisciplined field. Developments of the past two decades give hope that this perception is fading and that practitioners themselves are using and contributing to the growing scientific base of the field. In Chapter 2 we analyze the roles of diagnostician and evaluator developed in Chapter 1, and we extend the concept of the "diagnosing and experimenting practitioner" to measurements of quality and their application in formative evaluation (also called *process evaluation*).

In Part Two we tackle the issues of measurement at both conceptual and operational levels. Here we attempt to answer the question "How is the measurement to be done?" Chapter 3 begins with a review of measurement theory. Here we suggest ways of thinking about the connections between theoretical concepts and operational measures or test items, and ways to move back and forth, developing measures from theory and testing or interpreting theory from measurement results. In Chapter 4 we take measurement theory a step further with a display of the alternative ways the reliability of measurements can be estimated, and in Chapter 5, we do the same with the validity of measurements. In Chapter 6 we apply the concepts and methods reviewed in the three preceding chapters to the development of selection of measurement instruments for a diagnostic or evaluation study.

In Part Three we focus on how measurement should be applied in evaluation. Here we answer the question "How can the measurements and the things not measured be controlled?" Even with precise, quantitative measurement, the truth about health education needs, practices, or programs may not be known. Indeed, misplaced precision may be misleading. Mullen and Iverson make this point most forcefully in Chapter 7, on qualitative methods. This chapter identifies the ways in which quantitative methods need to be supplemented and extended in order to give more than numerical meaning to educational diagnosis and evaluation. We thank Patricia Mullen and Donald Iverson for adapting their excellent paper on qualitative methods for inclusion here. We are sure we could not improve on their paper in addressing the topic of qualitative methods in health education measurement and evaluation.

In Chapters 8 and 9 we propose alternative ways to organize quantitative and qualitative methods into evaluation designs that assure control of extraneous factors while assuring that health education practices or programs get a fair test. In Chapter 8 we give examples of the specific threats to validity in alternative designs applied to health education. Chapter 9 proposes a series of hierarchies that can be employed to set priorities among the alternative design choices, depending on the purpose and primary audience of the evaluation.

Chapter 10 suggests practical considerations and efficient methods for the sampling of subjects, patients, students, clients, groups, or communities for the measurement and evaluation of health education or health promotion methods or programs. This topic, often treated at the beginning of research textbooks or not at all in some evaluation texts, has been placed between design and analysis in this book. The discussion follows closely on the design chapters because sampling usually must be understood and applied in the context of a specific measurement and design strategy. Chapter 10 leads into a section on analysis because sampling yields the data to be analyzed.

Part Four concludes the book with two chapters on the analysis and interpretation of diagnostic measurements and evaluation data. Here we answer the question "How are the measurements analyzed and interpreted?" In Chapter 11 we present the theoretical and practical considerations peculiar to health education and health promotion data. In Chapter 12 we illustrate a step-by-step procedure for asking and answering each of the questions that can be answered in a logical sequence from evaluative data.

A "postscript" attempts to put all the foregoing in the perspective of understanding people's needs and our ability to help them meet those needs. In the final analysis our success depends on our ability to transfer these measurement and evaluation skills from scientists to practitioners, and from practitioners to the public.

Four appendixes offer examples of applications of the principles and methods described in the text. Appendix A presents a list of criteria for formal evaluation. Appendix B provides a case study of the measurement problems in a cross-cultural evaluation. Appendix C is a questionnaire based on a national survey of health knowledge, attitudes, and practices. In Appendix D, we have listed representative examples of the published evaluation literature. We hope these examples of alternative designs and measurements applied to various types of health education and health promotion programs will serve users as a bridge between the necessarily superficial and sometimes hypothetical examples given in the text and the case studies that original works themselves should supply.

A glossary of terms used in the text and not likely to be found in a standard English dictionary, at least not in the specific ways they are used here, is compiled at the end of the book. Many of the terms have yet to stand the test of comprehension and wider adoption by professors, students, and practitioners in health education and health promotion. Correspondence and advice from readers will be welcomed on this, as on any other aspect of the book.

ACKNOWLEDGMENTS

We are indebted for support at various stages to Johns Hopkins University, where we first collaborated; the National Heart, Lung and Blood Institute for postdoctoral research training grant no. T32-H10710-02 and high blood pressure education research grant no. R25-HL-17016-03, which supported our early work together; and to our teachers, students, and colleagues at Berkeley, Stanford, Hopkins, Harvard, Texas, and Washington, who inspired and encouraged this undertaking and in some instances suffered through early versions of the text and provided valuable comments. In particular, we want to thank Marshall W. Kreuter, Judith M. Ottoson, Kay B. Partridge, David M. Levine, Donald Iverson, Lloyd J. Kolbe, Patricia D. Mullen, Alfred McAlister, Chris Lovato, Richard McCuan, Robert L. Hanson, Patricia Hogan, and Janie Gordon; we also exonerate them from responsibility for the final manuscript (except for Mullen and Iverson's Chapter 7). Lansing Hays at Mayfield Publishing Company provided the encouragement that initiated this project, and he patiently allowed *Health Education Planning* to be completed first.

The text benefited from the professional assessments of the following academic reviewers: John P. Allegrante, Teachers College, Columbia University; Charles R. Baffi, Virginia Polytechnic Institute and State University; Gary D. Gilmore, University of Wisconsin; Donald C. Iverson, Mercy Medical Center, Denver, Colorado; and Ian Newman, University of Nebraska, Lincoln. The text also benefited from the editorial assessments of Lorraine Anderson and from the copyediting of Linda Purrington. Beverly Wright, Katie McGrath, Marty Lazzari, and Jennifer Green made possible the production of the manuscript.

Lawrence W. Green

Frances Marcus Lewis

MEASUREMENT AND EVALUATION IN HEALTH EDUCATION AND HEALTH PROMOTION

PART ONE

MEASUREMENT AND EVALUATION IN THE DEVELOPMENT OF PRACTICE

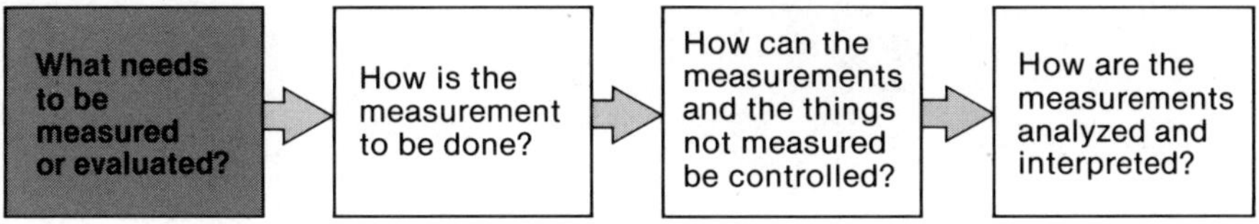

In these first two chapters, we set the stage and cast you, the main character, in several roles. The stage is set in Act One, Scene 1, with a flashback to 1945 when health education was just getting established. We review the progress made in measurement and evaluation through the four decades since then. We warn you of the traps and pitfalls you will need to avoid in the various roles you will play in measurement and evaluation—diagnostician, policy analyst, planner, manager, evaluator. In some roles, we suggest you will do well to maintain the attitude of a sympathetic critic. In all roles, we suggest that you establish yourself ideologically and operationally as a "diagnosing and experimenting practitioner." This posture will lend quality and credibility both to your measurement and evaluation and to your practice of health education and health promotion. It will also contribute to the development of quality practice by others.

Chapter 1

THE PLACE OF MEASUREMENT AND EVALUATION IN HEALTH EDUCATION PRACTICE

A noted public health physician and educator observed the beginnings of health education practice during World War II with some caution:

> A new "profession," known as "health educators," is arising. Too often these workers are without the restraint that comes from scientific training and are not well grounded in factual material relating to health and disease. They do, however, possess a stimulating enthusiasm and, in varying degrees, competence in catching the public interest. (Mustard, 1945, p. 176)

Mustard's early characterization of the developing health education field was not flattering, but he did acknowledge two difficulties in a scientific approach to health education: "Health education is an undertaking that produces its results slowly and these results are difficult to measure" (p. 175). These two problems of evaluation and measurement plague health education and health promotion even more today. With the shift in current emphasis to chronic and degenerative diseases (from the emphasis in 1945 on infectious and communicable diseases), current results require even more waiting and more sensitive measurement. Can we in fact claim to have advanced the state of measurement and evaluation in health education since 1945?

In this chapter we examine (1) the evolving needs for measurement and evaluation in health education and health promotion; (2) the capacity of health education specialists and various other health workers, educators, and behavioral or biomedical scientists to use measurement and evaluation in their practice of health education and health promotion that responds to these needs; and (3) the problems and potentials in merging the roles of evaluator and practitioner.

We are mindful, throughout, of Aristotle's warning to his Athenian students:

> Therefore in discussing subjects, and arguing from evidence, conditioned in this way, we must be satisfied with the broad outline of truth . . . for it is a mark of the trained mind never to expect more precision in the treatment of any subject than the nature of that subject permits. (Aristotle, *The Nicomachean Ethics,* Book One, pp. 63–67)

Undaunted, however, we recall that Aristotle also thought women were inherently "incapable of independence of character or position" (Durant, 1926). Like women, health education has come a long way.

THE CONTINUING NEEDS FOR MEASUREMENT AND EVALUATION IN HEALTH EDUCATION

In a background study for a World Health Organization (WHO) meeting in 1968, training institutions and ministries of health around the world were surveyed to determine the current status of measurement and evaluation efforts in health education (Roberts & Green, 1968). The survey showed the following results. First, most evaluation at that time was being carried out by health educators, nurses, and behavioral scientists trained in the United States. Indeed, the majority of formal demonstration and evaluation projects in health education were being conducted in North America. Those in Europe and Oceania were being conducted by Europeans, Australians, and New Zealanders, but most of those in developing countries were being conducted by U.S. investigators in collaboration with U.S.-trained nationals. Second, most of the measurement in developing countries was descriptive, rather than experimental, using survey methods, especially surveys of knowledge, attitudes, and practices (KAP) based on verbal reports from interviews with married people about family planning. Third, there had been little experimental evaluation except in a few isolated projects (e.g., Roberts, Mico, & Clark, 1963) in which the object of evaluation was more likely to be a technique than a program. Young's (1967a, 1967b, 1973) reviews of the 1960s literature, done for WHO, yielded similar findings. See Appendix B for examples of the state of the art in measurement and evaluation in the 1960s.

By the early 1970s, a turning point was developing, manifest in the nature of the measurement and evaluation being conducted in health education, as illustrated in Appendix D. It was also reflected in the redesign of training programs for health education specialists to give them greater skill in the use if not the conduct of research. The supply of behavioral scientists with greater interest and skill in evaluation of human service programs in collaboration with practitioners also was increasing (Mico & Ross, 1975; Steuart, 1969; World Health Organization, 1969a, 1969b).

The shift in emphasis from communicable diseases to chronic diseases marked a corresponding swing from nonexperimental evaluation of communication programs in immunization campaigns and family-planning programs in the late 1960s, to experimental and quasi-experimental evaluations of health education in clinical settings. These clinical settings offered opportunities for greater experimental control and randomized assignment of patients to experimental and control groups (Green & Figa-Talamanca, 1974). This shift brought many health education practices under much closer scrutiny than they had thus far experienced. It also provided health education with opportunities to gain scientific credibility with (1) the medical profession, which had always regarded health education as a humanistic but nonscientific enterprise, and with (2) health administrators, whose attitudes toward health education had not changed much since Mustard's statement in 1945.

The changes in the early 1970s heralded a growing awareness that societal resources were increasingly being allocated to human service programs, creating a concomitant demand for accountability to consumers and taxpayers. These shifts led to increasing requirements for evaluation in cost-benefit, cost-containment, and cost-effectiveness terms (Aujoulet, 1973; Green, 1974).

We can extend these developments through the 1980s if we improve and build on the best research, training, and practice in health education and health promotion, to strengthen the weak links, fill the gaps, and extend the centers of excellence.

Strengthening the Weak Links

In Mustard's time, health education had little credibility and even less fiscal support. The goals and methods of health education were diffuse and of questionable quality, resulting in modest or undetectable impact. When you cannot demonstrate the benefits of your programs, you cannot expect continuous or adequate support. Uneven fiscal support has perpetuated a cycle of poverty for health education, reflected on the left side of Figure 1-1. Only recently has that cycle been broken, particularly by evaluation, as seen on the right in Figure 1-1.

Like any other enterprise, when health education could not depend on a single source of revenue, it had to diversify its portfolio. Health education has had brief periods of greater support from one categorical health concern or another, such as immunization programs in the early 1960s, family planning and drug abuse in the late 1960s, hypertension in the early 1970s, alcohol and smoking in the late 1970s. But with these constantly

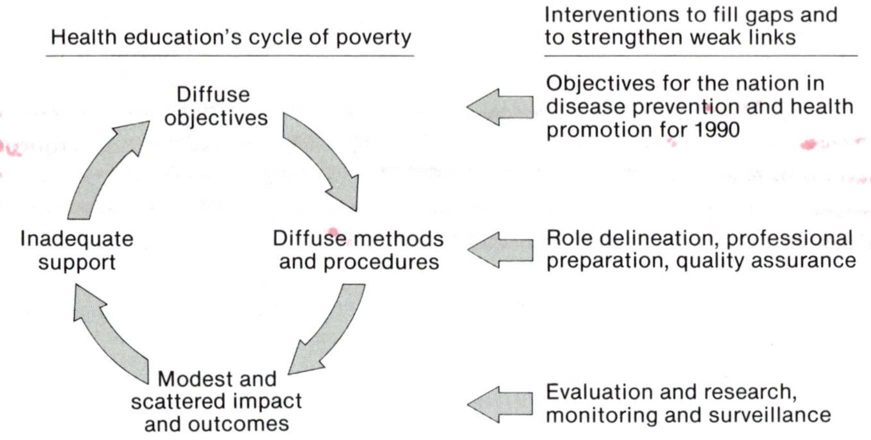

Figure 1-1 *The cycle of poverty for health education. Here the cycle is defined to emphasize the points of intervention addressed by current federal policy.* Source: *Adapted from Kreuter & Green (1978); Green, Kreuter, Deeds, & Partridge (1980), p. 153; Green (1981), p. 64.*

shifting priorities, long-term objectives were not pursued systematically and diligently; objectives remained diffuse. Professional training programs could not keep up with the changing job market and expectations for proficiency in the field. Hence the quality of practice suffered. Employers could not count on health educators trained yesterday to understand today's priorities. *Promoting Health, Preventing Disease: Objectives for the Nation* (U.S. Department of Health and Human Services, 1980) has strengthened the link between objectives and methods; role delineation, improved training, and quality assurance have strengthened the delivery of programs; and evaluation is providing the evidence of impact and outcomes required to generate increased support.

Strengthening the weak links requires a simultaneous shift in training and practice such that measurement and evaluation in health education benefit both from academic discipline and from practical experience. The need for such balance between rigor and reality is evident from the reviews of earlier research. Studies by practitioners, on one side, had little credibility because of weaknesses in the validity of their measurements and study designs. Studies by behavioral scientists, on the other side, had little credibility or influence with practitioners, administrators, and policymakers because their rigorous measurements and designs were limited in generalizability (Green, 1977, 1978; Hochbaum, 1960; Rosenstock, 1960).

Filling the Gaps

Three gaps in health education measurement and evaluation need filling. First, we need practitioners who are better trained in applying and interpreting measurements and evaluations. Second, we need a larger cadre of research specialists who can balance competence and experience in behavioral research methods and health education practice. Third, we need more effective translation of research and evaluation results into theory and policy to guide future training and practice in health education. All three needs must be addressed if the results of improved research and theory are to yield the benefits society expects from health education and health promotion.

Most expert committees and commissions on health education research or training have recommended more scientific training in one form or another. The Health Education Steering Committee of the Association of Schools of Public Health (ASPH), for example, included as one of eleven recommendations in 1965,

> that schools of public health give more attention and support to research in health education through adjustment in teaching and administrative loads of faculty, through the inclusion of the elements of scientific investigation in the master's program, and through the development of advanced graduate level programs for the preparation of research workers. (Boatman, Levin, Roberts, & Rugen, 1966, p. 25)

The Society for Public Health Education adopted guidelines on the functions and professional preparation of health education specialists, prepared in collaboration with the Professional Examination Service in 1977, noting that

> There are increasing opportunities for professional health educators to perform at more advanced levels of administration, supervision, consultation, organizational development, policy development, evaluative research, and cost-benefit analysis.... This creates increasing pressure to upgrade the curricula for the preparation of the master's degree person in order to provide these more advanced functions and therefore creates pressure to upgrade the preparation of the baccalaureate for entry-level health education practice. (Society for Public Health Education, Ad Hoc Task Force, 1977, p. 81)

The Guidelines for Baccalaureate Programs in Community Health Education, published simultaneously, included these in the list of competencies under professional preparation:

> Knowledge of and skill in the use of the problem-solving approach and scientific method; knowledge and skill in basic data collection

methods; knowledge and skill in using some commonly applied statistical methods; the nature of statistics and how to conduct small-scale studies. (Society for Public Health Education, Committee on Professional Preparation and Practice, 1977, p. 96)

Extending the Centers of Excellence

The guidelines of the ASPH Health Education Steering Committee and the SOPHE and WHO (1962, 1969a) recommendations for training of health workers for health education leave only one gap in the existing structure of research and practice. The group unlikely to be touched by most of these developments in training will be the current practitioners who received their professional training before the recommended curriculum changes were implemented in professional schools or who entered the practice of health education through channels of professional preparation that escaped these curriculum reforms. A program of extended publications, software, and continuing education for these practitioners must be included in a comprehensive approach to strengthening the scientific base of health education practice.

An example of reaching these practitioners was tested at various universities and by the National Center for Health Education in cooperation with the American Cancer Society in California. Practitioners were asked to identify an educational program, project, or activity that they expect to plan or evaluate in their unit. They were then brought together in workshops to develop their diagnostic measurement or evaluation designs in consultation with experts in measurement and evaluation in health education. This approach appears to have resulted in considerable professional growth and improvement in local health education practices even though the products were sometimes site-specific.

ASSUMING THE ROLE OF DIAGNOSTICIAN OR EVALUATOR

To assume that you can easily and quickly step into the role of educational diagnostician or evaluator is to ignore large areas of social and administrative reality. As a practitioner who seeks new data on the needs of a population to be served, you will arouse the suspicions of those who wish to maintain the status quo. As a planner or administrator attempting to play a dual practitioner-evaluator role, you will be suspected of conflict of interest or limited objectivity. If called in as an outside educational needs assessment expert or evaluator-consultant, you will need to know the questions that must be asked before the educational diagnosis or evaluation can begin. Whether you play the role of "inside" or "outside" evaluator, you must wrestle with your ability to (1) adopt a sympathetic critic stance, (2) answer questions about evaluator accountability, and (3) respond appropriately to the program's and sponsor's needs for information and feedback, keeping in mind the political arena in which priorities get set and programs get evaluated.

In the remainder of this chapter, we discuss these three skills you need to develop before you assume the role of policy analyst, diagnostician, or program evaluator. Passive or thoughtless adoption of those roles can lead to disappointments for you, for the program administrators, and for the program participants or constituents.

THE SYMPATHETIC CRITIC ROLE

Measurement and evaluation imply that objective data, in place of speculation and subjective judgments, are to be collected and analyzed at one or more of the six steps shown in Figure 1-2. You need to strike the professional posture of a sympathetic critic—sympathetic, yes, but unavoidably critical. The role requires that you judge the need for or value of a program, method, or activity—not merely verify a prejudgment. It is always possible that the program is not worth starting or continuing. You

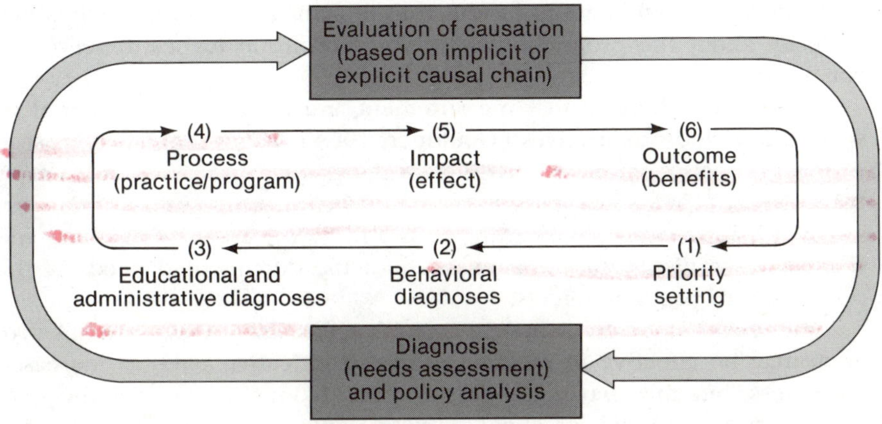

Figure 1-2 *The planning and evaluation cycle. Evaluation proceeds from left to right (from 4 to 6), but policy analysis proceeds from right to left (from 1 to 3) and is based on previous evaluation and theory and new diagnostic measures on the population in need.*

must keep in mind this possibility, in addition to the possibility that the program is or will be effective. If you do not seriously entertain both alternatives, you cannot pretend to be objective. Of course, professionals with any feeling or concern for the problem, the clients, the sponsor, or the staff of the agency probably can never be entirely disinterested and objective. Therefore the sympathetic critic role is a conscious, purposeful, self-disciplined role, not an inherent characteristic of the practitioner or evaluator.

Asking yourself if you can be a sympathetic critic calls for careful reflection. It also means seriously entertaining the possibility that "I cannot assume the diagnostician, policy analyst, or evaluator role in this situation." Recognizing the limitations as well as the potential benefits of health education and health promotion will help you serve as a sympathetic critic.

Acknowledging the Potential Effectiveness and Benefits of Intervention

Regarding a proposed program, can you believe that educational intervention can affect behavioral development or change and that these can result in improving or maintaining health? From your perspective, the program must have a chance of "winning," of achieving an impact or targeted outcome. It is not enough to orient cautiously toward the problem or the program. If in your mind the possibility of impact is nonexistent, you will have trouble adopting the role of sympathetic critic. A positive curiosity about the program's potential contribution to health serves all concerned.

People who believe that measurement and evaluation are neutral or value free delude themselves (Gouldner, 1964). Values enter every stage of the evaluation process: when specifying the problems and setting priorities and program goals; when choosing measurements of the targeted variables; when collecting, analyzing, and interpreting data; and when writing dissemination reports about the documented needs of the population or program effects.

Potential effectiveness and potential benefits are not the same. A program may be effective in meeting a limited objective, such as increased awareness, but may have no value in that it does not benefit the consumer, patient, student, or client, as with reduced illness or absenteeism. Conversely, the program may be ineffective in relation to some immediate objective but beneficial for reasons unanticipated by the planners, sponsors, or administrators of the program. It is possible to achieve a short-term or immediate effect that is irrelevant or trivial or that does not last long enough to yield the ultimate benefit intended. For example, a program may be highly effective in improving the health-related attitudes of its target audience, but these attitudes may not be translated into health practices that would actually improve or protect health. You need to maintain a balanced and comprehensive view of the needs, immediate effects, and ultimate benefits intended for a program.

Sustaining Doubts in the Midst of Enthusiasm

Taking the stand of sympathetic critic periodically requires renewed commitment. It is a position frequently challenged or eroded in the process of conducting the program or maintaining cordial cooperation with staff and clients. This is why physicians and lawyers are admonished not to treat or defend themselves or their own families. Program goals, objectives, and priorities must be understood sympathetically but need to be examined critically and frequently. You must be able to question their clarity, logical interrelatedness or contradictions, timeliness, consistency with the needs and outcomes expected by consumers or sponsors, and appropriate articulation with previous research and evaluation. An uncritical acceptance of program goals encourages short-term enthusiasm but undermines the ultimate result. Sound goals and carefully formulated objectives and priorities can stand the test of criticism; less sound ones benefit by repeated review, assessment of needs, and successive refinements before you collect final measurements of outcomes.

Accepting the evaluator role obliges you also to consider alternative explanations for results. Documenting the level of the program's impact does not end with the calculation of percentage change or mean score differences between groups. Many layers of evidence must be explored before you can justify firm policy statements on the basis of the documented findings (Green & Lewis, 1981). During data analysis, you need to "rule out" the alternative causes of observed needs or outcomes. For example, the outcome variables may show a meaningful and statistically significant gain on postprogram testing. You will need to ask repeatedly, "What variables or factors, other than the program, may have caused these results?" Positive results are the most difficult to view critically, because of the enthusiasm with which they are received. If you believe at the beginning, and in the absence of a perfect evaluation, that *only* this program could cause the obtained results, you will have failed as sympathetic critic.

If the content of the health education or health promotion program contradicts your own belief system, you will find it difficult to evaluate effectively. For example, if you view the program as too unconventional or too conventional, that attitude may turn your evaluation into a self-fulfilling prophecy. You may stack the cards unfairly, though unconsciously, against a positive result. For example, suppose that a medical staff or a clinic is trying to apply principles of operant conditioning in reinforcing patients' adherence to their antihypertensive regimens. Your role as evaluator would be to help plan and implement measurement procedures to document the impact of such a reinforcement program on hypertensive clinic patients. If a reinforcement (behavior modification) paradigm is dissonant with your value system, you will have difficulty sympathizing. In choosing among alternative designs, sampling procedures, data collection methods, and statistical tests, you may favor choices that are most likely to confirm your own covert hypotheses. Such problems are most likely to occur in programs in which the strategies for behavior or attitude change appear questionable, and in programs where consumer participation rights are short-circuited or involvement is not truly voluntary. A negative evaluator bias may also enter when you find unacceptable a major message of the educational component of the program or the sponsor. Such conflict may arise, for example, in educational programs regarding sexuality, birth control, alcohol and other drugs, nutrition, or parenting skills. And that conflict may be greater if the programs are sponsored by a reactionary (or a radical) group, or by an alcoholic beverage manufacturer's association, or the dairy industry, and so forth.

Sometimes you may not accept the potential efficacy of a program because the theoretical underpinnings of the framework are tenuous. The logic linking the program components with the program objectives may be weak, or the logic linking the program components with the client outcomes may be questionable. For example, a program may seek to affect a professional audience's attitudes toward cancer. The actual program, however, is only a two-hour-long slide and tape show on the cell physiology of cancer and a review of the national survey of attitudes toward cancer. Some evaluators would feel this proposed program suffers from weak links between program components and objectives. In this same example, let us say the program staff decide to measure the professional clients' cancer attitudes by measuring their anxiety scores and their fear-of-death scores on two standardized tests. To the extent that the evaluator questions that measures of anxiety and death-fear are appropriate indicators of cancer attitudes in professionals, the evaluator is successfully wrestling with the logic linking client outcome with program components. At best the study is a gamble; at worst it wastes the participants' time and energy and costs the program in reputation.

You may have difficulty accepting the strategies of the program because of underlying assumptions about what motivates the behavior of the target population. The assumptions may rest on a reductionist model, reducing human behavior to psychological or physiological stimuli and primitive response. The theoretical model may be based on theories or ideologies that have few roots in scientific research. The assumptions may cast humanity into a passive or irrational role, or they may characterize human motives as basically evil or basically benevolent. Whatever the assumptions, you will agree or disagree with them depending on your personal philosophy, and you may bias your evaluation accordingly.

You will need to ask, "Who delivers the health education in the field? Is this field delivery monitored and sufficiently supported by program administration? Is the entry or exit of field personnel controlled by the evaluator or by program staff or administration? To what extent, and in what forms, are contacts made and instructional or inservice support extended to field personnel? Are field personnel able to initiate contact with the evaluator or program administration, and on what issues?" Answers to these questions relate to the structural arrangements surrounding field implementation of the program. These areas of reflection are critical for the evaluator. To function as a sympathetic critic, the evaluator must be able to endorse the general approach as well as to reflect critically on the field arrangements for program implementation. Can you accept the qualifications of such people to deliver such interventions? A belief in the credential level of field personnel is important; discounting their educational preparation may cause, for example, a negative interpretation of their performance when the program fails to achieve its desired level of effect. You need to have some confidence in the agents of the intervention, or else you should offer to disqualify yourself as the evaluator.

BEING ACCOUNTABLE: TO WHOM AND FOR WHAT?

To whom are you accountable, and for what? This broadly phrased question narrows to two components in measurement and evaluation: (1) those individuals or groups to whom you must report and (2) the methods and procedures by which your reporting must take place.

To what governing council, funding agency, administrative body, or policy board are you accountable? By addressing this question early in the measurement or evaluation effort, you can minimize frustration and help fill the program's and the sponsor's needs for feedback. If employed by the organization or institution whose program, product, or service is being evaluated, you must confront questions of double jeopardy, conflict of interest, and credibility of the report. Regardless of "inside" or "outside" evaluation, by whom will the reports be seen and to whom will they be officially disseminated? Determine which persons may alter or otherwise interpret your analysis and interpretations. If your name will be appended to the report, you should have the right of final approval of the report's contents.

To what consumer of measurement or evaluation results are you accountable? Accountability takes several forms: accountability for purposes of professional, administrative, or policy decision; for information disclosure and channeling; and for budgetary monitoring. The following list shows potential audiences or clients for accountability:

- Board or legislative body with responsibilities for policy decisions
- Informal power groups
- Offices with information needs
- Scientific and professional community
- General public, taxpayers, consumers, and the press
- Administrator monitoring program's or evaluator's budget
- Program developers
- Sponsors of grant or contract support for the program or for the evaluation

Implied in all forms of accountability is the expectation of periodic disclosure to all interested parties (Lewis & Batey, 1982; Batey & Lewis, 1982).

Accountability for policy decisions to be made on the basis of your diagnostic studies or program evaluations may be to a single individual or to a governing council, board, legislature, or directorate. Such governing bodies make binding decisions about the program's initiation, budget, demise, or continuation. Often a board or council exists "above" the governing body, to which it must defer or "clear" its own decisions. The data required by this governing body must be made as explicit as possible and as early in the diagnostic or evaluation planning as possible. If this policy board has already predetermined the fate of the program, you need to know this. There is nothing quite so professionally painful as evaluating a program whose demise or continuation was decided by others beforehand. Such evaluation is futile and can entail a misappropriation of resources unless the results are useful to others. If you enter such a situation unaware, you risk a personally and professionally disillusioning experience.

Determining accountability for purposes of channeling information involves specifying which individuals or groups want or need progress reports and final reports from your diagnostic or evaluative studies. Such individuals or groups often possess a great deal of informal, but little formal power. They may be part of the agency or from an external influential group. These people can form coalitions, serve as pressure groups, and otherwise influence the resources at your disposal, including the cooperation of the public in your evaluation efforts. They do not make binding decisions that directly affect your activities, but this inability does not diminish their importance. Communicating with such people often can reduce anxiety, minimize program subversion, and provide a helpful channel of communication for information. Such advantages are particularly evident for providers in an agency where program evaluation decisions are formally made at upper administrative levels. Here, this group of individuals may include the professionals and volunteers actually implementing the program in the community.

You will be accountable to the administrator who monitors the program's budget or your data collection and analysis budget. This administrator frequently requests projected budgets for the diagnostic or evaluation planning and implementation phases, as well as reports on actual costs once the study is implemented.

Program developers are an additional group to whom you may find yourself accountable, particularly for diagnostic studies and in the initial steps of planning an evaluation. Interacting with program developers helps to specify projected program outcomes and to operationalize outcome measures in meaningful and valid ways (Hawkins & Sloma, 1978). Needs assessment and evaluation almost always involve selective, not exhaustive, measurement. The program developers can help you grapple with the issues of selecting measures that come closest to reflecting the types of needs they can handle and the outcomes they intend.

As your data come in, you may be accountable for providing the program personnel with diagnostic or evaluative information to improve or stabilize the program.[1] Here you need (1) to determine the timing and frequency with which the diagnostic feedback is to be given, (2) to specify the particular people who will be given the information, and (3) to clarify the most helpful forms in which this information should be given. A method of feedback that combines both a written summary and a face-to-face exchange is often desirable. Finally, premature feedback to staff can confound a diagnostic study of needs or a program evaluation if staff use the new information to alter public attitudes or to change the program for a "control group."

Issues of accountability raise sensitive questions that have potential repercussions. Are you willing to accept, for example, that the quarterly or final reports may be "modified" by others before they reach your administrator? Are you willing to accept an administrator's "editing" of the diagnostic or evaluation report before it reaches the offices of the funding agency? In short, will you want to be accountable for the report's contents despite its modifications by others? Are the reports used as a basis for dialogue and program development or revision, or are they merely filed away in an administrator's drawer? What about the summary report? Can you accept who will read and respond to it? Will it be

1. This provision of ongoing information raises a host of complex issues for evaluation, including the problems of mistimed program modification. Feedback may change the program en route, forcing it to exceed its predetermined limits of program variability. At that point, it is no longer clear what constitutes "the program." See Chapter 2 for a more detailed discussion of this problem.

filtered and strained by someone "above" you until the information is no longer based on the data you analyzed? Answers to these questions should influence your decisions about assuming the diagnostician or evaluator role.

How do you decide what form to give your evaluation? Cronbach (1983) suggests that, as evaluators, you are principally to be considered educators with the responsibility to teach your audience what you learn about the program through whatever means possible. These means may include verbal feedback and other forms of communication as well as written reports. Written reports require a lengthy development process, which often extends beyond the time line of needed information and therefore may be more useful for audiences who are in less immediate need for information about the program.

MEETING THE AGENCY'S NEEDS FOR INFORMATION AND FEEDBACK

Policy analysis, educational diagnosis, and evaluation breed institutional anxiety. Assessing needs or priorities and evaluation connote judgment, and judgment carries the possibilities of criticism, rejection, dismissal, and discontinuation. Although some cases may exist in which measurement and evaluation proceeded with minimum or no emotional overtones, these cases are the exceptions. True, evaluation may entail less anxiety today than before the rise of our current expectation that programs of any size, particularly if externally funded, should budget for program evaluation. Nevertheless, institutional anxiety, its sources, and its potential remedies remain issues of concern to anyone who steps into the role of policy analyst or program evaluator.

Institutional anxiety about diagnostic studies, policy analysis, and evaluation stems from program visibility and exposure, nonparticipation by key personnel or groups, the political climate underlying the measurement efforts, and the stakes various parties may have in the program's success or failure or in the study's implications for policy.

Visibility and Exposure

Measurement and evaluation require that aspects of the problem and components of the organization's practices be specified and made visible. Fulfilling this requirement makes practitioners and program planners more visible and therefore potentially more vulnerable to sanction. Program components that are made explicit and salient fall under the watchful eyes of everyone to whom the policy analyst or evaluator reports. This observation holds particularly for formative evaluation (see Chapter 2), in which frequent feedback is given to planners or directly to practitioners in the field.

Visibility makes the program and staff vulnerable, exposing them to negative as well as to positive analysis. Practitioners may worry: "Am I doing a good enough job?" "Will the program succeed or fail because of me?" "What happens if the evaluation measures my performance when I'm having an 'off' day?" "What happens if unexpected negative results occur?" Often staff do not realize the difference between program evaluation and personnel evaluation. They might erroneously equate the two and believe that they as individuals are being evaluated, not simply the program. Program visibility, of course, reveals both strengths as well as weaknesses, which presents difficulties for the program staff: it is one thing to display positive qualities, but another to divulge weaknesses.

Participation

Distance breeds suspicion. The more distance—physical or emotional—that people perceive between themselves and the policy analyst or evaluator, the more tension is generated. Getting potential recipients and staff members to participate in the diagnosis or evaluation is a key to eliminating this source of anxiety. Participation can come at almost all stages of the diagnosis and evaluation processes. Staff may wish to help specify the key outcomes and processes to be emphasized, the methods and frequency of data collection, and the record-keeping procedures, and to help edit or comment on the quarterly and final evaluation reports. You do not abrogate your responsibility when you allow staff to participate in these areas. Rather, you help ensure the stability, validity, and credibility of the measurement or evaluation. Work often limits the extent of staff participation, but using staff input enriches and lends the results a reality that is often missing when the evaluator has only an academic or theoretical understanding of the problem or the practice setting.

Political Climate

Policy analysis, needs assessment or diagnosis, and program evaluation occur within a political climate that affects the agency. This climate is influenced by factors at a national or an international level, as well as by internal agency pressures and local community pressures.

Tidy assessments wrapped up in smooth-reading final reports are not created automatically or effortlessly. They must be developed and nurtured. This part of the diagnostician and evaluator role begins with specifying objectives for measurement or evaluation. This process may be relatively straightforward, but usually it involves interviewing and discussing the objectives with many key members in the organization. Evaluators who are responsive to the organizational and political realities negotiate for the evaluation objectives (Hawkins & Sloma, 1978). For example, if the program funder's or administrator's objectives for an evaluation differ from those of the health staff, it is a good idea to uncover that fact early in the evaluation planning. Negotiation among organizational members can then take place. Uncovering the inevitable multiple purposes that exist for any measurement takes time, but it also has its rewards. Careful searching and negotiation in the early stages increase the usefulness and meaningfulness of data to all participants.

Identifying the multiple purposes for evaluation does not mean that you seek to align yourself with any one "camp." The diagnostician or evaluator role ideally is that of facilitator. Your purpose is to help identify and stratify the program's objectives to be used as standards of acceptability in the evaluation.

Policy Implications

The policy implications of a new health education diagnosis, new record-keeping procedures, or an evaluation can precipitate institutional anxiety. Both program continuation and program termination can provoke such anxiety, through hopeful expectation for success or through dread of the program being continued. People who hope for success are eager to hear how well "their" program has done. Yet they must realistically entertain the possibility of program failure. A new educational diagnosis of population needs can reveal that the program is no longer needed, whether it succeeded or not. Such possibilities can evoke protective, defensive behavior, and otherwise divert administrators, staff, and constituent energy. Moreover, program continuation does not always breed satisfaction. Sometimes program participants actually want the program to stop. They may want to build alternative health programs, redirect their program priorities, or carry out new needs assessments. The continued diversion of energy into the current program serves no useful purpose.

Likewise, the possibility of program termination, except where actually desired by program staff, can suck an entire agency down into tension or demoralization. This danger is particularly likely for program participants whose social as well as professional and financial sources of support revolve around the existing program.

Assessing anxiety regarding the evaluation is part of the role of analyst, diagnostician, or evaluator. Determining the expectations and hopes of program staff for the program's termination or continuation provides a basis for interaction between the health educator and other program staff.

Problems with Institutionalizing the Program

Among the principal roles in any measurement or evaluation effort are the roles of program advocate and critical analyst. Although budget constraints may push a single individual into both positions at the same time, these two positions ideally are held by independent parties. The assumption of both roles by a single individual or team can provide a sympathetic, useful evaluation, but requires rigorous attention to scientific methodology to assure that the evaluation be critical and credible.

The program planner has an ego investment in the program; the program manager "buys into" the program. This bonding or attachment makes these parties into advocates who are unconsciously blinded—if not outright defensive or even hostile—toward negative data or feedback about the program. The administrator *cares* for the program in every respect: it has been personally nurtured and, although it may suffer acknowledged weaknesses, it is, after all, "our" program.

In the stages of program development and implementation, these program advocates have engaged the energies of program staff. Staff roles are often expanded, the number of staff is increased, and entire formal or social networks are established around various aspects of the program. The program becomes institutionalized (Weber, 1949, [1949] 1982) and is reinforced by the work and exchange of many people. Issues and people begin to be guided on the basis of whether or not they support the program.

The staff, too, "buys into" the program. In part, their financial livelihood depends on the program's continuation. Such conditions make it difficult for such program advocates to evaluate their program objectively.

This situation is further complicated by still another factor: health education programs seldom yield a perfectly clear "landslide" evaluation, particularly when they are part of large-scale health programs (Green & Lewis, 1981). Evaluation data seldom clearly support either the unequivocal value of the program or its unquestionable failure. Even in the presence of statistically significant educational or behavioral changes, the evaluation may have difficulty establishing clinical importance or social significance. This problem of interpretation puts one further burden on the program evaluator: the implications of the study results must be teased out, because they are not obvious. In a situation of conflicting loyalties, the evaluator will probably either overvalue or undervalue the program's contribution.

We have no ideal solution to offer for this problem. Budgets seldom allow for both an inside program evaluator and a program director. When budgets do allow separation, part of the dilemma is solved. Moreover, in the case of a joint program planner-and-evaluator position, the budget may allow funds for outside consultation. Such consultation helps keep the individual more objective than he or she might otherwise be; however, the timing of the consultant's input is critical. For example, if the consultant provides input in the very early stages of the evaluation, while the population's needs or the evaluation's objectives are being specified, the consultant's influence enters the arena early but may have no impact on later evaluation phases. There is a long time lag between formulating the evaluation objectives and writing the final reports, and much can change in this time.

Finally, as we noted in the preface to this book, the risk of bias from program advocates who evaluate their own programs may be largely offset by the greater relevance and usefulness of their evaluation results. They are more likely to apply the results to the improvement of their own programs and practices if they conduct the evaluation themselves, or at least participate actively in it.

Substantive areas of influence for measurement and evaluation are chronologically listed as follows:[2]

1. Conducting needs assessment study
2. Determination of educational diagnosis
3. Formulation of theoretical framework between program elements and outcome and impact variables
4. Identification of program goals, objectives, and standards
5. Development or selection of evaluation instruments
6. Formulation of evaluation design and sampling procedures
7. Data collection
8. Data analysis (includes decisions about aggregation and the unit of analysis)
9. Interpretation of results (includes policy analysis)
10. Dissemination of results

THE DIAGNOSING AND EXPERIMENTING PRACTITIONER

In this book, we seek to encourage and to enable an approach to your everyday practice with a spirit of inquiry, treating your preconceived notions of what your clients need and what should produce effects as hypotheses rather than as ideologies. This challenge entails avoiding the pitfalls of blindly "buying into" a program, of assuming its value, or of prejudging its success or failure before it is tested. The objective position is extremely difficult to maintain. Human service professionals often eval-

2. The chronological ordering is a typical ordering. We appreciate, however, that evaluation research is not a rigid linear process. Instrument selection or development, for example, might occur earlier in the sequence.

uate programs they believe have unquestionable worth. But such an orientation encourages bias in selecting an evaluation design or method of data analysis, in executing experimental programs, in recognizing or accepting the result of "no effect," and in objectively and thoroughly interpreting results.

As an evaluator, you should not be intellectually committed to producing a positive result that is bound to a program ideology. Such commitment undermines the program, the credibility of individuals and institutions, and ultimately the intended beneficiaries of health education and health promotion. The experimenting practitioner recognizes that it is just as great a service to humanity—and sometimes a greater service—to discover that a widely accepted program or service is *not* working, as to "prove" that it *does* work. A report of negative results from even a much cherished or touted program can call into question the assumptions or the professional practices on which it is based, can help improve current practices or strengthen resources needed to make the program work, or can head off the waste of time, money, and misguided hope. As times change, circumstances change, so that the "truths" and principles of the past may need overhauling. The longer the deficiencies of a program go unrecorded and unreported, the greater will be the waste of resources, the lost opportunities to serve people more effectively, the lost potential in human development, and the disillusionment and disrepute when deficiencies eventually become visible.

The cornerstone of a professional's practice is a commitment to the outcomes achieved by the client. Professionals differ from technicians and artists in this regard. Technicians can be successful if their work or product meets technical specifications; artists, if their work satisfies esthetic tastes. In contrast, professionals must be concerned with more objectively defined needs and outcomes. A technician assigned the task of demonstrating a new syringe to a diabetic patient, or an artist producing a film on sexually transmitted diseases for parents, can rest or move on when the task is done. A professional also must be concerned with technique and esthetics, but has the added responsibilities of determining first that a demonstration or film is *needed* and later assuring that its intended effects were *achieved*. A major assumption in this book, then, is that you are concerned as much with the appropriateness and impact of your health education practices and programs as with your technique or materials.

Our second assumption is that your own professional contribution to the development or modification of health behavior will be part of a larger team effort or program, and that ultimately the combination of many educational, organizational, economic, and environmental supports for health behavior composes a program of sufficient scope to make a lasting difference in health outcomes. With this assumption, we concentrate in this book on measurement and evaluation of those aspects of health education and health promotion related to the more immediate concerns of

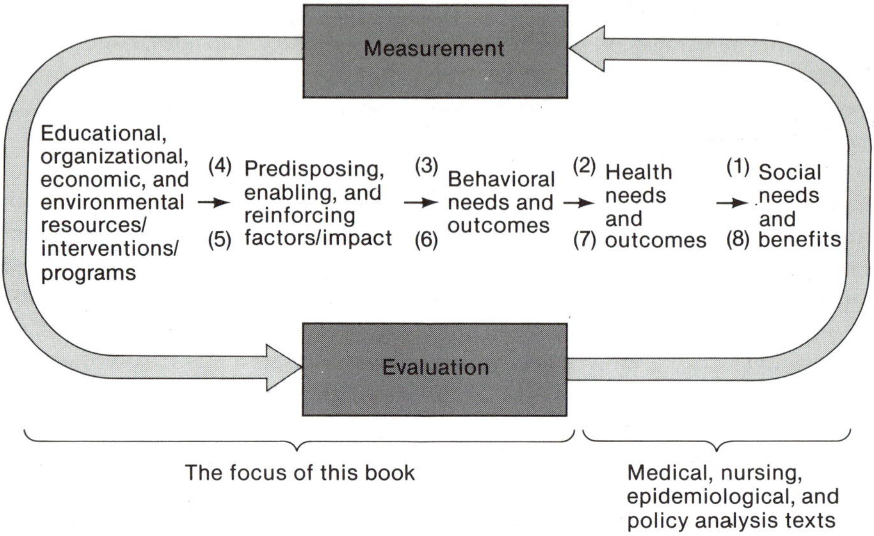

Figure 1-3 *The diagnostic evaluation model for measurement in health education and health promotion.*

practitioners and administrators, rather than on measurement and evaluation of the ultimate concerns of society, consumers, and policymakers. Thus when we speak of the diagnostic and policy analysis phases of measurement (Steps 1–3 in Figure 1-2; Steps 1–4 in Figure 1-3), we are referring here to the more immediate, local issues of behavioral, educational, and administrative diagnosis and assessment of priorities (Steps 2, 3, and 4 in Figure 1-3), rather than to the more global social and epidemiological diagnoses and policies (Step 1). This limitation is not meant to suggest that social and epidemiological diagnoses (Step 1) and evaluations (Step 8) should not be done locally. We only mean to acknowledge that much more has been written in textbook form on these issues and methods, and that the student or beginning practitioner in health education or health promotion is usually assigned to begin with diagnosis at Step 2 or 3, and to end with evaluation at Step 6 or 7.

In this model of planning and evaluation, adapted from the PRECEDE model (Green, 1974, 1976a, 1983, 1984; Green & Kansler, 1980; Green, Kreuter, Deeds, & Partridge, 1980; Green, Wilson, & Bauer, 1983),[3] the broad classes of variables to be measured in diagnosis and evaluation are

3. PRECEDE refers to predisposing, reinforcing, and enabling constructs in health education diagnosis and evaluation.

arrayed in their approximate causal relationship to each other. Policy analysts with broad responsibility for setting priorities begin with social and epidemiological diagnoses (Step 1). They end with cost-benefit evaluations on the social outcomes (Step 8). Most practitioners, on the other hand, begin their diagnostic measures with a given health problem (Step 2) and work back to specific interventions (Steps 3 and 4). Then they evaluate their efforts starting with process measures (Step 5) and work up to health outcomes to the right. This order of business is reflected by Figure 1-3, which shows the activities of diagnosis and evaluation in sequence. Each of these activities entails measurement.

Ideally, expert evaluators and statisticians work closely with expert practitioners (Baskerville, 1981; Finney, 1982; Moses & Louis, 1984), but if we had to choose between the two, we would seek to make practitioners more skilled in the evaluation of their own practice. Similarly, experts in the measurement and diagnosis of health education needs should develop these analytic skills on a foundation of experience in health education practice. If we must depend on policy analysts and evaluators for the measurement of health education needs and the assessment of health promotion programs, let them be experts who have some experience with the realities of implementation.

At the same time that we advocate self-monitoring and evaluation, we are painfully aware that practitioners are not the most objective observers and reporters when the object of evaluation is their own practice. As noted earlier, we believe that this risk is outweighed by the benefits of more relevant, immediate applications of measurement and evaluation when it is done by the same people who are responsible for the program. They are more likely to improve their own practice if they measure the needs of their own patients or clients and evaluate their own programs than if they read about the results of experiments conducted at some academic center. Their changes in practice are more likely to come about if they at least understand and participate in the diagnosis and evaluation than if somebody else independently assesses their clients' needs and evaluates their program or practice.

It follows, also, that one practitioner's evaluation of his or her own practice will not be very influential in changing the practices of many other health professionals. The findings of the diagnosing and evaluating practitioner may be inherently limited in objectivity, credibility, and generalizability beyond his or her own immediate situation, but the impact on practice then and there will be greater.

We recognize and sympathize with the trade-offs between service and research objectives. One can be maximized usually at the expense of the other. The trade-off, however, is often between short-term and long-term objectives, or between local and global objectives. When an immediate, local opportunity arises to contribute to long-term, global knowledge and development of the state of the art, more rigorous measurement and evaluation in the short-term, local situation seems justified, even if it entails some sacrifice of services. The trick is to be sufficiently conversant with the science and state of the art of health education to recognize the opportunity when it presents itself. For example, a local program on health promotion for the elderly may provide an optimum situation in which to test and expand aspects of the PRECEDE model.

CONCLUSION

The experimenting practitioner is devoted to the strengthening of the scientific base on which not only his or her own practice or programs are conducted but also on which the profession at large must build. The scientific base for professional practice must be a foundation for human development, a foundation that will not crumble every time a political wind blows against the programs erected on it. Therefore its weakest elements should be removed as new material is added. Much professional practice in all the human service fields rests on theory and professional judgment in the absence of concrete evidence. Those theories and professional judgments can be put to the test of evidence to determine their validity and to convert specific applications of theory into fact. The diagnosing and experimenting health educator diligently commits him- or herself to questioning client needs and professional practices, using methods of measurement and evaluation that will answer questions and serve as the arbiters of doubt.

Our choice of the terms *measurement and evaluation* rather than *research* in this book is intended only to emphasize practical rather than academic purposes. The terms are not mutually exclusive. As suggested in this chapter, good descriptive studies carried out for diagnostic purposes in health education practice can contribute to basic knowledge about health beliefs, attitudes, values, and behavior, as well as to epidemiological knowledge of the distribution and etiology of disease. Similarly, good evaluations can contribute to the store of research knowledge about the fundamental relationships between specific interventions and specific changes in comprehension, motivation, behavior, and health outcomes in specific populations.

SUMMARY

From its earliest roots to the late 1960s, health education had few people skilled in or devoted to measurement and evaluation. The limited pool of highly trained personnel in health education has since been expanded and can be extended further in usefulness and effectiveness by providing fundamental measurement and evaluation skills to practitioners in the field. Practice also will improve if the measurement and evaluation in the field concentrate on problems identified by the practitioners themselves. Practitioners can benefit from applying research methods to their practice, and they can help academicians develop and test theory. Following the principles and tools in this book, practitioners without extensive research training can integrate measurement and evaluation into their practice. With small successes in measurement and evaluation, practitioners may be expected to be more receptive to and more appreciative of the research literature and further development of their own skills in health education planning and practice. Measurement and evaluation in health education and health promotion can strengthen the weak links, fill some of the gaps, and extend the centers of excellence in practice. (In the next chapter, we present some more specific ways in which measurement and evaluation can strengthen practice first.)

The weak links in the cycle of poverty for health education and health promotion include diffuse objectives, methods, and procedures. These are being strengthened by national conferences devoted to obtaining consensus on objectives for the nation in disease prevention and health promotion, and consensus on the delineation of roles in health education practice and standards in professional preparation. Evaluation has strengthened the appropriate choice of methods and procedures.

The gaps in our capacity for measurement and evaluation are being filled. Better training of practitioners in the use and interpretation of measurements and evaluation; more research specialists who have experience in practice; and more effective translation of research and evaluation into theory and policy all have helped close the gaps in recent years.

The centers of excellence have been extended through the dissemination of measurement and evaluation results and skills to practitioners in the field through publications, software, and continuing education programs that reach out to settings where practitioners, vendors, and consumers of health promotion do not have access to research specialists.

The role of the educational diagnostician, policy analyst, or evaluator requires that you approach the practice setting as a sympathetic critic. It also requires that you have an open mind both to the possibility that the proposed program has great potential and to the possibility that it will fail. The role also requires that you sustain these open-minded hopes and doubts even while all the people around you may be demoralized or blindly enthusiastic.

You need to know who the potential users of your measurements and evaluation might be, to whom the program is accountable, and what decisions might have to be made from the report. The form and timing of feedback to administrators, staff, policymakers, and consumers can be threatening. The best way to lower the threshold of threat is to involve each of these parties in specifying the objectives and implications of the policy analysis or evaluation, discussing policy implications in advance, and separating advocacy and evaluation roles. Ideally, these roles would be occupied by different people, but practically the evaluator is inevitably called on to take a stand with regard to the policy questions.

When the stakes are high, an independent, expert evaluator can be brought in as a consultant or contractor to conduct a truly objective evaluation. Normally, the practitioner is left to his or her own devices to exercise as much skill and objectivity as possible in assessing needs and evaluating his or her own practice. The "diagnosing and experimenting practitioner" model we have suggested in this chapter emphasizes the latter situation. As we move through the chapters, we will come to the more global and academic purposes of measurement and evaluation.

Chapter 2

FORMATIVE EVALUATION AND MEASURES OF QUALITY

The term *formative evaluation* refers to the provision of short-loop diagnostic feedback about the quality and implementation of—and immediate responses to—methods, activities, or programs. Before contemplating eventual impact or outcome, the evaluating practitioner is concerned with the appropriateness and progress of the health education program, its ongoing refinement, and its reception at the field site. Formative evaluation is critical to establishing, stabilizing, and upgrading the health education program or curriculum.

The goal of formative evaluation in health education or health promotion is the control and assurance of quality in practice. Quality in health education is an elusive thing, however. Although we cannot define it so as to specify it for all time, we *can* conceive of ways to measure it.

After reading this chapter, you should be able to define formative (or *process*) evaluation and to elaborate its component parts. The traditional view of process evaluation merely provides measures of program implementation; instead, we take a broader view of formative evaluation that includes pretesting, making pilot studies, and forming *focus groups* before implementation, as well as seeking the immediate response of on-site people and agencies to the health education program. We also discuss when formative evaluation is indicated, and who should receive the information from formative evaluation. At the end of the chapter, we consider issues of quality control in health education.

Formative evaluation seeks to refine the implementation of the health education program and its support components to maximize the potential positive impact of the program or curriculum. Short-loop feedback is required because issues or problems identified in pilot studies or during the implementation of the program must be communicated quickly to the administrators and program staff, so that refinements and improvements can be made in the health education program. Thus the times between gathering information and analyzing it, and then disseminating it, are brief. In many cases this feedback loop is completed within a few days; in some cases, within a few weeks. These short loops necessarily limit the rigor and thoroughness of measurement and analysis, but if they are continued or repeated regularly they become routine. In formative evaluation, you are interested in diagnostic information that will improve the program continuously or repeatedly, as needed.

FIVE TARGETS OF FORMATIVE EVALUATION

Formative evaluation provides immediate diagnostic feedback about the implementation and the quality of the program. It includes feedback on one or more of five targets:

1. Program implementation
2. Site response
3. Recipient response
4. Practitioner response
5. Competencies of personnel

Some formative evaluation begins even before the program. Evaluation conducted *during* the program is often called *process evaluation.*

Program Implementation

Formative evaluation documents the extent to which a program is faithfully delivered as planned. What is actually occurring at the program implementation sites? Is the program being delivered? Are all program recruits involved to the same level or degree? Are the administrator and practitioners who present the program offering it as developed by the program planners, or are they making appropriate (or inappropriate) adjustments in its content or in the methods of prescribed delivery?

Such questions on program implementation anticipate an important reality in health education evaluation: the health education program delivery at the site will vary. The key job for the evaluator is documenting where such variability occurs and providing feedback when variability exceeds tolerable limits. In the final analysis, issues of program implementation deal with the appropriateness, integrity, and quality of the implemented program. What is eventually delivered and evaluated is seldom the original plan.

A "rule of thumb" for setting tolerable limits of variability in implementation is to allow greater variability when the population is larger, more heterogeneous, or more dispersed, and to allow less variability when the population is small, homogeneous, or cohesive. If the health education program is tightly articulated with a codified theory, you would not allow much variability, regardless of the heterogeneity of the population.

In evaluating field implementation, classroom operation, or clinical application, the first question is "How much can the program vary and still be labeled *program*?" Program variability may be affected by (1) instructor and instructional variability, (2) materials variability, (3) participant variability, or (4) site variability. Instructors may vary the health education program, for example, because they claim they get bored if the program is offered in the same way each time. Or different health educators may interpret the program materials differently to program recruits. These differences are instructional and instructor variability. Or there may be an inadequate supply of printed handout materials. Differences also emerge in the instructional materials to which participants are exposed. These differences are variability in materials. Participants may differ from one program to the next on such factors as receptivity, age, or educational background. This variability reflects differences in the type of program participant. The sites at which the program is implemented may vary in the degree to which they permit the program to be delivered in its original form. For example, light switches may not work (indeed, electricity may not be uniformly available), or round-table discussions may not be possible because of stationary aisle seating. These examples illustrate variability in the physical sites at which the programs are implemented.

Ideally, your determination of the tolerable limits of variability for a health education or health promotion program would be based on universal standards, but in reality such limits must be negotiated among the program's developers, implementers, recipients, and evaluators. When the tolerances for variability are exceeded, feedback must be provided to the deviating staff. The decision usually is to bring the implemented program back into the tolerable range. Sometimes, however, it is useful to measure systematically the impact of the variation.

A decision to measure the impact of the program's variability, rather than to impose controls on it, rests on two beliefs. First, program variability is to be expected and can be desirable. For example, the health educators in the field may "take possession" of the program components and may exercise discretionary judgments about needs for modification. Second, program variability is systematic, not random; it can be measured. Random or sporadic program changes are not at issue. Random variability is not especially useful to measure. The type of program variability at issue here is patterned and predictable. Understanding systematic variations in the implementation or delivery of a given program can provide immensely useful guides to the planners and administrators of the program in allocating resources, providing training and supervision, maintaining surveillance, and developing new programs.

Site Response

Health education and health promotion programs are seldom implemented in a benign or apolitical environment. What responses from people at the implementation site might subvert the program? What responses from staff of competing programs might set up obstacles? What do relevant consumer or professional groups in the community think about the program? Does any evidence exist of program subversion by community agencies or private parties who might perceive it as competing with their own programs? Subversion is more likely to be headed off by making appropriate adjustments in the program and negotiated administrative arrangements if such perceptions are understood early in the program (Moss, 1983). The increasing commercialization of health promotion, for example, makes vendor competition an aspect of many such programs. Organizational and economic trends constantly change any program; any program plan quickly becomes an inadequate description of actual implementation.

Recipient Response

Formative evaluation also addresses the quality of the recruitment and the progress of participants through the health education program. Recipient response to the program is judged from three perspectives: the participants' actual movement through the program, the quality of their progression, and their level of satisfaction with program components. Measures of progress through the phases of the program identify the number of entering program recruits (relative to the eligible population in need) and their completion rates, as well as reasons for attrition. Such measures include evidence of exposure to and understanding of the health education materials. Testing readability of written materials, audience response, and market share of mass media exposure are standard procedures in this phase (if they were not done earlier for the recipient population).

Your judgment of the quality of the participants' progress ideally is rendered on the basis of multiple performance measures. Emphasis is on easily and quickly documented measures of comprehension, perceptions, behavior, skills, and attitudes. You might include short written and oral tests and interviews, and might ask for behavioral demonstrations of skill. Throughout the information-gathering process, you are determining which participants show progress as planned. When participants do not progress as predicted, explore and analyze the reasons where, in the logic of the program, the learning seems to be breaking down. These tests are truly diagnostic, in the same sense as a trial run of computer software: if the results are not right, you know there must be a "bug" in the program.

Testing recipient response is not limited to gathering objective information about the program participants' progress. The emotional response of the program recruits is also important (Miller & Lewis, 1982; Risser, 1975; Ware, Wright, Snyder, & Chu, 1975). In what ways are the recruits evaluating their own experience in the program? How satisfied are they with the health educators and with the instructional materials? Are the materials emotionally appealing to special-interest groups or compatible with multiple ethnic groups? What meanings do the instructional materials impart to the program? Do program participants experience tension or dissonance with any aspect of the program or with behavior of the instructor? Such answers can be obtained through pretest questionnaires or focus groups (Romano, 1983) or through participant observation (Kurz, 1983; Spradley, 1980). Focus groups provide qualitative feedback by getting a group of eight to ten people from the target population to talk with each other freely and spontaneously about the program or the topic of concern.

Practitioner Response

Ideally, personnel are committed to carefully and systematically implementing the planned program. Moreover, ideally the same field personnel implementing the program also participated in its development. Field personnel implementing the program can contribute to its refinement and stability. They often identify weak areas in program structure as well as needed reforms. Their insights and feedback are absolutely essential information for the formative evaluation. While implementing the designed program, field personnel are in a unique position to observe inadequacies. Their feedback may uncover such a simple thing as the need to resequence a set of instructional slides or as vast a problem as inappropriate staff or a mismatch between program and participants. In either extreme, field personnel can offer their interpretation of the situation and recommend improvements. The field personnel themselves thus act as program participants. The field personnel, as well as the learners, respond both to the content of the materials being delivered as well as to the form in which they are delivered. Finally, the involvement of practitioners at this stage of evaluation also assures their greater likelihood of using evaluation results (Leviton & Hughes, 1981; Oman & Chitwood, 1984).

Competencies of Personnel

Formative evaluation provides feedback on the level of knowledge, skill, and attitudinal performance of the various professionals and nonprofessionals who deliver the health education program. In making a formative evaluation of personnel competence, you assess the staff and faculty's actual competencies in this program, as opposed to their expected or past competencies.

It is hazardous to assume that field personnel, once recruited, always stay the same. They too need updating, staff development, reinforcements, and feedback on their performance (Lewis, 1977a). Your purpose in evaluating personnel competencies is not to sanction or penalize personnel at the site. Instead, you apply a professional feedback model (Dornbusch & Scott, 1975) in which you encourage and support personnel to update and maintain their professional performance. This approach is consistent with the quality assurance perspective offered later in this chapter.

You can document the competencies of personnel with informal interviews, short quizzes, brief case analyses, and self-evaluations. On-site observation of staff performance may also be indicated. Audio or video recordings of interactions with clients, patients, students, workers, or consumers can become tools both for a more thorough analysis and for feedback (Inui, 1973; Roter, 1977).

The more geographically distant the field personnel are to the home agency, the more they need support and encouragement (Hongladarom, 1983). This correlation is particularly true when an implementation site has been nonsupportive; that is, a negative site response occurs. For example, an agency hosting a program in a nearby state may think the program encroaches on their agency's program goals. Agency personnel may act in ways that are not supportive. This correlation is also true when the program recipients' response to the program or to the health educators has not been enthusiastic.

INDICATIONS FOR FORMATIVE EVALUATION

When is formative evaluation indicated? Pilot studies, pretests, focus groups, and other preliminary data collection should precede any major program. Formative evaluation after the program is underway should be continuous but is most needed under four conditions:

1. In the initial implementation phases of a recently developed program
2. In the implementation of a refined program in which you have identified "bugs" or "rough spots"
3. In the implementation of a previously developed program that you import to a new site
4. In the implementation of a refined health education program that is experiencing new developments and variability

Recently Developed Program

Formative evaluation is indicated for a recently developed program being implemented for the first time. It is almost impossible to collect too much information for a recently developed program. Too little is usually known about the ways in which the health education program will be interpreted and implemented, the response of agencies and interest groups who cautiously watch the program's implementation, or the recruits' response. Seldom is much known about the judgments and views of the practitioners asked to implement the program, or about their ability to sustain the competencies required to deliver the program consistently.

Program with "Bugs" or "Rough Spots"

Some aspects or components of virtually every health education program are not well received. For example, program participants may identify problems with the complexity of the instructional materials; or the instructors may be perceived as nonsupportive or technically uninformed; or the sequencing of the health education intervention protocols may be experienced as inefficient or inappropriate. You can glean such information from a pilot implementation of the health education program, in which you conduct formative evaluation to "debug" the program. These "rough spots" in the program can then be worked out, and program solutions can be identified and integrated into a refined version of the health education offering.

Your goal with formative evaluation in a program with rough spots is to evaluate whether the program refinements directed at these spots did in fact handle the problems. For example, if the identified problem involved the technical competence of the instructional staff, do you now have evidence of staff competence? Did the bimonthly inservice training programs sufficiently update the health educators' technical knowledge, and is this update now demonstrated in the program delivery?

Imported New Program

The success of a health education program may be the result of the persuasive or charismatic qualities of the staff or other unique characteristics of the initial site, not a result of the content of the health education or promotion program. When you import such a program to your site in which new health education practitioners must implement the program, you need to evaluate the response and progress of the new program recruits, field personnel, and site response to the program (Padilla, Baker, & Dolan, 1975). Their response may differ significantly from the initial responses to the program at the previous site(s). If responses do differ, you need to identify causes and consider recommending alterations in the program.

For example, a typical problem arises in exporting innovative programs developed and tested in academic or research and development centers. The original research and development effort usually has included considerable supervision and monitoring of highly skilled graduate students or personnel hired specifically to carry out the demonstrations. In most service programs, you may not have graduate students or the time to provide such close supervision and surveillance, so the plan may require additional reporting requirements or more explicit instructions, protocols, and self-monitoring checklists for practitioners delivering the program under more isolated circumstances.

Sometimes practitioners in the initial health education program have had highly developed skills in persuasive techniques appropriate to group-based instruction. When you import the health education program to your site, however, the new health educators may be less skilled in either persuasion methods or group-focused instruction. The new practitioners initially may have been enthusiastic about endorsing the importance of the health education program, but the formative evaluation may reveal their inability to deliver the program as conceived.

Therefore, when evaluating an exported program, the experimenting health educator asks, "To what extent can the site easily implement the program as conceived? And to what extent is further adaptation of the program's design and methods needed?"

Continuous Development of Refined Program

The issue is not whether to carry out formative or process evaluation, but how much of the evaluation effort should be devoted to it. If you conceive of evaluation as a pie, your question will be "How big a piece should go to formative evaluation?" The larger the proportion of resources invested in formative evaluation, the fewer the resources that may be available for evaluating outcome or impact.

The best rule of thumb we can offer for this decision is to consider the existing evidence and relative certainty of the causal relationships between process (practices) and impact and outcomes, as represented by Arrows A and B in Figure 2-1.

In the example shown in Figure 2-1, the evidence is quite strong (indeed, practically irrefutable) that reduced smoking will reduce lung cancer (Arrow B). Therefore, you have little reason to devote scarce educational resources to evaluating outcomes. The evidence for the linkage between some behavior modification techniques and smoking cessation rates (Arrow A) is more tenuous, however, so your need to measure

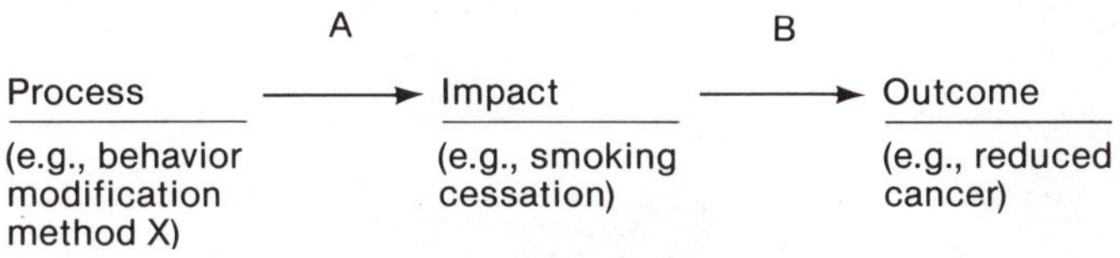

Figure 2-1 *Where to lay the emphasis in evaluation.*

smoking rates and to evaluate impact is much greater. For those methods of behavior modification (X) for which you have a reliable record of success in previous studies of smoking cessation, it may be sufficient to concentrate your evaluation efforts on process evaluation. This focus is made possible when you know with some certainty that if you carry out a behavior modification or educational method following certain standards, an impact of acceptable magnitude is likely to result.

CHANNELS OF COMMUNICATION IN FORMATIVE EVALUATION

At an early stage in the process evaluation, the health education evaluator asks, "To whom should what information from the process evaluation be given?" The answer to this question depends on the structure of the field staff and evaluation team and the political realities surrounding the evaluation. No universal rules are appropriate for all situations. You will do well to consider your own structures for each evaluation project.

An Example of an Organizational Structure

Let us envision a hypothetical but typical structure for implementing and evaluating a health education program. Figure 2-2 shows a four-site implementation (e.g., four schools, four clinics, or four worksites) with four health education practitioners, one in each site; a field coordinator from the central staff, who is a health educator physically removed from the implementation sites; an agency administrator; and a national funding agency that granted monies to evaluate the four-site project.

Seven people in this organizational structure might appropriately receive information gathered during the process evaluation. Let us work from the bottom up in Figure 2-2, beginning with on-site implementation. The health education practitioners are usually the first recipients of information.

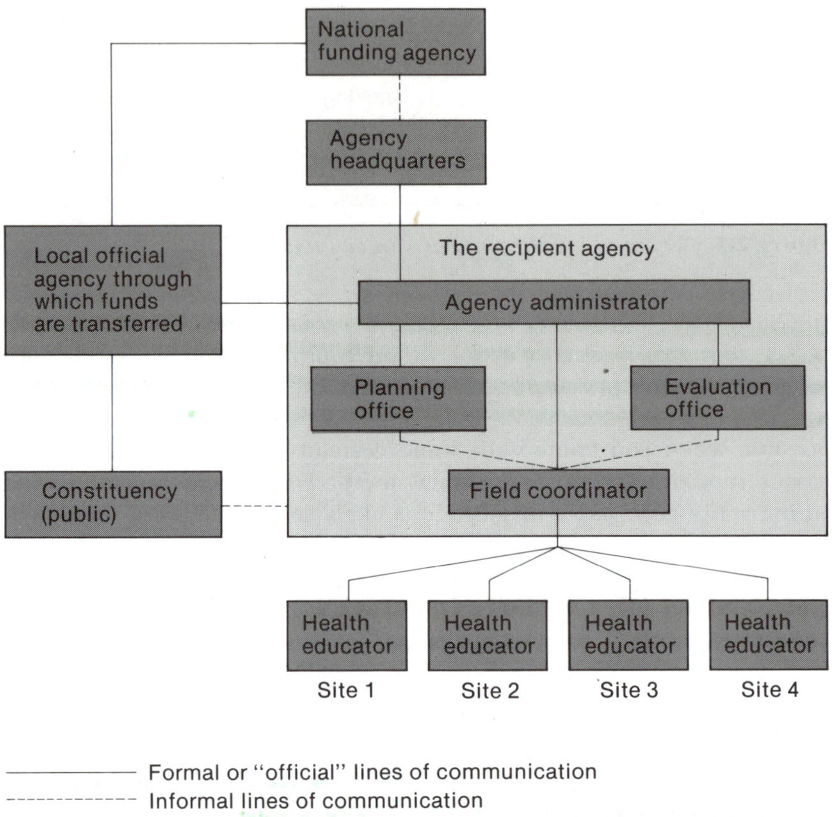

Figure 2-2 *Typical positions for reporting and feedback during process evaluation.*

On the "Firing Line." At the most basic level, the practitioners can collect information about the program from the program participants at the site. Typically this collection involves counting and logging in the daily activities, services delivered, and clients exposed; administering and reviewing satisfaction measures (Lewis, 1977b) or easily interpreted pencil-and-paper measures of the participants' progress; or observing behavioral demonstrations of the desired skills. Such short-loop feedback between practitioner and program participants provides a quick check on receptivity to the program and the gross progress of the participants.

Feedback specific to each health educator has limitations. Program participants may hesitate to evaluate the practitioner candidly; subjects may not want to threaten the educator with negative evaluations or to jeopardize their own eligibility for services through potential recrimination. If program participants do offer candid negative evaluations, practitioners in the field may be demoralized, may want to resign, or may show other symptoms of antagonism. If the site-specific evaluations will be seen by the program administration, health education practitioners may be tempted to underplay the importance of the negative evaluations and to highlight instead the positive evaluations. This bias may be particularly evident when the practitioner's positions, merit raises, or promotions are contingent on receiving favorable testimonials and positive formative evaluations. Also, in some instances health educators underestimate, not overestimate, their own performance.

Instead of each health educator collecting and separately reviewing their own evaluations, they can pool their evaluation forms and reflect on them statistically, as a group. This reflective process denatures the intensity of an educator-specific formative evaluation, yet provides some opportunity to examine the meaning of the feedback.

Putting Yourself in the Middle. In multiple-site implementation plans, a field coordinator can be designated to oversee either the implementation or the evaluation at each program site, or both. Usually such coordinators are assigned both responsibilities. This field coordinator can do any or all the following: disseminate and collect formative evaluation forms, carry out nonparticipant observations at the implementation sites, field-edit and tabulate information, and summarize the feedback for the health educators in the field. A key question you would ask if you were in this position is "To whom do I report what information?" Although you may want to provide feedback to the practitioners in the field, you may instead be required to channel a summary of the evaluation data directly to the central administration or evaluation staff, and to avoid direct feedback to the health educators. In other situations, the same information might go simultaneously to the practitioners and to the evaluation staff at the home site. In such situations, you may be caught in a crossfire when the responses come in.

Direct feedback from the field coordinator to the practitioners offers the advantages of quick ("short-loop") feedback: great reinforcement value of positive results, and possible immediate correction of negative findings. However, it can also result in premature, erroneous, or excessive adjustments in the program. Sometimes the field coordinator does well to report initial results to the central evaluator. The evaluator, in conjunction with the program development staff, can then summarize the evaluation data from several sites for several points in time and can recommend improvements or establish meetings in which the information can be discussed by the evaluation team and the site implementers. This process helps prevent overreactions to events in the field and assures greater continuity of program delivery. It also allows for counterbalancing adjustments in one part of the program with necessary compensations in other parts.

To whom at the central office should formative evaluation data be channeled? In some exceptional cases, no information needs to be regularly channeled to the home agency. Self-directed professionals may be given the authority to process the information on their performance independently and the discretion to initiate changes or adjustments in their own activities and program.

Under other conditions, central program staff, not the evaluation staff, receive information from your formative evaluation. They may, for example, learn that an entire instructional module is too abstract or is perceived as irrelevant. When such information is made readily accessible to them, they can create a new module (or refine the old one) and quickly cycle it back into the field for testing.

Under what conditions should formative evaluation data be relayed back to the agency administrator? Although no absolute guides exist, usually administrative personnel ask that only bimonthly or quarterly summaries of the formative evaluation data be submitted. For programs that are developing in essentially new conceptual terrain or in controversial areas, the administrator is well advised to receive weekly updates on the formative evaluation. Each administrator's needs for formative evaluation information should be assessed at the outset and periodically thereafter.

Under some conditions, the agency that funded the program, the local official agency or authority (e.g., the mayor) who authorized it, the headquarters of your agency, or the constituents who demanded the evaluation study *all* want to obtain regular and frequent reports on the process evaluation data. Their needs for both the timing and the scope of desired information should be ascertained at the beginning and repeatedly throughout the duration of the formative evaluation. For such consumers of formative evaluation outside the staff and administration of the program, the identity of staff whose performance is being judged should be routinely obscured and the confidentiality of client data ensured.

QUALITY CONTROL AND STANDARDS IN HEALTH EDUCATION

To be accountable for the resources that it absorbs, health education must demonstrate that potentially beneficial programs can be delivered with sufficient quality to ensure the potential benefits. This point is explicit in formative evaluation, with its emphasis on rigorous program implementation and on field personnel competencies. Standards and mechanisms for assuring quality in health education practice are often the least considered by medical, nursing, and allied health professions (e.g., Wilner, Winickoff, Schoenbaun, & Coltin, 1982). For health education specialists, such standards remain essentially undeveloped. Instead, quality in professional preparation has been emphasized more than quality in professional practice (Ross, 1976; Sills, 1976). We do not mean to say that professional preparation and practice in health education are without guidelines, principles, and even criteria and measures in some areas. These rules are not equivalent, however, to standards and institutionalized mechanisms to ensure quality. What is meant by quality control, and what is needed to ensure it?

Definition of Quality

The term *quality* refers to the appropriateness of a specific set of professional activities as performed in relation to the educational objectives they are intended to serve (Green & Brooks-Bertram, 1978). Quality is not determined by documenting impact or outcomes, which measure effectiveness and benefits, but rather by applying a set of *a priori* standards to the actual practice or performance of state-of-the art methods and skills. The term *quality assurance* refers to one aspect of professional accountability by which the relevant public—consumers, sponsors, providers, agency administrators—can be informed that professional activities are appropriately carried out (Batey & Lewis, 1982). Figure 2-2 illustrates various lines of communication in quality assurance. The term *quality control* refers to the surveillance system or procedures for providing feedback and sanctioning for the professional activities for which the health educator is accountable (Lewis & Batey, 1982; Dornbusch & Scott, 1975). Quality assurance and quality control may be influenced by, but usually cannot afford to await, measurement or evaluation of the actual impact on client outcomes of the health educator's professional activities. Quality assurance requires that standards of professional practice be applied even before the results or effects of the program are measured. (For example, a weekly report, a monthly staff meeting, and an annual audit can all serve as quality assurance mechanisms.)

Within this context, *standards* are the minimum acceptable levels of performance used to judge the quality of professional practice. When addressing quality and standards of practice in a process evaluation, you measure the *minimum* levels of performance required of those who deliver health education; the *degree* to which the program is implemented is unlikely to be measured unless the program has spelled out in great procedural detail all the educational steps and activities of each team member. Professional activities can meet minimum standards of practice only if those standards are explicit. Also, in some evaluation studies the evaluator and program sponsors or planners may require that practice exceed the minimum standards.

Developing Assessment Criteria

It would be ideal if both the institutional mechanisms for determining quality in professional practice in health education and the tools to measure quality were well defined and available. But they are not; both are evolving. If you are concerned with documenting quality in professional practice, you can choose criteria of appropriate practice using one or more of six approaches: exclusionary, problem checklist, consumer satisfaction, prescriptive protocol, general principles or process, or diagnostic-experimenting (Green, Kreuter, Deeds, & Partridge, 1980). Critical elements of these six paradigms are summarized in Table 2-1. Each paradigm or perspective from which to develop standards of practice for health education has its merits as well as its inherent limitations. Some combination of approaches is generally preferred.

The *exclusionary* approach defines health education restrictively and rules out everything that fails to meet the definition of a qualified method or practitioner. If we define quality of practice from an exclusionary perspective, we can proscribe specific technologies (e.g., electric shock), approaches (e.g., coercion), methods (e.g., aversive conditioning), or sources (e.g., hypnotists) of health education practice when they violate the definition (see Green, 1978). Although exclusion identifies practices and practitioners that should *not* be included in quality practice, this approach fails to specify at a procedural level the standards of practices that *should* be included. It thus becomes a form of professional birth control: we know what to rule out, but the approach does not specify what is appropriate.

The *problem checklist* model requires that we identify all the barriers to effective professional practice and then attempt to analyze each case of practice as to whether it commits these errors or effectively handles the barriers. With this approach, however, we still have little clue as to what quality health education should be other than free from these problems.

The third approach to defining quality of professional practice is the *consumer satisfaction* approach. This approach asks patients, clients, students, or trainees to rate their satisfaction with care, or, more specifically, asks their opinion of their instructor (Ware et al., 1975; Ware, Wright, & Snyder, 1976; Risser, 1975; Miller & Lewis, 1982).

The *prescriptive* approach, at the opposite extreme from the proscriptive or exclusionary approach, and sometimes called the "cookbook" or procedural approach, identifies the steps that should be taken in most

TABLE 2-1 Distinguishing elements in six approaches to standards of practice in health education

Paradigm	Distinguishing Features	Examples
Exclusionary	Defines quality performance by ruling out everything that fails to meet definition	Certification and licensure Exclusion of practices that are coercive, e.g., Green (1978)
Problem checklist	Defines quality performance in health education by identifying barriers or errors in practice	Squyres (1982) Weinstein & Stasson (1976)
Consumer preference	Defines quality performance on the basis of what consumers or patients prefer or demand, evaluated on the basis of market criteria or consumer satisfaction surveys	Byler (1969) Howard (1982) Miller & Lewis (1982) Ware et al. (1975)
Prescriptive	Defines quality performance in health education by listing the steps that should be taken in most situations	Podell (1975) Steckler, Dawson & Herndon (1980) Simmons (1977)
General principles	Defines quality performance by specifying the essential characteristics or principles of an educational program	Neufeld (1976) Ross & Mico (1980) Cleary, Kornacki, & Grancio (1980) Mullen & Green (1984)
Diagnostic-experimenting	Defines quality performance by the extent to which the instructional methodologies are theoretically justified and the targets are probable causes of the health behaviors based on diagnostic results	Green, Levine, & Deeds (1975) Green, Squyres, D'Altroy, & Herbert (1980) Bowler & Morisky (1983) Eriksen & Gielen (1983) Wilner et al. (1982) Zapka & Mamon (1982)

Source: Based on Green (1980c).

situations. Departing from these steps therefore requires justification. For example, in his *Physicians' Guide to Compliance in Hypertension,* Podell (1975) offers a list of eminently reasonable protocols for physician practice in patient education. Similar protocols have been offered for various medical settings (e.g., American Hospital Association, 1979; Breckon, 1982; Espenshade, 1979; Green, 1983; Madnick, 1980; McCormick & Gilson-Parkevich, 1979; Mullen & Zapka, 1982; Pritchett, 1977; Redman, 1980; Zander et al., 1978), worksites (Parkinson et al., 1982), and school settings (Anderson & Creswell, 1985; Bruess & Gay, 1978; Cornacchia & Staton, 1979; Jenne & Greene, 1976). Protocols apply best in institutional settings where the flow of people can be controlled.

Some combination of the consumer satisfaction and the prescriptive approach seems particularly appropriate for people expected to perform health education functions but who are not likely to have sufficient professional training in the discipline (for example, physicians in private practice). If algorithms or protocols can be developed for restricted health education problems and homogeneous client populations, the prescriptive approach to defining quality in practice is most appropriate (Green & Brooks-Bertram, 1978). For professionally trained health education specialists, this prescriptive approach restricts and constrains the discretionary judgments they are expected to exercise and may stifle innovation and experimentation. In the prescriptive approach, the lists can become tediously long and too detailed; the approach tends to ignore the motivational aspect of the professional's effort; the approach tends to be translated too literally and perfunctorily into information for patients; and prescribed procedures can become obsolete rather quickly. The creative needs and the autonomy of self-respecting professionals are challenged by overly prescriptive methods. In the extreme, practitioners either apply them ritualistically, or they abandon them (Green, 1980c). Combining the prescriptive approach with the consumer satisfaction approach helps offset some of these problems.

The *general principles* model identifies the essential characteristics or principles of an educational process or instructional program. Evidence obtained on the extent to which a given practice adheres to or implements these processes thus becomes the measure of quality. The only drawback of this paradigm for analyzing quality is that it often fails to distinguish the relative importance of the principles under different conditions. The principles thus become dogma or ideology rather than serving as a base on which to make more critical judgments (Mullen & Green, 1984; Mullen, Green, & Persinger, 1986).

The *diagnostic-experimenting* approach (Campbell, 1969; D'Onofrio, 1980; Green, 1974; Green, Kreuter, Deeds, & Partridge, 1980) assesses quality by the extent to which program activity is explicitly justified by and based on an *a priori* diagnosis of probable causes affecting the health

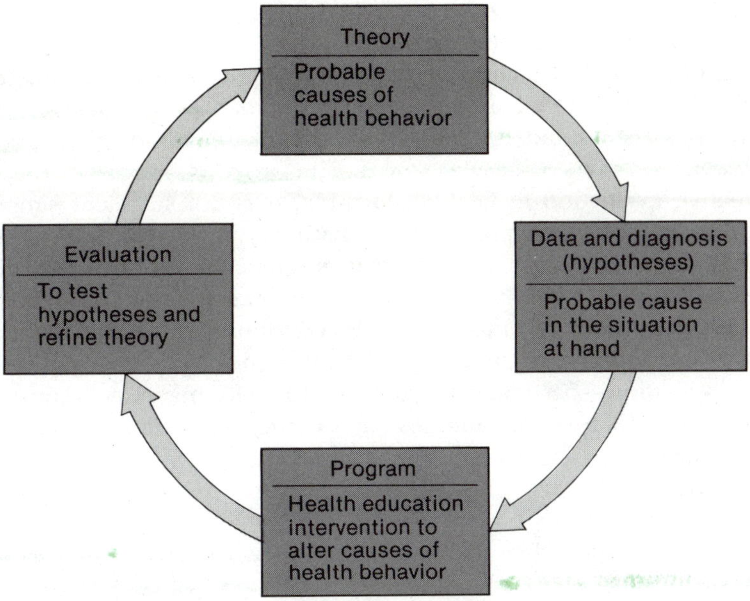

Figure 2-3 *The diagnostic-experimenting approach to health education.* Source: *Green (1980c), p. 143.*

behavior in question. The approach further specifies theoretically grounded strategies appropriate to alter the diagnosed causes. This model requires specifying for each program the assumptions that led to the intervention selection. The approach encourages pretesting, pilot testing, and experimentation to test these assumptions. The diagnostic-experimenting model links theory with evaluation from which results can elaborate the prior theoretical knowledge base in health education and health promotion. This cyclic process is summarized in Figure 2-3.

Examples of the application of the diagnostic-experimenting model of quality control have been published in relation to health education programs in breast self-examination (Zapka & Mamon, 1983), automobile child restraints (Eriksen & Gielen, 1983), blood pressure control (Bowler & Morisky, 1983; Chwalow, Green, Levine, & Deeds, 1978; Cleary et al., 1980; Fass et al., 1977; Green, Lewis, & Levine, 1980; Green et al., 1975; Green, Levine, Wolle, & Deeds, 1979; Inui, 1973; Levine, Green, Deeds, Chwalow, Russell, & Finlay, 1979; Morisky, Levine, Green, Russell, & Smith, 1980; Morisky, Levine, Green, Shapiro, Russell, & Smith, 1981; Morisky, Levine, Green, & Smith, 1982), and other areas of chronic disease management and self-care (Clark, Feldman, Freudenberg, Millman, Wasilewski, & Valle, 1980; Green, Werlin, Schauffler, & Avery, 1977; Maiman, Green,

Gibson, & Mackenzie, 1979; Parcel & Nader, 1977; Roter, 1977; Zapka & Averill, 1979; Zapka & Estabrook, 1976).

Regardless of the quality assurance paradigm chosen, the major assumptions common to all six perspectives are that quality can be defined in measurable terms and can be improved measurably, and that such improvements can influence the health outcomes of program participants. In formative evaluation in health education, it is not sufficient simply to claim "the program was implemented." Rather, you need to select a strategy for documenting quality within that implementation phase. Quality is not the opposite of quantity, is not to be equated with feelings or affect, and is not equivalent to outcomes. Any criterion of quality in practice is admittedly temporary, because times and circumstances change, but formative evaluation—particularly attention to field personnel competencies—demands that we develop, test, and refine such criteria.

Standards

The alternative approaches to quality just described yield *criteria* for assessing quality in practice, but they do not lead automatically to the establishment of performance *levels* that can be held up as *standards.* The minimum acceptable level of performance may be implicit in some approaches, but making standards more explicit is the task of a quality control study, mechanism, or system. Implicit standards, when made explicit, can usually be traced to one or more of the following sources: (1) historical comparisons with similar efforts in the past, (2) normative comparisons with contemporary activities elsewhere, (3) theoretical comparisons with some ideal conception, or (4) consensus among professionals, applying some combination of the first three.

On the basis of one or more of these sources, quantitative objectives may be set for (1) performance of professional activities; (2) deployment of resources, health services, or actions in priority action areas; (3) impact on accessibility of or satisfaction with resources and services, changes in behavior, or improvements of the environment; and these in turn are expected to contribute to (4) health outcomes expressed as objectives, such as those contained in the U.S. Surgeon General's Report, *Healthy People.* This entire sequence is detailed with 226 quantitative objectives in *Promoting Health, Preventing Disease: Objectives for the Nation* (U.S. Department of Health and Human Services, 1980). The relationships among these elements of quality control, program objectives, and broader goals are reflected in Figure 2-4. Some states and localities have adapted the national objectives so that they can be monitored for quality control at the program level (e.g., Texas Department of Health, 1984; Dumbauld, 1981). How such objectives or standards are derived, expressed, and applied, and how they may be refined and made more ex-

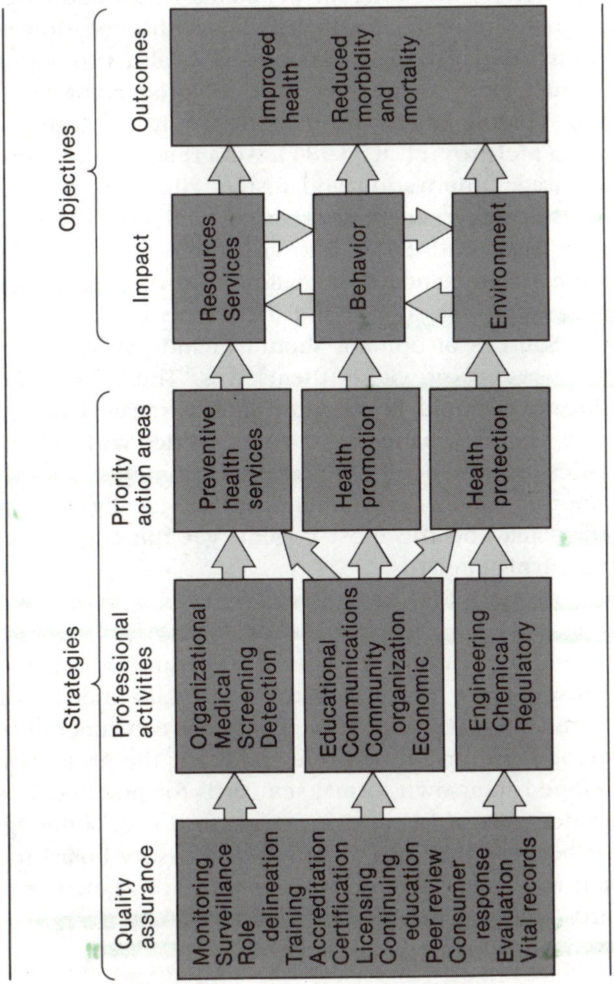
Strategies
Objectives
Quality assurance
Professional activities
Priority action areas
Impact
Outcomes
Monitoring
Surveillance
Role delineation
Training
Accreditation
Certification
Licensing
Continuing education
Peer review
Consumer response
Evaluation
Vital records
Organizational
Medical
Screening
Detection
Educational
Communications
Community organization
Economic
Engineering
Chemical
Regulatory
Preventive health services
Health promotion
Health protection
Resources
Services
Behavior
Environment
Improved health
Reduced morbidity and mortality

plicit in quality control procedures for health education, are discussed in the remainder of this chapter.

The most common, but often the least valid, standard for judging the appropriateness of health education or health promotion activities is tradition. When tradition is applied as the historical standard of acceptability, it may not account for new circumstances such as the changing scientific base for practice, the different problems being addressed, and the new organizational circumstances in which health education is practiced. We have seen this lag recently with new health promotion programs in the worksite. Many companies have adopted employee health promotion programs based largely on experience in clinical or other community settings (McLeroy et al., 1984). Adherence to tradition as a standard also discourages innovation and fosters ritualistic practice. On the other hand, tradition is at least time tested, and may thereby avoid judgments of quality based entirely on idiosyncratic opinion or fiat.

Opinion—an inevitable standard in quality control—can be useful if compiled from more than one source and if controls are applied against conflict of interest. Sources of opinion should include at least a balance of informed consumers and providers themselves. Thus, the self-evaluation of health educators should be checked at least against the perception of the students, trainees, patients, or communities with whom their professional activities are practiced. The opinions of employers or supervisors represent another kind of consumer standard. Finally, the opinions of professional peers may be the most cogent, yet the least developed, source of quality control standards.

Health education specialists have been very concerned with consumer involvement and representation in the planning of health programs. For this and other reasons, they have sometimes abrogated their professional responsibility to develop and to maintain their own standards of practice. The submission to surveillance by consumers has been a wholesome development for all the professions. For the professions that have not yet developed their own formal standards for practice, however, consumer surveillance cannot be an excuse not to do so. Some agencies have assumed that because they had a consumer advisory board they had met their obligation to regulate themselves. For those professions that have developed standards, consumer surveillance should complement, not substitute for, peer review and other methods of quality control.

EXAMPLES OF INSTITUTING QUALITY CONTROL

Health education has been largely without quality control, not only because the standards for judging its quality have not been sufficiently explicated, but also because it has not had resources set aside for this purpose. Health promotion is not yet identified as a professional discipline and, as such, has operated even further afield from professional standards. The commercialization of many aspects of health promotion has even resulted in some practices being made trade secrets subject only to market controls.

First, *accreditation* procedures applied to professional training programs in health education have not been consistently applied nor sustained (Wolle, 1976; Green, 1976c). Many programs would not submit themselves to accreditation review, and most of those that would, could not afford the cost of maintaining the required staff and procedures. The accreditation of HMOs (health maintenance organizations) for federal funding in the United States requires that thay have a health education component in their programs and services. The accreditation of U.S. hospitals now includes requirements for patient education programming. The accreditation of professional schools of dentistry, medicine, nursing, pharmacy, public health, and allied health have given increased attention in recent years to the behavioral science content of curricula.

Second, *certification* of health education practitioners has been limited to a few states that have laws requiring practitioners who are employed by government agencies or school districts to be graduates of specified types of academic programs, sometimes identified by their accreditation (Health Manpower Coordinating Committee, 1976). In a few states, examinations have been used in lieu of, or in addition to, the academic prerequisites for employment. These forms of quality control have been very unevenly applied, with limited participation by professional health education specialists in their development or application.

Third, *licensure* differs from certification mainly in the legal privileges and liabilities accorded the licensed professionals. No attempts have been made to achieve quality control through licensure of health education specialists, to our knowledge, although questions on health education may have appeared on the licensing examinations of dentists, nurses, pharmacists, physicians, and others. However, physicians, nurses, and pharmacists have been prosecuted for failure to inform patients adequately. The costs and the need for explicit standards are even greater in maintaining examination systems for certifying or licensing individuals than in accrediting institutions. However, the advantage of certification and licensure over accreditation is that they allow proficient individuals to enter the field even if they attended an unaccredited college or university program for their training, and they prevent some incompetent individuals from practicing, even if they received training at an accredited institution.

Fourth, *continuing education* has been tied to certification and relicensure in some professions as a means of quality control (Brown & Uhl, 1970). Ironically, health educators plan and administer continuing education programs for other health professions, but few such programs are designed specifically for health education specialists. The mid-year scientific sessions and the annual meetings of the professional societies provide the main continuing education opportunities. To the extent that quality assurance in health education practice depends on the adequate performance of health education functions by other professions, the maintenance of consultation, inservice training, and continuing education services for nurses, physicians, and others may be the best means of quality control at our disposal. Continuing education programs in health promotion, again largely commercial, have proliferated to meet the demand of professionals and institutions seeking to tap this new market.

Fifth, *advisory committees* with consumer representation or control provide another means for instituting quality control in both professional preparation and in practice. Our concern with this mechanism is that it has more important functions to serve in setting policy and priorities than to be burdened with quality control activities that are essentially managerial rather than policy problems. Moynihan warned against precisely this burden in his book *Maximum Feasible Misunderstanding* (1969), which attempted to explain what went wrong with the application of U.S. legislation in the early 1960s that called for "maximum feasible participation" of citizens and consumers in planning. Many agencies and programs in the "War on Poverty" turned too many managerial functions over to their consumer boards so that the boards had little time or energy left to grapple with the important issues of policy and priorities. The use of consumer advisory committees and control in health education and health planning has been analyzed extensively by Steckler, Dawson, Dellinger, & Williams (1981), Isley (1982), Tonon (1980), Freudenberg (1984), Minkler (1980–1981), and Zapka & Dorfman (1982).

Sixth, *peer review* has a long history in some professional organizations such as medical and legal associations. For health education also, peer review is a quality control process that, when combined with selected standards and mechanisms of assessment, can assure quality in professional preparation and practice. As a voluntary activity for health education, peer review provides an opportunity to develop quality control from within a faculty or program staff.

Peer review is an alternative to consumer surveillance that can be applied through several of the foregoing mechanisms of quality control, including advisory boards. This alternative is especially preferable to consumer surveillance when, as with most health education, the standards have not been sufficiently explicated to pass them on to nonspecialists in a form they can apply to quality control (Metsch, Berson, & Weitzner, 1975).

Mechanisms of peer review should have an identifiable structure that will facilitate their use by health education professionals within or between institutions or organizations. An identifiable structure for peer review in health education might consist of (1) uniform standards of quality that are established explicitly and that can be applied both to institutions and to individuals, (2) understandable standards of quality arrived at by consensus of health education professionals, and (3) current standards that are frequently revised to provide for growth and receptivity to innovations, both at the individual and the institutional levels.

Peer review is not suggested as an alternative to accreditation, certification, licensure, continuing education, or advisory boards. When combined with the positive features of these other mechanisms, however, peer review provides a productive channel for the input of health education specialists who are concerned with quality in the preparation and conduct of health education professionals and programs controlled by others (Wilner et al., 1982).

A good example of blending the peer review and the diagnostic-experimenting practitioner models is provided by Williamson and his colleagues (Williamson, Aronovich, & Simonson, 1975). They developed a system labeled "health accounting" as a quality assurance model of physician practice. After collaboratively developing a set of priorities with physicians who practiced together, initial outcome assessments were conducted in relation to those priorities, and then they obtained a definitive assessment of their practice. Afterward they conducted continuing education for the physicians and again reviewed the outcomes.

Williamson helped the physicians to estimate the results they expected if they were practicing correctly and if they were doing good patient education. They agreed that blood pressure control should be achieved in all but 5 percent of their cases. When they did the baseline assessment, however, they found that 36 percent of their patients were not achieving blood pressure control. Williamson then conducted continuing education directed at improving the physicians' patient education skills. This program reduced to 19 percent the patients who were not under blood pressure control. In a second round of studies, Williamson did the same thing, but added a patient educator with minimum educational background yet trained specifically to deal with hypertension patients. An even greater improvement in blood pressure control was achieved by patients educated by the patient educator (Williamson et al., 1975).

Inui (1973) followed Williamson's approach, combined with the diagnostic model (Green, 1974), but directed his efforts at tutorials for physicians, to improve their patient education practices. He established certain criteria about what should constitute quality patient education practice. One of Inui's criteria was that physicians ought to be more realistic about the extent of the patient compliance problem. Specifically, they ought to be able to make more realistic assessments of how many of their patients do not take their pills, do not adhere to their diets, and do not keep their appointments. As a result of his tutorial approach to educating the physician, he achieved a significant improvement in the percentage of physicians who more correctly estimated these three standards of compliance or noncompliance (Inui, Yourtee, & Williamson, 1976).

The second standard or criterion that Inui used to test physician behavior in the quality of patient education practice was that physicians would dedicate more time, proportionally, to educating the hypertensive patient than to physical examination and interim history taking. (This criterion, of course, applies to a patient population that previously has had rather thorough physical examinations and histories, so that interim history taking is really just a medical ritual that avoids talking to the patient.) Inui achieved a significant improvement in the percentage of time spent on patient education in the experimental group of physicians compared with the control, at the (appropriate) expense of time taken in histories and physical examinations (Inui, 1973).

The third standard or criterion of quality control that Inui employed was that the physicians should make more chart notations about patient education and about behavior. Again, significant improvement was obtained through his educational process in the percentage of charts on which physicians noted dietary recommendations, patient compliance, patient understanding of hypertension, and patient education. Significant improvement also appeared in the percentage of physicians who were making notes about patient education in the charts.

The fourth criterion Inui used was that some improvement should be displayed in the patients' knowledge, attitudes, and beliefs. On a variety of different criteria of knowledge and attitudes, he obtained significant improvements in the patients of the tutored physicians.

Finally (fifth), he thought that he should expect patient compliance behavior to improve as a result of this educational program. Indeed it did, at least for taking pills. Patient behavior did improve significantly between experimental and control groups. But it did not improve diet adherence and keeping appointments.

The bottom line was that Inui achieved very substantial increases in blood pressure control as a result of this intervention. The patients whose physicians did receive the tutorials showed significantly greater improvements in blood pressure control. Thus, quality in patient education can be defined in measurable terms, can be improved measurably, and such improvements can have a significant influence on health outcomes (Inui et al., 1976).

Another application of a combination of Williamson's health accounting approach and the PRECEDE model is described by Wang and her associates (Wang, Terry, Flynn, Williamson, Green, & Faden, 1979). Roter (1977) presents an example of mobilizing consumer surveillance as a quality control mechanism. Her hypothesis was that if the patients ask more questions, they will get more answers and that the doctor is more likely to offer information that he or she knows the patient wants. Roter carried out an educational diagnosis to identify the determinants of question asking. The predisposing factors she identified included belief in the acceptability of asking questions, the value placed on health, the salience of the question, and the expectations for information. The enabling factors she identified were the patients' ability to articulate questions and their ability to recall questions in the presence of the medical provider. Feedback from the question-asking process was expected to result in some reinforcement, such as encouragement by the doctor to ask questions, receiving answers, reduced anxiety from the increased information, and increased satisfaction from the information.

Roter then designed a patient education intervention in the waiting room, where she talked with individual patients, drawing out their problems and questions they were not likely to ask unless the doctor were to evoke them. She wrote the questions down for them, and she tried to convince them that it was very acceptable for them to ask their questions. The patients then went into the examining room with the physician, with the result that a statistically significant rise was achieved in the percentage of questions asked. Now, the one problem here is that we are in a transition period of history with this kind of quality assurance method. If we are going to create assertive patients, we have to expect some backlash. In fact, Roter found that while patient question asking increased, patient satisfaction did not increase. The patients came out of their session feeling somewhat shaky. She had tape recorded the sessions, with the doctors' and patients' permission. With a content analysis of the taped interactions, she found that the patients who had received the experimental treatment were involved in somewhat more acrimonious exchanges with their physicians. However, Roter did improve the behavioral outcome of appointment keeping. The experimental group patients were more likely to come back for the next appointment than were the control group members, who asked fewer questions (Roter, 1977).

Combining Quality Control Mechanisms

Various advantages and disadvantages are offered by each of the foregoing mechanisms for quality control and quality assurance in health education. The mechanisms that offer the greatest potential for quality *assurance* are accreditation and licensure, but greater advantages for quality *control* might come from peer review. The major disadvantages of each method are, to some degree, major advantages of others. Accreditation, for example, is expensive and is applied to a given program or institution only once every few years. But peer review can be inexpensively applied on a frequent or even continuous basis. A major weakness of using peer review alone is that it lacks consistency and official sanction or power to assure remedial action when deficiencies are found. And accreditation has these powers externally, but must depend on internal controls provided by peer review or administrative surveillance.

An ideal strategy for quality control in health education, then, would combine the essence of these mechanisms in some way to derive the benefits of several while minimizing the costs or risks of each. Implicit in all these mechanisms, when appropriately applied, are elements of others, including self-evaluation, consumer surveillance, administrative review, and budgetary audit. The "ideal" mechanism would also include these latter methods (Green & Brooks-Bertram, 1978).

Explicit Criteria and Standards

The cornerstone of the foregoing methods of quality control and process evaluation is the existence of criteria and standards. It is not enough to offer general guidelines for practice when the decisions to be made from the process evaluation are potentially damaging to the practitioners who are being reviewed. Experience with general guidelines in the accreditation process, for example, has shown that they tend to be interpreted to fit the variable perceptions and prejudices of the reviewers and the reviewees. Guidelines usually imply criteria, but the need in formative evaluation and quality control is for more explicit standards, if only for the self-evaluation of the reviewees. An example of combining criteria and standards has been worked out in detail in family planning (Hirschhorn, Goldy, Plager, Bell, Brier, Parenteau, McIntosh, & Robbins, 1984).

SUMMARY

Health education and promotion can demonstrate through formal evaluations of impact and outcomes their *potential* benefits, efficacy, and efficiency in preventing or reducing selected health problems. These potentials, however, can be assured only if the practice of health education is of a quality that brings appropriate methods and consistent performance of activities to bear on the problems addressed. Procedures exist to control and provide assurance of that quality.

Formative evaluation provides short-loop diagnostic feedback on the process and progress of the health education program. Early in the evaluation, the evaluator decides to whom results from the formative evaluation are channeled, and for what purposes. A key decision concerns the proportion of resources to allocate to formative evaluation and quality control. Committing resources to formative evaluation helps prevent moving too quickly into an outcome or impact evaluation before the program qualities and components are explicitly specified prior to stabilizing the program. Formative evaluation is particularly indicated for new programs but also makes an important contribution when refined programs have problem areas, when a previously refined program is imported to a new agency or site, and as a refined program develops. At such points, the program evaluator examines program variabililty, organizational response, recipient response, and the response and competence of personnel. Staff competence can be measured by a variety of quality control and quality assurance methods, each applying different criteria and standards.

Throughout the phases of formative evaluation, the health educator fills various roles in an investigative endeavor whose goals are development, feedback, and program improvement. Formative evaluations, including diagnostic studies, are a necessary first step in developing and stabilizing programs before evaluating behavioral or health outcomes. Such systematic development assures that the program is appropriately addressing needs, applying theory and state-of-the-art methods as consistently as possible under the circumstances, and providing information required to make administrative adjustments along the way.

PART TWO

MEASUREMENT: THEORY, OPERATIONAL CONSIDERATIONS, AND PRACTICAL APPLICATIONS

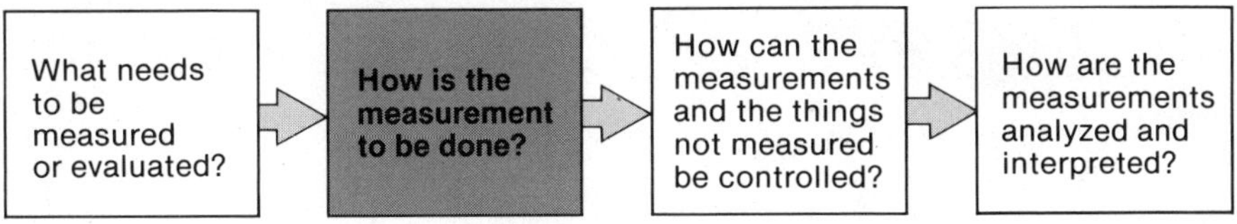

In this section we strike out on the turbulent sea of measurement opportunities and obstacles. To chart your way, we suggest in Chapter 3 that you develop a map of the connections between your theories or concepts and their possible dimensions and indicators. In Chapters 4 and 5 we suggest ways of estimating or judging the quality of your measurements. And in Chapter 6 we offer some guidelines and directions on the development of new measurement instruments and the selection of standardized measures.

Chapter 3

THE MEASUREMENT OF THEORY AND THE THEORY OF MEASUREMENT

Diagnosing educational needs and documenting program effects and processes both presuppose the use of measures that are relevant, valid, and reliable. Thus the health educator must understand the meaning of these three terms, as well as the cost he or she pays when measurement is deficient with regard to them.

Measurement need not be regarded as strictly technical and numerical. Esthetics and philosophy also enter into consideration when the health educator discovers the challenge, intricacy, and difficulty in "capturing truth" in the art of educational diagnosis and evaluation, and giving meaning to data. The health educator learns to take seriously as well as smile at Mephistopheles's taunt in Goethe's *Faustus:*

All theory is gray
my friend.
But life springs
ever green.

Nor is the experimenting, creative health educator done when his or her diagnosis or evaluation has captured some measure of truth. The health educator is an idealist as well as a naturalist, and as George Santayana has said, "The truth, which is a standard for the naturalist, for the poet is only a stimulus." Theories need to be refined, and programs improved, from the results of educational diagnosis and evaluation.

The road to the esthetic "greening" of theory and the poetic improvement of programs is paved with systematic observation. Attention to measurement forces you to examine carefully, and sometimes reconsider, just what is to be observed and how. Where does the road lead if you measure to the left or to the right; if you measure attitudes, beliefs, or behaviors that are more or less relevant to the health benefit intended? In addition to the hazards of measuring the wrong things, hazards arise in measuring the right things poorly. Measurement error decreases the confidence you can place in the data produced. If you cannot depend on your measures, you cannot depend on the results or implications of your measurements. Moreover, you cannot contribute to theory; nor can you confidently recommend changes in policy or in programs.

Our purpose in this chapter is to clarify what we mean by measurement. We define and elaborate measurement with relevance to health education diagnosis and evaluation. Before we address the specific issues of validity and reliability (in the next two chapters), we first need to introduce the terms *construct, concept, indicator,* and *variable,* as used in health education. These terms bridge the health educator's dual place in the world of theory and the world of empirical observations and actions.

Measurement in health education can be reduced to three issues: decisions about *what* to measure, decisions about *how* to measure it, and decisions about the quality of measures. This chapter addresses the first two issues. Chapters 5 and 6 address the issue of quality.

We also introduce the four levels of measurement—nominal, ordinal, interval, and ratio. An understanding of these levels of measurement tells you how the various forms of measurement set limits on the statistical procedures to be used in the data analysis phase of the evaluation.

This chapter lays the foundation for a more detailed presentation of measurement error (validity and reliability) to be covered in the following two chapters.

DEFINITION OF MEASUREMENT

Measurement in health education is based on concepts and principles similar to those for measurement in any other discipline. Measurement, by definition, is merely the assignment of numbers to objects, events, or people according to specified rules. For example, you can let the number 1 denote those clients who value their health, and let the number 2 denote those clients who do not value their health. This example assigns the numbers 1 and 2 to subjects according to a rule; that is, whether or not the person values his or her health. Further specification of the rule requires you to clarify such terms as *health* and *value.* It also requires making explicit the way to assign numbers (e.g., 1 and 2 differentiate subjects who value their health from those who do not). In short, the definition of measurement requires that the health educator clearly specify the objects to be measured, the numbers to use, and the rules by which the numbers are assigned to the objects.

CONCEPTUAL MODELS IDENTIFYING OBJECTS OF MEASUREMENT*

Your first task is to place the objects of interest for your measurement in perspective as to their presumed relationship to other objects, including interventions (methods, personnel, programs), processes of change (cognitive, motivational, organizational, environmental, economic, behavioral), and outcomes (physiological effects, morbidity, mortality, fertility, or social benefits). The following discussion of models in medicine, public health, behavioral sciences, school health, health education, and health promotion attempts to locate factors or variables implicit in these models, in response to the first question of measurement: what is to be measured? The model you develop also determines your answers to subsequent questions about expected relationships among the things you measure.

Biomedical and Public Health Models

When medical and public health workers speak of *function,* they refer generally to the assumed or expected relationship between an intervention and a health outcome. The quality, effectiveness, and efficiency of an intervention, which may be a technique, strategy, program, or institution, are assumed to be justified or measured on the basis of its causal relationship or contribution to "saving" lives (usually meaning the deferring of death), improving health (usually meaning the removal or control of symptoms), or preventing disease or injury. For any given intervention, this relationship is more or less supported by "hard" evidence, meaning controlled trials in which subjects selected at random who received the intervention showed significantly better health outcomes than did subjects, also selected at random, who did not receive the intervention. Most interventions, except for FDA-approved drugs, immunizing agents, and medical appliances, have not met this test of evidence (Perry, 1982). Instead, they are defended on the basis of an implicit model of indirect or *mediated* causation. Thus the simple medical and public health models,

(a) medical intervention → individual health outcome
(b) public health intervention → population health outcome

are elaborated with assumptions and evidence concerning the primary impact of the intervention on some immediate impact or series of effects. These impacts in turn are assumed or known from other studies to be directly related to the intended health outcome:

(c) intervention → impact → outcome

*Adapted with permission of Hospital Research and Educational Trust, Chicago, from L. W. Green, Some challenges to health services research in children and the elderly, *Health Services Research* (19(6):793, February 1985, Pt. 2.

Biobehavioral Models

The "impact" variables range from specific, physiologically documented risk factors, such as blood pressure control, to theoretical constructs for which the only evidence of their existence is subjective, self-reported statements, such as attitudes or beliefs. The latter are typically embedded in more elaborate hybrids of behavioral science and biomedical science models, in which the number of intermediate impact variables multiply into complex chains of causation with some strong links and some weak ones. For example,

```
(d) intervention → impact → impact
                 ↘  ↓ ↑       ↓
                   impact → impact → outcome
```

is a generic form of model in which the intervention is assumed or expected from diverse data and experience to set into motion a series of actions and reactions, direct and indirect effects, leading ultimately to the desired health outcome. Some of these intermediate variables are cognitive, some attitudinal, some behavioral; some have to do with factors in the social, physical, or economic environments. The complexities of measurement proliferate in such models.

Health Education Models

Among the foregoing models, medicine has had a distinct advantage because its interventions are subject to more immediate and controlled testing for health outcomes than those of public health. Within both medicine and public health, patient education and community health education have required more complex and difficult-to-test models because of the necessary linkages of cognitive, environmental, and behavioral variables, each of which is variously and sometimes tenuously related to the others and to health outcomes. A generic health education model, as defined in the preface to this book, contains a "combination of interventions designed to predispose, enable, and reinforce voluntary adaptations or behavior conducive to well-being":

```
                      predisposing factors
                    ↗                      ↘
(e) educational
    interventions → enabling factors → behavior → health → quality of
                                                            life
                    ↘                      ↗
                      reinforcing factors
```

School Health Education Models

Within health education, school health education has had an even more complex path to define between its interventions and the expected health outcomes. Documenting the relationships between classroom interventions and health outcomes has been difficult (and, some would say, unjustified) in school health education (Coates, Peterson, & Perry, 1982; Green & Iverson, 1982; Kolbe, Green, Foreyt, Goodrick, Williams, Ward, Korton, Karacan, Widmeyer, & Stainbrook, in press; Kreuter & Christianson, 1981; Mechanic, 1979). Nevertheless, an impressive record of impact on health behavior has accumulated in the past few years, as documented in a number of recent reviews (Evans & Raines, 1982; Evans, Hill, Raines, & Henderson, 1981; Green, Heit, Iverson, Kolbe, & Kreuter, 1980; Iammarino, Weinberg, & Holcomb, 1980; Levy, Iverson, & Wahlberg, 1980; McAlister, 1979, 1984; Olsen, Redican, & Kruz, 1980; Schaps, DiBartolo, Moskowitz, Polly, & Churgin, 1981; Thompson, 1978). The most impressive record, however, has been achieved with improvements in knowledge, attitudes, and skills assumed to be important in decision making and in the subsequent development of health behavior. In this hierarchy and temporal sequencing of effects lies an implicit model that could be imposed on school health education:

cognitive development ↗ ↘

(f) curriculum → affective development → behavior → health

↘ skill development ↗

This model, like the public health education model (e), places ultimate importance on health outcomes and the behavior necessary to achieve them. The problem is that schools are neither medical institutions nor public health agencies and have never adopted the same mission and goals. School health educators have worked valiantly to address some of the same health problems as their colleagues in public health education, but in recent years they have been fighting an uphill battle with the "back to basics" movement. The schools simply cannot be held accountable for solutions to all the ills of society (Green, 1980b; Kolbe, 1979, 1982; Kolbe et al., in press). The line is now being drawn more severely between the educational mission of the schools and the functions other agencies would like the schools to serve. Measurement and evaluation must be sensitive to these conceptual and organizational differences in purpose.

Comprehensive School Health Program Models

One response to this recognition that the classroom could not be expected to accomplish behavioral and health outcomes by itself was to return to a basic model of school health programs, derived not from medical or public health models but from education. The generic model of school health programs combines (1) health teaching with (2) school and community health services and (3) interventions in the school and community environment, to produce that level of health outcome necessary to assure that students can perform effectively in school and achieve academically. The two significant departures of this model from the preceding models are (1) the combination of education with school and community services and environmental interventions to promote health, and (2) the emphasis on health as a means to an educational end rather than as an end in itself.

The relationships among concepts in the comprehensive school health program model would look something like the following:

(g) school health services ↘ (to health)
↓ (to behavior)
curriculum → behavior → health → performance
↑ (to behavior)
school health environment ↗ (to health)

Community Health Promotion Models

The comprehensive school health model (g) approximates in two ways at the school level what has come to be associated with health promotion at the community and national level. First, the combination of health education with organizational and environmental services and resources in support of health behavior in both the school health model and in the health promotion model (see Figure 2-4) removes some of the unrealistic expectation that health education alone should accomplish behavioral and health outcomes. Second, the recognition that health is not necessarily an end in itself, but may serve other values and social goals or quality of life concerns, corresponds with the positive concepts of health as "physical, mental, and social well-being" heralded in the earliest approaches to health education in the World Health Organization (1954) and in the more recent formulations of policy in health promotion (Green, 1980a, 1981; Green & Johnson, 1983; U.S. Department of Health, Education, and Welfare, 1979; U.S. Department of Health and Human Services, 1981b).

This instrumentality of health is reflected in one of the resolutions of the World Health Assembly of 1977 (World Health Organization, 1981, p. 1): "The main social target of Governments and WHO in the coming decades should be the attainment by all the citizens of the world, by the year 2000, of a level of health that will permit them to lead a socially and economically productive life."

Worksite Health Promotion Models

Where the World Health Organization, the U.S. Surgeon General, and the schools speak of "socially productive lives," employers initiating worksite health promotion programs speak of "productivity on the job." Where the school health model speaks of combining education with school health services and interventions on the school environment, WHO defines "primary health care" as consisting of these three elements, and the U.S. Surgeon General's initiative in disease prevention and health promotion consists of parallel elements in preventive health services, health promotion directed at behavior, and health protection directed at the environment, as reflected in Figure 2-4. The model of health promotion emerging in occupational settings reflects a convergence of these elements: traditional occupational safety and health bring the environmental and health services together with the new emphasis on health and fitness behavior or lifestyle.

MAKING CONCERNS EXPLICIT FOR MEASUREMENT

We said at the outset of this chapter that the first rules of evidence in educational diagnosis and evaluation are that the measurements should be relevant, reliable, and valid. By developing "maps" of the presumed or hypothesized relationships among the concepts, factors, or variables implied by professional activities and programs in health education and health promotion, we make explicit what lies implicit in health education practice. This mapping opens the relevance of our assumptions to question and to measurement.

Besides the signposts implied by the factors identified in the foregoing models, and the relationships implied by the arrows, the health promotion "movement" suggests some more immediate benefits to be appreciated from lifestyle modification than most health professionals and scientists would normally count as health outcomes. Some would not be counted because they are too subjective, such as "feeling good," "feeling alert," and "feeling more energetic." Others would not be counted because they are considered to have more to do with cosmetic, economic, or social norms than with objectively defined health. Such outcomes of "healthier" lifestyle include weight control, agility, endurance, concentration, efficiency of movement, muscle tone, and independence or performance in activities of daily living.

Together, these and related "intangibles" make up a large part of the "quality of life" or social concerns that are considered a consequence of health in the public education model. They are given prominence there because public health education begins "where the people are" as a matter of principle or philosophy, and because educational research, especially on adult populations, has demonstrated that people who are committed to a program's goals are more likely to participate, cooperate, or otherwise behave in response to a program. Recognizing that the most important concerns of a population are seldom expressed in terms of health, public health education has typically worked to show people how health can contribute to their quality of life or social concerns. These factors deserve as much measurement attention in some health education and health promotion programs as the emphasis generally accorded measures of physiological change, morbidity, or mortality.

Schools are not obliged to justify their attention to performance and achievement in terms of their contribution to health, just as teen or senior citizen centers need not justify their recreational programs on the basis of any relationship to health. Yet both contribute to health through education and behavior and therefore could be construed as health education and health promotion. The wider range of interventions implied by these new models of school and community health promotion places an additional burden on the health educator or evaluator to specify the placement of interventions relative to the many effects and relationships they are expected to mobilize. Where, for example, does the school's driver education program fit in the broader context of state licensure laws in controlling teenage automobile injuries (Green, 1980b)?

AN EXAMPLE OF MERGING MODELS FOR EVALUATION OF HEALTH PROMOTION

As portrayed in the foregoing review of models and assumptions, the major difference between those derived from the health fields (biomedical, public health, biobehavioral, and public health education) and those derived from education (e.g., the comprehensive school health model) and recreation is where they place health—as an end or as a means, as an ultimate outcome or as an instrumental outcome. Part of the related disagreement over this placement stems from the missions of the various sectors—health, education, and recreation. With the increasing complexity of etiologies and causal pathways for specific diseases and health problems (Stallones, 1980), the health establishment seems ready to entertain more complex models of intervention as related to health outcomes. The growing interest in disease prevention and health promotion attests to this. At the same time the schools and their constituencies are demanding greater "time on task" and improved achievement scores of their students. Employers installing worksite health promotion programs are expecting increased productivity and morale, and reduced health care costs, in addition to the health benefits usually touted to employees. The convergence of these trends suggests a new rationale for health promotion measurement, in which the variables targeted for the short-term outcomes are behavioral and performance variables:

(h) intervention → lifestyle → performance → achievement

Employers and the education establishment lean toward this model more or less, depending on the evidence available on the association between lifestyle and performance as measured in educational or industrial productivity terms. Substantial evidence can be mustered in some areas of lifestlye: drug and alcohol abuse, sleep, exercise, diet, and stress (Kolbe et al., in press; McAlister, 1982; McLeroy, Green, Mullen, & Foshee, 1984; Parkinson, Green, McGill, Eriksen, Pearson, Merwin, Ware, Collings, & Beck, 1982). Their influence on performance in the worksite or school makes them good candidates for measurement and evaluation in worksite health promotion and school health education.

To maintain the interest and possible support of the health establishment, this model needs to be extended to show its potential contribution to health outcomes. The main argument and body of evidence affirming the relevance of this model to health is the pervasive and inescapable correlation between educational attainment and health (Bachman, O'Malley, & Johnston, 1978; Mechanic, 1979; Breslow & Enstrom, 1980). The connection of educational attainment to health is most logically explained in behavioral terms, although genetic and economic factors undeniably enter into both the educational attainment and the health behavior of children and their parents. The empirical evidence supporting the causal link between educational attainment and health behavior is consistent but tenuous in that it is not experimental. Similarly, the link between health behavior and long-term health outcomes is widely documented and accepted, but nearly impossible to establish experimentally.

With these caveats in mind, we propose the following model for measurement and evaluation in schools and worksites:

(i) health services ↘ (→ lifestyle, → performance)

health education → lifestyle → performance → achievement → health

health environment ↗ (→ lifestyle, → performance)

This model, of course, is highly simplified, leaving out the "exogenous" influences of other aspects of the curriculum on performance, factors other than performance on achievement, and factors outside the school or worksite, including coordinated community health services and community health promotion efforts, on all the outcomes. Our purpose is simply to specify the essential elements linking health education and related interventions with health outcomes in a causal chain that recognizes and gives primacy to the productivity outcomes, which are the main, if not the sole, concern of schools and worksites.

DECISIONS ABOUT WHAT TO MEASURE

Early in the staging of the program's evaluation, the evaluator asks, "What should I measure?" This simple question is best answered by determining the objects of interest to the sponsors or consumers of the evaluation and the standards of acceptability that they will apply to those objects. The objects of interest may be any of the factors identified in the foregoing models, or one or more elements of process, impact, or outcome, as shown in Figure 3-1. We addressed formative or process measures in the previous chapter, so we concentrate here on impact and outcome measures. In nonmedical fields of evaluation, the terms *impact* and *outcome* are sometimes used in reverse: *outcome* refers to the more immediate effects of programs, methods, or professional activity; *impact* refers to the distant or ultimate effects of social programs. The usage here is intended to conform to the established use of *outcome* in biomedical and health services research traditions to refer to physiological changes and subsequent consequences in terms of quality of life and economic benefits. In educational diagnosis, impact and outcome variables are the primary and secondary causes of ultimate social goals or quality of life concerns.

At one extreme, the object to be measured can be an isolated clinical outcome, such as blood pressure, or indicators of a set of behaviors, such as diet management. The objects or variables can vary on their degree of abstractness. Behavior and even diet management are broad abstractions of human actions. Less abstract would be specific actions such as number of calories consumed in a day, specific vegetables consumed, last purchase of butter or margarine. At the other extreme, the phenomena of interest are the complex relationships among concepts in the cause-and-effect chain of a larger conceptual framework. This interest may entail (1) a broad concern with the relationship between knowledge and attitudes, or between health beliefs and health behavior; or (2) a specific relationship between recall of a specific fact (e.g., peanuts can cause cancer) and attitude toward an object (e.g., eating peanut butter). In both cases, it is necessary to understand what is meant by a concept and an indicator in health education.

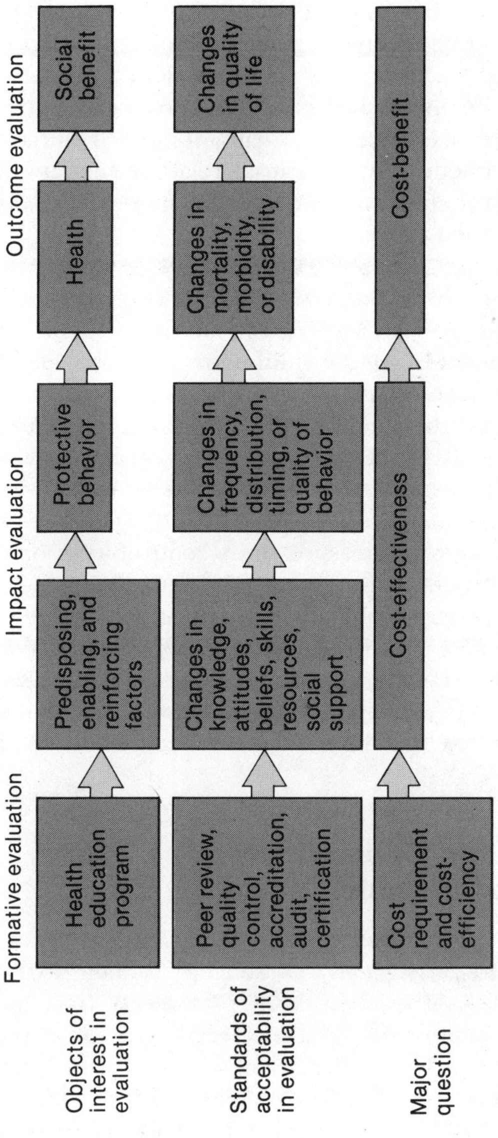
Formative evaluation
Impact evaluation
Outcome evaluation
Objects of interest in evaluation
Health education program
Predisposing, enabling, and reinforcing factors
Protective behavior
Health
Social benefit
Standards of acceptability in evaluation
Peer review, quality control, accreditation, audit, certification
Changes in knowledge, attitudes, beliefs, skills, resources, social support
Changes in frequency, distribution, timing, or quality of behavior
Changes in mortality, morbidity, or disability
Changes in quality of life
Major question
Cost requirement and cost-efficiency
Cost-effectiveness
Cost-benefit

Program effects to be measured may include one or more of the projected or predicted outcomes the program is expected to have in its target population or their environment. Ideally, the assumed link between program effect and program elements is implied by the underlying conceptual framework or theory of the health education program. In the framework, the relation between the program elements and the projected outcomes is understood within some causal model that theoretically links the various elements in the health education program to their intended impact, which in turn are linked to their anticipated outcomes. Figure 3-2 illustrates a hypothetical set of causal relationships among program elements (process), their initial impact, and the subsequent outcomes. The arrows represent assumed cause.

The objectives of the health education program usually specify what needs to be measured. If the program objectives are sufficiently detailed and logically developed, they often direct attention to the specific program impact and outcomes. At the minimum, they provide the parameters or identified boundaries of the potential areas to measure. They should at the very least suggest the scope or breadth of outcomes to be affected by the program. The more specific the program objectives are, the more guidance they provide in deciding *what* to measure. Loosely or capriciously conceived program objectives provide little guidance. Worse, they can mislead the evaluator to measure the wrong objects or to misplace the emphasis onto detailed measurement of trivial effects.

With or without program objectives to guide the choice of measures, you need also to stand back from the program assumptions to ask what theory or conceptual framework has guided the program. Knowledge of the theoretical basis for a program can suggest additional concepts or variables to be measured that may not have been listed as objectives in the program.

From Concepts and Constructs to Indicators and Variables

In health education, as in other applied behavioral sciences, most concepts cannot be measured directly. A concept is merely an abstraction created by a generalization drawn from particulars. It is induced from particular situations, statements, gestures, responses, or observations. As an abstraction, a concept is not directly observable or measurable. Examples of concepts relevant to health education include (1) locus of control, (2) health beliefs, and (3) reinforcing factors. When a concept has been selected or developed for use in a conceptual or theoretical framework, it is called a *construct*. A construct is a concept adopted for use in scientific formulations (Kerlinger, 1973). Because a construct is a type of a concept, by definition it too is a nonobservable. Constructs correspond-

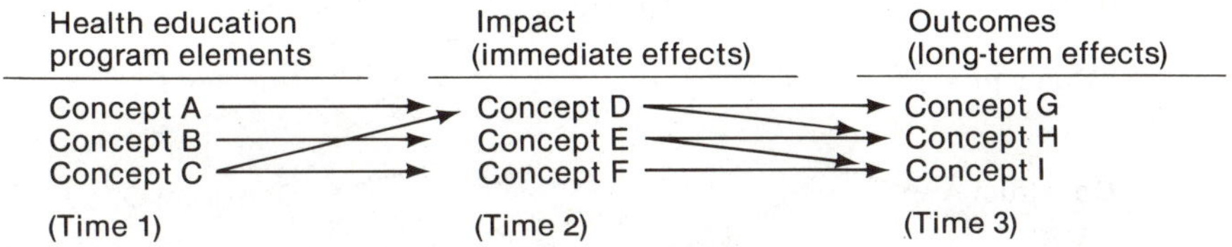

Figure 3-2 *Example of conceptual linkages among program elements and outcomes.*

ing to the examples of concepts just given are (1) health locus of control, (2) belief in seriousness, and (3) social support.

As nonobservables, constructs have no direct measures. Rather, the health education evaluator chooses measures or instruments that provide a range of scores or indicators for the construct, and the evaluation infers that he or she has measured the construct. These specific measures are called *indicators*. Indicators are observable phenomena that are inferred measures of concepts or constructs. Other labels for indicators include *indices, operators,* and *indicants*. For each of the previous examples the indicator might be (1) a single answer in a questionnaire, (2) a total score adding or subtracting answers to a series of interview questions, or (3) a rating based on observation of a behavior.

Measurement involves measures, not of the concept or construct, but of their *properties* (Kerlinger, 1973). Concepts and constructs each have multiple properties or dimensions. For example, health beliefs (constructs) include beliefs in seriousness, in susceptibility, and in efficacy of prevention or treatment. Belief in seriousness includes dimensions such as fear, knowledge of risks, and attitudes toward risks (properties) for any given disease or health threat. Indicators, then, serve as surrogate measures of some of the properties of a concept or construct. From Figure 3-3 you will also note that more than one indicator serves as a surrogate measure for any one property or variable in a given construct. Usually multiple indicators are used for any variable or construct. Several questions would be asked, for example, to generate a variable to indicate internal health locus of control, or belief in seriousness of a given disease, or positive peer support. (Figure 3-3 illustrates only two or three indicators for each of two properties, to simplify the chart.) The task of the program evaluator is to choose the best indicators from among a possible set of indicators.

The word *variable* is often used inappropriately as a substitute for *concepts*. A variable is an observable property that varies—that is, takes on different values—and to which numbers are assigned. In the present discussion, a variable may be equivalent to an indicator or may consist of

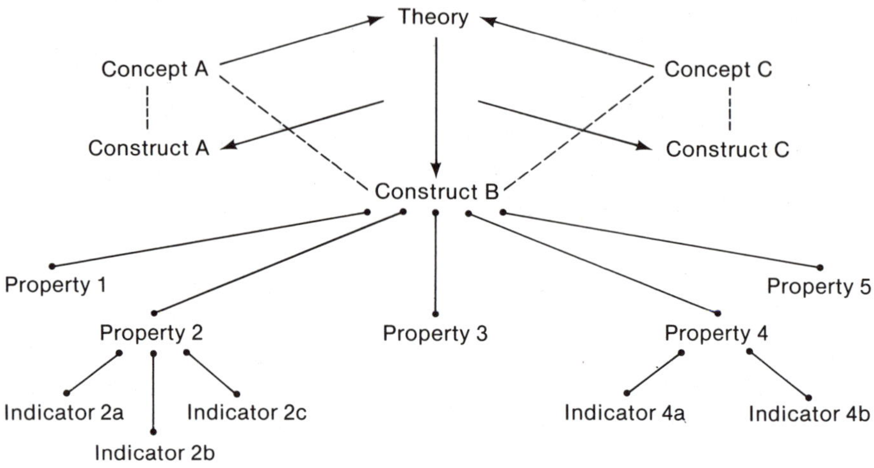

Figure 3-3 *Theory, constructs, concepts, properties, and indicators.*

several indicators combined to measure a property or a dimension of a construct. The variables for the preceding illustrative constructs might be scores on a scale of 1 to 5 in response to a single question, or total scores from 5 to 25 in response to five questions or interview items. The relations between theory, concept, construct, property, and indicator are illustrated in Figure 3-3. A variable may be created to serve as the measure of a specific indicator, or as the combination of two or more indicators to measure a property or dimension of the construct, or as the combination of two or more properties to estimate the relative standing of a individual or group on the construct itself.

In the actual measurement procedure, the analyst assigns numbers to the accepted indicators after making observations (e.g., through questionnaires) of the indicators. The assigned numbers associated with the indicators are then used in subsequent statistical analysis (see Figure 3-4). Examples of concepts, constructs, properties, indicators, and variables in health education evaluations are shown in Table 3-1, listed in the approximate order of immediate to ultimate outcomes (see page 72).

Several consequences in health education follow from this discussion of concepts, constructs, and indicators. First, you can never claim to measure directly either a concept or a construct. Rather, in health education evaluation, as in other studies involving measurement, you always measure indicators, or approximations, of the concepts. The evaluator who claims to have measured locus of control and belief in seriousness is technically incorrect. In practice, measurement is not made of these concepts but of the accepted indicators of these concepts. Evaluators can only infer the existence of the concepts from the measures of indicators.

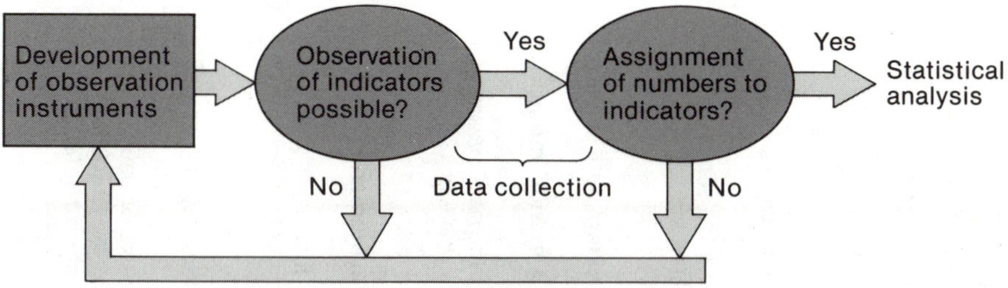

Figure 3-4 *Measurement procedure.*

For example, you may decide, on the basis of the program objectives, to measure self-esteem in a smoking prevention program for adolescents. Self-esteem, you decided from theory and previous research, is a key determinant of long-term behavior (resistance to smoking) and ultimately of health outcomes. Thus self-esteem is the concept linking the program to the intended benefit. In this case, it is also a construct. The question you now face is "How do I measure the participants' self-esteem?" Because various potential ways exist for measuring self-esteem, your decision is really among multiple indicators. A review of the literature will reveal many paper-and-pencil tests measuring self-esteem. Self-esteem may also be measured by interviewing all program participants and analyzing the content of their responses. Using informed reports from the adolescents' teachers, friends, or family is another way to measure the participants' self-esteem. Projective techniques and behavioral measures could provide additional indicators of self-esteem. The point is that *specifying what to measure includes specifying both the object to be measured and the exact means by which it is to be measured.*

A second implication of measurement is that in choosing what to measure, you decide between measuring short-term or more long-term phenomena. This choice is sometimes an issue of focusing on quickly forgotten information or behavior change versus what is retained. Short-term phenomena or measures of impact are usually evident during or immediately after completion of the health education program. But evidence of their continued presence over time is difficult to obtain. This difference is particularly obvious, for example, with technical knowledge. The more technical the knowledge and the less rehearsed its content, the shorter the time over which it will be retained.

The third important implication of measurement for health education is that seldom do single indicators exist that are accepted as definitive measures of a concept or construct. Rather, the evaluator must virtually always deal with multiple indicators of any concept or construct. In eval-

TABLE 3-1 Examples of concepts, constructs, properties, indicators, and variables in health education evaluation

Concepts/Constructs	Properties (Dimensions)	Indicators[a]	Variable
Predisposing Factors			
Locus of control	Internal vs. external	Questionnaire items	Sum of ratings
Health beliefs	Belief in susceptibility	Checklist items	No. of positive responses
Enabling Factors			
Decision-making skill	Ability to estimate risks	Simulation	Test performance score
Access to resources	Ability to pay for services Distribution	Income	Monthly salary
Reinforcing Factors			
Peer support	Perception of support	Interview of subject	Rating of support on a scale of 1 to 10
Social norms	Expectations of friends	Interview of peers	Average of 3 friends' ratings
Health Behavior			
Utilization	Use of dentist	Frequency	No. of visits in past 2 years
Self-care	Flossing teeth	Self-report	No. of times per week
Health Outcomes			
Risk factor	Blood pressure	Control	Mm Hg on 2 sphygmomanometer readings
Morbidity	Disabling illness	No. of sick days	No. of days lost from work
Mortality	Deaths from stroke	Stroke as primary cause of death	Age-specific death rates
Social Benefits			
Economic benefits	Reduced medical care expenditures	Hospitalization	No. of hospital days for stroke
Quality of life	Autonomy	Independent functioning checklist	No. of activities of daily living performed on checklist
Productivity	Output	Absenteeism	No. of days absent/total days paid

[a]The terms *indicators* and *variables* are used interchangeably by different authors.

uation research, the program evaluator should therefore anticipate the critics' challenge that the appropriate indicators were not chosen in any particular study or that the chosen indicators were not appropriate or sufficient reflections of the underlying concept. For example, self-reported "compliance" with prescribed medical regimens is often criticized as a weak measure of the patient's adherence to the prescribed regimen. The best protection against such criticism is to have multiple indicators of each major effect expected of the program.

Recall from the discussion of models in the first part of this chapter a fourth implication of this discussion of concepts, indicators, and variables. Program evaluation in health education can and should be viewed from both a conceptual and an operational perspective.[1] Dual attention is needed on both the underlying concepts and the indicators. It takes only a little reflection to realize that most health education programs have as their major purpose not the altering or modifying of some isolated specific attitudinal or even behavioral indicator, but instead the changing of some larger pattern of behavior better represented in a more general concept or construct, such as participation in planning, lifestyle, self-care, delay, prenatal care, or use of health services. Even the program administrator with minimum theoretical training in health education often has, if only vaguely, some causal chain in mind that relates program components to its outcomes. Elements in this causal chain are concepts, not indicators.

When you conceptualize your measurement problem at both a conceptual and operational level, specific advantages accrue. Any concept, because of its multiple properties or dimensions, has different aspects that you may wish to consider in order to document program effect. By sorting out the relative change in specific indicators, you might find that your program achieved a considerable increase in fear of a disease but little improvement in knowledge of the actual risk. Such specificity in relation to the construct of "belief in susceptibility" could be very helpful in modifying the program design. Attention to *only* the operational measurement level, however, easily results in "missing" some salient properties of the overriding concept. This result, in turn, may cause you to document only trivial program effects, at least from the broader (conceptual) perspective of the program objectives. In addition, casting the program evaluation within a conceptual perspective permits you to identify a larger set, and a more detailed set, of hypotheses about the program and its effects because it puts the evaluation in touch with a richer body of literature and previous research on the broader concepts.

1. This position sharply contrasts with one that sees much of program evaluation totally at the operational level; that is, a position in which the indicators as indicators are all-important. In such a position, theoretical formulations and constructs receive little if any attention. For further elaboration of this position, see Suchman (1967), p. 330.

Finally, it should be clear that empirical results from most health education evaluations are more or less removed from the full representation of the underlying concepts. Conclusions by implication must be carefully interpreted and reported as approximations of the effect of such a program on "health beliefs," or "locus of control," or "peer support," or "lifestyle as measured by ______."

The Relevance of Measures

The ideal measuring instrument is relevant in addition to being valid and reliable.[2] Relevance concerns issues of applicability[3] and economy.

A *relevant* instrument has applicability to all the people on whom it is administered. Such relevance implies that every subject for which the measuring device was chosen can potentially obtain any score, including the highest or the lowest score, when measures are taken. This capacity implies that the full range of scores must be potentially applicable to every person on whom it is used. Every subject is potentially describable in terms of that particular characteristic or attribute. It would be inappropriate, for example, to ask a set of attitudinal questions about the use of over-the-counter drugs with respondents whose culture does not recognize the use of external chemical agents in symptom reduction. It is similarly inappropriate to administer an instrument measuring food management skills to the institutionalized elderly, who depend on others for meal preparation.

Relevant measures are also economical, because they obtain some degree of meaningful information from all subjects in the evaluation study. Because the measures are applicable to most if not all the clients, information is obtained, so use of the "not applicable" response category is minimized or unnecessary. The amount and usefulness of information yielded by each observation, measure, or question should be commensurate with the cost of collecting the information.

UNITS OF OBSERVATION AND LEVELS OF MEASUREMENT

The subjects of measurement may be events, individuals, families, groups, organizations, communities, or some other population unit, depending on the level of aggregation of smaller units.

2. Technically speaking, validity and reliability are not categorical properties of measurements. As will be seen in the next two chapters, measurements possess varying degrees of validity and reliability.

3. Relevance may also be discussed in terms of the measuring instrument's correspondence to reality. Such discussion borders on issues of specificity as part of validity (see Chapter 6).

If measurement is the assignment of numbers to subjects or objects according to certain rules, then different rules can specify different levels of measurement for any given unit of observation. Four levels of measurement—nominal, ordinal, interval, and ratio—are listed in Table 3-2, along with definitions. Table 3-2 summarizes some of the permissible statistical tests appropriate for each level of measurement.

We discuss levels of measurement first, then units of observation (under the heading "Levels of Aggregation of Measurement").

Levels of Measurement

Nominal classification is merely the coding of characteristics into categories such as female or male. For example, let the number 1 denote a female and let the number 2 denote a male. These assigned numbers, 1 or 2, have no numerical meaning and as a consequence, they cannot be added, subtracted, or rank ordered. Indeed, letters or symbols from any alphabet could be used as codes. The numbers or other codes serve merely to designate the assignment labeling, or placement of each program recruit into one of the two or more categories. Such coding makes manual or computer tabulation and data management more efficient than the descriptive words for each category, especially as the number of categories becomes large. Postal zip codes are an example of numerical classification of a large number of categories (place of residence). As such, zip codes represent a nominal measure of residence that cannot be added, subtracted, ranked, or otherwise numerically manipulated except to classify people by region, state, city, and postal zone.

Ordinal-level measurement rank orders the phenomena or objects of interest. The numbers assigned to the objects of interest reflect a ranking, not some absolute numerical quality. For example, a health educator may be asked to rank order the relative ability of twenty adolescent boys who complete a program on diabetic control. Each boy would receive a number from 1 to 20. The assignment of this rank is based on the program recruit's ability to perform on some selected criterion variable, as compared to the performance on the same variable of the other nineteen. These same assigned numbers indicate a ranking of the twenty boys with respect to each other, but the numbers themselves do not contain an absolute numerical quantity. As a result, numbers based on rank orderings cannot be added or subtracted.

Interval-level measurement assumes that all the distances or magnitudes between one assigned number and the next are equal in length or size. As such, numbers assigned at an interval level of measurement can be added or subtracted. It is important to realize, however, that the intervals, not the absolute values of the numbers, have meaning in the calculations. Temperatures on the Fahrenheit scale are interval measures, because

TABLE 3-2 Levels of measurement and examples of numerical procedures appropriate to each

Levels[a]	Comments	Permissible Numerical Procedures and Statistics[b]
Nominal	Categorizes subjects, events, or objects. Numbers assigned have no numerical meaning—i.e., cannot be added or rank ordered.	1. Frequency counts 2. Frequency statistics—e.g., chi square, percentages, contingency coefficients[c]
Ordinal	Rank orders subjects, objects, or events. Numbers indicate rank but not absolute numerical quantity. As such, numbers cannot be added or subtracted.	1. Frequency counts 2. Frequency statistics—e.g., chi square, percentages, contingency coefficients[c] 3. Ranks determined 4. Rank-order measures—e.g., rank-order correlation coefficient; Kendall's W
Interval	Distances between number are assumed to be equal in size. Intervals can be added or subtracted but only with understanding that it is intervals, not absolute numbers, that are involved in computations.	1. Frequency counts 2. Frequency statistics—e.g., chi square, percentages, contingency coefficients[c] 3. Ranks determined 4. Rank-order measures—e.g., rank-order correlation coefficient; Kendall's W 5. Summated ratings 6. Mean, t-tests
Ratio	Scale has an absolute or natural zero point that possesses empirical meaning. Numbers on scale represent the *actual* amount of property measured. Numbers can be added and subtracted as well as divided and multiplied.	1. Frequency counts 2. Frequency statistics—e.g., chi square, percentages, contingency coefficients[c] 3. Ranks determined 4. Rank-order measures—e.g., rank-order correlation coefficient; Kendall's W 5. Summated ratings 6. Mean, t-tests 7. Analysis of variance 8. Correlation analysis and all other parametric tests

[a] Levels are ordered from the lowest (nominal) to the highest (ratio) level of measurement.

[b] The list of statistical operations is suggestive, not exhaustive.

[c] For a detailed discussion of statistical assumptions underlying nonparametric statistics, see Siegel (1956).

the difference between 99 and 100 is the same as the difference between 100 and 101, but zero has no absolute meaning on this scale.

Ratio-level measurement is the highest level of measurement. In ratio-level measures, the scale has an absolute or natural zero starting point that has empirical meaning. The numbers on the scale represent the actual amounts of the measured property. Ratio-level scales are scarce among impact measures at the cognitive and attitudinal level in health education evaluation, but common in counts of behavior such as number of clinical visits, number of missed appointments, months of prenatal care received, number of calories consumed, number of days per week in vigorous physical activity, number of cigarettes smoked; and changes in risk factors such as pounds lost, serum cholesterol level, or sodium, sugar, alcohol, or other substance consumed, as measured in blood or urine samples.

The key question for the program evaluator with regard to levels of measurement is "What level of classification or measurement is possible, economical, and reasonable?" The answer to this question comes from two sources: (1) a measurement perspective and (2) a practitioner-oriented perspective.

From the measurement perspective, the level of measurement chosen should maximize discrimination among subjects on program effects. In addition, higher levels of measurement—for example, interval and ratio-level measures—permit the use of a greater variety of statistics in the data analyses. It is often to the evaluator's advantage to choose the highest level of measurement that the indicator and data collection procedures allow. When lower levels of measurement are chosen, some information is lost and consequently program facts may be missed.

The practitioner perspective in selecting measurement level offers an alternative or complementary perspective to the strict measurement perspective. The practitioner perspective demands clinical or administrative meaningfulness from the measurement level you choose (Green & Lewis, 1981). From this perspective, it may be clinically and socially meaningless to distinguish between fine levels of the impact or outcome variable. For example, the evaluator may develop a health education program whose purpose it is to affect the participant's blood pressure. Although interval scales can be constructed to measure diastolic and systolic blood pressure readings to the nearest millimeter, such differentiation may not be clinically meaningful. Instead, it may only be important that the subject is "in" or "out" of blood pressure control, using some nationally recognized blood pressure criterion. It is even less likely that clinicians or health administrators will find much meaning in attitude scale scores elaborated to the second decimal. Such misplaced precision can be costly and distracting.

In summary, your choice of measurement level for both the impact and the outcome variables in health education diagnosis and evaluation should balance scientific and practical concerns. The same balancing will be seen throughout this text as we move from measurement to evaluation.

Levels of Aggregation of Measurement

In health education and health promotion, the community health perspective approaches the problem of needs assessment as an initial step in *program* planning. The assessment is carried out with the intent of developing a composite package of health education interventions that will be most appropriate and cost-effective for a *population* of patients, clients, students, or consumers, rather than the perfect intervention for each individual. This diagnostic perspective is distinguished from the medical model of individual provider-patient encounter, in which diagnosis is intended to pinpoint the specific problems of that patient in order to tailor a treatment plan for that patient. Educational and behavioral interventions are characterized in the literature and in clinical settings by one or the other of these two perspectives and orientations toward measurement (see Table 3-3).

The health educator who has a community or population perspective is more likely (than one without such a perspective) to use sociological and epidemiological methodologies that emphasize a survey approach to data collection. Instruments often have structured, standardized questions and preestablished categories of response. In the most rigorously technical situations, instruments are piloted, normed, and tested for their psychometric properties in advance of their administration for diagnostic study. In contrast, the clinician's methodologies emphasize intensive, open-ended interviewing. Open-ended questions are preferred, particularly in the early diagnostic stages. Structured or standard questions exist, but the response categories are often not predetermined. Emphasis is on individualized analysis of medical records and patient responses.

The health educator with a community or population perspective *aggregates* or *summarizes* the data from individual patients or other subjects sampled, attempts to gain objective distance from them, and tries to construct a composite picture of educational needs. These identified needs are based on a particular study variable, or on a statistical difference observed between groups of patients, students, workers, clients, or consumers. Attention goes to identifying epidemiological *patterns* that appear in the aggregated data. Data for the health educator adopting a community perspective include percentages, rates, measures of central tendency, contingency tables, and various types of coefficients. Within such aggregated data, the individual virtually "disappears." Idiosyncracies and unique characteristics are absorbed and masked.

TABLE 3-3 Contrasting perspectives in diagnostic and evaluative measurement

Community Health Perspective (Social-Epidemiological Model)	Clinician's Perspective (Medical Diagnostic Model)
Methodology emphasizing a survey approach with standardized instruments	Methodology emphasizing intensive interviewing and individualized content analysis
Aggregate data used	Case data used
Data collected from several sources	Data source limited to patient
Summary measures and statistics used	Individual data (e.g., patient's lab tests) used
Idiosyncratic data minimized	Idiosyncratic data influential
Tends to focus on a given disease or problem early	Initially attempts to "rule out" several diagnostic possibilities
Diagnosis based on patterns in data summarized across patients	Diagnosis based on inference from data on individual patient
Treatment consisting of a program of varied interventions for different categories of patients, clients, or consumers	Treatment consisting of a specific intervention to achieve a specific effect tailored to the patient
Diagnostic process finite; generates new hypotheses or diagnostic probabilities only if surveillance system is installed with program	Diagnostic process continuous or repetitive; generates new hypotheses or diagnostic possibilities over time through trial and error

Source: Green, Lewis, & Levine (1980), p. 89.

For clinicians, such summarizing of data violates the very purpose for which as students they so dutifully studied such things as differential diagnoses and detailed family or personal histories. They are inclined to see data aggregation as an "organizational" matter and leave it to hospital administrators.

In an attempt to be efficient or for reasons of mandate, the community health educator tends to focus on a given problem relatively early in the diagnostic phase. The expectation of problem-oriented planning is that, once identified, the problem's cause can be appropriately "ruled in" and can be effectively targeted by the educational program. This expectation stands in contrast to the clinician, who attempts to "rule out" several diagnostic possibilities before "ruling in" the cause of the problem. For the clinician, the diagnostic process is continuous, even after the initial therapy or intervention is begun. For the community health educator, the opportunities for repeated surveillance or monitoring are more limited after program implementation has begun.

The origin of the educational diagnosis is different for the community health educator. For the clinician, treatment consists of a tailored intervention targeted to achieve a particular behavioral response specific for a unique client. This approach frequently mobilizes diverse educational modalities that are cycled only once in a particular sequence. In contrast, the community health educator develops a systematic treatment program that consists of multiple standardized interventions for different categories or types of clients. The tailoring of the educational intervention is limited by the fit between the standardized program package and any particular individual's unique learning needs.

Unlike the community health perspective, idiosyncracies in the data and the patient's individuality are critical in formulating a medical treatment plan and course of therapy. This plan is influenced by informal observations of the particular patient's demeanor, his or her intelligence and maturation, as well as the clinician's experience with patients who share certain characteristics with the presenting patient. We (the authors of this book) believe that, with responsible data collection (sampling design, instrumentation, and field administration) and analysis, an educational diagnosis from aggregate data can assure as much validity in designing a patient education program for a population of patients as could be assured from a diagnosis based on the sum of individually tailored interventions from clinical assessments of each patient's educational needs. The main advantage of the former method is efficiency. These two perspectives can be complementary, as illustrated in some case studies (Cernada, 1982; Green, Gustafson, Griffiths, & Yaukey, 1972; Green, Lewis, & Levine, 1980; Zapka & Mamon, 1982).

SUMMARY

Clear conceptualization, appropriate design, and adequate measurement are key elements in any diagnosis or evaluation in health education or heath promotion. Measurement is the assignment of numbers to objects, events, or people according to specific rules. As such, measurement requires careful specification of the objects to be measured, the numbers to assign, and the rules by which the numbers are assigned. The objects to be measured are specified according to alternative conceptual models. Categories of models include the biomedical and public health models, biobehavioral models, health education models, school health models, the community health promotion model, and the worksite health promotion model. These models help health educators develop "maps" of the theoretical links among concepts and indicators, including the relationship between program interventions and outcome or impact variables. Ultimately, the frameworks help us decide what to measure.

Concepts are abstractions created from particulars and are not directly observable. Indicators are specific measures of concepts that are observable. In reality, the health educator assigns numbers to the indicators or variables after making observations of the objects of interest. These numbers are then used in subsequent data analyses.

Levels of measurement are based on the rules by which numbers are assigned to the observed objects of interest. Nominal measures merely assign an observation into two or more categories. Ordinal-level measurement rank orders the objects of interest. Interval-level measurement assigns the observed objects to numbers, assuming that the distances among all adjacent numbers are all equal in size. Ratio-level measurement involves the assignment of numbers to a scale in which there is an absolute zero point that has empirical meaning.

The evaluator needs to maintain perspective on both the short- and the long-term objectives, on the conceptual and the operational, on practice and policy questions, and on individual and aggregate levels of measurement. In approaching the subject of measurement, the health educator does well to maintain both a theoretical or a conceptual perspective as well as an operational one. If the evaluator loses sight of the overall conceptual framework or implicit cause-and-effect chain linking program activity to health outcomes, measurement can stray into irrelevant and costly realms. By keeping the larger picture as well as the immediate operations and effects in view, you can balance the distribution of indicators and the relative investment in their measurement in such a way that the evaluation can inform both your practice and your policy decisions.

Chapter 4

RELIABILITY OF MEASUREMENT

The ideal measurement is both valid and reliable.[1] A *valid* instrument or procedure measures exactly what you want it to measure, and a ***reliable*** one does it consistently. Such ideal measurement is totally free from error.

Such a "perfect" instrument has not, does not, and will never exist. Measurement, like most things, has limitations. This recognition need not cause dismay; it only reflects reality. As a practitioner or an evaluator, you proceed with an awareness of any instrument's limitations and the level of confidence you can place in the information obtained from it. Instead of discouragement, your awareness of the instrument's limitations should cause both reflection and action. You might well ask, "What is meant by 'valid and reliable instruments'? What do different types of reliability tell me about my evaluation instrument? How do I interpret the various reliability coefficients for a set of measures? If my budget and timetable allow, what can I do to maximize the reliability in my set of measures?"

This chapter challenges you (1) to understand what is meant by reliability, (2) to interpret estimates of reliability in a set of health education measurements, and (3) whenever possible, to modify the instrument or methods of its administration in order to improve the obtained reliability estimates.

Imagine yourself a health educator interested in systematically evaluating the effects of a nutrition program on its participants. You have developed a twenty-item paper-and-pencil questionnaire. Before using it, you wonder, "Are all twenty questions measuring aspects of food habits?" You next wonder, "Would each person's answers to the questionnaire be the

1. It is technically more accurate to apply estimates of validity and reliability not to an instrument or set of measures, but to a set of *measurements*. This distinction is made because these estimates depend on three things: (1) the measuring instrument itself, (2) the population sample, and (3) the conditions under which the instrument is administered (Guilford & Fruchter, 1973). As Cronbach (1971, p. 447) stated, "One validates not a test, but an interpretation of data arising from a specified procedure."

same if I gave the test now and once again a week later?" You then ask, "If someone else administered the questionnaire, would the results be the same?" These questions relate to three types of reliability. The first question relates to ***internal consistency;*** the second addresses ***stability*** or ***test-retest reliability;*** the last question relates to ***interrater reliability.***

We begin with an introduction to the classical theory of measurement error. This theory forms a basis for understanding the operational forms of reliability, namely internal consistency and stability reliability. Readers interested in a more mathematical introduction to classical test theory or measurement error theory are referred to Chapter 17 in Guilford and Fruchter (1973), Lord and Novick (1968), or Chapters 13 and 14 in Guilford (1954). Theoretical details on measurement error are presented in Chapter 6 in Nunnally (1967), Chapter 26 in Kerlinger (1973), and Chapter 6 in Selltiz, Wrightsman, and Cook (1976).

INTRODUCTION TO MEASUREMENT THEORY

Reducing the amount of error or "noise" in an instrument increases its reliability. The greater the amount of error, the less reliable the measurements. The less reliable the measures, the lower the degree of confidence you can have in the obtained diagnostic or evaluation results. Reducing error in the instrument or set of measures increases the evaluation's credibility and value.

A Tale of Two Errors

Two types of error creep into a measuring instrument: (1) constant or systematic error and (2) random error. A ***constant error*** is one that systematically affects the characteristic being measured or the measurement process itself. It produces ***bias*** in the measure because it constantly tilts the results in one direction or another. A ***random error,*** on the other hand, results from temporary conditions in the person, situation, or measurement procedures that vary in direction or magnitude from time to time. This variability in measurement occurs even though the underlying characteristic being measured remains the same. The first goal of the diagnostician or evaluator is to minimize the amount of random measurement error in the set of instruments to be used.

Validity estimates, considered in the next chapter, are affected by both constant or systematic error as well as by random error. Reliability is influenced only by random errors. Table 4-1 summarizes the association of random and systematic error with reliability and validity.

TABLE 4-1 Categories of error for validity and reliability

	Random Error	Constant or Systematic Error
Reliability	Applicable	Not applicable
Validity	Applicable	Applicable

Theoretical Conceptions of Reliability: Classical Error Theory

An individual's score on a set of measures is composed of a "true" measure and an error component. The obtained score or the total score on the measuring instrument is a combination of both components, as represented in Table 4-2.

The total score is the score you actually obtain on a measuring instrument—for example, a questionnaire or knowledge test—for any particular person in your study. The "true" score is the score the same individual would obtain if all conditions of administration were ideal and the measuring instrument were perfect. The error score represents either an increase or a decrease from the "true" score. This error score arises from several factors responsible for errors in measurement.

As with a particular person's score, so it is with an instrument. Any measuring instrument has three types of variances: total variance, "true" variance, and error variance. These types are summarized in Table 4-3. Error variance is distinguished from sampling variance. Error variance results from imperfect measuring procedures, while sampling variance results from deviations from population values when samples are drawn. Sampling variance is discussed in a later chapter.

If reliability is defined as the opposite of error variance, then an estimation of error variance in a set of measures can reflect the measurement's reliability. The reliability of a set of measurements is the proportion of their variance that is "true" variance or what would be obtained if the

TABLE 4-2 Components of an obtained score for a particular person

		Total Obtained Score or Measure		
		True Score + Error Component		
Total Score (Obtained Score)	=	*True* Score (Unobservable)	+	*Error* Score

TABLE 4-3 Components of the variance in an instrument's score				
Score's Total Obtained Variance				
Total Variance (Obtained)	=	True Variance	+	Error Variance (Unobservable)

set of measurements were totally free from error. Reliability can be defined as the ratio of "true" to total variance. As illustrated in Equation 1 in Table 4-4, the larger the "true" variance, the greater is the reliability in a set of measurements.

Reliability is usually expressed in the form of a coefficient that ranges from 0 to 1, and Equation 2 in Table 4-4 will yield a value between 0 and 1. Equation 2 shows that larger error variances act to reduce the size of the reliability coefficient. If all the variance in the observed score results from measurement error, the reliability coefficient will be 0 (zero). With no measurement error, the reliability coefficient will be equal to 1.

OPERATIONAL FORMS OF RELIABILITY

Reliability reflects the consistency and dependability of a set of measurements. When assessing reliability, you ask, "Can I rely on my set of measurements repeatedly and consistently to yield the same results under similar conditions? Will the measurements yield the same ranking or ordering of individuals in the population on the characteristic of interest?" Your operational criterion of the measurements' repeatability will be stability or test-retest reliability. The operational test of the degree to which the instrument measures one phenomenon in a consistent manner will be internal consistency reliability.

Each type of reliability estimate provides a different piece of information about the basic behavior of the measurement instrument. This idea is represented in Figure 4-1. Knowledge about the stability reliability of a set of measurements, for example, does not tell you anything about the set's internal consistency reliability. Some methods provide a more com-

TABLE 4-4 Reliability as proportional variance

Equation 1	Reliability	$= \dfrac{\text{True Variance}}{\text{Total Variance}}$
Equation 2	Reliability	$= 1 - \dfrac{\text{Error Variance}}{\text{Total Variance}}$

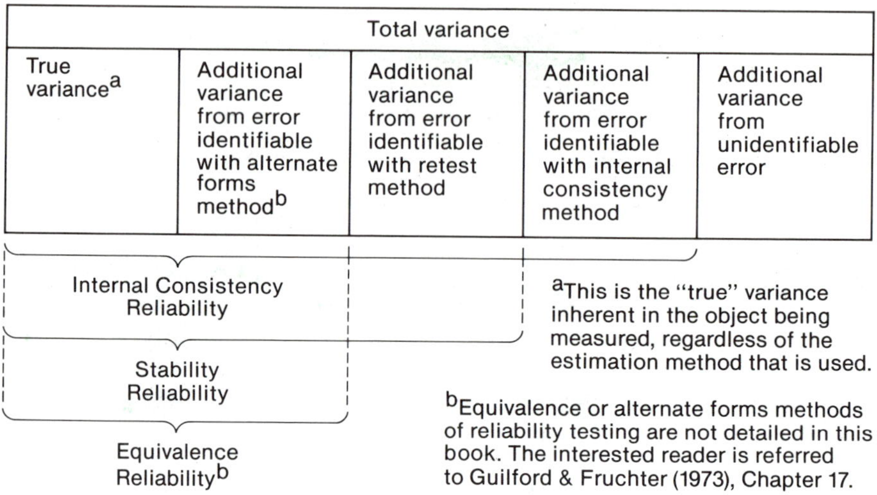

Figure 4-1 *Categories for estimating reliability and related error variance.* Source: *Adapted from Guilford & Fruchter (1973), p. 404.*

prehensive but less specific estimate of reliability. As a result, there is no "best way" to estimate reliability. Rather, you obtain information on the different types of reliability when that information is (1) relevant to verifying the value or merit of the set of measurements for the immediate purposes of the evaluation, (2) important in making the same measures usable in replications and other applications of the instruments, and (3) obtainable given the form of data available from the actual evaluation study.

Internal consistency, split-half, and stability reliability reflect the amount of internal measurement error in the instrument. Interrater reliability reflects external or coder error.

There are several ways of obtaining estimates, usually expressed as coefficients, of these various forms of reliability. Variations on these coefficients make up the technical aspects of reliability testing, but the concept is essentially the quest for dependable and consistent measures. Reliable measurements increase the level of confidence you can have in the results of your assessments of health education needs, impact, or outcomes.

Internal Consistency Reliability

Internal consistency reliability examines the intercorrelations or covariance of all the individual items making up the instrument. It is an indication of the extent to which each item in the instrument relates to the other items. The higher the intercorrelations among items, the greater is the instrument's internal consistency reliability.

In evaluating an instrument's internal consistency reliability, the instrument or scale is assumed to be linear or summative (see Nunnally, 1967, Chapter 2). This assumption implies that the instrument is developed as representing only one aspect or dimension of the characteristic being measured. For example, the evaluator might be interested in a measure of control the program participants have over their health. Multiple aspects to control include, but are not limited to, cognitive, behavioral, decision making, and attitudinal control (Lewis, 1982a, 1983a, 1983b). In examining internal consistency, the evaluator chooses to focus on one aspect or dimension at a time. Individual items can be summed into a single score because they are all measuring the same characteristic of interest and they are all of a similar nature. This similarity between the items on the instrument can be examined logically by checking to make sure that all items appear to be of equal difficulty and that they appear to reflect the same aspect of the property being studied. Item similarity can also be examined statistically; see Bohrnstedt (1970), for example, for more detail.

Cronbach's Alpha. The most popular approach to estimating internal consistency reliability is based on the Kuder-Richardson formula (Richardson & Kuder, 1937) and their generalizations, particularly Cronbach's alpha (Cronbach, 1951). Cronbach's alpha is a summary measure of internal consistency based on a calculation of the amount of intercorrelation or similarity of all items examined simultaneously.

The calculated Cronbach's alpha coefficient theoretically ranges from 0 to 1. Values close to 1 denote greater internal consistency reliability in the scale. In computing the alpha coefficient, you seek a statistical estimate of the degree to which all the individual items in the scale are consistently measuring the same underlying concept, property, or characteristic of interest. Let us review a few examples of published reports on the internal consistency reliability of a scale.

An evaluation form for group-led classes in health education was developed to measure two hypothetical dimensions of a health educator's performance: technical competence and interpersonal skill (Miller & Lewis, 1982). Using data collected from 157 respondents, an initial forty-nine-item preliminary version of the Instructor Evaluation Instrument was refined to twenty-seven items. Table 4-5 presents the interitem correlations for both the Technical Competence and the Interpersonal Skill Scales for the final version of the instrument. The alpha reliability for the Technical Competence Scale was 0.89; for the Interpersonal Skill Scale, 0.90. In addition, interitem correlations for the total scale were computed; correlations ranged in size from 0.25 to 0.47. The alpha coefficient for the total scale was 0.94 (Miller & Lewis, 1982, p. 61).

TABLE 4–5 Interitem correlation matrices for items on Instructor Evaluation Instrument

Item	1	2	3	4	5	6	7	8	9	10	11	12	13	
Technical Competence Scale														
1	1.00													
2	.39	1.00												
3	.38	.43	1.00											
4	.27	.25	.23	1.00										
5	.33	.34	.35	.30	1.00									
6	.30	.27	.39	.34	.12	1.00								
7	.34	.40	.40	.45	.26	.47	1.00							
8	.36	.28	.43	.49	.42	.43	.39	1.00						
9	.41	.28	.40	.43	.36	.54	.56	.61	1.00					
10	.37	.46	.51	.29	.49	.29	.37	.51	.38	1.00				
11	.36	.27	.33	.37	.38	.38	.41	.47	.55	.45	1.00			
12	.49	.28	.46	.30	.43	.42	.36	.53	.50	.57	.53	1.00		
13	.28	.31	.45	.39	.34	.35	.43	.45	.49	.45	.43	.44	1.00	
Interpersonal Skill Scale														
1	1.00													
2	.30	1.00												
3	.36	.44	1.00											
4	.36	.29	.41	1.00										
5	.28	.42	.47	.40	1.00									
6	.26	.51	.53	.40	.62	1.00								
7	.32	.31	.48	.33	.34	.48	1.00							
8	.26	.41	.35	.29	.47	.44	.40	1.00						
9	.41	.27	.39	.45	.42	.48	.37	.39	1.00					
10	.30	.35	.39	.34	.34	.38	.30	.54	.42	1.00				
11	.37	.28	.31	.34	.24	.36	.30	.27	.45	.38	1.00			
12	.37	.37	.38	.31	.35	.33	.36	.39	.38	.60	.36	1.00		
13	.55	.46	.45	.44	.48	.45	.44	.42	.49	.51	.50	.61	1.00	
14	.40	.45	.35	.40	.44	.51	.33	.44	.43	.47	.36	.41	.53	1.00

Source: Adapted from Miller & Lewis (1982), pp. 61–62.

Psychometric testing of scales relevant to the Health Belief Model offers another example of the use of internal consistency reliability (e.g., Maiman, Becker, Kirscht, Haefner, & Drachman, 1977; Green, Levine, Wolle, & Deeds, 1979; Dielman, Leech, Becker, Rosenstock, Horvath, & Radius, 1980). In a study of mothers with obese children, a multiple-item questionnaire was constructed to measure each component of the Health Belief Model; responses contained a six-choice rating scale of agreement (Maiman et al., 1977). Single items of the questionnaire that were assumed to be different aspects of the same underlying theoretical concept (based on the Health Belief Model) were combined to form subscales for each of the dimensions of the Health Belief Model. Each subscale was therefore assumed to be measuring a single aspect or dimension. Five specific components of the model were measured: (1) general health motivation, (2) perceived susceptibility, (3) perceived severity, (4) perceived benefits, and (5) perceived barriers.

In computing each subscale's reliability, the covariance among all the items in each subscale was examined simultaneously. Table 4-6 summarizes the consistency coefficients for selected dimensions of the subscales. Note that the subscales had internal consistency reliability coefficients that ranged in size from 0.47 to 0.96.

KR-20 Coefficient. The KR-20 reliability coefficient is an estimate of the internal consistency reliability of a scale composed of dichotomous items (Richardson & Kuder, 1937). In the simplest cases, correct or preferred

TABLE 4-6 Selected measures of internal consistency reliability for parent's Health Belief Model components and dimensions of adherence to diet prescribed for an overweight child

Five Dimensions and Nine Subscales of Health Belief Model	Consistency Coefficient
General Health Motivation	
General health concern for child	0.77
Special health practices for child	0.86
Perceived Susceptibility	
Child's general susceptibility to illness	0.91
Likelihood of contracting specific illness	0.91
Perceived Severity	
Seriousness of overweight	0.85
Worry about child's illnesses in general	0.96
Perceived Benefits	
Likelihood physician can cure specific illness	0.87
Likelihood diet will help child's overweight	0.47
Perceived Barriers	
Likelihood of diet-related problems	0.51

Source: Maiman et al. (1977), pp. 220–221.

answers are assigned one point, and incorrect or nonpreferred answers are assigned zero points. The scoring of the Moos Family Environment Scale (Moos & Moos, 1976; Moos, Insel, & Humphrey, 1974) is an example of an instrument with dichotomous items. Items are true-false; respondents are scored with one point for each "correct" answer. Like Cronbach's alpha coefficient, the KR-20 theoretically varies from 0 to 1. Again, values closer to 1 denote greater internal consistency reliability.

Item-Total Correlations

The item-total correlation shows the degree of association between each individual item on a measuring instrument with the total score on the same instrument. Item-total correlations, like Cronbach's alpha, are a function of the degree of interrelatedness of all items in a unidimensional scale. Unlike Cronbach's alpha, the item-total correlation is not a summary statistic for all items in the scale. Rather, it is a correlation coefficient for *each* item in the scale. This statistic, computed most often as a Pearson correlation coefficient, represents the degree to which that item correlates with the remaining items comprising the total scale (calculated with that item deleted from the total score).

Item-total correlations are often used diagnostically to refine an instrument during its developmental stages. Items are chosen for inclusion in the scale when they correlate most highly with the total scale score. Obviously, the items that correlate most highly with the total scale score are also those items that correlate most highly with each other. Sometimes a criterion level of correlation is established—say, .25 to .35—below which items are excluded from the scale.

Table 4-7 offers examples of item-total correlations in the refined version of the Instructor Evaluation Form described earlier (Miller & Lewis, 1982). The authors specified the set of rules they used to decide which items to retain or to delete. Specifically, they deleted items that were inversely correlated with other scale items, that had low interitem correlations with three or more retained items (i.e., $r \leqslant 0.10$), and whose corrected item-total correlations were low (i.e., $r \leqslant 0.40$) for the total scale or $r \leqslant 0.50$ for the item's relevant subscale (Miller & Lewis, 1982, p. 60). Decision rules may vary according to the study's purpose and the level of measurement error you can tolerate. Dishman and Ickes (1981), for example, used an item-total criterion of .30 for deleting items for an initially large questionnaire pool.

At the very least, you must decide on the error level or on the magnitude of correlation desired to retain items. An arbitrary decision on the cutoff level oversimplifies the evaluator's task. Decisions to delete or retain scale items are both conceptual as well as empirical issues. Recall

TABLE 4-7 Interitem correlation for 27-item instructor evaluation form

Item	Item-Total Correlation
1. The instructor puts high priority on the needs of the class participants.	.51
2. The instructor makes a lot of mistakes in class.	.52
3. The instructor gives directions too quickly.	.52
4. The instructor helps me feel that I am an important contributor to the group.	.55
5. A person feels free to ask the instructor questions.	.61
6. The instructor should be more friendly than he/she is.	.58
7. I could hear what the instructor was saying.	.65
8. The instructor is a person who can understand how I feel.	.57
9. The instructor focuses on my physical condition but has no feeling for me as a person.	.65
10. Everyone who wanted to contribute had an opportunity to do so.	.57
11. There was too much information in some sessions and too little in others.	.52
12. Just talking to the instructor makes me feel better.	.60
13. The purposes for each session were made clear before, during, and after the session.	.50
14. Covering the content is more important to the instructor than the needs of the class.	.60
15. The instructor asks a lot of questions, but once he/she gets the answers she/he doesn't seem to do anything about them.	.62
16. The instructor held my interest.	.68
17. The instructor should pay more attention to the students.	.69
18. The instructor is often too disorganized.	.67
19. It is always easy to understand what the instructor is talking about.	.61
20. The instructor is able to help me work through my problems or questions.	.62
21. The instructor is not precise in doing his/her work.	.60
22. The instructor understands the content he/she presents in class.	.68
23. I'm tired of the instructor talking down to me.	.60
24. The instructor fosters a feeling of exchange and sharing between class participants.	.58
25. The instructor is understanding in listening to a person's problems.	.72
26. The instructor could speak more clearly.	.60
27. The instructor takes a real interest in me.	.62

Source: Adapted from Miller & Lewis (1982), pp. 63–64.

that any concept has multiple aspects or substrata, each of which has multiple indicators, as discussed elsewhere in this chapter. Deleting items with relatively low correlations may result in "missing" key aspects of the concept you want to measure. This awareness will cause you to adjust the error level downward or to form subscales on items with relatively low correlations. In measurement, always balance theoretical and operational considerations.

Split-Half Reliability

The split-half method estimates reliability as the magnitude of the correlation of scores between two halves of an instrument. Items in the instrument are divided into two halves, typically using either an odd-even method or random method, and these half-tests are then correlated with each other to obtain an estimate of the instrument's reliability. Then the Spearman-Brown prophecy formula is often applied to the obtained correlation coefficient in order to correct for the number of items in the scale.

Although a popular early approach to estimating reliability, the split-half method has not been systematically employed. The method of dividing the test into halves is not standardized. Some researchers split the instrument by dividing the items into odd and even items; others use the preferred method of randomly assigning the total number of items to one or the other of two half-tests. With each division, however, there is potentially a different reliability estimate. For example, an instrument containing ten items has a possible 126 different splits. Some of these splits will overestimate, and some of them will underestimate, the instrument's reliability.

When to Measure Internal Consistency Reliability

Knowledge of the internal consistency reliability of the outcome or impact measures is the minimum amount of information you need before placing any confidence in the results obtained from a measurement instrument that uses composite scores from multiple items. Without an estimate of the instrument's internal consistency, it is virtually impossible to place any degree of confidence in the obtained results. Instruments with a low reliability coefficient can be refined in order to improve consistency prior to final data collection. The more you want to document program effect with accuracy, the more attention you should pay to internal consistency reliability.

There are probably only three circumstances in which estimating the internal consistency reliability is unnecessary. First, if the outcome measures were knowingly composed of single-item measures, each assumed to represent an isolated concept, there is no justification in estimating the internal consistency reliability. The measures simply were not conceived as unidimensional, composite scales.

Second, in the case of a one-shot program whose demise is guaranteed, estimating the internal consistency reliability misallocates resources. In such cases, the program evaluator usually wants only a general notion of the relationship between the health education program and the expected outcomes and is frequently pressured to offer the program and the evaluation under time constraints. Taking time to pilot the instruments and estimate their reliability is neither appropriate nor cost-effective.

Third, when you are concurrently evaluating multiple program offerings, knowledge of a particular program's effect may be desirable but in the long run is less important than other evaluations. Here the issue is a matter of program and evaluation priorities. Piloting and estimating an instrument's reliability takes both time and money. If competing program and evaluation demands exist, you may find that reliability testing goes to instruments in programs given highest importance.

Whenever you are either (1) concerned with the precision or accuracy of a multiple-item instrument that intends to measure an underlying concept, or (2) concerned about estimating the size of the relationship or the significance of differences between program and nonprogram (control or comparison) groups, you can justifiably allocate resources for internal consistency reliability estimation. As Suchman (1967, p. 119) pointed out, "the more important it is to know the degree of difference, the more attention must be paid to unreliability." Remember, the usual effect of unreliability in the measures is to attenuate the true relation between the program and the outcome variables. In other words, unreliable measures tend to understate the impact or importance of the variables measured.

Table 4-8 offers a summary of guidelines for the standards to be applied to internal consistency reliability. These guidelines should be viewed as tentative signposts against which to judge the precision of an evaluation measure. They are not prescriptive standards. Cronbach earlier argued for the potential value of a measuring tool with high validity that was known to be multidimensional; the known dimensionality may cause low internal consistency reliability coefficients. Every evaluator decides the trade-offs for each particular study.

Stability Reliability

Stability reliability is the degree of association between sets of measurements collected at two or more points in time. Stability reliability is reliability measured in a test-retest situation. The test-retest method of estimating reliability tells you about the stability in the rank orders of in-

TABLE 4-8 Guidelines for standards of internal consistency reliability: measure, standard, and source

Measures of Reliability	Standard	Comments	Source
Cronbach's alpha coefficient	.50–.60	Represents "modest reliability" in "early stages of research"	Nunnally (1967), p. 226
	.64	"Low reliability" but no reference given to length of scale or stage of research	Bohrnstedt (1970), p. 97
	.80	Standard for *basic* research	Nunnally (1967), p. 226
	Greater than .80	Standard appropriate in many *applied* research settings	
	.90–.95	Standard appropriate where major clinical or policy decisions are made on the basis of exact score obtained on instrument	Nunnally (1967), p. 226
Split-half reliability	Greater than or equal to .65	"Reasonable split-half correlation for a 16-item scale, uncorrected for scale length"	Bohrnstedt (1970), p. 87

Note: This table is offered as an approximate set of guides for establishing an acceptable level of reliability for evaluation instruments. Guides are suggestive only, not prescriptive.

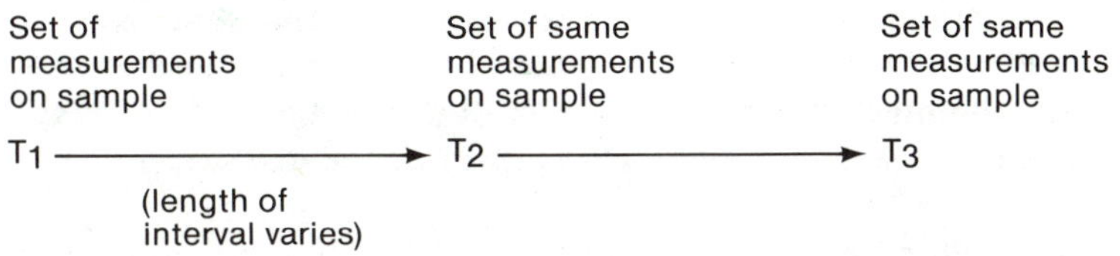

Figure 4-2 *Stability reliability: Measurements of sample at multiple points in time.*

dividuals over time (Guilford & Fruchter, 1973, p. 408). A high stability coefficient reflects two things. First, the subjects changed their relative positions very little, if at all, within their population on their status of the characteristic between the time of the initial and subsequent measurements. Second, the instrument itself measures the same characteristic at the initial and follow-up measurements—that is, at Time 1, Time 2, or Time 3.

To examine stability reliability, you administer an instrument to a specified sample at one point in time and then remeasure the sample of subjects at a subsequent point or points in time. This procedure is illustrated in Figure 4-2. The duration of time between measurements may vary. The ideal goal is to have the length of time maximum but not so long that an outside event occurs and causes a change in the characteristic measured by the instrument. In some studies, test-retest coefficient time intervals range from less than an hour to months or even years (Lewis, Firsich, & Parsell, 1979; Wallston, Wallston, Kaplan, & Maides, 1976).

Stability reliability is expressed as a simple zero-order coefficient. This coefficient may be presented in the form of the Pearson product-moment correlation coefficient, the Spearman rank correlation coefficient, or as other parametric or nonparametric correlation coefficients. As with any statistic, the evaluator chooses the measure of correlation on the basis of whether the data can meet the statistic's underlying assumptions.

When to Examine Stability Reliability. The more you know about the behavior of your set of instruments, the better equipped you are to judge the results you obtain. In this sense, knowledge about stability reliability, or about all other forms of reliability, is important. But budgets and time constraints often limit the information you can obtain about the measurements. Knowledge about stability or test-retest reliability is particularly important to obtain under six conditions: (1) when you have serious reason to believe that the characteristic of interest is itself unstable over time, (2) when the characteristic is assumed stable but very little documentation of that stability exists, (3) when the stability of the characteristic is known to vary differentially in different populations, (4) when the health education intervention is expected to affect a feature otherwise known to be stable, of the program participants, (5) when the health education program is administered over a long period of time, and (6) when the evaluation design does not include a control or comparison group.

Problems of Reactivity and Time Intervals. An individual's level of responsiveness to a set of measures may be affected by the actual measurement itself. This effect constitutes a problem of reactivity (Webb, Campbell, Schwartz, Sechrest, & Grove, 1981), a problem particularly relevant to the discussion of stability reliability. Thus, a subject measured by an instrument at Time 1 (see Figure 4-2) may gain an increased level of interest in the phenomenon measured by the instrument because of (1) the measuring process itself and (2) change with regard to this phenomenon. Measurement of the variable at Time 2 or 3 will subsequently reflect this heightened interest, and the score on the variable will show an increase or decrease because of the subject's reaction. This reactive effect to the measuring process affects the size of the stability coefficient and is independent of the effects resulting from the health education program.

In addition to reactivity, different stability correlation coefficients are obtained as a function of the duration of the time interval between the measurements. Longer time intervals between Time 1 and Time 2 tend to lower the reliability estimate because of the increased probability of an actual change in the characteristic of interest. Shorter time intervals can increase the chances of actual recall to the responses at Time 2. This recall factor could inflate the size of the stability reliability correlation coefficient.

Heise (1969) offers an estimation method for determining change caused by unreliability and change caused by actual change in the characteristic of interest. Heise's method requires observations at three points in time.

To the extent that you can argue against reactivity between measurements as causes of subsequent scores on an evaluation measure, you can place that much more confidence on the meaning of the stability reliability coefficient. In general, the more technical or specialized the information obtained on a test, the more difficult it is to claim that heightened interest alone affected the subsequent scores. Technical or specialized material requires a significant amount of self-study or instruction to affect subsequent scores.

Interrater Reliability

Our examination of error variance in an instrument has led us to discuss internal consistency reliability, split-half reliability, and stability or test-retest reliability. Now, in these cases it may be helpful to think of the source of error as "in" the instrument. Interrater reliability, on the other hand, estimates the amount of error in an instrument's score that is caused by the observation, rating, or coding processes. Error of this type is not "in" the respondent or in the measures, so much as it is "in" those individuals doing the measuring or the coding. Interrater error affects the level of accuracy with which two or more people document or code the characteristics of interest. In that sense, interrater reliability deals with external error—that is, error arising from the fallibility of human observation and documentation. It tells the evaluator the extent of the error that is introduced into the measurements because of differences in human perception and coding.

Interrater reliability is typically measured as either a percent agreement score (see Appendix B) or as a correlation coefficient. Recent work by Goodwin and Prescott (1981) employed analysis of variance to estimate interrater agreements.

An estimate of interrater reliability is relevant to situations in which a coder, observer, or rater is documenting or coding the performance, attitudes, or perceptions of others or is coding self-reported data of the respondents. Obviously, this description includes most evaluation situations.

Interrater reliability is an issue worth your frequent attention. Initial estimates of the level of interrater reliability provide a diagnostic base to retrain raters or observers and to determine either that the external error is sufficiently low or that the error level is excessively high. The determination of "high" or "low" levels of interrater error is determined on the basis of standards you establish for a tolerable level of error. Interrater reliability standards are commonly set at 80 to 100 percent. In the situation in which the error level is sufficiently low, you may be tempted to relax and proceed with data collection or the coding phase, no longer mindful of the potential introduction of rater error. This misguided sense of security, however, ignores the fact that interrater reliability tends to change as rater or observer fatigue increases or interest decreases. You will do well to ask, "How many times and at what times in the total course of the evaluation should I allocate resources to document the level of interrater reliability?"

As with any quality control method, there are no pat answers to the question of when and how often to document interrater reliability. Indeed, "spot checks" might best be done at random. Clearly, the initial estimate of interrater reliability is ideally calculated prior to the full-blown data collection phase. Subsequent estimates can be calculated at any interval thereafter, depending on the introduction of factors you believe could potentially affect the precision of the observations or their coding. Because factors such as the rater's level of fatigue or boredom increase

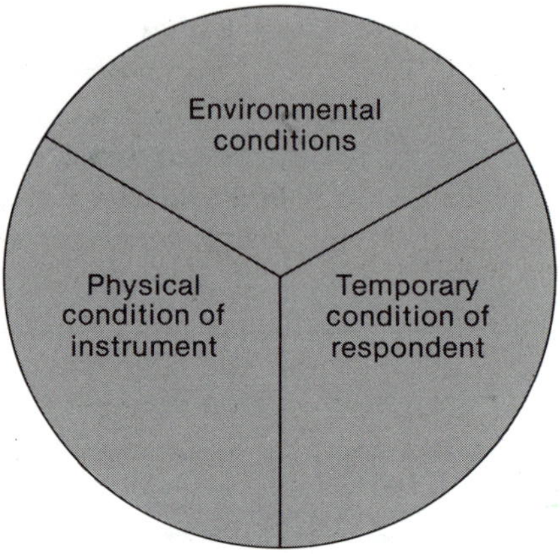

Figure 4-3 *Three components of measurement variance attributed to random error.*

over time, you do well to reevaluate interrater reliability. Retraining raters or observers may be needed. Often the source of interrater reliability can be pinpointed on one or two items that two observers or raters tend to perceive differently. Such sources can be most readily adjusted with additional training, supervision, more detailed coding rules, or a third rating to break the ties on items that most often disagree.

Reducing Error Variation

Random error, applicable to both reliability and validity (refer to Table 4-1), is a disturbance that results from a multitude of factors. This random error has three components (see Figure 4-3): (1) the physical condition of the instrument, (2) the environment or testing conditions under which the instrument is administered, and (3) the temporary condition of the respondent. By controlling, to varying degrees, one or more of these random error components, you are actually defining different true scores and different residual or error scores (Lord & Novick, 1968, p. 39). The goal in improving an instrument's reliability is to maximize the variance of the individual's differences while simultaneously minimizing the error variance.

Physical Condition of Instrument. Item wordings should be unambiguous. Avoid compound sentences that contain more than one idea or alternative. Use simple and easily understood words. Avoid catchy phrases, complex or uncommon words, and double negatives. Ambiguous items can be interpreted in many ways and thus allow random error variance to be introduced. The instrument should be legible and type size adjusted for readability for the target population—small print and light-colored ink may not suffice.

If the instrument is composed of a small number of items and is not reliable enough to meet your standards, add additional unambiguous items that are assumed to be similar to the initial set. In most cases, the addition of more "like" items improves the reliability coefficient. The relative improvement for each additional item, however, decreases markedly after six or eight items when reliability on the existing set of items is between .50 and .70 (see Bohrnstedt, 1970, and Cronbach, 1970, for details on this upper limit in adding "like" items). Improving an instrument's reliability by adding "like" items means that you are more thoroughly sampling the content domain of the concept or characteristic of interest. Chapter 3 addressed this point. More thorough sampling by multiple items makes each error by the respondent in choosing a response for a single item less important.

Standard instructions are necessary. Directions should be clear and short, not complicated and lengthy. If instructions are ambiguous, error variance again increases. If instructions are given orally, delivery should be loud and clear enough for all to hear.

Environmental Testing Conditions. Error variance increases when the testing environment fluctuates, is unpleasant or disruptive, or is not standardized. Instrument administration should occur under carefully controlled conditions. Room temperature, lighting conditions, comfortable seating, adequate writing surfaces, noise levels, and ambience all can affect a responder's score on the instrument. Controlling these conditions can reduce errors of measurement.

Temporary Condition of Respondent. The temporary physical and emotional states of the program participants affect the obtained scores. Personal distress and high anxiety, for example, are known to affect the quality of performance. To the extent possible, measurements on or completed by program participants should be completed when personal symptoms or distress are controlled or within a tolerable range. The obviously distressed, in pain, or suffering person is a weak source for a reliable measure.

SUMMARY

Reliable instruments are dependable and consistent. They can be relied on to rank order a person similarly on the characteristic of interest with repeated measures under like conditions. In health education and health promotion diagnoses and evaluations, reliable instruments yield a more dependable measure of the relevant baseline, impact, or outcome variables. Estimates of instrument reliability allow you to place varying degrees of confidence in the obtained information.

Measurement error in an instrument decreases the amount of confidence an evaluator can have in the study results. By minimizing measurement error, the evaluator can achieve a higher degree of assurance in the obtained measurements. Both systematic or constant error and random error are broad classes of measurement error. The current chapter emphasizes the importance of estimating the amount of random error associated with internal consistency reliability, stability reliability, and interrater reliability.

Internal consistency reliability reflects the degree of association, correlation, or covariance of a set of measurements that are developed to measure a single or unidimensional concept. Cronbach's alpha reliability coefficient represents one of the most common summary statistics of internal consistency reliability. Stability or test-retest reliability is the degree of association between sets of measurements collected at two or more different times. Stability reliability is typically operationalized as a zero-order correlation coefficient. Interrater reliability is the amount of error in the measurement that is due to error in observation, coding, or data entry processes. As such, error related with interrater reliability is not "in" the measure; rather, it is in the measurement process or in those people who are doing the measuring. Interrater reliability may be reflected in a percent agreement score between two or more independent raters.

Chapter 5

VALIDITY OF MEASUREMENT

The *validity* of an instrument represents the extent to which the instrument adequately measures the concepts under study. Although a reliable measure can be used to rank order subjects *consistently* on the characteristic of interest, a valid instrument reflects the extent to which the instrument *correctly* measures the characteristic. A consistently incorrect measure is reliable but invalid. If an instrument is not judged valid, the instrument is not measuring what you intended to measure. If an instrument is judged valid, it implies that you can use the instrument to measure correctly the variable or concept of interest.

Imagine that you want to construct an inventory of items measuring beliefs in personal vulnerability to illness episodes. One of the first questions you face is the meaning and scope of the term *personal vulnerability.* On superficial reflection, this concept includes at least three dimensions: perceived susceptibility, emotional vulnerability, and personal risk. Clearly, the concept is multidimensional. A literature review or even a reflective analysis of the concept and its components thus engages you in the process of establishing the *content* validity of the inventory.

You might also wonder about the inventory's ability to predict illness episodes in an adult clinic population. Does the score on the personal vulnerability inventory actually predict the frequency with which adults come into the clinic? Such a question relates to the *criterion validity* of the inventory; more specifically, to its *predictive validity.*

Now let us say that another health educator, modeling her thinking on the Health Belief Model, has constructed and piloted a scale to measure belief in susceptibility. You might wonder to what extent scores obtained on your personal vulnerability inventory relate to the scores obtained in the same clinic population on the susceptibility scale. Asking such a question addresses a second kind of criterion validity of the inventory—namely, its *concurrent validity.*

And if personal vulnerability as a concept is theoretically composed of other concepts, and if these relationships are empirically tested, you are measuring its *construct validity.*

The current chapter offers an expansion on the meaning and definition of validity as well as outlines the operational forms of validity. Validity of measurement differs from validity of design, analysis, and interpretation, discussed in later chapters, but all depend to some extent on validity of measures.

MEANING OF VALIDITY

Validity deals with the accuracy with which you specify and measure the concepts under study (Atwood & Hinshaw, 1977). In the broadest terms, validity in measurement addresses the degree to which the concept or concepts under study are accurately represented by the particular items on your questionnaire, test, self-report form, or other measuring device. Valid instruments "minimize variance resulting from specification error due to poorly indexed concepts" (Atwood & Hinshaw, 1977). "In the crudest terms, we say that a test is valid when it measures what it is presumed to measure" (Guilford & Fruchter, 1973, pp. 424–425). Blalock (1982) contends that "unless very careful attention is paid to one's theoretical assumptions and conceptual apparatus, no array of statistical techniques will suffice."

About validity you are really asking, "Does my set of measures accurately tap the underlying phenomena or concepts in which I am interested? Do the measures actually 'get at' the predisposing, enabling, or reinforcing factors I need to diagnose, or the impact or outcome variables for which I need evidence?" To do so, the set of measures must have a low level of "noise" (i.e., random error), but it must also adequately represent or reflect the underlying variable or concept.

Systematic Error

Validity particularly concerns systematic error. Systematic error creeps into measurements because of relatively stable characteristics of the respondent that do not vary from situation to situation for that individual, but do differ from the typical person for whom the test was developed. These characteristics may bias the respondent's answers, and the respondent's measures will therefore be a result not only of the variable under study but also of the respondent's other characteristics. Intelligence, sex, educational level, social status, and other such nonrandom variables may act as biasing factors. Two particular biasing factors—social desirability and acquiescent response set—are discussed extensively in the literature.

Social Desirability Bias and Acquiescent Response Set

The term *social desirability* is used to describe a biasing factor that results from the respondent's attempt to demonstrate behavior that is socially desirable or preferred (Phillips, 1971; Edwards, 1957). The term *acquiescent response set* describes an effect, sometimes called "yea-saying bias" or "nay-saying bias," that results from the respondent choosing a particular pattern of behavior that does not vary in response to the measurement stimulus (Phillips, 1971). For example, a respondent may select all extreme answers, may zigzag across response options, or may choose only the most neutral response options. Valid instruments minimize the amount of systematic error contained in the measurement. Systematic error is also known as *biasing* or *constant* error. An instrument that adequately identifies the underlying structure of the concepts minimizes constant or systematic error. To the extent that the items on the instrument measure *only* the concept—and not some biasing factor—to that extent you can claim your instrument is valid.

Let us expand this idea by reflecting on the concept of self-care practices. When concerned about validity, the evaluator is asking, "Do my measures actually reflect self-care practices?" Focusing still further, the evaluator asks, "Do my measures of self-care practices adequately document those particular aspects of self-care that the literature, other researchers, and my own reflection have identified?"

Once the domain or scope of the concept is addressed, the evaluator wants to make sure that the actual items in the instrument are closely linked to the concept—that is, represent the concept. As Atwood and Hinshaw (1977) argue, validity is often an imaginary or theoretical correlation between the concept and its measures or indicators, namely the instrument's items. Unless there is an independent, objective measure of the concept, the instrument's validity can only be inferred from three types of test, namely, content, criterion, and construct validity.

Whether the measures adequately cover the parameters or specific aspects of a concept is a test of the content validity of the measures. If the instrument approximates another measure of the same phenomenon, you have a test of its criterion (predictive or concurrent) validity. When you test the interrelatedness of the items in the instrument with other variables, all of which are assumed to relate theoretically, you have a measure of the construct validity of the measures.

With this overview of validity, let us address the operational forms of validity.

CONTENT VALIDITY

Content validity indicates the degree to which the instrument has adequately sampled the total possible meanings or substrata of a concept. Unlike the other operational forms of validity, you assess content validity during the scale's early development, not after its completion. As such, your tests of content validity provide a "road map" against which the scale is developed. The "road map" specifies the definitional boundaries of the concept, its various aspects, dimensions or substrata, and the scale items relevant to each substratum. The following are examples of substrata of the concept of adherence to a medical regimen: keeping appointments, taking the medicine even when feeling better, taking the medicine even when feeling worse, reporting side effects, keeping a record at home or work, avoiding specific foods or drinks while taking medicines, continuing medication to the end of the prescribed supply, and taking the prescribed number of pills each day, properly spaced, before or after meals.

For each of the substrata for adherence, you could include several possible items or measures. In focusing on the content domain, the evaluator actively and prospectively decides on those particular aspects of adherence that are relevant to the current diagnostic study or evaluation project. You are only one of many potential decision makers in the study. Program administrators, clients, clinical specialists, and other health education practitioners will have insights and perspectives on the concept, its substrata, and items that tap into them (Green, Lewis, & Levine, 1980).

When content validity is approached systematically, you can think of five steps, summarized in Table 5-1. Although listed as sequential steps, Steps 1 through 4 usually occur concurrently.

Content validity assumes a literature search and review in an attempt to document the meaning of the concept of interest. This review often reveals additional aspects of the phenomena of interest for which you had no previous awareness. You may discover particular items or tools that measure these different aspects of the phenomenon or concept.

Personal reflection is a crucial part of establishing content validity. The evaluator asks, "What particular aspects of the concept exist? Which aspects do I want to be sure to measure in the current diagnosis or evaluation? Which aspects of the concept exist but are not relevant to our current project?"

The professional and scientific literature can give you new insights into the concept. These insights come from the synthesis of the literature as well as from your own creative conceptual leaps. As the alternative meanings of the phenomena multiply, so do their substrata or dimensions. For those substrata or particular aspects of interest to your study, you need to generate, or adapt from existing instruments, multiple items (e.g., seven to ten) for each relevant substratum. Gradually you reduce

TABLE 5-1 Aspects of establishing content validity

1. Literature Review
   - Previous use by experts
   - Empirical research
   - Practitioner papers
2. Personal Reflection
   - Dialogue and exchange
   - Exposition of new facets of concept
   - Synthesis of literature
   - Critique and expansion of literature
   - Reconstruction of literature
3. Identification of Substrata of Concept
   - Break multidimensional concept down into unidimensional substrata
   - Exhaust meanings in domain
4. Identification of Items
   - Series of items
   - Measure substrata
   - Choose from substrata
5. Empirical Analysis of Items
   - Cluster analysis or factor analysis
   - Rating by experts of relevance of each item to the intended substratum or concept

these multiple items, through logical analysis, review by an expert or panel of judges, or empirical analysis. Empirical analysis assumes the administration of the set of items to respondents, and then an examination of item correlations between and within the preestablished substrata. See Bohrnstedt (1970) and Bohrnstedt and Borgatta (1981) for more detail on cluster analysis for content validity. Diagnostic information on the relatedness of the intended items can also be provided by factor analysis, item analysis, or simply "eyeballing" a series of cross tabulations or a matrix of correlations between pairs of items measured in a pretest or pilot sample of people.

When to Measure

Content validity applies to any attempt to construct scales or composite measures in health education.[1] The amount of effort required for an adequate literature search and the time needed to specify the substrata of the concept and to identify multiple items for each substratum are often too much for the pressed health educator. Admittedly, they may be costly

1. Some would argue that an attitude, as one type of predisposing or impact variable, cannot be elaborated from a content map perspective. Namely, the parameters of an attitude's content domain cannot be identified. See Cronbach's (1971) attention to this objection in discussing the concept of "ego ideal."

steps (Alkin & Solmon, 1983). Budgets are often restricted for an instrument-planning phase. If such a planning phase is impossible, you need to specify (at least at a cursory level) what aspects of the concept you intend to measure. The evaluator also does well to document those aspects of the concept that are intentionally *not* included in the measures. The issue is one of *how much* effort goes to specifying the content domain, not *if* any effort goes into it. The usual safeguard against the effects of having no time to develop your own instrument is to borrow existing scales and instruments from similar projects done elsewhere.

Face Validity and Consensual Validity

Both face and consensual validity provide ways of judging content validity. In both, content validity is judged by an external expert. In the instance of face validity, the instrument is judged by an expert in the field who logically determines if the instrument "looks like" what it is supposed to measure. Here the external reviewer judges the significance or meaningfulness of the measures. Face validity of the instrument is judged after it is constructed; it is a check on the completed product. Consensual validity extends face validity from one expert to a *panel* of experts who examine and rate the appropriateness of each item in the completed instrument. An agreement score can be calculated on the extent to which the members of the external panel agree on the appropriateness of the measures.

Face validity should be established as a minimum standard for content validity. This standard can serve to protect the credibility of your instrument in the eyes of potential critics. Both a theoretical as well as a clinical or practitioner perspective should be represented in the expert panel of reviewing judges.

CRITERION VALIDITY

Criterion validity is the degree of correlation of the measure with another measure of the same phenomenon. Typically, you choose a criterion measure believed to represent the "same thing" as the measuring instrument to be used in the evaluation study. You may, for example, employ a self-report scale on medication adherence and correlate the obtained scores with a physician's or nurse's rating of the respondent's medication-taking practices, with a pill count, or with blood or urine tracers from laboratory tests.

Depending on where you turn for an alternative measure, your criterion validity will be one of two types: *concurrent validity* or *predictive validity.* Concurrent validity measures the degree of correlation of two measures of the same phenomenon administered at the same point in time—that is, at T_1. Predictive validity measures the degree of correlation of a present measure with a future measure(s) of the same phenomena—that is, the degree of correlation between measurements obtained at T_1 and T_2. Predictive validity is usually reserved for long-range predictions—for example, over a period of days to years. Concurrent validity is typically limited to the correspondence of measures taken at essentially the same point in time.

Both concurrent and predictive validity can be summarized as a simple zero-order correlation coefficient. A more helpful way to express the results if the criterion is an objective measure is as the percentages of false-positives and false-negatives produced by the new instrument compared with the criterion. Subtract each of these measures from 100 percent to produce measures of specificity and sensitivity, respectively.

When to Measure

In many health education studies, information on the criterion validity of the instruments is optional, and can be easily sacrificed if budgets are limited. However, you should not pass up the opportunity to document the concurrent validity of an instrument when (1) the instrument is newly developed; (2) when long-range plans include the instrument's use in additional future studies; (3) when one of the goals is to present the instrument as a "better," a "revised," or a "new" version of an instrument with an established history of use in health education; or (d) when the nature of the instrument lacks credibility with one or more constituencies or sponsors of the evaluation.

Additional Comments

If alternative measures are readily available, you will probably not bother to develop and validate a new instrument. However, you will often experience difficulty in finding an appropriate criterion measure. The problem is particularly acute in health education because the literature offers few standardized instruments developed in the past (Green, 1976a). As a result, you may be forced to choose a criterion that only approximates the same phenomenon. This incongruence obliges you to exercise caution, especially if you get a relatively low correlation. A questionable criterion should not force inappropriate decisions about the validity of the measure under study. Even in the case of an appropriate criterion, you may get a low correlation because of unreliability either in the scale under study or in the criterion measure. This awareness should temper your overreaction to the size of the correlation coefficient. You can correct mathematically for attenuation due to unreliability.[2]

CONSTRUCT VALIDITY[3]

One goal of science is to confirm or disconfirm assumptions about relationships among variables. A composite measure includes multiple items measuring alternative but related substrata or dimensions. Their relationship is tested by *construct validation*. As health education moves in the direction of codifying its knowledge base, construct validation becomes increasingly important in testing not only the relationship among constructs within a measurement instrument, but also the relationships among constructs within a total program of health education. Construct validation is the process by which you test the theoretical relationships among the underlying concepts against the hypothesized relationships and then revise the theoretical formulations or the measures accordingly.

Using the construct of health locus of control (HLC) to illustrate, construct validation requires evidence on questions such as the following: "Does the HLC scale actually reflect an internal belief state, or does a higher score (more external) simply imply less personal interest or investment by the respondent in his or her health (Lewis, Morisky, & Flynn, 1978)? Would higher scores correlate with a lower frequency of health-seeking behavior (Wallston, Wallston, Kaplan, & Maides, 1976)? Do low-scoring respondents of differing ethnic backgrounds have the same generalized health expectancies?"

Theory informs and is informed by construct validation. Each health education diagnosis and program evaluation not only measures program effect but also contributes to theory development, modification, or extension. The theory in question is that which guides the program and predicts its impact or outcome. You may develop, elaborate, or modify various components of the program and evaluation methodology (e.g., program intervention, instrumentation, procedures of administration or design) in order to test some aspect of the underlying construct or the hypothesized interrelationships among concepts.

2. See Bohrnstedt (1970) for a general discussion of some of the dilemmas and debate surrounding the correction for attenuation due to unreliability.

3. Attention to construct validation is not without controversy, even in the nonapplied or non-service-oriented professions. Effectively, the opposition clings to an extreme operationalist perspective and claims that a construct has scientific value only when it is analogous (seen as the same as) to a particular indicator. The interested reader can follow an interpretation of this argument in Cronbach (1971), especially pp. 480–484. Original sources include Weber (1982). See also Bernstein (1976).

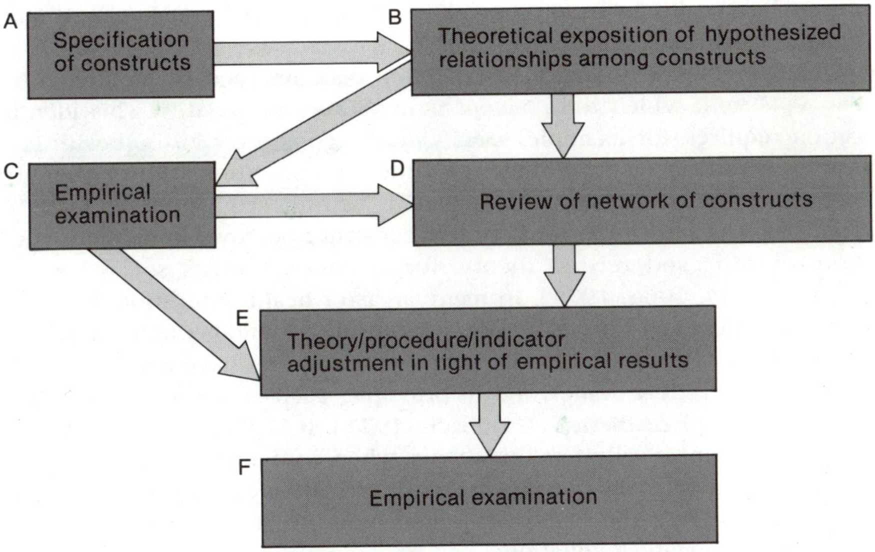

Figure 5-1 *A simplified representation of selected processes in construct validation.*

As a process, construct validation (1) is never "once considered, forever handled"; (2) always involves multiple studies over many situations with many populations; and (3) is a complex process, but accessible to even the beginning health education practitioner.

At the risk of oversimplifying the intellectual complexity of construct validation, one can conceive of it as a set of processes. These processes are graphically presented in Figure 5-1. The level (A to F in Figure 5-1) at which the program evaluator engages in construct validation depends partly on the maturity (previous research and validation) of the construct (e.g., belief in seriousness has been more extensively validated than health locus of control). It depends also on the degree of confirmation of the network of constructs (e.g., health belief model versus Rotter's original locus of control theory).

At the beginning stages of construct validation, you assume (hypothesize) that an instrument measures a specific concept. This specification of a new construct requires more than a new label—it requires a definition and delineation of the construct. You attempt to answer the broad question, "What is meant by the construct?" The construct of health locus of control or multidimensional locus of control is a relevant and current example in health education (Wallston et al., 1976; Wallston & Wallston, 1978; Wallston, Wallston, & DeVellis, 1978). When you specify what is meant by "health locus of control in a respondent," you begin to spell out the construct's meaning.

Still in the early stages of reflection, you proceed to identify other concepts with which the concept is hypothetically related. This identification requires, for example, specifying the constructs in the health education program (e.g., confidence-building communications) that are hypothesized as affecting the impact construct (e.g., internal locus of control). The health locus of control construct borrows initial constructs from existing and related theory; for example, Rotter's social learning theory (1954, 1966, 1975). In many areas of health education, however, we can expect (and hope) to see responsible ground-breaking activity in which health educators identify new constructs that have a minimally developed theoretical framework. In principle, each construct is embedded within a complete theory (Cronbach, 1971). It is the evaluator's task to specify and empirically test this theory when committed to construct validation. In some cases the statements interrelating the constructs are relatively vague; in some cases they might be quite precise, even taking the form of mathematical equations.

Empirical testing is an unavoidable step in construct validation (Level C in Figure 5-1). Logical or philosophical reflection is insufficient, although necessary. In the initial studies, empirical evidence, often in the form of simple correlation coefficients, is brought to bear on the hypothesized or predicted relationships among the constructs under investigation. The magnitude and utility of the correlations between the specified indicators are examined, not just their statistical significance (Green & Lewis, 1981). This initial study is often primitive (Lewis et al., 1979), and even the inexperienced reader can offer alternative explanations for the observed behavior, explanations that do not rely on the hypothesized underlying construct(s).

The empirical results offer confirmation or disconfirmation to the hypothesized relationships (see D and E in Figure 5-1). These data cause reflection on the part of the evaluator and may result in modifications of any one or more of the following: specified constructs, including abandonment or synthesis of new ones; accepted indicators of the underlying constructs; hypothesized relationships among the specified concepts; and/or method of obtaining measures of the underlying constructs.

Your reflection on the empirical results in light of their theory base engages you in theory construction, not just in empirical evaluation. You constantly ask, "What concepts or variables account for the program recipients' observed behavior? Is the explanation consistent with the hypothesized relationship as originally identified? Have I ruled out alternative explanations (e.g., other constructs or situational phenomena) that can account for the observed program results? What relationships among impact constructs can account for some of the observed results?"

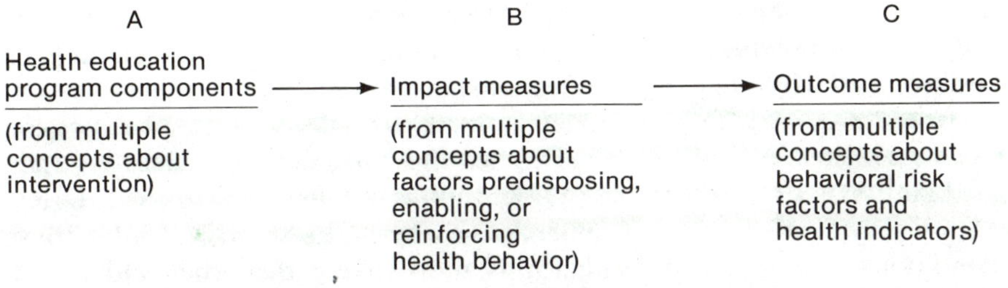

Figure 5-2 *Sources of concepts in health education diagnosis and evaluation.*

Now empirical examination begins again. You then proceed to carry out one of the activities that result from reflection on the initial empirical results, such as experimental studies or further correlational studies. In construct validation, your attention is always on the total network of constructs, their indicators, and the hypothesized interrelationships.

When to Measure

In a real sense, any commitment to a theoretically based educational diagnosis or evaluation is an investment in construct validation. Any time you attempt to specify *a priori* the nature of the relationships in Figure 5-2 within A, within B, within C, or between A and B, B and C, or A and C, you engage in at least the conceptual stages of construct validation. Empirical testing and reexamination must also follow.

If you take a strictly practical or pragmatic orientation, your job is to describe rather than to explain, and is characterized by the atheoretical selection of predictive or outcome criteria.[4] You can ignore construct validation of ways in which B links A and C. Just measure A or C, or both. Efforts in pragmatic evaluation go toward judicious selection of at least clinically meaningful outcome criteria. You can justify a pragmatic, nonexplanatory orientation in early ground-breaking efforts where either the meaningful impact variables or the program variables have yet to be identified. Time or budgetary constraints may also push you toward a descriptive perspective and away from a construct validation perspective. You may be forced (unless you are using time or budget restraints as excuses for avoiding theory) to "grab" what reliable measures you can in

4. Although admittedly the lines between pragmatic health education evaluation and theoretically oriented evaluation are not always sharply drawn, the *intent* of the evaluator can be specified at the outset.

order to document program effect. Attention to a theory may be possible only after completing the program evaluation. Then you might stand back and ask the "why" and "how" questions.

Construct validation deserves greater attention in health education when extramural funding supports such evaluation efforts, when randomized clinical trials research is feasible, or when quasi-experimental design, particularly with multiple comparison groups, can be used. Under these conditions, the research evaluator is more likely than the field practitioner-evaluator to have the resources to attend to construct validation. This advantage is especially evident when one considers the need for a multimethod multitrait approach to construct validation, to be discussed in the next section.

However, this view need not force practitioners to be shortsighted. The professional involvement of field practitioners in construct validation cannot be dismissed. Recall (see Figure 5-1) that construct validation, particularly in its earlier stages, typically engages the investigator in some firsthand observations and pilot studies in the clinical, classroom, worksite, home, or other field setting. The field practitioner is a potential contributor to these initial studies, and, to the extent that they are guided by a theory-testing focus, they constitute important initial efforts at construct validation.

Measures of Construct Validity

No single measure summarizes an instrument's construct validity. Rather, multiple measures, taken together, provide a more or less comprehensive profile of the construct validity of an instrument. Again, these measures should always be seen as situationally specific to the population and time period sampled and open to repeated examination.

Convergent and Discriminant Analysis: Multitrait Multimethod Approach. Program participants who score high on one impact measure should also score high on other measures of the same underlying construct. This idea is at the base of *convergent analysis,* which may apply therefore to criterion validation as well as construct validation. Data are collected as a result of a diagnostic or evaluation study, and you examine the data for convergence of the various measures of the construct. (A full treatment of this subject can be found in the seminal paper by Campbell & Fiske, 1959).[5]

5. The Campbell and Fiske paper is also reproduced in the reader edited by Summers (1979).

Indicators of the same underlying construct may depend variously on direct observations, self-report forms, medical record data, and informant responses. In studying the convergence, the evaluator is looking for zero-order positive correlations with varying levels of magnitude. High correlations are not necessarily expected because of an instrument's dependence on such things as situational, administrative, or personal characteristics.

As you examine the convergence of indicators supposedly measuring the same construct, you also can examine the degree of relatedness of indicators supposedly measuring different constructs (Campbell & Fiske, 1959). Constructs, in other words, should be distinguished from each other. It follows that their indicators should be also. In studying discriminability, you seek relatively low correlations or negative correlations between measures of independent and contrary constructs.

Factor Analysis. Factor analysis provides a quantitative means to put convergent indicators into empirical rather than *a priori* theoretical constructs or factors. Items intended to measure the same underlying construct should converge and load high (e.g., r equals .35) on one factor and not load high on any other factors (Cronbach, 1971). Indicators that have substantial loadings on more than one factor are, by definition, impure (Nunnally, 1967). An example of a 6-factor solution of child health beliefs is summarized in Table 5-2.

Analysis of Variance Components. In an attempt to identify both the nature of the sources of variance and the magnitude of their effect on any instrument's score, you may adopt an analysis of variance (ANOVA) perspective in construct validation. Although it is typically reserved for advanced analysis of experimental results (Jaeger, 1983), we introduce it here as a method of examining construct validity. An analysis of variance perspective allows you to extract and partition components of the total variance of any hypothesized construct. The underlying model for the ANOVA requires measures on one or more variables obtained from each respondent. One-way ANOVA allows you to compare the variance within individuals to the variance between individuals on one variable. Suppose you have collected the data by two methods, or you have the data coded or scored by two or more people. The analysis separates out the effects on the impact measure of the timing of the measure, the content of the instrument, the data coder or scorer, and the various interaction effects. "It thus indicates the magnitude of each 'impurity' in the score and tells how closely the score corresponds to the hypothesized general stable . . . ability" (Cronbach, paraphrasing Coffman & Kurfman in Cronbach, 1971).

TABLE 5-2 Selected items of six-factor solution for child health belief factors

Items Loading Primarily in Each Factor	Factor Loading Value
Factor I: Specific Health Concerns (11 items)	(Alpha = .77)
When you are sick, how much do you worry about it?	.39
How worried would you be if you got a cold?	.67
Factor II: Perceived Susceptibility (5 items)	(Alpha = .67)
How much of a chance do you think there is that you might get a fever?	.41
How much of a chance do you think there is that you might throw up?	.52
Factor III: General Health Concerns (7 items)	(Alpha = .56)
How much do you worry about your health?	.40
How much do you worry about getting sick?	.60
Factor IV: Perceived Parental Concern (4 items)	(Alpha = .26)
What things do you do that aren't good for your health?	.25
How much does your mother/father seem to worry about you when you get sick?	.55
Factor V: Perceived Seriousness of and Susceptibility to Disease (5 items)	(Alpha = .43)
How worried would you be if you were feeling dizzy?	.27
When you're sick how bad do you usually feel?	.38
Factor VI: Perceived Susceptibility (General) (7 items)	(Alpha = .65)
How often do you get sick compared to others your age?	.59
When others in school have colds, do you usually catch a cold also?	.28

Source: Dielman et al. (1980).

CONCLUSION

No instrument is totally valid and reliable. Validity, like reliability, is always a function of the instrument, the conditions of administration, and the population being measured. As such, an instrument is never categorically "valid." Rather, it is "valid" to a certain extent and within a context, under certain conditions of administration, and with a particular sample of respondents. The extent of its validity can only be stated meaningfully in comparison with alternative measures of the same concepts or constructs.

Instruments, like good health education programs, are not developed for "one-shot" uses. You develop and refine instruments over many applications and use them to measure inputs and outcomes in multiple populations. Under these conditions, validity evolves. This cumulative approach places less burden on any one diagnostic or evaluation study to estimate all operational forms of validity coefficients.

Striving for perfection is never easy and in the final analysis is futile. The burden of this chapter is knowing that the establishment of an instrument's validity is always "in process" and limited to a particular context. Attention to estimating and improving an instrument's validity has distinct advantages. It makes the program evaluator more confident in just what phenomenon or concept is being studied; it facilitates the exchange of measures and results; it begins to establish credibility for the obtained diagnostic results or program outcomes or effects.

SUMMARY

The validity of an instrument is the extent to which the instrument adequately measures or indexes the concepts being studied. In a general sense, validity focuses on the degree to which the concepts are accurately represented by the measurements used in a study. Validity is affected both by specification or indexing error and by social desirability bias.

There are three broad types of validity: content, criterion, and construct. Content validity focuses on the degree to which the instrument has adequately sampled from the total possible meanings of a concept. Subtypes of content validity include face validity and consensual validity. Criterion validity is the degree of relationship between two measures of the same phenomenon. There are two types of criterion validity: concurrent and predictive. Concurrent validity assesses the degree of correlation between two presumed similar measures at the same point in time. Predictive validity assesses the degree of correlation of a current measure with a future measure of a presumed similar phenomenon.

Construct validity is the extent to which the hypothesized theoretical relationships between the concepts and their measures are verified or not verified on the basis of obtained data. As a process, construct validation is an ongoing effort in which relationships between concepts are tested and revised on the basis of repeated studies.

Chapter 6

DEVELOPMENT AND SELECTION OF MEASUREMENT INSTRUMENTS AND DATA SOURCES

In this chapter we present a framework for the selection or development of a set of measures for diagnosis or evaluation in health education. From the two previous chapters, you have some idea of what instruments are acceptable for measuring or evaluating health education. The task of instrument selection is easier when relevant instruments exist with tested validity and reliability. Even when measures exist for your purposes, you must decide if they meet the requirements of your task. Adequacy is determined by a set of additional questions. When you find no existing measures appropriate for your specific purposes, you may need to develop and pilot test a new set of measures. When you *can* select from already existing instruments or measures, consult this chapter for a framework to assess both instrument relevance and adequacy. When you must develop and test new sets of measures, the chapter provides a developmental framework for instrument construction. Building on the preceding chapters on reliability and validity, we now consider ways to improve the quality of data from instruments in terms of error reduction within time and budget constraints.

SEVEN STAGES IN DEVELOPING AND TESTING INSTRUMENTS

The development and testing of a set of measures can be organized into seven stages, summarized in Figure 6-1. The explanation of these stages represents an elaboration of the framework summarized by Lindeman (1976a, 1976b).

These stages in instrument development are sequential, but not rigidly so. Reflection during the earlier stages minimizes error and facilitates

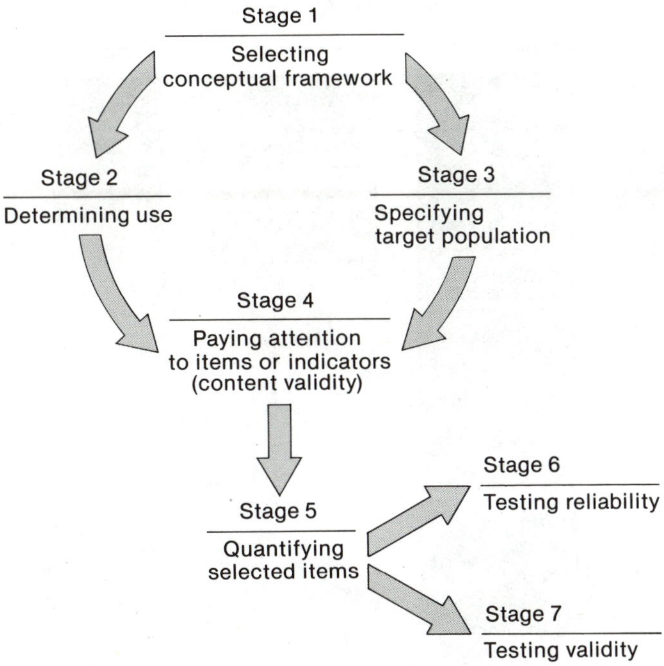

Figure 6-1 *Stages of instrument development.* Source: *Adapted from Lindeman (1976a, 1976b).*

work in later stages. You may be pressured into identifying items or indicators of the desired variables (Stage 4) before carefully specifying the study's overall framework (Stage 1). The population of subjects to be studied (Stage 3) often, of necessity, has been specified by policy prior to the onset of the study, rather than coming midway in the instrument's development; content validity, however, needs consideration early in the development of the instrument. Validity testing (Stage 7) may await final evaluation of a program. Nevertheless, the sequential nature of the framework provides stages through which your work can proceed.

Stage 1. Selecting a Conceptual Framework

What conceptual perspectives, theories, or assumptions guide the overall program design or evaluation? We have outlined a series of alternative models in Chapter 3. The selection of theoretical or conceptual perspectives for instrument development occurs at two levels of specificity, within any of these alternatives. These levels are illustrated in Figure 6-2.

Level 1: Example of an overall framework for structure of evaluation [a]

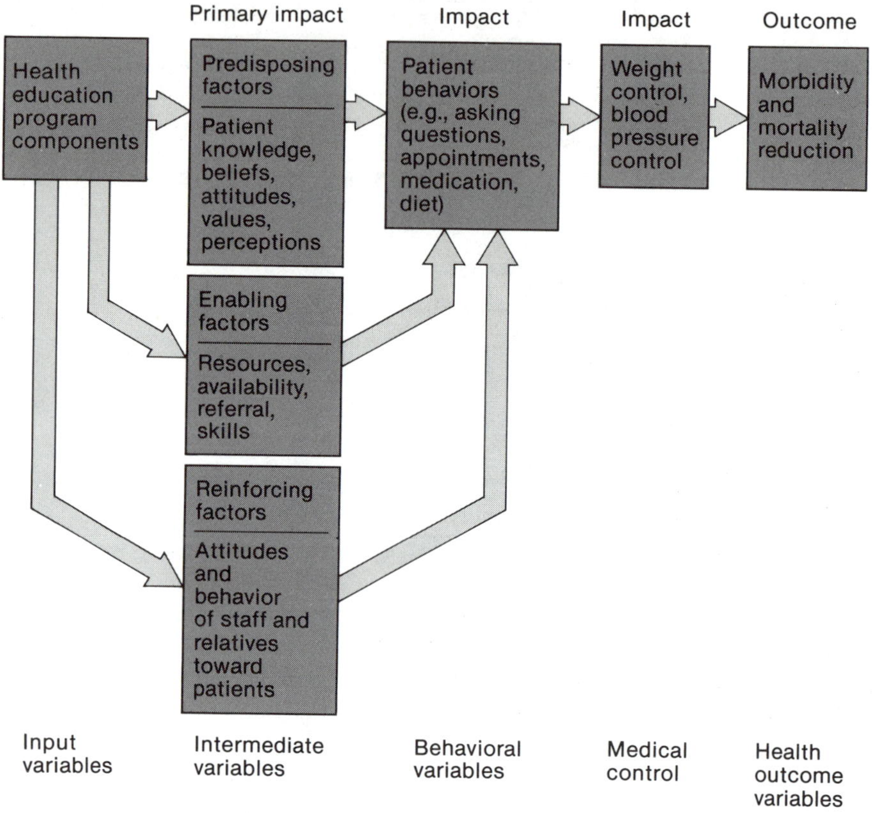

[a] Green, Levine, & Deeds (1975), p. 420.

Figure 6-2 *Two-level framework for instrument development.*

At the first level, the framework outlines the broad categories of variables or "objects of interest" to the program or the study, and it specifies at an abstract level the presumed causal relationships between the categories of variables (Green, 1974). In Figure 6-2, Level 1 illustrates the more abstract level of an educational diagnostic model applied to a patient education program for poor, inner-city, hypertensive patients. In this framework, the predisposing, enabling, and reinforcing factors are the immediate effects of an educational program. Predisposing, enabling, and reinforcing factors, in turn, affect behavioral impact measures that are hypothesized to relate in turn to medical control of weight and blood pressure, which contribute to health outcome measures (Green et al., 1975).

Level 2: Example of four levels of more detailed theoretical or conceptual structure for linking particular program components with particular impact measures[b]

2a: Application of locus of control constructs

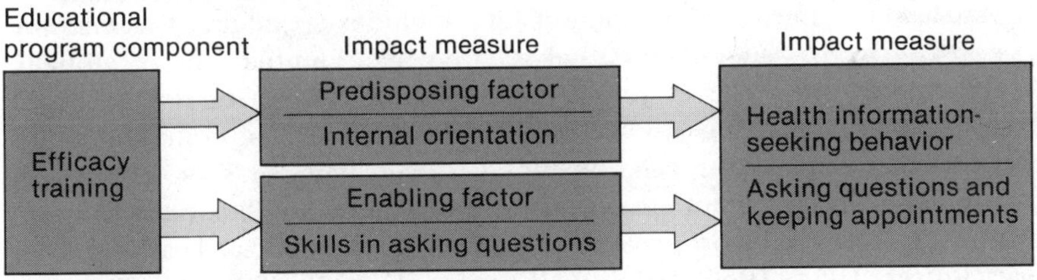

2b: Educational diagnosis: Major factors

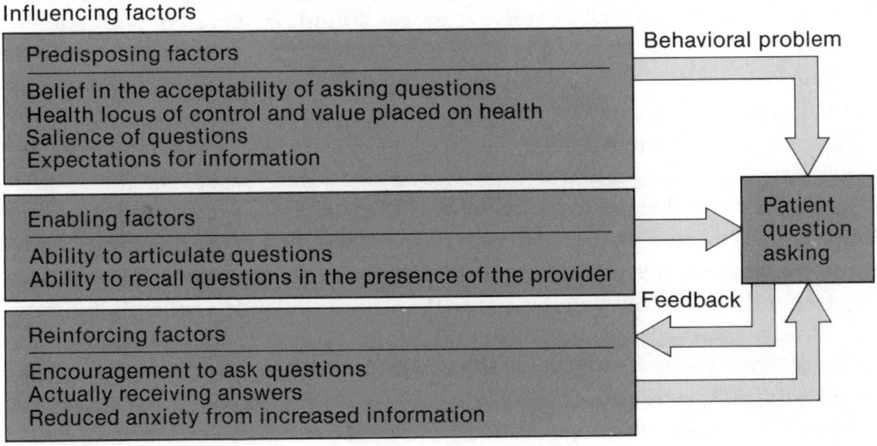

2c: Patient behavioral change process

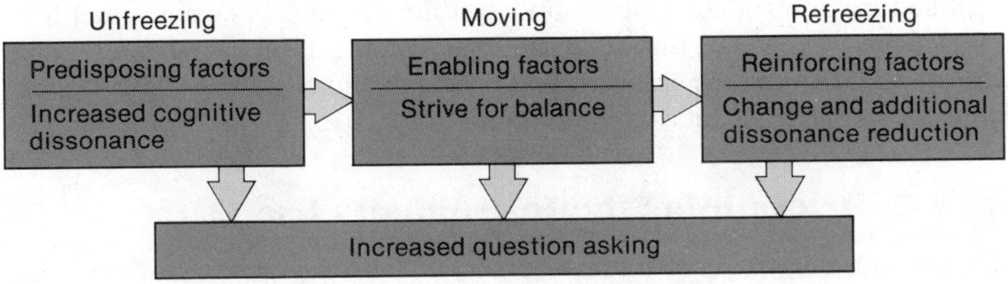

2d: Hypothesized relationships among interventions and effects

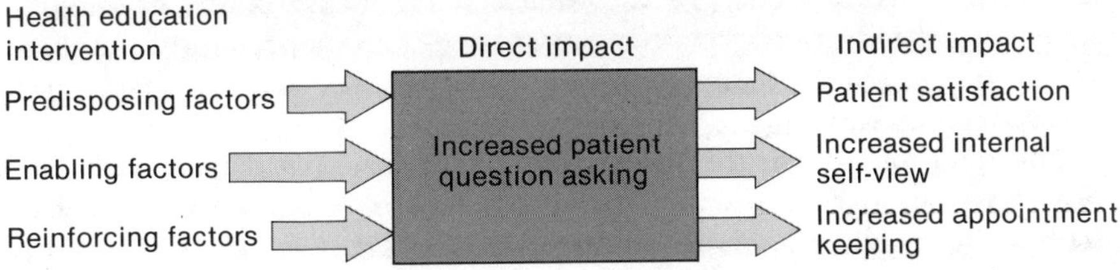

[b] Roter (1977).

Level 2 in Figure 6-2 shows a more detailed representation of the presumed or hypothesized relationships between specific program components (no longer broad categories of variables) and specific impact measures. Elaborating these relationships includes specifying the *mediating variables* that affect the causal relationships identified more globally in the framework at Level 1. Selecting a framework at the second level actually entails selecting a more specific theory or set of complementary theories that explain the relationships between pairs or sets of program components and program effects. Level 2 of Figure 6-2 illustrates the second level of a framework, based on part of Rotter's Social Learning Theory (Rotter, 1954, 1966, 1975; Wallston et al., 1976; Wallston, Wallston, & DeVellis, 1978). Other examples of further specification at Level 2 of the same framework as Level 1 can be found in Eriksen and Gielen (1983) and in Madnick (1980).

The importance of selecting a framework to guide the measurement or evaluation cannot be overemphasized. A conceptual framework determines the scope of the measures, specifies the main concepts of interest, offers a structure in which to organize the sets of measures, facilitates the identification of irrelevant concepts and measures, and specifies, at either Level 1 or 2 (see Figure 6-2), the ways in which health education program components may affect the impact or outcome variables.

Depending on the specific content of the theory or concepts guiding your study, you will develop or select impact measures related to specific types of knowledge, attitudes, or behavior, including psychomotor skills, social supports, perception, or values. Decisions about measures of effect also include decisions about outcome measures, both short- and long-range medical or health outcomes. The former type of medical outcome is exemplified by controlled diastolic and systolic blood pressure, normal levels of urinary glucose, or a normal tidal volume range. The long-range type of health outcome is represented by morbidity and mortality rates, reduced disability, or increased functional capacity.

Stage 2. Determining the Instrument's Use

The second stage of instrument development or selection answers the question "For what use or purpose is the instrument designed?" This question has two aspects: (1) For what type of measurement or evaluation effort—diagnostic, formative, summative, or comprehensive evaluation—is the instrument intended? (2) Who will directly administer and interpret the instrument?

The decision to use the instrument for educational diagnosis or formative evaluation requires that the instrument be efficient. Efficiency is necessary to provide diagnostic information and rapid feedback about the program. You can increase efficiency by making the instrument portable, by ensuring that it can be easily administered with minimum training, by simplifying data collection and recording, by ensuring that responses can be easily coded, by making scores or summary measures quickly and easily computed with minimum or no transformation or item weighting,[1] and by making measures directly interpretable. Efficiency also means that you require low levels of inference in moving from summary measures or scores to preliminary judgments or decisions about the program's content or impact. You achieve this requirement by making the measures concrete and self-evident, rather than abstract or dependent on a highly trained specialist for interpretation. For example, be sure scores run from low numbers to high numbers for positive outcomes; convert mixed scales to a common denominator, preferably 100, so that they can be compared as averages or percentages.

Formative evaluation and diagnostic studies do not demand the same degree of precision in the choice of instruments as do summative evaluation studies. Educational diagnosis and formative evaluation emphasize description of the target population and process feedback for diagnostic purposes for program developers or implementers, and do not emphasize the thorough documentation of program effects. Impact measures are needed merely to describe general trends, using past experience or preliminary results. Outcome measures are seldom examined in educational, behavioral, or administrative diagnosis or in formative evaluations.

In summative evaluation, the stakes are higher for measurement error. You need only reflect on the effect of measurement error in attenuating the predicted relationship between program components and effects. As a result, summative evaluation studies commit the evaluator to the selection or development of refined instruments for documenting effects.

In determining the instrument's use, you also need to ask, "Who will directly administer the instrument?" This decision may affect the type of instrument selected or developed. If field workers or health education practitioners will administer the instrument in the course of their daily work, this fact should be reflected in the choice of the instrument. If specially trained research assistants or a professional polling organization are to administer the instrument, more complexity in administration and format may be allowed. If the eventual goal is to develop the instrument for future long-term or widespread use by health education practitioners, the practicality of administering the instrument should also reflect that goal.

1. Data transformation and item weighting are made easy with the use of computers. In formative evaluation, however, feedback data, including measures of preliminary impact variables, may be collected and analyzed in the field setting. It may be inefficient and ineffective to use a computer for handling such data. With the growing use of microcomputers, even this exception may crumble.

Stage 3. Specifying Client Population

For what group of clients are you developing or selecting the set of measures? For instrument development efforts, you usually need to define the patient or client population restrictively (homogeneously) rather than broadly. The more homogeneous the population, the more the variability in the clients' responses may be attributed to differences in their status on the impact or outcome variables measured, not to other sources.[2]

Your attempt to obtain a homogeneous client population for testing an instrument may present difficulties. Defining the client population too narrowly—for example, "forty- to fifty-year-old men experiencing angina without prior history of myocardial infarction"—often limits the number of potential clients that can be recruited from any one site at any one time. This narrowness consequently limits the number of clients available for piloting the instrument. However, defining the client population too broadly allows too many sources of variability in client response. Usually you must compromise by defining the client population as narrowly as possible, but broadly enough so that a sufficient number of subjects can be recruited for instrument testing within realistic time and budget constraints.

Under optimum conditions, you have the liberty to develop and refine the set of evaluation measures before their actual use for educational diagnosis or program evaluation. If so, the measures should be pretested on a sample of people representative of the target population that will eventually receive the health education program. You can assure similarity between the referent test sample and the final program participants by drawing a probability sample of subjects from the target population (see Chapter 10). Systematic random sampling of the target population is not always feasible. In such cases, you must generate alternative samples for pilot testing the evaluation instruments. Chapter 10 summarizes some of the alternative sampling methods you can use for piloting the measurement instruments and the inherent strengths and weaknesses in each approach.

Although use of a probability sample from the target population is the clearly desired alternative, each of the other alternatives has important information to offer. It is always better to have some information on how subjects respond to your instruments than to have no information. This preference commits you to some order of pilot testing, even if a probability sample cannot be obtained.

2. Excessive homogeneity among factors predisposing, enabling, or reinforcing the behavior or health outcomes in the population might restrict the amount of variability in the responses to the study instruments. This homogeneity, in turn, would attenuate the internal consistency reliability of the measures.

When selecting among instruments developed by others, you need to ask whether the instrument was tested on a sample of subjects "similar to" the sample of subjects about to experience your health education program. Under the most desirable circumstances, data will show that the instrument was tested on a random sample of subjects from the same defined population. Such congruence is rare, however. Usually you are left to decide on the applicability of someone else's pilot test or basis of standardization to your current target population.

Stage 4. Paying Attention to Items or Indicators

Your selection or generation of items or indicators is the fourth stage in instrument development. The conceptual or theoretical perspective and variables selected earlier in Stage 1 specified the major concepts of interest, and the task now is either (1) to select from existing measures specific items that best represent the concepts or (2) to generate new items.

At this point you choose between already developed standardized instruments and developing your own new instruments. The choice involves trade-offs. Developing valid and reliable instruments *de novo* is costly in terms of staff salaries, training, supervision, and supplies. Consultants may be needed at several points. If you turn the instrument's development over to subcontractors, fees for service, if not energy for quality control, are involved. In instrument development, you need time and energy to access subjects for pilot testing, including appropriate clearance through the institutional committee for the protection of human subjects, as well as for actual data collection and analysis. If the instrument requires a high degree of precision, you may commit your funds and time to many pilot studies, not just one.

The choice to develop your own instrument makes the instrument particularly vulnerable to critique. The probability of critical rejection of the instrument is greater (1) the larger the scale, or (2) the more visible the evaluation effort, or (3) the greater the clinical or policy implications to be derived from the study's results. An assault on the instrument's integrity is ultimately an assault on the evaluator's conclusions. However, you are in a better position to report and defend your own procedures if you have developed your own instrument thoroughly.

Already developed standardized instruments are not a panacea, but they do provide some advantages over homemade instruments. Some of these advantages are summarized in Table 6-1. Already developed standardized instruments permit comparison of results among studies. Such comparison, in turn, helps advance the scientific base of health education practice. Without such comparison and repeated use of standardized instruments, health education studies lack the cumulative quality essential to codifying knowledge and developing theory and policy.

TABLE 6-1 Relative advantages and disadvantages of previously developed instruments versus homemade instruments

Developed Standardized Instrument	Homemade Instrument
Permits comparison of results across studies	Limited use of instrument does not permit comparison across studies
Usually less costly than the development and testing of new instrument	Usually more costly than already developed instrument
May reflect historical dependence and be inappropriate for current time period	Relevant to current time or period
Better documented validity and reliability under different testing conditions	Documentation of validity and reliability limited to current pilot test results
Often contains excess number of irrelevant items	Contains only relevant items
Changes in wording to fit local situation might alter comparability	Tailored to local situation
Higher credibility with other health educators	Credibility limited to investigator's reputation and reported procedures
Instruments may be refined without justification	Instruments open to critique based on reported testing procedures
Response options in questions may not fit with population to be studied	Response options accurately capture range of population's responses

Developed standardized instruments, even though fees are required for copyrighted instruments, usually prove less costly to use than developing a new set of measures. Time is also saved if pilot tests reveal that reliability is sufficiently high on the evaluation's population to permit ready use of the developed instrument.

Standardized instruments usually have more extensively tested and better documented validity and reliability than do newly developed instruments. Such information comes from repeated use of the instrument with a variety of populations in different studies under different as well as similar conditions of administration. An excellent example of this cumulation of data on a single instrument is given by studies using and testing both the unidimensional and multidimensional Health Locus of Control Scale, a scale initially developed and tested by Wallston and her associates (1976), which builds on theoretical work by Rotter (1954, 1966, 1975). Repeated testing of these scales, under different methods of administration in different studies, and with different client populations, results in a body of information about the scale's reliability and validity.

Tables 6-2 and 6-3 summarize some of this information. Only by repeated use of such a standardized instrument can such data be accumulated and serve as a basis of choice for future health education studies.

The use of previously developed instruments also has some drawbacks. Previously developed instruments frequently contain an excess number of items that have no relevance or bearing on the salient concepts in the current evaluation. This problem is only partly avoided by choosing items from among the larger set of items. The psychometric properties (reliability and validity) of the subset of items chosen for your purposes usually are not known, or are not reported. Although you can then test the subset, you are no further ahead than if you had started from scratch, except for comparability of items. Caution must be exercised not to remove a subset of items from a standardized instrument while assuming that the original properties of measurement persist.

Even if the instrument does not suffer from an excessive number of items, you may find it unacceptable for other reasons. Items developed by someone else may not have face validity for your purposes. You may find the relationship between the concept to be measured and the standardized questionnaire items for that concept unacceptable. The most common problem of this kind in health education is with standardized tests for values or beliefs that do not relate clearly enough to the type of health problem or behavior of concern in your population. You sense that some of the items are "not quite right," or do not quite measure what needs to be measured for the purposes of your program or study.

Items or measures in health education and health promotion are usually time dependent or historically bound to some extent. This limitation may present problems for the evaluator choosing from already existing instruments. Measures of the concept to be evaluated may reflect a particular period in time and may therefore be inappropriate for the current period. For example, attitudes toward nuclear power developed and standardized during the early 1980s may refer to President Reagan or Prime Minister Thatcher. When you choose to use them again, other national leaders need to be substituted—but it may not be sufficient merely to insert their successors. History may change the key decision-making nations or positions.

At this point the evaluator asks, "Are the items appropriate to use, even with their current limitations?" You can sometimes compromise, by developing some measures as well as using some previously developed items that meet at least minimum criteria for adequacy.

The fourth stage of instrument development involves both *responsible reflection* and *creative endeavor* (Lewis et al., 1978). Responsible reflection occurs when the evaluator engages in a systematic literature review of available instruments. These instruments may be found most

TABLE 6-2 Selected reliability coefficients of the Health Locus of Control Scale (HLC) and the Multidimensional Health Locus of Control Scale (MHLC)

Reliability	Value	Scale	Comments	Investigator
Internal Consistency				
Cronbach's alpha	.72	HLC	Established on 98 presumed healthy college students	Wallston et al. (1976)
Cronbach's alpha	.40–.54	HLC	Established on subsequent samples	Wallston et al. (1976)
Cronbach's alpha	.36	HLC	Established on 318 adult hypertensives. Modified response scale; administered as an interview, not self-administered	Lewis et al. (1978)
Cronbach's alpha	.80	HLC	Established on 115 female cancer patients	Bloom (1979)
Cronbach's alpha	.51	HLC	Established on 57 late-stage adult cancer patients	Lewis (1982a)
Cronbach's alpha	.67–.86	MHLC	Established on 115 respondents ≥ 16 years old	Wallston et al. (1978)
Cronbach's alpha	.58	HLC	Established on hospitalized patients	Meyers et al. (1982)
Stability (test-retest)	.71	HLC	Established over 8 weeks	Wallston et al. (1976)
Stability (test-retest)	.69	HLC	Established on sample of schoolteachers and administrators at 4-week interval	McCusker & Morrow (1979)

TABLE 6-3 Sources of selected tests of validity for the Health Locus of Control Scale (HLC) and the Multidimensional Health Locus of Control (MHLC) Scale

	Criterion Validity		
Content Validity	**Predictive**	**Concurrent**	**Construct Validity**
HLC (Wallston et al., 1976)	MHLC (Wallston & Wallston, 1978)		HLC (Lewis et al., 1978)
		HLC (Wallston et al., 1976)	HLC (Wallston et al., 1976)
		MHLC (Thomas & Hooper, 1983)	HLC (Snow & Thurber, 1983)
			HLC (McCusker & Morrow, 1979)
		MHLC (Wallston & Wallston, 1978)	HLC (Seeman & Seeman, 1983)

TABLE 6-4 Instrument compilations

Aday & Eichhorn (1973)
The Utilization of Health Services: Indices and Correlates
Anderson (1981)
Assessing Affective Characteristics in the Schools
Andrews & Withey (1976)
Social Indicators of Well-Being: America's Perception of Life Quality
Berg (1974)
Nursing Audit and Outcome Criteria
Buros (1975)
Personality Tests and Reviews. II.
Buros (1974)
Tests in Print
Chun, Cobb, & French (1975)
Measures for Psychological Assessment: A Guide to 3,000 Original Sources and Their Applications
Clearinghouse of Health Indexes (periodic listing by Division of Analysis, National Center for Health Statistics)
Elinson & Siegmann (1979)
Socio-Medical Health Indicators
Green, Wilson, & Bauer (1983)
Data Required to Measure Progress on the Objectives for the Nation in Health Promotion and Disease Prevention
IOX Assessment Associates (1983)
Seven "evaluation handbooks for health education programs": (1) *Smoking*, (2) *Alcohol and Substance Abuse*, (3) *Diabetes*, (4) *Exercise*, (5) *Immunization*, (6) *Nutrition*, (7) *Stress Management*
Morris (1979)
Measuring the Condition of the World's Poor: The Physical Quality of Life Index
Pinckeny & Pinckeny (1982)
The Encyclopedia of Medical Tests
Population Council (1967)
Selected Questionnaires on Knowledge, Attitudes and Practices of Family Planning (2 vols.).

directly by reviewing books of compiled instruments. Table 6-4 lists some compilations and broadly outlines the nature of their contents. Most major university libraries contain these books, or you can obtain them through interlibrary loan programs. Full bibliographic citations are given in the reference list at the back of this book.

In addition to published compilations of instruments, certain professional journals often include articles devoted to the development and testing of valid and reliable measures. The measures are often explicated within a theoretical context. Relevant journal papers can be identified most efficiently through various computerized or bound indexes and abstracts. Examples of these include *Medline, Index Medicus, Behavioral Medicine Abstracts, Sociological Abstracts, Psychological Abstracts, Cur-*

TABLE 6-4 Continued

Rand Series "Conceptualization and Measurement of Health for Children and Adults in the Health Insurance Study"
- Eisen, Donald, Ware, & Brook (1980)
  Conceptualization and Measurement of Health for Children
- Spolsky, Kamberg, Lohr, & Feldman (1983)
  Measurement of Dental Health Status
- Ware, Brook, Davies-Avery, Williams, & Stewart (1980)
  Model of Health
- Ware, Davies-Avery, & Donald (1978)
  General Health Perceptions
- Ware, Johnston, Davies-Avery, & Brook (1979)
  Mental Health

Reeder, Ramacher, & Gorelnik (1976)
Handbook of Scales and Indices of Health Behavior

Robinson, Athanasiou, & Head (1969)
Measures of Occupational Attitudes and Occupational Characteristics

Robinson & Shaver (1973)
Measures of Social Psychological Attitudes

Solleder (1979)
Evaluation Instruments in Health Education

Sorochan (1976)
Personal Health Appraisal

Stine, Pacanowski, Roffman, & Heald (1974)
Two Health Questionnaires for Adolescents

U.S. Department of Health and Human Services (1981c)
Health Risk Appraisals: An Inventory

Ware, Wright, & Snyder (1976)
Development and Validation of Scales to Measure Patient Satisfaction

Wilson & Iverson (1982)
Federal Data Bases for Health Education Research

rent Awareness in Health Education, and the *Cumulative Index to Nursing Literature.* Particular journals are noted for their publication of instrument development articles. Examples of such journals from the basic sciences as well as from the professional fields are listed in Table 6-5.

Creative endeavor is an important and significant part in the fourth stage of instrument development. Because existing instruments are often not appropriate for direct adoption, you usually have little choice but to generate additional items or to modify existing items. If you develop new items, generate multiple items for each major concept to be measured. Brainstorming items with a panel of experts can be very helpful. Your expert panel can be composed of health education practitioners, other health professionals, content experts, curriculum or education specialists, measurement experts, and health consumers. In generating the measures, they need only initially concur on the list of major concepts to be measured and on a theoretical definition of the concepts.

TABLE 6-5 Journals that include relevant articles on instrument development

Journal	Comments
Addictive Behaviors	Measures of drug and alcohol abuse
Adult Education	Quarterly articles on evaluation
American J Public Health	Monthly articles on health measures
Behavior Research and Therapy	Quarterly articles on behavioral measures
British J Addiction	Semiannual articles on alcohol, drug, and smoking measures
British J Educational Technology	Three issues per year, from London
Child Development	Quarterly articles
Health Education Quarterly; formerly *Health Education Monographs*	Quarterly articles related to health education measures
Human Relations	Monthly articles on social psychological measures
J Abnormal and Social Psychology	Bimonthly articles
J American Dietetic Association	Monthly articles on nutrition measures
J Applied Behavioral Analysis	Quarterly articles on experimental measures
J Applied Behavior Science	Quarterly articles on organizational measures
J Behavioral Medicine	Frequent articles on behavioral measures
J Clinical Psychology	Quarterly articles on personality measures
J Community Health	Occasional articles on behavioral, health, and economic measures
J Comparative Family Studies	Canadian, three issues per year
J Consulting and Clinical Psychology	Psychological or social measures
J Counseling Psychology	Monthly articles on counseling measures
J Drug Education	Regular articles on measurement
J Educational Research	Regular articles on measurement
J Health and Social Behavior	Quarterly articles on social measures
J Medical Education	Monthly articles on measurement and evaluation
J Nursing Education	Very occasional articles on knowledge and attitude measures
J Personality and Social Psychology	Monthly articles on psychological measures
J Personality Assessment	Frequent articles

Note: This list is suggestive, not exhaustive.

TABLE 6-5 Continued

Journal	Comments
J Psychosomatic Research	Bimonthly articles
J School Health	Occasional articles on child health education
J Studies on Alcohol	Monthly articles on alcohol measures
J Youth and Adolescence	Quarterly articles, social, and psychological measures
Medical Care	Monthly articles on measurement and evaluation issues
Milbank Memorial Fund Quarterly on Health and Society	Occasional articles on health economics
Nursing Research	Bimonthly articles dealing with measures of physiological as well as psychosocial outcomes
Patient Counselling and Health Education	Quarterly articles on measurement and evaluation in patient education
Perceptual and Motor Skills	Bimonthly articles on enabling factors
Preventive Medicine	Quarterly articles related to health promotion measures
Promoting Health	Occasional summaries of recent research and evaluation
Psychosomatic Medicine	Bimonthly articles related to stress
Public Health Reports	Occasional articles
Rehabilitation Quarterly	Articles on guidance measures
Research in Nursing and Health	Occasional articles on instrument development
Review of Educational Research	Bimonthly articles on educational measures
Scandinavian J Social Medicine	Three issues per year, in English
Small Group Behavior	Quarterly articles on group process measures
Social Science and Medicine	Frequent articles on sociomedical and economic measures
Sociometry	Quarterly articles on social measures
Western J Nursing Research	Occasional articles on instrument development and outcome measures

Item generation is an intriguing as well as difficult step in the instrument development process. Remember that there are no truly definitive measures of variables, and there are always alternative measures for any one concept. The ideal is to generate a large number of possible items to measure the concept—that is, to generate a large pool of items and then to apply systematically a set of criteria that allows the evaluator and the expert panel to choose from this larger set. Each panel may develop their own criteria for review, but they may include criteria for clarity, clinical meaningfulness, thoroughness or scope, degree of abstractness, and potential for variability across the program participants.

As items are generated, reexamine the theoretical definitions of the concepts (Stage 1). These definitions help delete measures that have minimal or no theoretical relation to the current work.[3]

Stage 5. Quantifying Items

At this stage, the goal is to achieve a level of measurement that allows you to categorize or score people with as much discriminating power as the study requires without exceeding the limits of precision that the measurement circumstances will tolerate or justify. The extremes are a simple dichotomous (yes or no, true or false) classification, or a tediously long, painfully detailed questionnaire, interview, or physical examination with repetitious items in which thoughtful judgments are required on a scale from 0 to 100. The first extreme is misplaced brevity; the second is misplaced precision.

How much precision will the circumstances of measurement tolerate? Few rules specify the tolerable limits of human endurance, which are subjective and circumstantial. People will tolerate measurement procedures that are more invasive and tedious if they have voluntarily submitted themselves to the time and place than if they have to be "captured" in a surprise phone call or street-corner interview. Workers will tolerate longer questionnaires if their employers have given them release time from their duties than if they have to fill out forms during their lunch hour; patients, if they are bedridden; students, if they can do it on class time; or anyone, if comfortable and recognized or rewarded for the contribution of time and effort.

How much precision will circumstances justify? The best rule of thumb here is to be sure your level of precision does not exceed your number of subjects. For example, your conclusions will appear fatuous if you report twenty variables on ten subjects; or if you report subjective statements (attitudes, beliefs) on a scale of 0 to 50.

Stages 6 and 7. Testing Reliability and Validity

Stages 6 and 7 follow the procedures outlined in the two previous chapters. We regret to report that relatively few tests and measures used spe-

3. An alternative to deriving items from theory is to allow the responses to open-ended questions in a pilot survey of a study sample to generate items for the structured instrument.

cifically in health education have been submitted to these final steps. Often those measures for which validity is claimed by their authors have undergone only the most cursory of tests, such as a casual check of face validity by one or two experts other than the author. Recently, the Center for Health Promotion and Education of the Centers for Disease Control contracted with IOX Assessment Associates (IOX Assessment Associates, 1983) to develop seven handbooks on measurement and evaluation of health education in smoking, diabetes, and five other areas (see Table 6-4). In collecting the hundreds of instruments or batteries of questions and measurement procedures on these, the contractor found few in which their psychometric quality was adequately established.

In a quantitative review (to be described in the last chapter) of fifty-seven evaluations of patient education for chronic conditions published between 1971 and 1984, only 61 percent explicitly defined the behavioral outcome measured. Most of those twenty-one studies that measured knowledge (comprehension, recognition, or recall) paid little or no attention to the reliability or validity of their measures (Mullen & Green, 1984; Mullen et al., 1986).

These examples indicate more clearly than further admonitions from us the need in this field for reliability and validity testing. Having stated the need in a variety of ways and having offered two chapters on concepts and methods in testing reliability and validity, we are, nevertheless, still concerned that the subject remains too abstract. In Appendix A, therefore, we have reprinted a concrete example of the specific procedures followed in examining the reliability and validity of interview data in an experimental evaluation of a family-planning project in a developing country.

USE OF EXISTING DATA SOURCES*

To show the rich resources available for measurement and evaluation of community, state, and national health education and health promotion programs, let us consider the national quantifiable objectives for disease prevention and health promotion. The tracking of national progress and setbacks in relation to these objectives has required systematic development of data sources for monitoring, surveillance, and periodic surveys. New data are being collected by government agencies to measure progress on many of the objectives through additions to existing local, state, and national reporting requirements; health surveys; and state registration systems. Before collecting original data for your own projects, consider

*Adapted with permission of the *American Journal of Public Health* from Green, Wilson, & Bauer (1983).

the existing data systems available through these government agencies and private sector sources. The sources and the quality of available data are examined in the remainder of this chapter.

Description of the Objectives for the Nation

The 226 objectives reflecting the consensus of experts on priorities for the United States in disease prevention and health promotion are detailed in *Promoting Health, Preventing Disease: Objectives for the Nation* and in *Strategies for Promoting Health for Specific Populations* (U.S. Department of Health and Human Services, 1980, 1981b). The objectives relate to fifteen priorities, grouped under health promotion, health protection, and preventive health services, as follows:

- *Health promotion* objectives relate particularly to behavioral concerns such as reducing smoking, reducing misuse of alcohol and drugs, improved nutrition, exercise and physical fitness, and stress and violence control.
- *Health protection* objectives relate particularly to environmental concerns, including toxic agent control, occupational safety and health, accident prevention and injury control, fluoridation and dental health, and infectious disease control.
- *Preventive health services* objectives relate particularly to high blood pressure control, family planning, pregnancy and infant health, immunizations, and sexually transmitted diseases (STD).

The implied hierarchy of objectives within each of the fifteen priorities can be seen as a causal chain of events and outcomes that must be achieved in order to accomplish the broad goals previously outlined in *Healthy People: The Surgeon General's Report on Health Promotion and Disease Prevention* (U.S. Department of Health, Education, and Welfare, 1979; see also U.S. Department of Health, Education, and Welfare, 1978). Five categories of objectives were listed for each of the fifteen areas: (1) improved health status, (2) reduced risk factors, (3) increased public and professional awareness, (4) improved services and protection, and (5) improved surveillance or evaluation systems. The objectives in all five categories are relevant to the evaluation of health education, as suggested by Figure 6-3, but those under Categories 3 and 4 are the most directly related to health education.

The approximate relationships among the objectives are shown in Figure 6-3, omitting the set of objectives for improved surveillance and evaluation systems. Health status objectives, on the right in Figure 6-3, were broadly stated in *Healthy People* for each of five age groups and more specifically stated in *Promoting Health, Preventing Disease: Objectives for the Nation* (U.S. Department of Health and Human Services,

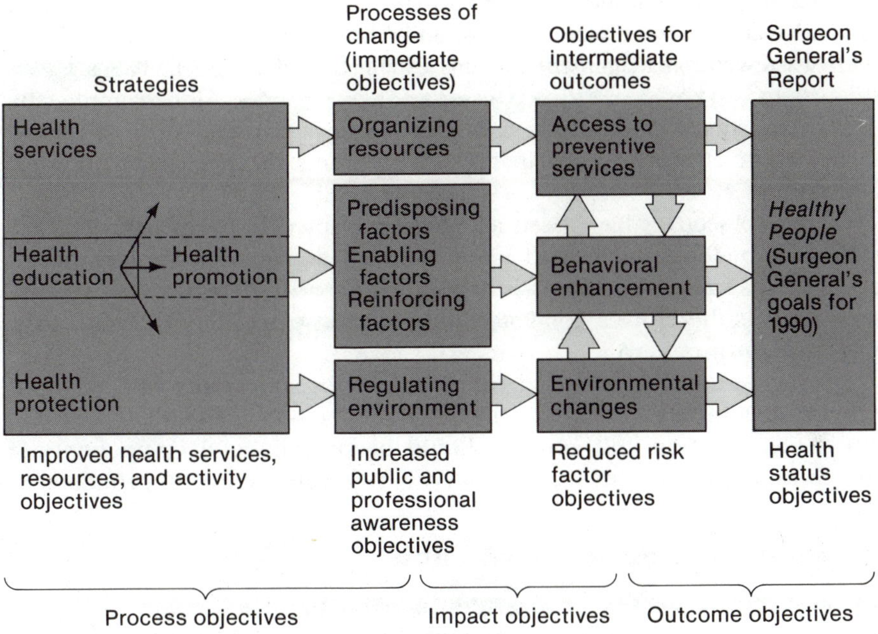

Figure 6-3 *Structure and logical relationships of* Objectives for the Nation *in disease prevention and health promotion.* Source: *Green, Wilson, & Bauer (1983), p. 24. Used by permission of the American Public Health Association.*

1980) for each of the fifteen priority "actions for health." These 56 health status objectives are expected to be achieved through the reduction of risk factors, many of them behavioral, as expressed in 46 intermediate objectives (on the right in Figure 6-3). The reduced risk factor objectives, in turn, are to be accomplished through processes of change expressed by a set of 42 more immediate objectives for increased public and professional awareness. These processes of change, in turn, are to be set into motion with strategies expressed in 46 objectives for improved services, resources, and activities (on the left in Figure 6-3).

Objectives are stated in several ways. Most are expressed as an absolute reduction in a rate—for example, "By 1990, the fertility rate for fifteen-year-old girls should be reduced to 10 per 1,000. (In 1978, there were 14.2 births per 1,000 for this age group.)" Others are expressed as an absolute reduction in a number—for example, "By 1990, the incidence of compensable occupational dermatitis should be reduced to about 60,000," or call for the complete elimination of a hazard—for example,

"By 1990, there should be virtually no preventable contamination of ground water, surface water, or the soil from industrial toxins associated with wastewater management systems established after 1980." Finally, goals relating to improving data sources are not quantifiable—for example, "By 1990, data should be available with which to evaluate the short- and long-term health effects of participation in programs of appropriate physical activity."

These objectives have been adopted or adapted in the policies of most state health departments and many national and local voluntary health agencies. Reference to the national objectives or the corresponding state document is therefore a good starting point for quantifying the objectives of your own program.

Some terms used in the national objectives statements require more precise definition before they can be quantified—for example, "By 1990, stress identification and control should become integral components of the continuum of health services offered by organized health programs."

Types of Data Systems Available

Various existing data systems used in tracking prevention goals are adaptable for measuring, estimating, or evaluating local health education needs or programs (Wilson & Iverson, 1982). The range of possible data systems includes (1) *regulatory or quasi-regulatory systems* such as those operated by the Food and Drug Administration (FDA) or the Environmental Protection Agency (EPA) and suggested to be used in relation to the objectives for toxic agent control; (2) *surveillance and monitoring systems,* such as those established by the Centers for Disease Control (CDC) for surveillance of sexually transmitted diseases, nutrition, and infectious diseases, and the environmental monitoring systems established by EPA; (3) *population-based surveys* such as the National Institute on Drug Abuse's biennial national survey on drug abuse, and the National Center for Health Statistics's (NCHS) National Health Interview Survey (NHIS) and National Health and Nutrition Examination Survey (NHANES); and (4) *data systems based on records,* either a sample of records, such as the National Ambulatory Medical Care Survey and National Hospital Discharge Survey of the NCHS or a complete count of records as in the birth and death registration systems. Some of these record-based systems use administrative data, such as the Medicare claims and enrollment files.

Most of the data systems for tracking goals are federal systems. Some are aggregations of data from state health agencies, such as the Vital Statistics Registration System. A few are in the private sector, such as the data from the Professional Activities Survey of the Commission on Professional Hospital Activities.

Surveillance systems based on voluntary reporting, or at least not enforced reporting, of all events of a given kind (such as the CDC reporting systems for sexually transmitted diseases or the childhood illness reporting systems) can be used for comparing trends in your program with trends in national data.

The types of data sources for the currently measurable objectives of the four levels of process, impact, and outcome rely heavily on administrative records and surveillance systems. Data for the health status objectives come particularly from the National Vital Registration System's death statistics and the *Morbidity and Mortality Weekly Reports* of CDC. The risk reduction objectives heavily rely on interview surveys of health practices, whereas the improved services measures derive about equally from surveys, surveillance, and administrative records (Aday, Sellers, & Andersen, 1981; Cornell, Landis, Zemach, Manela, Wainstock, & Gardner, 1980; Roos, 1975).

Recommended Survey Questions for Health Promotion

Most of the health promotion objectives must be tracked with data collected by surveys based on self-administered questionnaires, face-to-face interviews, or telephone interviews. Goals for stress, nutrition, exercise, family planning, hypertension, and smoking, alcohol, and drug abuse all require at least some interview data on personal health behavior or public and professional awareness. Such data can be collected under existing data systems. Behavioral and cognitive data are required to measure progress toward the goals in nutrition, hypertension, and stress. Measures of trends in public awareness and behavior are particularly sensitive to wordings in precise questionnaires. The NCHS's National Health Interview Survey has done little to measure health beliefs in past surveys, but will probably do more in the future. State surveys have been conducted most consistently with an instrument developed cooperatively by the CDC and the Office of Disease Prevention and Health Promotion. Results from the cooperating states are published periodically in CDC's *Morbidity and Mortality Weekly Reports.* These data provide current norms against which to compare local populations or program results. For this reason we commend the items from this survey to health educators to replicate in their own measurement and evaluation. The questionnaire for the NCHS National Survey of Personal Health Practices and Consequences is reproduced in Appendix C.

Problems with Trend Data

Data on health behavior are easy to compile from surveys, but the stability of questions repeated over a number of years is jeopardized by several factors. The state of the art in survey methodology continually advances, or at least the changes usually are offered as advances, and it is difficult, if not impossible, to resist applying these advances to later surveys, thus reducing comparability over time. Even if identical question wording can be maintained, other factors subject to change include the context in which the questions are asked, interviewer training, instructions, sample design, coding, editing, and data-processing errors. All these changes can affect comparability. Questions on cigarette smoking have become somewhat standardized over time, but as the emphasis changes from investigating the *relationship* between smoking and health to studying more detailed aspects of changes in smoking behavior itself, it is easy to foresee further efforts to "improve" question wording on smoking habits, again affecting comparability. Experts disagree on what standard questions to ask for measurement of alcohol consumption, but serious efforts are underway to develop national consensus on such measurement issues. Diet and nutrition questions, physical fitness measures, and stress, coping, and quality of life measures all await such consensus development, but will be even more difficult to standardize over time because of their sensitivity to cultural and lifestyle changes, technological changes, and growing knowledge.

Although the problems of comparability are most at issue with trend data from interview surveys, other trend data are not immune to those problems. For example, the measurement of blood pressure in the National Health and Nutrition Examination Surveys differed in procedures between the first survey of adults and the later surveys. Periodic changes in the international classification of diseases can result in some comparability problems, although efforts are made to limit such changes to more detailed classifications that can be recombined for trend analysis. The recent ninth revision of the *International Classification of Diseases* (1980), for example, added more specific diagnostic categories for sexually transmitted diseases, to permit better monitoring of such diseases.

Definitional Differences

Sometimes you can use data bases from more than one source. For example, one agency's 1985 survey might serve as baseline data and to establish objectives and to set goals, and another agency's similar survey in 1988 might provide the "posttest" measures you need to compare with trends in your community where you conducted an innovative health education program in 1987. Be sure to examine the compatibility of variables that are assumed to be similar.

Several of the occupational injury objectives, for example, are focused on the reduction of work-loss days attributed to injuries. Two sources of data are frequently used for this measurement: the Bureau of Labor Statistics (BLS) data based on reports from industry, and data from the National Health Interview Survey. Both these sources are used in National Safety Council reports. While both BLS and NHIS use the measure "work-loss days," the BLS definition includes only days lost from work beyond the day of injury, while the NHIS definition includes any day on which at least half of a normal workday is lost. The impact of such definitional problems may be less significant than other aspects of the two data bases, such as how the data are collected (e.g., records versus interviews), but definitional differences add confusion and complexity to the analysis and interpretation of data from multiple sources.

Evaluating Surveys and Data Systems

An irony arises in the process of evaluating the usefulness of sample survey data for monitoring goals, as opposed to other types of data. Large statistical data systems based on probability samples usually are accompanied by detailed descriptions of their methodology, indicating both the strengths and limitations of the data derived from such systems. These limitations are often not described for some of the less rigorous data-gathering mechanisms. There is a tendency, when data systems are compared, to emphasize the limitations of a data system when they are clearly acknowledged, but to overlook limitations of other systems when they are not clearly identified. Hence, more precise data systems often receive less credibility than do less precise systems.

Examine alternative systems on the same criteria. Before accepting one system at face value, ask the same questions of it as the other survey or data system has asked of itself. For example, if one system acknowledges a high refusal rate (low response rate) in certain subgroups, inquire whether the other survey was subject to the same problem and whether that problem was even reported.

Measuring Incidence

Systems for measuring and monitoring the incidence of selected diseases, such as hypertension, or conditions related to certain toxic agents are scarce. In *Promoting Health, Preventing Disease: Objectives for the Nation* (U.S. Department of Health and Human Services, 1980), many of these goals were stated in terms of *developing the measures* rather than reducing *incidence*. Incidence—the number of new cases of a disease occurring in a given period of time—requires information on the onset of the disease as well as the population at risk. Onset information is difficult to obtain in interview data and often does not exist in record data. When data from physician and hospital records are used to measure incidence, you must also make adjustments for people who receive medical care from multiple sources. Also you must make a distinction between new cases of a disease and newly *diagnosed* cases.

Converting National Goals into Subarea or Subgroup Objectives

National data bases exist to track many of these goals and objectives, but if the objectives are to be tracked for smaller geographic areas, such as a state, county, or town, or for subgroups of the population, such as specific minority groups, you need to develop baseline data and trend data. The major exception is the birth and death data from vital records, but even here, up-to-date population data for the denominators are rarely available for particular subgroups or geographic areas for years other than the U.S. Census years (1970, 1980, etc.). In addition, the relatively small number of certain events, such as maternal mortality, in a small geographic area makes the application of percentage reduction goals questionable.

Surveillance systems will continue to be available to track certain diseases and processes at the local level. A number of these systems have been developed by CDC and have been in operation for many years such as those in sexually transmitted diseases and for some of the childhood diseases. It is necessary, however, to evaluate the completeness of reporting in these systems because they are frequently based on voluntary reporting. Sources participating in these systems may include all providers of medical care, as in the case of certain reportable sexually transmitted diseases, or providers from a limited number of sites such as laboratories or clinics. The sites may or may not have been selected as representative samples of all such sites. Data derived from these systems are published as "reported cases of" (for example, reported cases of gonorrhea or of measles).

Such types of data pose several problems when used to monitor objectives. First, the proportion of cases that are reported may vary by the type of disease and perceived significance of reporting. For example, many physicians do not report childhood diseases through the appropriate public health channels. Although the actual level of reporting in the surveillance system is often lower, the trend patterns are usually very similar to those from sample survey data. Both the surveillance and the survey data reflect periods of increased activity and public concern.

A second problem that can arise is the possibility that the level of underreporting in a surveillance system can change over time. As more public attention is given to a specific disease—for example, through a major prevention program, or through publicity accorded a condition such as AIDs—the completeness of reporting can improve. Therefore, the data used to monitor progress will show increased levels of incidence, when in fact only an increased proportion of the actual cases is being reported. The greater the degree of underreporting, the greater the potential for this ballooning to occur.

Future Data Plans

In the years ahead, watch for several new developments in the use of data bases. First, the National Center for Health Services (NCHS) and the Center for Health Promotion and Education of CDC are developing the capability to conduct telephone surveys primarily by using random-digit dialing sampling techniques. This breakthrough has opened up the possibility to collect certain health behavior and health knowledge data from national and state samples on a periodic basis. NCHS has conducted for the Office of Health Information and Health Promotion two waves (1979 and 1981) of a National Survey of Personal Health Practices and Consequences (NSPHPC) using this technique (Wilson & Elinson, 1981; U.S. Department of Health and Human Services, 1981a; Gottlieb & Green, 1984). An abbreviated version of this instrument is reproduced in Appendix C to encourage replication of its items.

The NCHS's National Death Index (NDI) will be linked with the NSPHPC to relate health behavior prospectively with causes of death. The NDI is also a potential data source in toxic epidemiological studies. This data system—or, more precisely, research tool—is scheduled to be available from NCHS with a user's manual. The first year of deaths recorded in this index was 1979. This index will help researchers determine if people in a study sample have died in subsequent years.

In monitoring pregnancy and infant care objectives, you need to match birth and infant death records. Most states already have at least a numerical match between these two types of records, which makes the next step of actually linking the data easy.

The National Survey of Family Growth by NCHS provides much of the tracking data for the family-planning objectives. This survey, last conducted in 1982, is projected to be repeated about every five years. While the past surveys have been restricted to every married woman or single woman who has offspring in the household, the 1982 and future surveys include all women ages fifteen to forty-four in their samples. This range will make the survey more useful in providing norms and trends on teenage pregnancies and abortions in all ages.

The family-planning objectives reflect the need for data on socioeconomic status of births. The new one-time National Natality Followback Survey conducted by the NCHS provides such data for a sample of 10,000 live births occurring in 1980. In addition, the National Fetal Mortality Survey now provides normative data on 7,000 fetal deaths of twenty-eight weeks' gestation or more occurring in 1980.

Several of the objectives require data collected in the National Health and Nutrition Examination Survey. For example, data on objectives related to dental caries, height and weight, obesity, and hypertension are available in this periodic survey. The National Health Interview Survey will continue to collect data periodically on cigarette smoking. Questions on alcohol consumption were on the 1983 and 1985 NHIS. CDC has undertaken to stimulate the needed attention to methodological studies and use and analysis of existing data files in relation to the *Objectives for the Nation.* The Center for Health Promotion and Education of CDC, the NCHS, and the Office of Disease Prevention and Health Promotion conduct seminars for investigators around the country, and (with Health and Welfare Canada) compare national and regional data sets. These agencies also cosponsor grant programs, along with National Center for Health Services Research, the National Institutes of Health, and other federal agencies to support secondary analyses of existing data sets.

In all, agencies are collecting or compiling national data on the approximately 110 measurable objectives in disease prevention and health promotion, or developing measures on another 80 objectives by adding to their surveys, surveillance, or administrative record systems. In addition, state and local agencies are monitoring progress on their own adapted versions of the national objectives. Most of these data are collected at the taxpayers' expense and are in the public domain, which means you have access to them and should be encouraged to use them. Seldom will they meet all your measurement and evaluation needs, but seldom should they be ignored. At the very least you will do well to consult the form of their data collection methods and the wording of their survey questions (see Appendix C) so that your own measurements can be compared with regional or national norms.

NORM-REFERENCED AND CRITERION-REFERENCED MEASURES

The existing data systems just described provide measurements on large populations or estimates of population parameters based on representative sample statistics. Such population-based data can be considered *normative* insofar as they represent the norm. They are useful in diagnostic studies or evaluations of health education needs or outcomes in subpopulations in that they allow direct comparison of an object of interest in your population against a standard of acceptability in the larger population.

What you are saying, in effect, when you compare the status of your target population against the norm of the larger population of which they are a part, is that your criterion of reference or your criterion of success is the status of the larger population. This criterion has been particularly suitable for public health agencies because they could reasonably settle for a level of health or health behavior for their constituency that was at least as good as the norm for the nation. Schools settled for norm-referenced testing for a long time because it was enough to assure parents that their children were getting "above-average" grades and test scores.

Something happened in the 1960s to change this attitude toward criteria and measures of adequacy and success. The history of the shift in perspective in medicine and public health, and more generally in public policy, is traced most cogently by McGinnis (1982). With McNamara's introduction of "management by objectives" techniques in the Defense Department came a new orientation to planning and evaluation against criteria other than tradition, historical experience, or national norms. The question became "What should we be able to accomplish if we applied our knowledge, skills, and resources more effectively?"

For schools, Glaser (1963) posed the same question another way. If we keep grading or scoring "on the curve," using norm-referenced tests, we run the risk of failing to aspire to the learning outcomes of which schools with new instructional technology are capable. Unfortunately, Glaser's worst-case scenario has materialized. The norms against which students have been graded in school or scored in standardized achievement tests (SATs) have slid to the point that a national commission had to conclude in 1983 that "For the first time in the history of our country, the educational skills of one generation will not surpass, will not equal, will not even approach those of their parents" (National Commission on Excellence in Education, 1983). The students passed, based on normative tests, but they failed based on criteria other than norms.

Criterion-referenced testing has gained considerable ground in measuring comprehension and cognitive skills (Berk, 1980; Brown, 1980; Hambleton, Swaminathan, Algina, & Coulson, 1978; Hambleton & Eignor, 1978; Messick, 1981; Millman, 1974; Popham, 1981) and in attitudinal and other affective dimensions of educational outcomes (Anderson, 1981; Popham, 1978). More extensive application in health education is advocated (Iverson, 1984; Popham, 1982).

Essentially, criterion-referenced testing requires specifying in advance of the test what level of result is required to "pass" or to meet the standard of acceptability. In other words, the criterion in criterion-referenced measurement is a quantified objective. Hence, for broad-scale evaluation of health education and health promotion we come full circle to the objectives for the nation as a logical starting point in developing measurement criteria and selecting measurement tools.

At the individual level, a criterion-referenced approach to the same health promotion objectives is the health hazard appraisal instrument, or *health risk appraisal (HRA),* as it is more commonly known. The HRA was designed as an educational tool to help people recognize their personal or individualized health risks. A typical HRA asks questions about habits such as smoking, exercise, and diet. More extensive instruments collect additional information, including a medical history, environmental influences, blood pressure, and other physical measurements. These risk indicators are then compared to epidemiological and age-specific mortality data to yield information on an individual's expected longevity or risk for disease. The term *risk factor,* often used interchangeably with *risk indicator,* refers to the probability that a given disease, condition, or death will develop or occur within a certain time period; for example, smoking is a risk factor that increases the risk for lung cancer and death. Most HRAs also predict which specific risk factors may shorten an individual's life span, and many suggest ways to reduce specific risk factors (Bauer, 1978; Beery, 1981; Faber, 1980; Faber & Reinhardt, 1982; Farquhar, 1978; Goetz, Duff, & Bernstein, 1980; Hall, 1980; Hall & Zwemer, 1979; Ratcliffe, 1978; Robbins & Blankenbaker, 1982).

Health risk appraisals continue to be refined. One aim of current research is to increase the accuracy of HRAs, both by updating the statistical data base and by improving the methods used to compute risk factors (Safter, 1982; Wagner, 1982). Researchers are also working to develop appraisals that are appropriate for specific populations, such as adolescents and blacks (Center for Health Promotion and Education, 1983b). Another concern is the educational impact of HRAs—how they can best be used to help people to change their habits. Some recommendations for implementing HRA programs, entitled *Guidelines for Health Risk Appraisal/Risk Reduction Systems,* have been issued by the Society of Prospective Medicine, the professional group most responsible for advancing the technology and application of HRAs.

At least forty-four versions of HRAs are currently available. They come in three forms:

- *Computer-scored HRAs,* which are mailed to a central computer facility for batch processing. These are usually the more complex and detailed appraisals.
- *Microcomputer-based HRAs,* which can be processed by a microcomputer at home, in schools, or in offices. Some of these are interactive, meaning that the user can type responses directly into the microcomputer, and results are displayed or printed immediately.
- *Self-scored questionnaires,* which are usually brief and do not involve a computer; they are scored by the user. Most of these are not HRAs in the strictest sense.

However, vendors should always be consulted for more detailed ordering information; for example, there may be a minimum required for batch processing. In addition, many vendors offer related services such as group and custom profiles, technical assistance, and health promotion programs (Beery, 1981; Hall, 1980; Sorochan, 1976; Vickery, 1979).

As a criterion-referenced measure, the HRA comes as close to a standardized instrument as any broad-scale measure of individual health practices or lifestyle. The major criterion against which most of the more statistically grounded instruments are referenced is probability of death. This fact causes some to miss the point of health promotion concerning quality of life, energy, productivity, and other benefits of health and healthy behavior besides delaying death. Nevertheless, enough variations exist in the HRAs available to avoid this pitfall. The latest compilation of HRAs is available from the National Health Information Clearinghouse (see U.S. Department of Health and Human Services, 1981c).

CONCLUSION

As in all good things, you need to heed some cautions in tapping existing data systems and standardized measurement tools. Most of these cautions have to do with the appropriate fit with your own conceptual model, target population, and program objectives. To ensure the best opportunity for an appropriate fit, we suggest using the national objectives in disease prevention and health promotion as a criterion-referenced starting point. These objectives will need to be adapted to your own setting and target population, but by referring to them at the outset, you stand a better chance of linking your measurement as well as your program efforts to the mainstream of policy, scientific and professional development, coordinated programs, and data systems.

In the next part of this book we stand back from the details of quantitative measurement and ask, "What else is needed in structuring observations and collecting data to assure that we are not misled by the apparent precision of quantitative results?"

SUMMARY

There are seven stages in which to develop and test a set of measures. Stage 1 involves the selection of a theoretical or conceptual framework that will offer, at minimum, the definitions of the variables to be measured. At best it also offers a set of hypothesized or potential interrelationships between the health education program components, the health determinants, and the outcome and impact variables. Stage 2 requires that the evaluator identify the purpose of the instrument. Stage 3 requires specifying the target population on which the set of measurements will be tested. Stage 4 involves specifying the content map or conceptual domain of the instrument's measures. Stage 5 forces the evaluator to quantify the selected items. Stages 6 and 7 engage the evaluator in reliability and validity testing respectively.

Sometimes data are available through existing data systems that can be used instead of or in conjunction with data generated by instruments developed by the evaluator. A review of the *Objectives for the Nation* provides a backdrop against which to view these data bases. These data bases can sometimes be used to measure, estimate, or evaluate local health education needs or programs; regulatory or quasi-regulatory programs; monitoring data systems; population-based surveys; and record-based data systems. In addition to the norm-referenced measures implied in the existing data systems, the evaluator may consider criterion-referenced measures. Criterion-referenced measures bring us full circle back to the *Objectives for the Nation.*

PART THREE

DESIGNS FOR EVALUATION

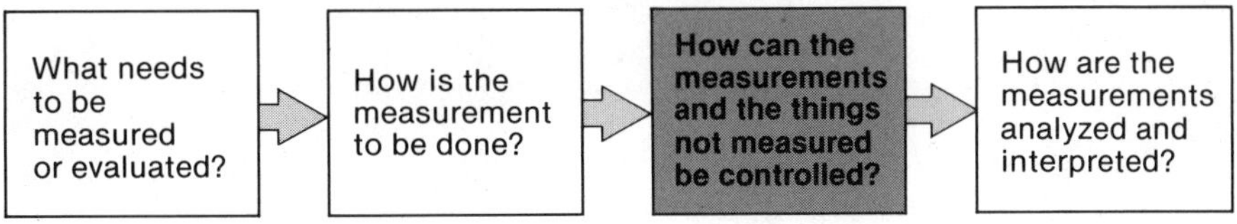

Once you have relatively reliable and valid measurement instruments, you might assume that the important work is done. In fact, however, precise quantitative measurement can be misleading if it has not been supplemented and applied under circumstances that allow for qualitative assessments and experimental controls through design and sampling. The chapters in this part of the book offer qualitative methods, experimental and quasi-experimental designs, and sampling methods particularly appropriate to diagnosis and evaluation in health education and health promotion. The elements of experimental design can be stratified as to relative importance in controlling various threats to evaluation validity. This capacity allows us to offer a series of decision hierarchies to help you select the design that best fits your evaluation purposes.

Chapter 7

QUALITATIVE METHODS

The previous chapters have concentrated on quantitative measurement, and the following chapters focus on experimental and quasi-experimental designs. Such methods and designs emphasize quantitative measures, outcomes, and use of baseline statistics and control groups as standards of comparison. These approaches have provided the field a more substantial base for practice and for legitimacy, and they have contributed to standards of accountability. Their preeminence, however, has overshadowed other ways of "knowing" and other evaluation models. This emphasis has led to some disappointment in the results of evaluation studies. Not surprisingly, experimental approaches have come under criticism as being inadequate and unsuitable as the *exclusive* tools for construction of our knowledge base in social programming (Weiss, 1972; Cronbach, 1975; Patton, 1978; Gebhardt, 1980; House, 1980). In the words of experimentalist Donald Campbell, "It is with regret that I report that in U.S. program evaluations . . . [the] sensible joint use of [qualitative and quantitative] modes of knowing is not yet practiced" (1979a, p. 53). Many other evaluation theorists and practicing evaluators now advocate including both quantitative and qualitative methods in the evaluator's repertoire (Cook & Campbell, 1979; Reichardt & Cook, 1979; Patton, 1980; Guba & Lincoln, 1981).

This chapter bridges the preceding and following chapters. Here we offer a definition of qualitative methods, delineate six functions of qualitative evaluation, and indicate the types of information that can be generated by such methods. We then describe, in relation to the six functions, selected qualitative evaluation approaches that have potential for serving your needs in health education and health promotion.

DEFINITION OF QUALITATIVE EVALUATION

The concepts underlying qualitative and quantitative evaluation methods differ on far more than specific data collection techniques. Yet the exact nature of the differences is subject to some debate (Rist, 1977; Filstead, 1979; Reichardt & Cook, 1979; Patton, 1980). The debates stem primarily from historical differences in both philosophy and methodology (Habermas, 1971). A fundamental distinction between qualitative and quantitative methods lies in their goals. Quantitative methods have developed largely to confirm or verify theory, whereas qualitative methods have been developed to discover theory.

Evaluation approaches differ along several dimensions, as summarized in Table 7-1. A given approach may not "qualify" on all dimensions. For example, the goal-free evaluation technique developed by Scriven (1972) may use quantitative data but still can be classified as qualitative.

You take a qualitative approach when you use methods to interpret the meanings of the program participants (and nonparticipants), of program planners and implementors themselves, and of the multiple realities they bring to a given situation. Such meanings are assumed to be socially constructed or learned (Berger & Luckmann, 1967; Schutz, 1973). As such, they are a prime object of qualitative study.

The scope of inquiry with qualitative methods is generally broader, unconfined by a presumed reality or program objectives. When using quantitative methods, objectivity (i.e., reliability) is foremost, stemming in part from the assumption that meaning is intrinsic and independently

TABLE 7-1 General characteristics of qualitative and quantitative methods

	Method	
Dimension	**Qualitative**	**Quantitative**
Intent	Discovery of theory, understanding of phenomena under study	Verification of theory, statistical prediction
Assumption about the origin of meaning	Socially constructed and conferred on objects and acts	Inherent in objects and acts
Scope	Holistic, rich in context, emphasizes interactions	Particularistic, guided by program objectives
Measurement	Qualitative data	Quantitative data
Data gathering	Semistructured or unstructured response options, observation	Fixed response options
Analytical techniques	Inductive	Deductive

embedded in "reality." You use qualitative methods in research to understand phenomena and situations as a whole (Schatzman & Strauss, 1973; Psathas, 1973), whereas in evaluation you use qualitative methods to understand programs as a whole (Broadhead, 1980; Parlett & Hamilton, 1976). An understanding of a program's setting, goals (as held by a variety of key figures or groups), and actual implementation processes is essential to understanding the program. This richness of context often gives qualitative methods the edge on validity.

Qualitative measures tend to produce data in the language of the subjects, rarely with numerical values attached to observations. This language is thought to be crucial in capturing and conveying the participants' systems of meaning. Open-ended questions, semistructured interviews, observational methods, primary and secondary documents, and a range of audio and video or film methods are commonly used to collect qualitative data. Quantitative measures rely on more standardized data collection and reduction techniques, using predetermined questions or observational indicators and established response options. These different goals and measures require different analytical techniques. Qualitative data are usually but not always analyzed inductively—concepts are generated from data. Thus, an evaluation of the impact of an education program on sexually transmitted disease, given in a high school, may reveal ways of viewing STD symptoms and meaning systems that were not anticipated. Quantitative data tend to be analyzed by deductive methods, although inductive methods such as some applications of factor analysis are not uncommon.

FUNCTIONS OF QUALITATIVE METHODS

Qualitative methods can significantly aid decision making and contribute to the understanding and improvement of programs. Specifically, at least six functions of qualitative methods exist in evaluation: (1) developing and delineating program elements before a quantitative evaluation is begun, (2) boosting the power of quasi-experimental designs, (3) broadening the observational field for program effects, (4) analyzing processes and individual cases to explain the "how" and "why" of an outcome, (5) generating theory, and (6) taking the place of quantitative approaches.

Tool for Developing and Delineating Program Elements

The precision of quantitative methods is wasteful and inefficient when applied to immature programs or when based on inadequate delineation of the assumptions underlying program elements. This problem commonly occurs when quantitative instruments become the routine method of measuring a construct such as self-esteem, resistance to persuasion, health beliefs, or locus of control, without the construct itself being understood in the context in which it is being measured. Qualitative methods systematically applied at the outset can help avoid the perfunctory or ritualistic adoption of the wrong measurement tools.

Qualitative approaches are especially important in the developmental stages of a program or an evaluation. Many programmatic issues are raised by a decision to institute a demonstration program that uses, for example, a group teaching and discussion process to help asthmatic children manage their regimens and conditions. The issues in such complex undertakings include the current practices, attitudes, and values of both the children and their parents; the forcefulness of the group leader(s); and myriad other factors, many of which enter into planning models (e.g., Green, Kreuter, Deeds, & Partridge, 1980). To later answer the question of *what* program operated on *which* population to produce *what* effects, you must first specify the program elements. Failure to do so clouds inferences about which specific elements of the program contributed to the long-range impact and clouds inferences about the program's generalizability to other populations. It also truncates the feedback loop to corrective action. The specification work you must do in planning an evaluation includes delineating the preexisting conditions, program components, intervening events, and program outcome and impact.

Preexisting conditions include not only the usual demographic descriptors for the target population (age, sex, marital status, and socioeconomic distributions), but also the social context in which the new behavior would be initiated, the organizational context of the program, and its interdependence with other programs and activities of the organization. Program components include inputs such as the program objectives, intensity and timing of the interventions, staffing patterns, the leadership styles of group leaders, and interactional patterns of counselors. Also included are the relationships among program activities—for example, the interaction between physician referral and the school health service program.

Intervening events may modify the program or its organizational context enough to change the intervention description. The next section, on the role of qualitative models in strengthening quasi-experimental designs, elaborates this point. Finally, you must delineate impact and outcomes (both intended and unintended). Here, qualitative assessments help to specify which quantitative instruments should be used, and if they are not currently available, the qualitative assessment can be the basis for instrument development. By discovering and sorting out actions and reactions, you can plot sequences of hypothesized effects from the program inputs as in Figure 7-1, which presents an example of a home visiting program for hypertensive patients. These hypothesized relationships, based on qualitative methods of observation and inference, then provide a map of causal pathways that can be confirmed or verified with both qualitative and quantitative tools.

Power Booster for Quasi-Experimental Designs

Too often the administrative and operational processes of the program under evaluation are restructured artificially to meet experimental requirements. Overemphasizing outcomes has frequently limited the measurement to exclude those processes that presumably cause the outcome. Such measurements contribute little to understanding where, in a complex web of causation such as shown in Figure 7-1, the program broke down. Without that information, an evaluation can offer little guidance to program improvement.

Variations on experimental design and many quasi-experimental designs, as will be seen in the next two chapters, have been advanced to reduce the rigid control requirements imposed by the full experimental designs. Cook and Campbell (1979) have described a deductive process through which the less rigorous but more workable designs can retain "specific" credibility by ruling out threats to validity, although the narrow focus on outcomes is left unchanged. Alternatively, contextual or naturalistic approaches—which rely primarily on qualitative methods—focus on program processes as well as outcomes and shore up the "trustworthiness" of evaluation designs by examining the dependability and stability of methods (Suchman, 1967). The confluence of both the experimental and contextual models produces a mixture of desirable elements for program evaluation.

Qualitative methods can play a valuable support function that allows a quantitative design to be altered to fit program circumstances. Called "intervening variable analysis" (Suchman, 1967), "implementation assessment" (Shortell & Richardson, 1978), and "internal analysis" (Deniston & Rosenstock, 1973), these methods have not been widely used, nor until recently have they been recommended in design options as practical alternatives to experimental designs. See Chapter 8 for further discussion of these methods.

Some quasi-experimental designs require only measurement of outcomes (posttest), with a "matched" comparison group. Matching is usually based on a few demographic characteristics (e.g., age, sex, socioeconomic status), behavioral status (e.g., smoking of *X* intensity and *Y* duration), and some indicator of motivation (e.g., similarly enrolled in a smoking cessation group). This choice of design implies that a pretest has been ruled out for practical reasons (e.g., cost), ethical problems (e.g.,

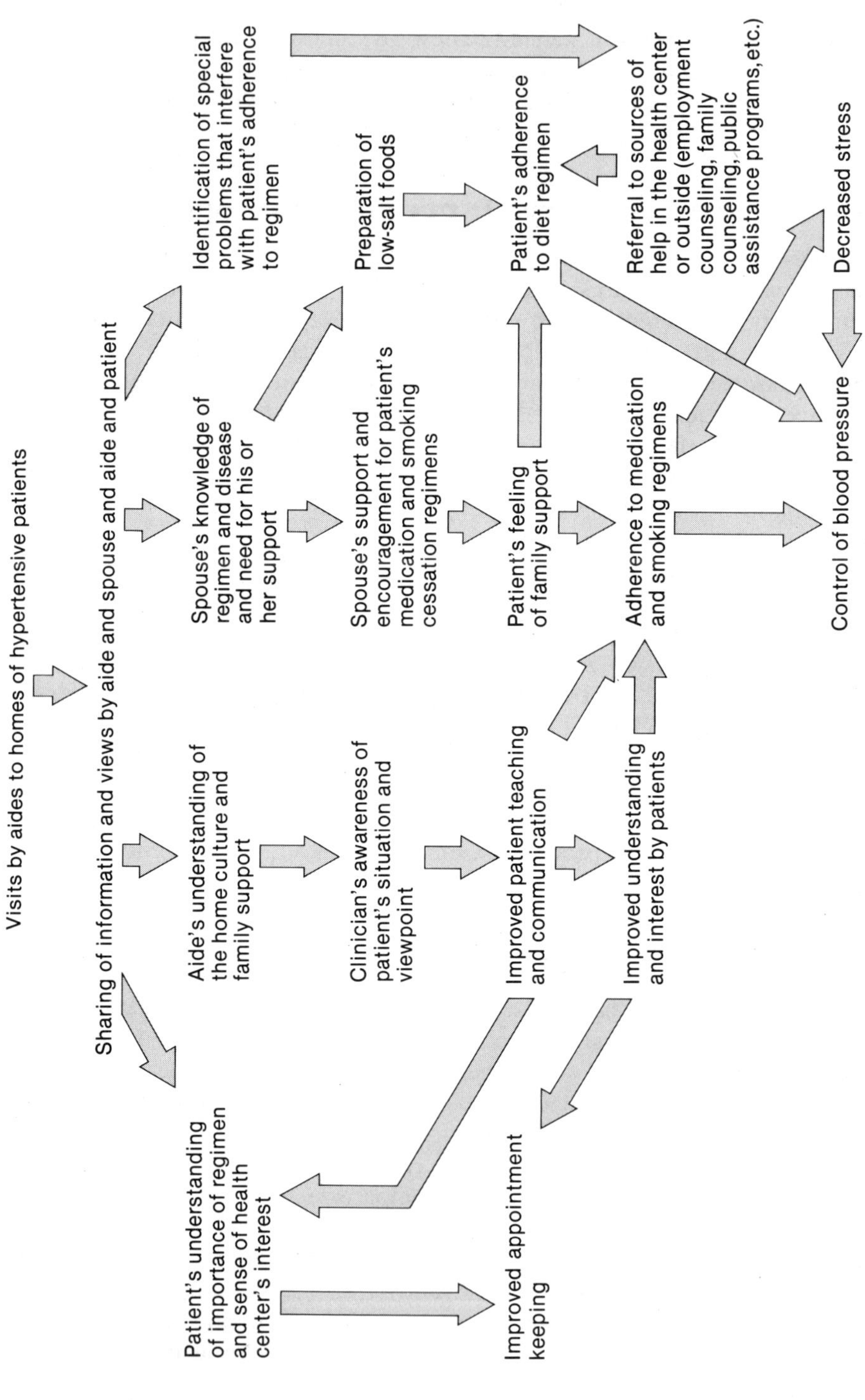

Figure 7-1 *Flow chart showing the possible sequences of action and reaction, some intended and some unintended, identified by qualitative analysis.* Source: *Mullen & Iverson (1982), p. 13.*

delaying the intervention), or research considerations (e.g., intrusiveness of the pretest). This matched control group design could compensate for the absence of pretests with the addition of qualitative measures. If you conducted probing, semistructured interviews with a subsample of each group, you could ascertain retrospectively the quality of the behavior, factors operating in changing or maintaining it, and the rough chronology of influences and decisions. Such information would help substantiate the degree to which the groups were similar initially and with respect to any subsequent events that might have influenced the outcomes. A single-group design with pretests and posttests could, of course, be strengthened by adding observations or asking members of the group to calculate extraneous effects. Campbell (1979b) has argued for the validity of the case study under these circumstances, and several authors have offered guidelines for conducting case studies (e.g., Guba, 1978).

Enlarger of the Observational Field

Specification of program goals and objectives is sometimes presented as the *sine qua non* of successful evaluation. In the case of an experimental program, however, restricting the measurement to the intended effects may mean that other significant effects are overlooked. Not only do some programs produce effects opposite from those intended (e.g., programs to instill independence and personal competence may produce chronic organizational dependents), but also some programs that effect their intended goals successfully have undesirable side effects. Theory may fail to predict main effects, or program planners may apply theory inadequately and set objectives that reflect only a part of the actual effects that could have been predicted. In such instances, goal-based measurement will be inadequate. Scriven (1972) first identified this pitfall of goal-based evaluation in classroom studies. In some programs where positive outcomes were achieved (increased reading scores, mastery of difficult mathematical concepts), there were also other effects—on teacher morale, student interaction, student achievement in other areas. However, not all these unintended effects were negative.

Qualitative approaches can help broaden the observational field to capture *actual* effects, not just those envisioned by the program planners. In addition, "perspective discrepancy assessment" (Mezirow, Darkenwald, & Knox, 1975) can help expand the list of program objectives beyond those stated by a single set of actors in the situation, such as the funding agency, the program planners, larger constituencies, or the actual clients. For example, one investigator who reviewed the evaluation studies of continuing education programs for nurses found that, among other deficiencies in measurement, no study evaluated the programs in terms of one of the major political agendas of the nurse continuing education "movement"—namely, higher status for nurses (Ottoson, 1981). Likewise, the evaluator who undertakes to evaluate a program that lacks well-specified objectives might use qualitative methods to measure actual effects and to generate a more complete list of objectives (Weiss, 1972).

Process and In-Depth Analysis

Sources of failure to find detectable differences or effects have been pointed out in discussions of ways to guard against wrongly concluding that a program is ineffective (Suchman, 1967; Green & Lewis, 1981, p. 49; Weiss, 1972). The program may not have been set in motion adequately, the program may have been implemented according to plan but may not have been theoretically appropriate for the problem or the population, or perhaps a theoretically sound program was indeed implemented, but the measures or sample size were not sensitive enough to detect change. Collecting qualitative data could help explain such causes.

Cronbach (1975, p. 127) has noted the tendency to ignore descriptive data, thereby increasing the possibility of Type II (false-negative) errors:

> The time has come to exorcise the null hypothesis. We cannot afford to pour costly data down the drain whenever effects present in a sample "fail to reach significance." . . . Let the author file descriptive information, at least in an archive, instead of reporting only those selected differences and correlations that are nominally "greater than chance." Descriptions encourage us to think constructively about results from quasi-replications, whereas the dichotomy significant/non-significant implies only a hopeless inconsistency. The canon of parsimony, misinterpreted, has led to the habit of accepting Type II errors at every turn, for the sake of holding Type I [false-positive] errors in check. There are more things in heaven and earth than are dreamt of in our hypotheses, and our observations should be open to them.

You should continue such description or delineation of the program components throughout the evaluation period as the first line of defense against the inability to interpret your findings or to pinpoint sources of Type II error. Programs tend to drift away from their protocols. The program personnel, anxious to achieve success, may make midcourse corrections based on early perceptions of how well they are doing. A harried clinical staff for whom the program represents extra work may slacken their effort. You need qualitative data to detect these changes.

Process analyses are useful in large, diffuse programs where the source of program effects is unclear. Such analyses are helpful in replicating the program later, in improving it, or in pruning unnecessary components. An excellent example of an outcome evaluation paired with a process analysis comes from two studies of an alternative treatment center for juvenile schizophrenics. Results from the quantitative study showed that the center achieved significant improvements in long-term functioning as compared to conventionally institutionalized patients (Mosher & Menn, 1978). The qualitative study showed *how* those effects were achieved through an infrasocial controlling process that replaced traditional mental hospital controls (Wilson, 1982).

You should also collect qualitative data to learn as much as possible about how, why, and under what conditions a program brings about certain outcomes (including no effect). Process analysis, then, encompasses more than the functioning of the program. It answers the question "What happened?" by applying an ongoing analytical approach captured in the present progressive mode: "What is happening?" (Deutscher & Gold, 1978, p. 227).

Flow charts (e.g., Figure 7-1) produced in advance of the evaluation should be verifiable through a mix of quantitative and qualitative data. Such hypothesized linkages will guide process analysis. Where the sequence of effects is not laid out in advance—or where the results show that the hypothesized paths were not taken, or did not lead to the expected destination—qualitative data will help make sense of the results.

How useful such methods can be was made clear by an intensive public education campaign aimed unsuccessfully at changing public attitudes toward the mentally ill (Paul, cited in Suchman, 1967). Because project personnel conducted a series of intensive interviews before and after the educational campaign, because they took note of the changing reception they received, and because they used a social science frame of reference and procedures of inductive analysis to interpret their observations, they were able to analyze the process that led to the failure of the campaign. The qualitative findings assured that the study produced an adequate explanation of the program effects.

In-depth examination of selected cases—individual clients, staff members or program sites—is also helpful in certain studies. Analysis of unusual failures, successes, or dropouts; close observation of especially effective or ineffective clinicians or instructors; reconstruction of the patterns of outstanding clinics, outreach programs, or local units—all may give you or the program decision makers a better picture of how the program "really works." The ability to make crucial comparisons allows you to develop ideas about how the program can be improved. Case studies might be done, for example, with new types of clients, enabling you to recommend new service delivery mechanisms, including outreach and staff communication styles.

Theory Generator

Many programs and their evaluations have been undertaken without theory, a lack that greatly diminishes the explanatory power of evaluation. To compensate, interpretation of findings has tended to rely on *post hoc,* and often undisciplined and unexamined qualitative knowledge. Such insights and interpretations can be extremely valuable. They deserve to be acknowledged, planned, and conducted legitimately and systematically.

We tend to think of programs as applications of theory, and to think of evaluations as tests of theory. Yet evaluative research can present excellent opportunities for generating theory as well as deliberate efforts to intervene in ongoing social processes and under closely scrutinized circumstances. Such opportunities are particularly well presented by large, multisite evaluations, because varying conditions, larger numbers, and more complex data sets afford rich possibilities for generating theory (Mullen, 1981). The process evaluation of the alternative treatment center for young schizophrenics just described generated substantive theories of the processes at work for staff, for patients, and for the management of an organization in a hospital setting (Wilson, 1982). Similarly, a study of Chicano patients and their dealings with various health care providers yielded valuable theories about the roles of significant others as coaches and arbitrators (Hayes-Bautista, 1979).

Few evaluation studies operate within a formal social psychological or social structural model. In fact, theory in itself receives little attention among evaluation researchers. One study of federal evaluation programs noted that "only 18 percent (N = 43) of our total studies were operating within a formal social-psychological, social structural, or economic model" (Bernstein & Freeman, 1975). A qualitative analysis approach would bring theory-generating objectives to the evaluation project (Deutscher, 1977; Broadhead, 1980). One objective is to discover empirically and articulate the operational theory of a program itself, a theory that is seldom explicit or well developed. In the words of Broadhead (1980, p. 31), this objective is

> to generate... competing or rival theories which account for the meaning and purpose of a program in larger sociological [or psychological, anthropological, or other social science] terms. An official ideology of what a program "is" is one thing; interpretations and observations, possibly shared by many staff members or concerned publics, of what a program "is," and what it "does," may reveal an entirely different perspective. The multiple realities of a given program constitute the program itself, and such realities and interpretations need to be theoretically conceptualized in order to discover a program.

A second theoretical objective is to generate theories that identify and explain both the intended and unanticipated consequences of any given program. For example, the ways in which clients use and interpret programs, and the ways in which communities, schools, and other organizations respond to them, are frequently unknown or perplexing to staff members. Generating theoretical understanding of such events, as well as programs themselves, is an essential and important evaluation activity.

Alternative to Quantitative Designs

Should qualitative analyses ever be used alone in evaluative undertakings? Despite our best attempts to confine program aims to measurable objectives, some programs, at least initially, are "broad-aim programs" (Weiss & Rein, 1972). Their goals are diffuse—a "more responsive institutional system," an "energized family," "empowered patient," "informed consumer"—and may be misrepresented if they are reduced prematurely to narrowly defined criteria. Measures may need to be operationalized in many different ways, and even then they may miss the mark. Some of the community and school health programs with the greatest potential for significant achievement fall into this classification, and unfortunately they have been ignored in the past decade, partly because they were not considered to be evaluatable. Other difficulties with the application of experimental or quasi-experimental designs to broad-aim programs arise from the essential uncontrollability of the situation (e.g., a unique or a rapidly changing organization or community), and nonstandardized and emergent interventions. Such cases demand an approach that aims "to develop a coherent and appropriately-near-to-complete description of the relevant community systems prior to the intervention of a new program, of the nature of the intervention, and of the new system which then develops in which the intervention is a dynamic constituent" (Weiss & Rein, 1972, p. 243).

QUALITATIVE EVALUATION MODELS

Six distinguishable approaches to qualitative evaluation are summarized in Table 7-2. This table also displays their relationship to the six functions of qualitative evaluation. These examples introduce you to a wider range of models (House, 1980; Madaus, Scriven, & Stufflebeam, 1983).

The illuminative Parlett and Hamilton (1976) and Stake (1973) approaches are chief examples of the transaction model of evaluation. The

TABLE 7-2 Selected qualitative evaluation approaches

Approach Functions (Authors)	Description	Data Collection Techniques	Functions
Illuminative Evaluation (Parlett & Hamilton, 1976)	Provides for an intensive study of the program as a whole—its rationale, operations, achievements, and difficulties. The model has 3 steps: observation, inquiry, and explanation.	Observations (with and without checklists), structured and semistructured interviews, open-ended questionnaires	6, 3, 1, 2, 5, 4
Stake Model (Stake, 1973)	Combines qualitative and quantitative methods to describe and judge a program. It structures the comparison of program intents with observed events and present criteria. These comparisons are made at several points in the program.	Historical records, questionnaires, interviews, scientific instruments, standardized tests	1, 6, 3, 4
Grounded Theory Method (Glaser & Strauss, 1967; Glaser, 1978)	Uses comparative analysis to generate concepts and hypotheses and to interrelate them into a middle-range theory. Data gathering and analysis are interactive.	Records and documents, semistructured interviews and questionnaires, and observation	5, 4, 1, 2, 6
Goal-Free Evaluation (Scriven, 1972)	Requires the collection of data on a broad array of actual effects and judgment of their relative importance in meeting demonstrated needs. Ideally, evaluator does not know the objectives of the program.	Interviews, observations, questionnaires, standardized tests, and records	3, 6, 1, 4

CIPP Model (Stufflebeam, 1973)	Focuses on information for decision making via description and analysis of components: Context, Input, Process, and Product (CIPP).	Open and closed questionnaires, standardized tests, records, needs assessments, and observations	1, 3, 2, 4, 6
Client Analysis (Reiner, Reimer, & Reiner, 1963)	Focuses on the relationships between the target population's wants, recognition of these wants and needs (by others), eligibility to receive services to satisfy wants and needs, actual receipt of the services, and benefits.	Records, structured and semistructured interviews, observations, standardized tests, questionnaires	3, 1, 2, 6

Note: 1 = tool for development and delineation of program elements; 2 = power booster for quasi- and preexperimental designs; 3 = enlarger of the observational field; 4 = process and in-depth analysis; 5 = theory generator; and 6 = alternative to quantitative designs. Functions are listed here according to how well the approaches fulfill them, if at all.

transaction model concentrates on program processes via various informal methods of investigation and has been drawn increasingly to the case study as the major method. The grounded theory approach (Glaser & Strauss, 1967; Glaser, 1978), with its focus on process, may also be considered an example of the transaction model. Goal-free evaluation (Scriven, 1972) is considered a separate type of qualitative evaluation, and Stufflebeam's CIPP model (1973) is a prime example of the decision-making model in which the evaluation is structured by the decisions to be made. Client analysis (Reiner et al., 1963), the last model presented, is a hybrid of quantitative and qualitative approaches that starts with a goal-directed focus and works backward from any "shortfalls" in target population goals.

Illuminative Evaluation

Illuminative evaluation (Parlett & Hamilton, 1976) is used for innovative or developing programs. It provides for intensive study of the program as a whole, and it relies almost exclusively on qualitative data collection techniques. The questions you address in the illuminative approach include

- How does the program operate?
- How is the program affected by various situations?
- What do program personnel consider the program's strengths and weaknesses to be?
- What is it like to be a program participant?
- What are the most significant features of the program?
- What do the primary effects of the program appear to be?

Answering these questions provides a thorough understanding of the instructional system or program and the sociopsychological and material environment in which the program operates.

The three distinct stages of illuminative evaluation are (1) observation, (2) inquiry, and (3) explanation. In the observation stage, you become familiar with the day-to-day operations of the program, using checklists, for example, to record client-staff, client-client, and staff-staff transactions. During this stage, your chief test is "to unravel . . . [the program], isolate its significant features, delineate cycles of cause and effect, and comprehend relationships between beliefs and practices and between organizational patterns and the responses of individuals" (Parlett & Hamilton, 1976, p. 147). In the inquiry stage, you select specific phenomena, occurrences, and opinions as targets for further investigation via observation, structured and unstructured interviews, questionnaires, tests, and documents. In the final (explanation) stage, you seek general principles underlying the organization of the program and the patterns of cause and effect within its operation.

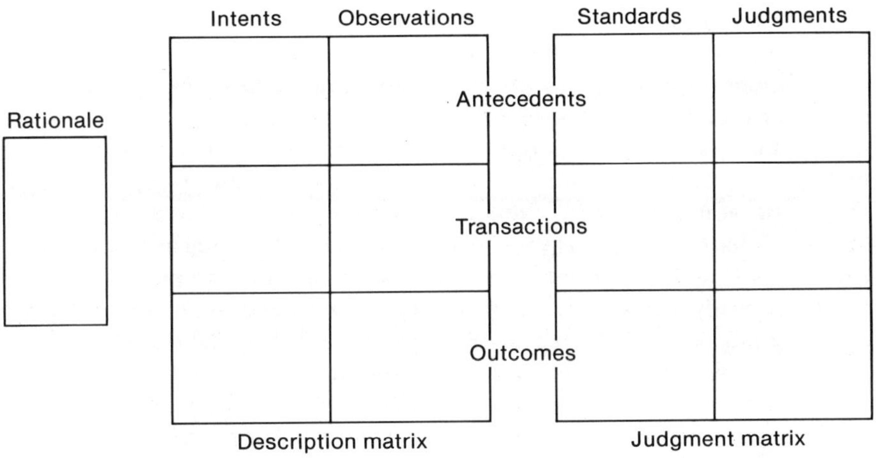

Figure 7-2 *A layout of statements and data to be collected by the evaluator of an educational program.* Source: *Stake (1973), p. 108.*

Stake's Model

Stake (1973) recognized the importance of both describing and judging a program and believed that evaluations are incomplete if both processes are not included in the evaluation effort. To facilitate the inclusion of both description and judgment in the evaluation process, Stake proposed the framework depicted in Figure 7-2. The rows represent three types of data: antecedent, transaction, and outcome. An *antecedent* is any condition existing before the initiation of the program that may relate to outcomes; for example, the motivation of the participants or the qualifications of the instructor. The *transactions* are the encounters between program staff and clients that comprise the process of the program. The *outcomes* are the intended benefits to be gained through program participation such as positive changes in attitudes and beliefs, skill development, behavior change, and improved health status. You might also anticipate outcomes for staff, organizational effectiveness, and in the program's interaction with the environment.

Now you examine the program across the two broad evaluation matrices—description and judgment. The description matrix includes the components of intents and observations. Intents refers to "the planned-for demonstrations, the planned-for coverage of certain subject matter, etc., as well as the planned-for student behavior. To be included in this three-cell column are effects that are desired, those hoped for, those anticipated, and even those feared" (Stake, 1973, p. 114). Your listing of intents should include all effects that may logically happen—not just that which the sponsors or staff hope will happen.

Multiple observations of the environment and program events that you select for focus include those described in the intents column but should not exclude other observations. An important step in the evaluation process occurs after the evaluator has completed the description matrix. At this point, you can test for theory and implementation failure. You examine the cells in the description matrix and test for congruence between the rows of intents and observations—that is, did the intended actions or events actually occur? This step estimates the success in implementing the program. Your next step involves examining the relationships or contingencies among the cells in the description matrix. For the intents column, examine the sequence from antecedent to transaction to outcome to determine if the flow is logical. To make such a judgment, you must be well versed in the principles of the program area. If the sequence is not logical (in theory), the program will probably not be successful. You can test your judgment by examining the empirical relationships among the antecedents, transactions, and outcomes. This step involves a comparison of the observational data for the three rows. You can then examine the observational data from either outcomes to antecedents, or vice versa. These two steps indicate the level of theory and implementation failure.

With these steps completed, you now enter the judgment matrix and set public standards for antecedents, transactions, and outcomes. These standards may be either absolute or relative, the latter based on what the program has achieved in the past (historical), on what other programs of this type usually achieve (normative), or on what change occurs in a group not receiving the program (control). Different standards of acceptability may be used for each of the three rows, but they must be described in advance of the evaluation.

The final step involves your judgment of success. You compare the observations against the standards and describe the program's position relative to the standard. Recommendations specific to the three levels should be made to facilitate and guide program growth.

Grounded Theory*

The grounded theory method was developed and refined by Glaser and Strauss (1967) and Glaser (1978). This approach uses comparison as an analytical tool to generate concepts and hypotheses. It then interrelates these concepts and hypotheses through core variables that are both effi-

*This description is based on Mullen and Reynolds (1978).

cient in explaining more than one phenomenon and broad in scope. The final goal is middle-range substantive theory in a specific content area such as dying, pain management, and recovery after a heart attack. It can produce formal theory generalized over a number of specific areas such as status passage (e.g., from teenager to adult) or lifestyle redesign.

In the first stage of a grounded theory study, you discover categories into which data can be coded. You inspect incidents and definitions in the data by asking the question "Of what concept is this finding an indicator?" In the early part of the study, you attempt to discover many categories and to compare them with new indicators, to uncover their characteristics and relationships. Then you compare indicators with other indicators, to establish underlying patterns and their varying conditions. Next you compare the concepts to new indicators, to generate more theoretical properties of the concept and new hypotheses and to verify the concept. A third level of comparison is concept-to-concept comparison. This step establishes the best-fitting concept(s) for a set of indicators.

Substantive categories or codes are of two kinds: (1) codes taken from the language of the people who were observed or interviewed, such as "budgeting oneself" and "convincing"; (2) implicit codes, such as "social loss" and "conditional dependence," that are constructed by the researcher based on behavioral and social science concepts.

Your data gathering should be directed purposefully through theoretical sampling to obtain more comparison groups. In later stages of a study, after identifying a basic social process or other core variable, focus sampling directly on the developing theory. This mix of comparisons soon allows you to construct theoretical properties of categories and permits major categories to emerge. Coding thus leads to conceptual reorganization. Core variables provide your organizing focus and are selected on the basis of pervasive and meaningful relatedness to other categories and frequent occurrences in the data. In grounded theory studies, core variables are most often social processes, because qualitative data frequently have a time dimension. The analysis then traces the emerging process to identify its stages, dimensions, and the characteristics and conditions that vary it.

Goal-Free Evaluation

The goal-free evaluation strategy was proposed by Scriven (1972) after he observed the restrictions of goal-based evaluation and the tendency for an evaluator to want to find effects, once he or she knows what they are supposed to be. Goal-free evaluation gathers data on a broad array of actual effects and evaluates their importance in meeting demonstrated needs. Goal-free evaluation also avoids classifying side effects and unanticipated effects as second-class interests, when they may well be the crucial achievement, particularly in terms of new priorities.

For example, some years ago in a pilot study of educational programs for heart attack victims in the coronary care unit, investigators found that patients retained little of the information they were given. This aspect of the program was almost scrapped until it became clear that patients' anxiety was reduced. This finding led to greater emphasis on anxiety and has in fact been the chief mechanism through which patient education has assisted surgical and heart attack patients.

Scriven felt that working within a goal-oriented framework reduced interest in looking for other effects. And then, less evidence is demanded, creating a situation "which is extremely unsatisfactory with respect to the many potentially very harmful side-effects that have turned up over the years" (Scriven, 1972, p. 1).

A goal-free evaluator can remain untroubled by midcourse shifts in program goals. By using goal-free evaluation in its purest form, you avoid all discussion of program goals. This method is classified as qualitative because it is holistic and inductive; it suspends judgment about what the program is trying to do and focuses instead on what actually happens. Also, it relies heavily on description and direct experience with the program. You simply measure as many likely effects of a program as possible, using a mixture of quantitative and qualitative data-gathering instruments. You base the estimates of the program's likely effects on inspection of the program itself, on the program's anticipated operation, and on the literature and prior experience of practitioners and evaluators with this type of program. For example, having learned from another study that a programmed economics text did not teach economics better than standard methods but that it did improve reading scores, the School Health Curriculum Project evaluator was alerted to examine reading scores in addition to health knowledge and beliefs. (In fact, the project also had a significant impact on reading scores.)

What can you do when the program is your own and you cannot ignore the objectives? A practical alternative is to apply general interviewing and observation techniques, and to obtain ideas about possible side effects from people who doubt that the program will work, from colleagues who have tried similar programs, and from the literature.

CIPP Model

The CIPP model was advanced by Stufflebeam (1973), who defined evaluation as "the process of delineating, obtaining and providing useful information for judging decision alternatives" (1973, p. 120). The acronym CIPP stands for four steps: context evaluation, input evaluation, process (or formative) evaluation, and product evaluation. Each step is designed to produce timely information to help with decision making.

Context evaluation provides a basis for determining program objectives. Specifically, it defines the environment in which the program is to operate and the desired and actual conditions pertaining to that environment. It identifies the unmet needs and unused opportunities within the environment and diagnoses why they go unmet and unused. The question you address in this step is "Should the program be developed, and if it is to be developed, what should the focus be?" Qualitative data (observation, unstructured interviews, analysis of archival data) are more frequently used, but quantitative data (questionnaires) may be useful.

In input evaluation, you identify and assess relevant capabilities of the agencies involved with the program, strategies for achieving program objectives, and methods of implementing selected strategies. You accomplish these tasks using consultants and expert committees as well as the professional literature. As a general rule, the more important the program (from a political or investment perspective), the more important is this phase of the evaluation.

The context and input evaluations usually occur before the program begins. If, however, the program began without access to this type of information, it is prudent to conduct these evaluations prior to the process (or formative) and product evaluations to assure the program's compatibility with the environment and available resources. After a course of action is selected and the program has begun, begin process (or formative) evaluation. Stufflebeam believes that process (or formative) evaluation detects or predicts defects in the procedural design or its implementation during the early phases of the program, provides information for program decisions, and maintains a record of the program's implementation.

As you will recall from Chapter 2, formative or process evaluation is designed to provide continual and in-depth information on the program and its component parts. This information guides the process of program modification. You collect regular feedback from staff members and information on user participation, user and staff interaction, user satisfaction, and appropriateness of procedures.

Product evaluation—the last component of the CIPP model—measures and interprets program attainments during and on completion of the program. In this step you are likely to apply more quantitative methods. If the first three steps in the evaluation process are completed successfully, the product evaluation should yield relevant information on program effectiveness, and, in some instances, program efficiency. This information helps program personnel decide on program continuation, termination, or modification. In this last step you devise operational definitions of the program objectives; secure data pertinent to the criteria that reflect the objectives; compare the data with predetermined, absolute, or relative standards; and interpret the outcomes using the context, input, and process information.

Client Analysis

Client analysis is a technique for measuring program effectiveness in a population (Reiner et al., 1963). The model has substantial applicability to public health programs, especially those mandated by law. This evaluation model is unusual in that the procedures are intended to stimulate, and in some situations, force debate on the intents, merits, and consequences of the program. A number of public health programs—ranging from general programs for children such as Head Start and the Early and Periodic Screening, Detection and Treatment Program (EPSDT) to specific programs for high-risk populations such as community-based weight control and smoking programs—are well suited to the client analysis approach.

Client analysis investigates the relationships between the needs and preferences of a population, the accessibility and acceptability of goods or services in satisfaction of these needs, actual receipt of the services, and the benefits, if any, resulting from the services.

In the first step in this approach, you specify the target population and the benefits and services to be provided under the program. For mandated programs, specific criteria may be attached to the benefits and services described in the legislation and regulations. For programs without enabling legislation, you can extract information on the target population and intended benefits and services from primary sources such as articles of incorporation, or board and committee minutes.

You then compare the legally eligible or epidemiologically appropriate population—the "client population"—with the "clients" or group using the services. You can identify the clients on a cross-sectional basis during a representative time period or on a longitudinal, cumulative basis. From agency records and small-scale studies, you should stratify clients by types and amounts of services used. In the comparison, you look for demographic differences between the two groups, including such characteristics as age, sex, income levels, education, and residence.

Next you seek to understand the differences between the eligible client population and the clients, by making a detailed study of the conditions under which services and benefits of each program are offered and received. In general, the ratio of clients to client population depends on the selection standards that govern access to the program and the standards of service that govern program acceptance. Examine written policies to determine the nature and specifics of the administrative selection standards. Techniques such as observation, structured and unstructured interviews with clients and staff, and questionnaires with open-ended questions provide vital additional data. You should also assess the program's standards of service, including the quantity and quality and features such as cost to client, if any; location of facility and other considerations of convenience; and the characteristics and performance of the service staff.

Comparisons of data from the eligible client population and the actual clients will reveal any differences that require further investigation. For example, members of the eligible client population may say that they did not use the service because staff seemed hostile toward them, and yet this perception may not be shared by the actual clients. Is it because members of the client population were predominantly Spanish-speaking, for example, or were less well groomed than the clients, or were unorthodox in the use of health services? This step is essential in the evaluation, because the standards of service often present the greatest barriers to program use.

Assessing the number of clients who experienced some gain from the program yields a group who "effectively benefited." You need to determine the degree of benefit and distribution of benefit within the population. This step provides you with a comprehensive view of the program so that problems, inequities, and benefits can be described for various populations. This information should help in developing specific recommendations. If no serious problems exist with the program, the last four steps in client analysis can be used to estimate future program needs and benefits.

SUMMARY

It is difficult to envision a health program that would not benefit from the inclusion of qualitative methods. The question is not whether to use qualitative or quantitative methods. Rather, it is how to establish the appropriate balance between the two. Comprehensive program evaluations always include both methods, and the balance is determined on the basis of program needs, program maturity, and available resources. In some situations, qualitative methods will dominate the evaluation process; in others, quantitative methods will receive greater emphasis.

As a tool for developing and delineating program elements, qualitative methods surpass quantitative methods in their capacity to take into account a wider range of elements, some of which would be difficult or unreasonably expensive to measure quantitatively. As power boosters for quasi-experimental designs, qualitative methods address the dynamics of change, while quantitative methods tend to be focused on the outcomes of change. Qualitative methods enlarge the observational field by spotting unintended effects and unanticipated outcomes. And qualitative methods provide additional data for in-depth analysis of processes that quantitative methods were too insensitive to measure.

As theory generators, qualitative methods allow you to draw from the experiences that were not anticipated—and therefore not measured quantitatively—insights that will revise, expand, and create theoretical perspectives and concepts to explain the change process.

Six approaches to qualitative evaluation represent alternative models or ways of viewing and analyzing situations. Illuminative evaluation takes a holistic approach to a program, attempting to assess the distinctive features, processes, and transactions between clients and staff, among staff, and among clients.

Stake's model emphasizes the importance of describing as well as judging a program, including its antecedents, transactions, and outcomes.

Grounded theory uses comparison as an analytic tool to generate concepts and hypotheses. Relating these concepts through core variables, the method seeks to produce "middle-range" theory in such specific content areas as dying, pain management, and lifestyle redesign following a heart attack.

Goal-free evaluation avoids focusing on objectives and seeks to document the full range of effects produced by a program, including unintended "side effects" and serendipitous benefits.

CIPP is concerned primarily with weighing options for decisions. At each of four levels implied by the acronym—context evaluation, input evaluation, process evaluation and product evaluation—information is sought to assist with decisions required in each phase of program development.

Client analysis seeks to stimulate debate between providers and recipients on the purposes, merits, and consequences of a program, and between policy makers and implementers of programs as to the degree they are serving the intended clients.

Chapter 8

INTRODUCTION TO DESIGNS FOR QUANTITATIVE EVALUATION

Having considered the range of qualitative information useful in evaluation, you may still find that the questions to be answered in your program call for statistical comparisons against some standard of acceptability. This need calls for quantitative designs. In this chapter we first review definitions, criteria, measurement techniques, and designs that you have encountered in previous chapters. These key concepts are summarized here, along with some elaboration, to frame our approach to evaluation objectives and designs. We then discuss the validity of designs and present and describe the major threats to external and internal validity in quantitative evaluation design. We suggest ways to prevent or control each threat, and we discuss their implications for evaluation in health education.

Our five objectives in this chapter are to enable you (1) to identify the three basic elements of evaluation (comparison, object of interest, standard of acceptability), (2) to isolate independent and dependent variables comprising the objects of interest in your health education programs, (3) to recognize (connect) the standards of acceptability implicit in different methods of comparison, (4) to state an evaluation problem in the form of a testable hypothesis, and (5) to recognize some threats to validity in moving the state of the art of health education toward theoretical standards of acceptability.

COMPONENTS OF EVALUATION

For a definition of *evaluation,* we suggest, "Comparison of an object of interest against a standard of acceptability" (Green, 1974). This simple definition identifies the three essential components of evaluation: (1) a comparison, (2) an object of interest, and (3) a standard. Without comparison of some kind, even if it is only comparison with an imaginary ideal or a purely subjective preference, there can be no evaluation, just as no evaluation can exist without an object to compare, or some standard, however implicit or vague. These essential concepts provide a framework for understanding alternative designs for evaluations, to be presented in Chapter 9.

Comparison

A comparison is usually made by measuring two or more observations of the object of interest. Standards of acceptability against which comparisons are made are ideally made explicit as *objectives* expressing (1) how much, (2) of what outcome, (3) is expected in whom (which population, group, or individuals), (4) by when. Objects of interest become objectives when they are expressed with these four questions answered *in advance* of the actual observation or measurement of effects. By stating explicitly (in writing) in advance what you expect to achieve from, or find in, an object of interest, you commit yourself to a standard of acceptability against which you or the program or the object of interest can be held accountable.

For example, in evaluating the *quality* of a pamphlet, your objective might be to assure that it requires "no higher than an eighth-grade reading level when pretested in a sample of patients before the program." When evaluating the *effectiveness* of the same pamphlet within the context of a patient education program, the objective might be "To achieve a 50 percent increase in average scores on a twenty-item knowledge test in ambulatory adult clinic patients tested immediately before and one day after exposure to the pamphlet."

Objects of Interest

Objects of interest in evaluation may be anything from a specific element of a program (such as a pamphlet, a message, the timing of communication), to a complex relationship between one or more of these inputs and one or more desired outcomes of a program. In Figure 8-1, each variable within each box could be an object of interest. Or, any of the arrows representing a relationship between two or more variables could be evaluated in a patient education program.

Objects of interest such as health education methods that are programmed or manipulated in a specified way (X) under controlled circumstances may become the *independent variables* in an evaluative research design. Objects of interest that are observable (O) and measurable may become the *dependent variables* in an evaluation if they represent possible effects or outcomes of the independent variable(s). In Figure 8-1, any variable in the first box on the left could be an independent variable in

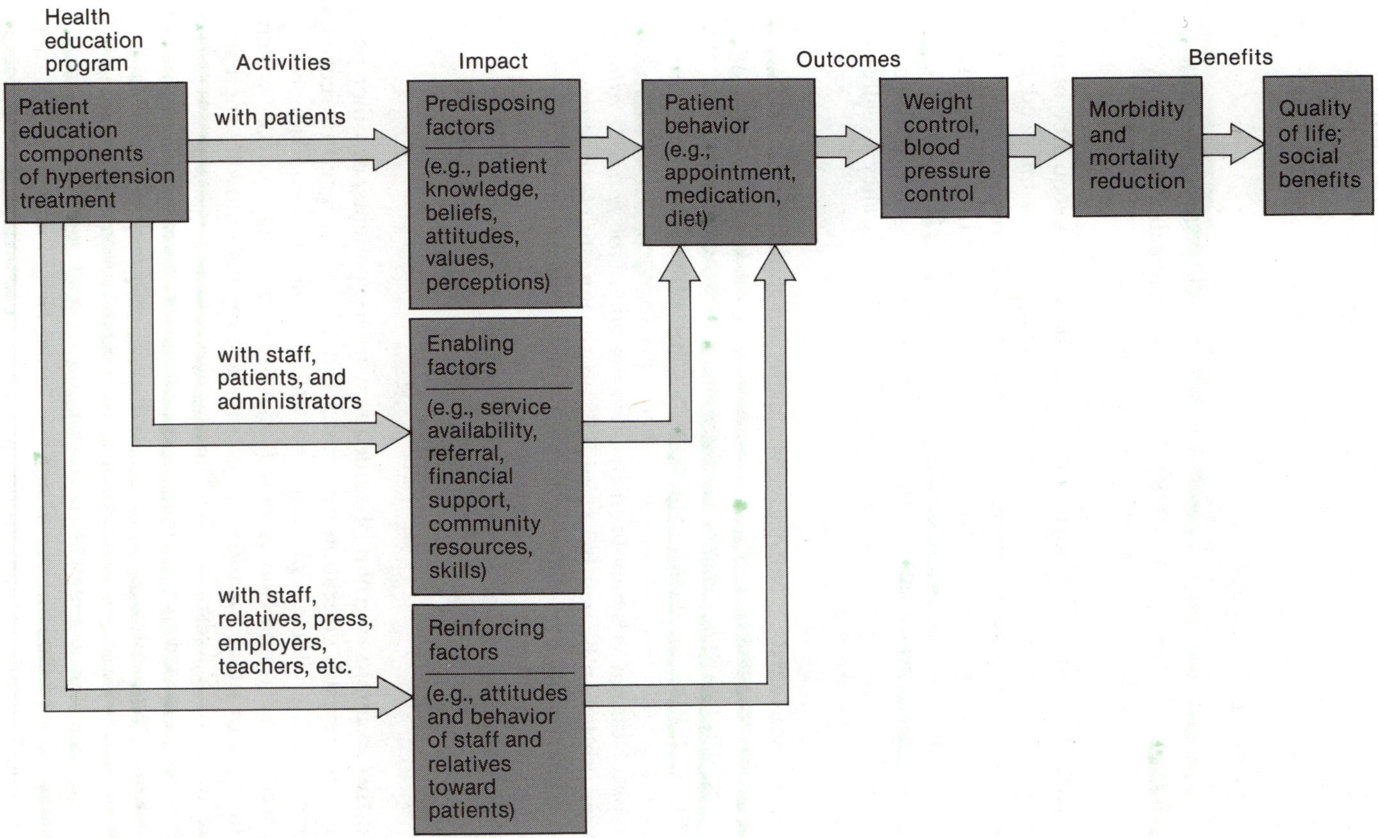

Figure 8-1 *Objects of interest in the planning and evaluation of a patient education program for hypertension outpatients. Independent variables to the left are presumed to influence dependent variables to their right.* Source: *Green, Levine, & Deeds (1975), p. 420. Used by permission of Academic Press.*

the evaluation of a patient education program. Any one or more of the variables to the right of the arrows could be dependent variables in the evaluation.

Standards of Acceptability

Comparison of achievements may be against one or more of the following standards (Green, 1974, 1978). Statistical significance tests may be used as the criterion in any of the comparisons.

Historical Standards. The symbols O_1 X O_2 describe a sequence of pretest observations (O_1) followed by an intervention (X), followed by a posttest (O_2). In the next chapter we present specific pretest-posttest and longitudinal designs recommended for evaluation of health education. Historical standards generally ask, "How did you perform this month compared with last month?" or "How did this year's program results compare with last year (when we didn't have a program)?" They usually are graphed as in Figure 8-2.

Normative Standards. Normative standards are applied when you compare one group against another, your program against another, your program against national averages, and so on. "Control" groups are the ultimate, all-purpose comparison group because random assignment (R) of patients to different educational treatments maximizes comparability. This type of design is symbolized by showing an R (for *random allocation*) on the left, followed by X_1 and X_2 on separate lines, to show that different interventions or different forms of the independent variable were applied to different groups. The trailing O in each line shows that posttest observations were conducted in each group:

$$\begin{array}{ccc} R & X_1 & O_1 \\ R & X_2 & O_2 \end{array}$$

In this example, a group of students, workers, patients, or other participants in a health education program are randomly assigned to receive either X_1 or X_2, which represent two forms of health education being compared. The comparison is based on observations O_1 and O_2, which may be tests or other measures taken on the subjects following their exposure to X_1 or X_2, respectively. The standard of acceptability is normative because the measures of impact or outcome taken on one group are the norm against which the measures on the other group are compared.

Usually normative comparisons are made with groups of people who receive no special intervention or educational program, but who do receive "usual care" if they are patients (or "usual classroom routine" if they are students). People in such groups provide a "pure control" only if they

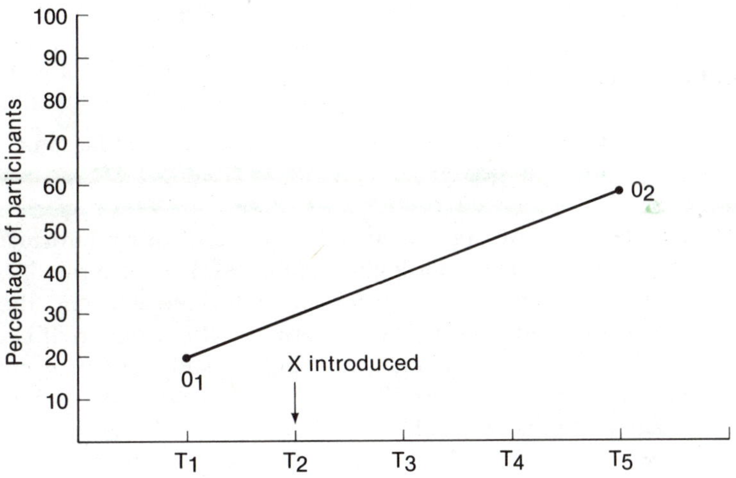

Figure 8-2 *Graph of historical standards. The typical historical comparison involves one or more pretests* (O_1) *and one or more posttests* (O_2) *with the experimental educational interventions* (X) *between.*

receive no information or education on the topic. But such circumstances can only be obtained in highly contrived communication laboratories, so the term "pure control" is avoided in most health education evaluation.

Normative standards also apply when a population has been sampled and representative scores have been obtained on some area of knowledge, attitudes, or practices for the population, with or without prior exposure to a program designed to influence that area of knowledge, attitudes, or practices. In this instance, the measurement instrument has been "normed" on the population. Any subsequent use of the instrument in samples of the same population who are exposed to your program allows you to compare their posttest scores against the normative scores of the population. Recall the discussion of norm-referenced tests versus criterion-referenced tests in Chapter 6.

For example, adolescents may be asked to complete a cancer prevention attitude scale. Descriptive statistics are thereby obtained on a "nontreated" sample. In another state, a federally funded intervention program may be in place to positively affect cancer prevention attitudes in another sample of adolescents. It may be possible to use the scores obtained on the nontreated adolescent sample as a normative standard against which to compare the adolescents who are experiencing the federal intervention program. As standardized scales of outcome or impact variables become the norm rather than the exception in health education, we will undoubtedly see an increase in the use of normative standards in evaluation studies.

Absolute Standards. When you resort to absolute standards of acceptability, you are demanding complete success: 100 percent achievement is the standard, and the actual percentage achieved is the comparison. The absolute standard is only applied in the absence of other information or in extreme political or epidemiological situations. For example, if lawyers or consumers insist on full disclosure and informed consent, then 100 percent comprehension may be the objective of the program. If everyone must be immunized against a highly contagious and virulent agent, then 100 percent awareness and behavioral adoption may be necessary objectives and standards of acceptability.

Theoretical Standards. Theoretical standards are the expected results of a program if everything went right, based on the best evidence from previous research and theory. If methods employed in the classroom, or in the field, were applied as in prior research studies, then the same results theoretically should be obtained. This kind of standard is implied when you know from controlled clinical studies on attitude change that a specific fear arousal message can achieve an average of 50 percent acceptance of a specific diet in men and 60 percent in women, and so you set 55 percent as the objective for your program.

Negotiated or Compromise Standards. When you combine two or more of the preceding standards, negotiated or compromise standards result. This kind of standard of acceptability is implied when consumers want 100 percent (absolute) and providers expect 50 percent (based on historical experience), so they agree on a goal of 75 percent.

DEVISING A TESTABLE HYPOTHESIS

In evaluation, the test of a relationship should be directed by hypotheses stating the expected forms of the relationships between the input or program (independent variable) and the impact or outcome (dependent variable). These variables should be operationally defined in terms of the observational or measurement procedures to be used, and the specific standard of comparison for the dependent variable should be made explicit.

An example of the simplest hypothesis for the historical comparison implied in Figure 8-2 might be "The patients exposed to the education

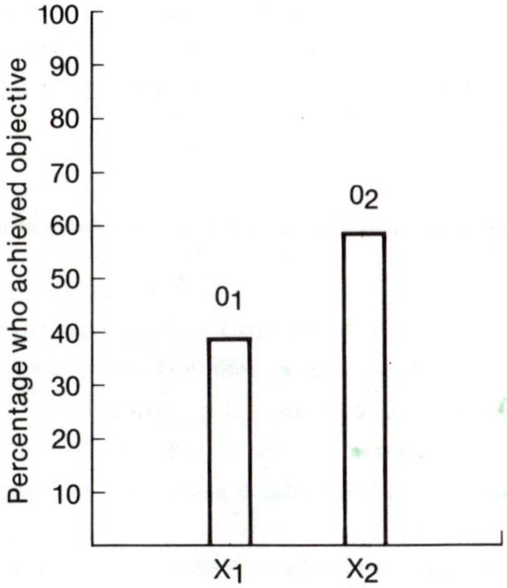

Figure 8-3 *Graph of normative standards. The typical normative comparison involves posttest measures* (O) *taken on the groups of people exposed to different amounts or forms of* X.

will have higher knowledge scores after exposure than before." This simple hypothesis reflects a minimal objective of *direction*—in this case, of increased knowledge, without specifying how much increase or even that the increase should be "significant."

A second level of specification for a test of a hypothesis, then, can be based on *how much* improvement is expected. "The patients exposed to the education will have significantly higher scores after exposure than before," as reflected in Figure 8-2, or "significantly higher scores than those not exposed," as reflected in the normative comparison of Figure 8-3.

You are aware from elementary statistics, of course, that statistical significance can be obtained on even trivial differences by simply increasing the sample size. Hence, a third level of specificity in a testable hypothesis for evaluation is to state the amount of change or degree of difference required to achieve educational, behavioral, or clinical significance. Thus, your hypothesis could read, "Group A will have a 20 percent greater mean score than Group B" or "The percentage of the population exposed to the education who adopt the practice of not salting their food at the dinner table will increase from 20 to 50 percent by the sixth month after exposure."

One additional means of increasing the specificity of the hypothesis is to operationally define the dependent variable in terms of the conditions of measurement. The operational definitions in the preceding examples would be added as follows: "Group A will have a 20 percent greater mean score on a twenty-item true-false test of comprehension than will Group B," and "adopt the practice of not salting their food at the dinner table, *as measured by* a series of three questions in a telephone interview."

VALIDITY OF DESIGNS

The specific problems of reliability and validity in measurement were discussed in Chapters 4 and 5. The problems of validity in relation to the *design* of evaluations pose the same basic question: Can you say with certainty that the results are true? Methods of convergent validity in relation to measurement depend on cross-checks against supplementary sources of data that should yield the *same* result, whereas most methods of assuring validity in designs for evaluation depend on supplementary sources of data that should yield *different* results, as in discriminant validity of measurement instruments. The question for validity of designs can also be phrased: "Can you say with certainty that the result you wish to attribute to the health education method or program is truly *caused by* the method or program, or could it be caused—at least in part—by other forces?"

An Inventory of Competing Explanations

And what other forces? The results of any evaluation can be attributed variously to factors other than the health education method or program being evaluated. These factors are sometimes referred to as *threats to validity.* They have been summarized most efficiently by Campbell and Stanley in their original monograph (1963), with more recent extensions by Cook and Campbell (1979). These studies provide the classic reference point for most discussions of validity of evaluation in education and the human service fields. Our experience, however, is that most students plead for supplementary explanation and examples in their own field. We offer here an explanation of the validity concepts particularly adapted to evaluation in health education. Specific applications in alternative designs are provided in Chapter 9.

Internal Versus External Validity

The term *internal validity* refers to the assurance that the results obtained from an evaluation can be attributed to the intervention being evaluated: Can you plausibly infer that your program caused the observed results? The term *external validity* refers to the assurance that the results obtained from an evaluation can be expected to apply anywhere else under typical conditions. Internal validity is threatened when the evaluator does not have sufficient data or control to rule out competing explanations for the results. External validity is threatened usually when the evaluator exercises *too much* control or collects so much data from people that their behavior is influenced in ways that would not be the same if they were exposed to the same health education under usual circumstances.

EXTERNAL VALIDITY

External validity of evaluation designs has three components: (1) generalizability across alternative *measures* of the program or the outcomes; (2) generalizability *to* other people, settings, and time; and (3) generalizability *across* people, settings, and time (Cook & Campbell, 1979).

Three Ways to Generalize

Generalizability across alternative measures of the program or outcomes asks, "To what extent would the obtained result occur were you to measure either the program or the outcome or effects in a different way?" Cook and Campbell (1979, p. 65) argue for the importance of multiple measures of the program's impact or outcome measures. They also highlight the value, in order to maximize the external validity of the design, of purposefully varying two or three examples of the program or its components "where possible" (Cook & Campbell, 1979, p. 65).

Generalizability *to* other populations is the basis for statistical inference. It relates to whether results obtained from a particular study can be generalized to others within the specified target population.

Generalizing *across* other populations is distinguishable from generalizing *to* populations. Generalizing across population depends on which separate identifiable subpopulations have been affected by the health education program.

A prenatal education program, for example, may positively affect all primiparous women who participated. A more differentiated analysis of the data, however, may reveal that women living as part of a couple situation fared far better on your measures of health than did women not living in a couple situation. Such results would show that the effects of your health education program could not be generalized across all subpopulations of the primiparous women, even though you could still agree that the results could be generalized to the population of primiparous mothers from which you drew the probability sample.

Threats to External Validity

The threats to external validity or generalizability are sometimes referred to as "reactive effects," in that the evaluator is causing the subjects to react to the experimental situation as well as to the health education. This reactivity is a major problem in health education (Green, 1977). It takes several forms:

The Hawthorne Effect. An early experiment in industrial hygiene at the Hawthorne electrical plant obtained a curious result. Workers seemed to increase their productivity when the lighting was increased, *and* they increased their productivity when the lighting was lowered. The evaluators concluded that the workers were responding favorably to the attention being paid to them. This interpretation has been debated, but the possibility of making your results unrepresentative by paying too much attention to your subjects remains a threat to external validity.

The Social Desirability Effect. Closely related to the Hawthorne effect is the reactive effect created by experimental situations in which the subjects want to please or impress the evaluator, so that they give answers or demonstrate behavior that they think is expected of them. This effect is especially common in situations where the evaluator is also the teacher, doctor, employer, or other person controlling rewards for the subjects.

The Placebo Effect. People often improve because they believe in the treatment or provider. This effect is so common in medical research that control groups are routinely given a placebo treatment to equalize their tendency to respond favorably to the belief that any treatment given by the doctor will improve their condition. In health education, the placebo effect may occur even without medicines or surgical procedures if the health educator has sufficient authority to change attitude or behavior apart from the educational effect. When the believer is the educator, the effect is called the Pygmalion effect.

The Pygmalion Effect. Pygmalion, the mythical Greek king who sculpted a woman statue so ideal that he fell in love with it, was blessed when Venus turned his stone beauty into a real woman. Ever since, the Pygmalion effect has been defined as the belief that if one expects something to happen strongly enough, it can and will happen. Both positive and negative applications of this effect have been shown. For instance, during the Great Depression of the 1930s a sound and substantial bank could be ruined in a matter of hours if a rumor were started about the bank's possible instability. The rumor was acted on by the people *as if* it were true, so these actions actually caused the rumor to *become* true.

Applied to people, the Pygmalion effect works in this way. Generally, one person projects a certain behavioral expectation onto another person, and comes to expect a person to behave accordingly. If the subject of this projection does as expected, then positive reinforcement results. (The reverse is also true.) People generally do not like to be proven "wrong" in their predictions about another, so they will consciously or unconsciously arrange situations or hold beliefs that support their view. Even people who believe themselves to be fair and unbiased when interacting with others have been shown to influence others according to their preconception or projection. If the teacher believes that a certain group of children is brighter than a randomly selected control group, evidence suggests that these children will not only react as if they were brighter, but will indeed do better when their performance is measured. These results are explained more simply by the character Eliza Doolittle (in the musical *My Fair Lady,* one of many stories based on the Pygmalion effect): "The difference between a princess and a flower girl is not how she behaves, it's how she's treated."

The Novelty Effect. Many innovations in health education, especially with educational technology such as teaching machines and instructional television, or with tools such as health risk appraisals (see Chapter 6), have been evaluated under conditions that make them unusually attractive because of their novelty. In the field and under routine educational conditions, they are less effective. The threat to external validity in this instance is the reactive effect of evaluating a novelty that captures the interest and attention of the teachers and subjects more than it may be expected to do in normal use.

Interaction of Experimental Conditions with Educational Methods. This set of threats to external validity overlaps with some of the foregoing threats but deserves a residual category to accommodate the multitude of subtle ways in which the evaluator may bias the educational circumstances. These ways include causing subjects to respond more positively, attentively, avidly, negatively, passively, or otherwise to the educational treatment (*X*). The interaction of testing and *X,* for example, represents the threat to external validity introduced by the pretesting of subjects, which makes them more "tuned in" to the educational content than would be the case in the usual administration of the program. Some programs or curricula, on the other hand, routinely require pretesting of the students. In such cases, the interaction of testing and *X* is not a threat to external validity. Health risk appraisals, for example, are now routinely used both as a pretest for data gathering and as a lead-in to health education about lifestyle risks (see Chapter 6). Evaluations of the HRAs have benefited rather than suffered from this interaction of testing and *X.*

Ways to Counteract Threats to External Validity

The safeguards against reactive effects and interaction of experimental conditions with *X* apply variously to the specific threats, so they do not match up in a simple one-to-one listing. The best advice we can offer you is to consider all the following as possible ways to counteract any one or more of the foregoing threats to external validity. The blinding procedures can also help protect against some threats to internal validity, such as the tendency of participants (educators or subjects) to compete or to compensate if they think they are receiving less desirable treatments.

Blinding. There was a time when evaluation could be carried out without the subjects even knowing they were part of an experiment. They were "fully blinded," in the parlance of experimental research. Now, given current informed consent requirements, subjects must at least know the purposes, risks, and alternative forms of involvement they might face as participants in a study. (This requirement does not apply in some routine evaluations of ongoing service programs.) It is still possible, nevertheless, to obtain informed consent for participation in the study before randomizing subjects to experimental and control conditions. Hence it is possible to keep subjects blinded to whether they are in the "special" educational treatment or in a usual treatment control group, as long as they are not too familiar with the usual educational treatment.

Double-Blinding. When the threats to validity include both the subjects and the people delivering the education, it is sometimes possible to arrange for blinding of both parties to their experimental or control group assignments. If the health education method being tested, for example, is one of several methods in a total program, the subjects and the educators can be rotated to various combinations of methods without knowing which one is the object of interest in the evaluation.

Triple-Blinding. The evaluators or data gatherers also can bias the results of an evaluation. If they might do so by influencing the responsiveness of subjects, it is sometimes possible to mask which ones are in experimental or control conditions from all three parties. By using code numbers, collecting data by mail or telephone, having subjects enter their responses on an interactive computer keyboard, and other such short-circuiting of the interaction among the three parties, all three can be blinded to the place of subjects in the experimental assignments, at least until the education is done and possibly until the data collection is completed.

Unobtrusive Measures. The best way to reduce the reactive effects of testing and other forms of observation and measurement is to make them nonreactive. In the past, the use of participant-observers was a popular nonreactive procedure (Spradley, 1980). This method lost favor after some of the informed consent and privacy provisions of recent regulations governing research and evaluation—at least federally sponsored research. One-way mirrors are still used in educational laboratories and some clinical situations, but the subjects (or their parents, if the subjects are minors) must consent, which offsets the nonreactive advantage. But experience indicates that after giving their consent to be observed, taped, or filmed, subjects sometimes forget about the window-mirror, the tape recorder, or the video camera, so that they participate in the health education experience more freely than they would with pencil-and-paper tests or interviews imposed periodically. A wide range of even less obtrusive measurement strategies is available (e.g., Webb et al., 1981).

Sampling. We devote an entire chapter (Chapter 10) to sampling, but it deserves at least being listed here as a way to counteract the major threat to external validity, which is posed by selecting, for evaluation of a program, a sample of people who do not represent the intended usual recipients of the program.

THREATS TO INTERNAL VALIDITY

Now you know how to avoid threats to external validity of your evaluation—but why bother generalizing results that cannot be attributed with some certainty to the health education method or innovation that you would export with your results? This question brings us to the problem of internal validity. We will say more in the next chapter about the tradeoffs between internal and external validity in selecting the best design for evaluation. This chapter concludes with an assessment of the threats to internal validity and the basic techniques to control them.

History

History is the most pervasive threat to designs that depend entirely on historical standards of acceptability, including simple pretest-posttest designs without control groups. The term *history* here refers to any *secular trend* or *extraneous event* occurring before or during the health education program that could account for some or all the resulting knowledge, attitudes, behavior, or health improvements measured after the program. In the design implied by Figure 8-2, the increase from O_1 to O_2 could be attributed to X, but it could also be attributed to a trend in that direction that started before O_1, or to a television program that was aired on the same topic during the time between O_1 and O_2.

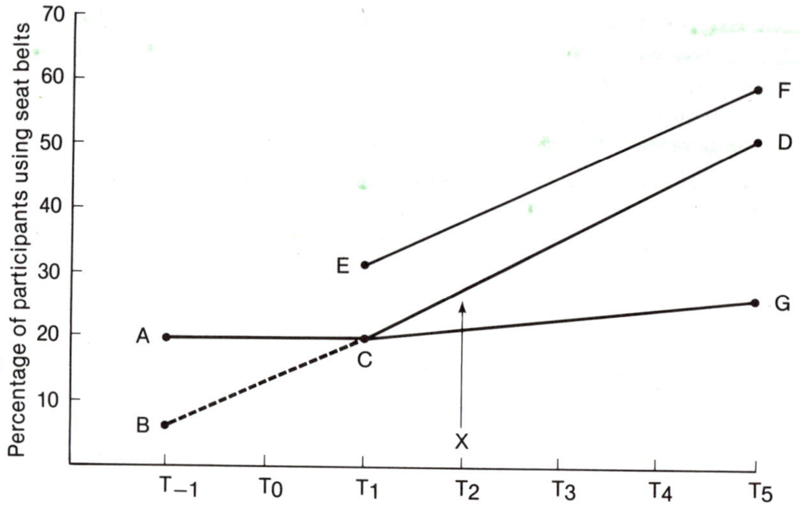

Figure 8-4 *A retrospective extension (C to A) of data from Figure 8-2 (represented by slope CD) to establish that the increase from 20 percent to 50 percent was not merely a continuation of a secular trend (BC), so that it can be attributed with greater certainty to Intervention* X. *Slopes EF and CG are from comparison populations.*

Two corrections or safeguards exist for this threat to internal validity. One is for secular trends only (see Figure 8-4); the other, for both secular trends and extraneous events (see Figure 8-5). In Figure 8-4, we employ a method to rule out secular trends as a competing explanation for the result observed in Figure 8-2. First we go back in time, as shown in Figure 8-4, to gather earlier data on the same outcome variable in the same population. If it is an outcome variable on which data are routinely collected, such as morbidity or mortality, or number of visits per month to a clinic, then it is easy to collect the additional retrospective data by digging further back into the same chronological record system. If the data are from interviews or questionnaires, then it may be necessary to ask additional questions about the month or year prior to the interview at T_1. The example in Figure 8-4 shows two possible results of a retrospective analysis of seat belt usage in a population exposed to a seat belt campaign (X) at T_2. We might find that the percentage of the population using seat belts at T_0 (say, one year ago) was only 8 percent. This finding would create the slope BC from T_0 to the original pretest survey at T_1, shown by the dotted line. Such a result would confirm the suspicion that CD, the increase observed from before to after the campaign, was merely a secular trend and cannot be attributed to the educational campaign.

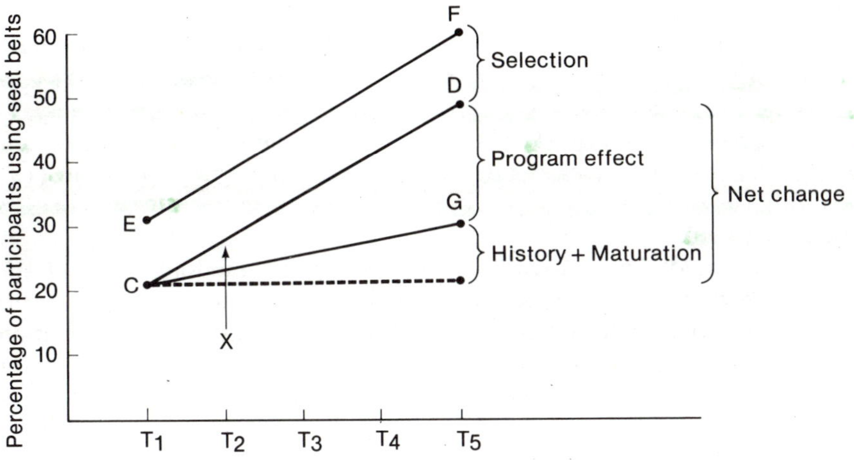

Figure 8-5 *The estimated contribution of selection, program effect, and the combination of history and maturation, based on posttest differences between the nonequivalent comparison group (EF) and the experimental group (CD), the experimental group and the randomized control (CG), and the pretest-posttest change in the control group (G − C).*

If, on the other hand, we find that 20 percent were using seat belts a year before the campaign, the same percentage as just before the campaign, then we can draw slope AC and conclude with greater certainty (though not total certainty) that CD is attributable to the educational campaign (X).

The remaining uncertainty concerns the other historical threat to internal validity—the possibility that some *extraneous event,* such as a bad accident in the community or an unexpected national television special on the subject of seat belts, occurred during the period between T_1 and T_5. The best way to rule out or to confirm this alternative explanation for the increase is to have simultaneous measures on an identical population that did not receive the educational campaign. This ideal group is virtually impossible to obtain in community or institutional health education programs because of educational *spillover,* sometimes referred to as "contamination" of the control group or, more flatteringly, the "diffusion," "imitation," or "halo" effect. Broad-scale health education programs, especially of the campaign variety, tend to leave few people unexposed.

The next best solution is a matched comparison group from another community or institution, or at least from another classroom, building, or floor within the same institution. Such a nonequivalent control group produces a "quasi-experimental design," which is an improvement over the "preexperimental design" represented by the simple historical (pretest to posttest) comparison shown in Figure 8-2. By adding simultaneous measures in an unexposed comparison group such as a neighboring community, we may find that there was a similar change during the campaign period, shown by Slope EF in Figure 8-4. This finding leaves us to conclude that the increase in our educational campaign population (CD) could have been caused by the same extraneous events that caused the increase E to F.

If we could create a true control group with randomization of subjects *within* the target population, we would have a true experimental design and could rule out or confirm both of the historical explanations for our results, as well as most of the other threats to internal validity we discuss next.

Maturation

Maturation, like history, is a threat primarily to designs that depend on pretest-posttest comparisons. Unlike history, maturation involves changes taking place within the individuals being measured over time, rather than the extraneous (nonprogram) events or changes taking place in the environment. The term *maturation* refers to intrinsic changes associated with growth and development. It is most dramatically a threat, therefore, to evaluations of programs for children and youth, in whom maturational changes are more rapid. But it also plagues longitudinal studies of change in adults, especially studies centered around life span transitions such as graduation, marriage, family formation, divorce, "midlife crises," retirement, relocation, and widowhood.

Cognitive skills change most rapidly in childhood; attitude changes and physical changes are most dramatically associated with narrow age ranges of maturation in adolescence. These are important threats to the internal validity of evaluation that is attempting to relate change in such things as knowledge, attitudes, or skills to health education or health promotion programs.

With a health behavior such as seat belt usage, as with other risk- or safety-related practices, we know that the behavior increases with age through adulthood. Part of the maturation process, according to one theory, includes taking fewer unnecessary risks with one's life and limb. Whether this theory of maturation is correct or not, the association of some risk-taking practices with age remains and must be taken into account in evaluations that have, as their standard of acceptability, changes over time in such risk-taking behavior.

In our example in Figure 8-4, it is possible that the change from C to D could be attributed to the maturation of the population between T_1 and T_5. Some reassurance could be found in a retrospective analysis showing that the change in a prior period (AC) had not been so rapid. Some additional test of the maturation explanation could be had from a comparison group not exposed to the program whose change during the same period was similar (EF) or different (CG).

The major question left unanswered in relation to the maturation hypothesis in both these analyses is whether the comparisons are with truly comparable populations in terms of age and life transitions. If the population exposed to the seat belt program at T_2, for example, consisted of high school seniors who were pretested on their seat belt use when they were high school juniors (C) and posttested three years after graduation (D), we have a population that is undergoing considerable maturation in relation to practices such as seat belt use. Suppose the comparison group were seniors when they were pretested (E). This fact might account for their higher starting point (30 percent, compared with 20 percent in juniors), but this difference is rather large for a one-year maturational difference in seat belt usage. The pretest difference (C versus E) is so great that we must face another threat to validity if we use them for comparison.

Dropout or "Mortality"

Any tendency for people to drop out of experimental groups at different rates creates a difference between the groups at the time of the posttests. Such differences cannot be attributed entirely to the intervention but rather must be understood as a process of selection. As such, the loss of people from either experimental or control groups threatens internal validity. It is a special case of the "selection" threat, which we will examine in more detail now.

Selection

The selection threat to internal validity refers to the problem of comparing apples and oranges. If we try to compare the seniors with the juniors in terms of their seat belt usage five years later, we will be unable to say whether the difference (F − D) is attributable to their age, their maturity, their different experiences, or a host of other possible factors that might explain the difference. All we can say with certainty is that we have a "selection effect." Selection, then, is a threat to internal validity whenever the comparison groups are not identical. Any differences between the groups might account for their final differences on the dependent variables, so that results could not be attributed solely to the intervention of *X*.

This threat can be partially offset by using pretest data to control for the differences between the two groups. But this control is only as good as the thoroughness and completeness of the pretest data set in covering all the potentially infinite number of ways in which the initial differences between two groups could account for their eventual differences on a complex outcome of a health education program.

The alternative safeguard against a selection bias or threat to internal validity is equal assignment of prospective subjects to experimental and control groups to assure their equivalence. Randomization is the most sure-fire, all-purpose equalizer of groups. Other methods of equalizing, such as matching pairs of experimental and control subjects on selected "important" characteristics such as age, sex, and socioeconomic status, tend to fall short of achieving equivalence on other characteristics. It becomes increasingly difficult to match people on more than two or three characteristics, so that matching groups on the basis of some individual characteristics leaves them unmatched on many more.

Random assignment is the most secure way to achieve equivalence of groups and thereby to offset the selection bias. The assignment problem particularly plagues health education evaluations in which people are left to sort themselves into experimental and control groups on the basis of their interest in the subject or the medium. Such self-selection produces the most troublesome motivational bias because the results are left ambiguous as to how much of the change or difference between groups can be attributed to *X* and how much to prior motivation.

Returning to our example in Figure 8-4, note that the difference between C and E, the pretest results for the experimental and comparison groups, is substantial. This difference was only the tip of an iceberg of other differences between the two groups, any of which might produce a selection bias. The two groups gained converts to seat belt use at the same rate, even though the nonequivalent control group did not receive the educational program. Are we to conclude, therefore, that the educational program was ineffective? No, we can only conclude that the educational program did not achieve more change than the progress achieved in another population of somewhat older, possibly higher socioeconomic individuals. This conclusion leaves open the question of whether the experimental group would have changed less without the program.

Turning to Figure 8-5, we have added a randomized control group whose adoption of seat belt usage is reflected by the change from C to G—that is, from 20 to 30 percent. Note that the starting (pretest) percentage for this control group is *equivalent* to that of the experimental group. This equivalence will usually exist, give or take a few percentage points depending on the number of subjects randomized. The larger the number randomized, the more certain you may be that the comparison groups will be equivalent on pretest characteristics.

Insofar as the experimental and control groups were equivalent on all but the one distinguishing feature—namely that the experimental group received the seat belt education campaign and the control group did not—

we can attribute the difference between their posttest percentages (D − G = 50% − 30%) to the program *with a high degree of certainty.* This degree of certainty is not based on statistical significance, although a significance test will assure us that such a large difference could not have occurred by chance in more than 5 in 100 experiments. Our certainty is based, rather, on the fact that with the pretest-posttest, randomized experimental design we have ruled out or controlled for the major competing explanations for the result. We have ruled out selection by assuring equivalence of the groups with randomization. We have controlled for history and maturation by having posttest measures on an equivalent control group who went through the same period of history, in the same locale, and with the same maturation possibilities.

Figure 8-5 shows some increase (10 percentage points) in seat belt use by the randomized controls (G − C). This increase can be attributed to maturation and history. This amount also can be subtracted from the net change in the experimental group (D − C = 30 percentage points) to yield an estimate of the true program effect (30 − 10 = 20 percentage points). What could there possibly be left to worry about?

Testing

There remains one nagging problem, especially in health education, even with the all-powerful randomized pretest-posttest design. This problem is the threat to internal validity created by testing subjects twice—once before and once after the intervention. The problem is that people become test wise and are able to perform better on the posttest if they have taken the same test before. This effect is especially true of conventional tests of knowledge and skills (Lana, 1969; Rosnow & Suls, 1970). With attitudinal and behavioral measures, people become acquainted with what the evaluator is seeking and may score better on the second testing even if their own attitudes and behavior have not changed. Even with some physical measures, people may be cued and even motivated to change their behavior quite independent of the health education intervention in order to control the risk factor if they know they are going to be tested again. People may stop smoking, lose weight, change their diet, or increase their exercise as a result of a health professional weighing them or asking them an incriminating series of questions before a program.

This effect differs from reactive effects only in the sense that here we are concerned with its influence on *internal* rather than external validity. It threatens internal validity when no control group exists in which to measure its effect on the dependent variable. With a control group, we can subtract this effect, along with maturation and history effects, from the total change observed in the experimental group, as we did in Figure 8-5. Indeed, we can add "Testing" to "History + Maturation" in Figure

8-5, because the change observed in the equivalent control group is a product of all three factors.

If we can control for it, why is testing a problem? The randomized design controls for it along with history and maturation, thereby eliminating it as a threat to internal validity, but it does not distinguish the effects of testing from those of maturation and history. In health education we are interested in this distinction because pretesting is an optional part of most health education programs, and it is sometimes expensive, time consuming, or otherwise bothersome for students, patients, and other recipients. So we would like to know how much pretesting adds or subtracts from the total program effect. There are two answers to this problem.

One response to the issue of the expense of pretesting, both for evaluators and for educators, is to drop pretesting from the evaluation design. "Horrors!" say some traditional experimentalists, especially from the clinical fields. "How can you be sure the control group is equivalent if you do not have pretests?" This reaction betrays a lack of confidence—not to say faith—in random assignment as an adequate equalizer. If you cannot trust random assignment to equalize the groups, why do it? And if you find that the groups are unequal in some respect, are the minor statistical adjustments you can make worth the expense of the pretesting? These retorts are a bit harsh, but the truth is that little is gained by pretests, especially relative to their costs. Indeed, a posttest-only randomized design is just as good as a pretest-posttest randomized design for controlling all the threats to internal validity. And the posttest-only design will be half as expensive.

The second response to the problem of pretests is to go to the opposite extreme of *adding* two groups to the basic pretest-posttest randomized design. This addition results in a Solomon four-group design, the purpose of which is to give a quantitative answer to the question "How do pretests influence educational outcomes?" (Solomon, 1949). Let us review the elements of design that we have accumulated in our successive solutions to the various threats to internal validity to see how they come together in the Solomon four-group design.

We started with the understanding that evaluation is the comparison of an object of interest (X) against a standard of acceptability, which we symbolize with an O to represent an observation or an outcome measured against an objective for X. To represent a historical standard of acceptability, we suggested the sequence:

$$O_1 \quad X \quad O_2$$

and graphed the comparison with a frequency polygon as illustrated in Figure 8-2. To control for the effects of history, maturation, and selection, we added a control group and recommended randomizing:

R	O_1	X	O_2
R	O_3		O_4

Now we have suggested that with true randomization we should not need the pretests, because the groups can be assumed to be equivalent at the outset:

R	X	O_1
R		O_2

If this last combination does everything that the previous combination does, except to introduce pretests, then it can serve as a control for the previous combination to determine the effects of pretests. Hence, the Solomon four-group design is as follows:

R	O_1	X	O_2
R	O_3		O_4
R		X	O_5
R			O_6

The last two groups, in effect, are a control for the first two in an experiment to determine the effect of pretests with and without the educational intervention (X). Our interest in the effects of pretests in health education, however, is usually in relation to the intervention. How do pretests interact or combine with the intervention to enhance or detract from the educational outcomes? To answer this question more specifically and efficiently, we recommend a three-group design that properly conceives the combination of pretest and educational intervention (OX) as one experimental treatment, the intervention alone as a second experimental treatment, and the posttest-only group as the control:

R	(OX)	O_1
R	X	O_2
R		O_3

This design answers all the same questions answered by the Solomon four-group design except one: What is the effect of the pretest *without* the intervention? We fail to see many practical uses for the answer to that question, at least in health education, so for most purposes in which the effect of pretesting is of concern we recommend the three-group alternative, for the sake of economy, efficiency, and less wear-and-tear on subjects.

Instrumentation

Although we have now covered all the experimental variations necessary to eliminate or control virtually all the threats to internal validity, a few other threats should be understood so that if one of the weaker designs is used (a design other than randomized experimental designs) the potential risks of interpretation can be taken into account. The term ***instrumentation*** refers to the problem created when the pretests are not exactly the same, or are not conducted under exactly the same circumstances, as the posttests. Instrumentation differs from testing bias in that it involves changes in characteristics of the test or testers, whereas testing bias involves changes brought about in the subjects themselves. Both result in differences between pretests and posttests that may not be attributed to the intervention (*X*)—hence their threat to internal validity.

Examples of instrumentation problems are changes in the wording of questions between pretest and posttest; changes in the skill, interest, morale, or energy of the people collecting or coding data and thus in their performance; and changes in the setting in which data are collected. For example, blood pressure measures taken in the home are known to be lower, on the average, than blood pressures taken in the clinic. If the pretest measures were taken in the home and the posttest measures in the clinic, the actual improvements in blood pressure would be at least partially masked. Similarly, the answers patients give to their physician differ from answers they give to some of the same questions from nonmedical interviewers. A change in interviewers from pretest to posttest can thereby create changes in data that are not attributable to the interventions.

The best cure for instrumentation problems is not to conduct pretests. We have already rested our case for the advantages of posttest-only randomized designs over pretest-posttest designs, so let us not rub salt in the wounds of pretests. They do have their uses, as seen in discussing the last two threats.

Regression Artifacts

The easiest way to understand this threat to internal validity is to think of it as a law of nature, as are most statistical phenomena: What goes up must come down. This formulation is an exaggeration if applied to individuals, but when applied to groups, as in experimental and control groups, it is predictable that exceptionally high average scores for a group at Time 1 will be followed by lower scores, on the average, at Time 2. It is equally true that unusually *low* pretest scores will tend to be higher, on the average, at posttest. In short, extreme scores in either direction will tend, over time and independent of any intervention, to regress toward the mean. The change in scores for extreme groups between pretest and posttest, therefore, cannot be attributed entirely to *X,* so the change threatens internal validity.

This phenomenon bodes especially troublesome in health education programs directed at high-risk groups, which is typical of most public health programs. If you select a target population on the basis of high scores on any risk factor such as blood pressures greater than 100 mm Hg diastolic, or smoking more than two packs a day, or cholesterol greater than 250 ml, you may expect that the average score for the group as a whole will be lower at a later date. Even though some people will persist in their eating or smoking behavior and some will get worse, the *mean* score for your extreme group will be closer to the population mean at a later date, with or without health education.

This regression obviously poses the greatest threat to pretest-posttest designs that lack comparison or control groups. If the result shown in Figure 8-2 had occurred in a target population in which childhood immunization levels were as low as 20 percent at the beginning of the program, the fact that they were at 50 percent at the end of the program could be attributed as much to regression to the population mean as to the intervention.

A nonequivalent comparison group could be even more misleading if it should happen to have extreme pretest scores in the opposite direction from those of the experimental group. Consider our example of seat belt education for high school juniors, with a nonequivalent comparison group of seniors at a different high school. If the 20 percent pretest level of usage in the experimental group was exceptionally low relative to the national average, and the 30 percent pretest level in the seniors was unusually high relative to the national average for seniors, we should expect to see their slopes converge. We have drawn the slopes in Figure 8-6 to show how subtle the process might be, especially in relation to a moving average such as a national trend. But the results of some designs for evaluation could be misleading in several ways. First, the regression to the mean might not be detectable in a short period. Second, the trends for nonequivalent groups might converge at the posttest, giving the impression in a posttest-only design that there were no differences between the two groups. This confusion illustrates the one undeniable value of pretests, namely to establish the preintervention differences between nonequivalent comparison groups. We remind you that if the groups had been created by random assignment from a single population (e.g., one high school and one grade), the comparison groups would not have been different at pretest, and pretests would therefore be unnecessary.

Finally, you should consider the other forms of regression to the mean that might occur in nonequivalent comparison groups. These forms can apply to knowledge tests, attitude scales, behavioral measures, skill tests, physical measures of vital signs and risk factors, and measures of morbidity and mortality. Consider also that the regression phenomenon can interact with history, maturation, dropout or "mortality" of subjects, testing, and (most of all) selection, to produce compounded threats to validity. In Chapter 11, on analysis, we address other examples in health education of handling these various anomalies.

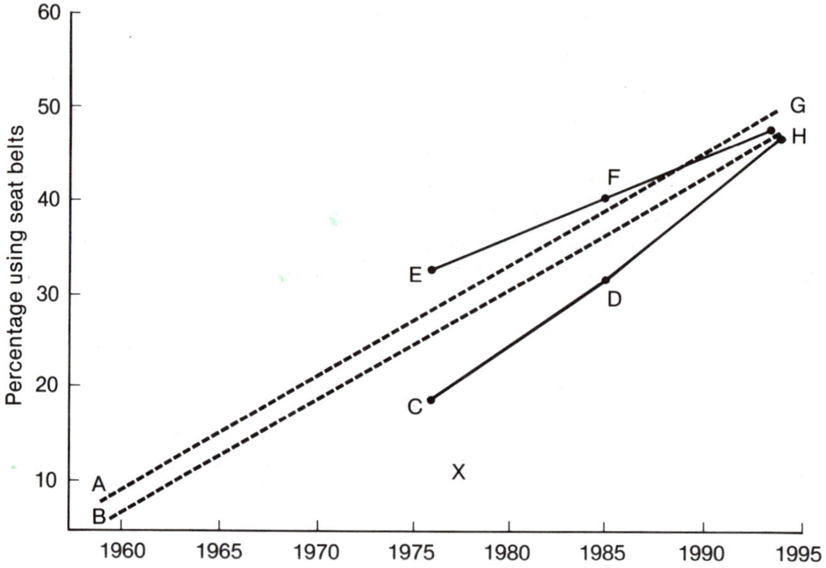

Figure 8-6 *Hypothetical slopes for trends in adoption of seat belts by high school seniors (AG) and juniors (BH). The dashed lines show the national averages in percentage who use seat belts regularly. The solid line CH shows the regression upward toward national averages for the group that started out below the mean for juniors. Line EF shows regression to the mean for the group that started out above national averages for seniors.*

SUMMARY

The three evaluation components are *comparison, objects of interest,* and *standards of acceptability.* (Methods of comparison are discussed elsewhere.) Objects of interest can be reduced to independent variables (*X*) and dependent variables (*O*). Independent variables may be any object of interest in the planning or conduct of health education, ranging from specific instructional techniques, materials, or messages to complex combinations of these into strategies, interventions, or programs. Dependent variables may be any observable or measurable result—ranging from immediate impact (changes in knowledge, attitudes, or beliefs) to ultimate outcomes (behavioral risk factors, morbidity, mortality, or social benefits)—that was an objective or presumed effect of the independent variable.

Standards of acceptability take several forms, depending on the information available and consulted in setting objectives, and depending on the politics of emphasizing or discounting certain kinds of information. Program managers usually prefer historical standards; sponsors prefer normative standards; consumers prefer absolute standards; academic consultants prefer theoretical standards. The outcome of their negotiations will often result in some compromise standard, depending on the distribution of power and control among these parties. For most evaluation purposes, however, the rules of evidence require that the independent variable (X) be judged on the basis of historical or normative standards, or some combination of the two.

The various ways in which the evidence concerning the value or effectiveness of X can be compromised are called *threats to validity.* Such threats can undermine (1) external validity or (2) internal validity. Threats to external validity are ways in which the circumstances of evaluation can limit the possibility of generalizing the conclusions to other places or times. Threats to internal validity are ways in which the circumstances of evaluation can limit the certainty that the changes observed in the dependent variables (O) can be attributed to the influence of the independent variable (X).

There are ways to protect against or control for each threat to validity. You will not, however, always be able to employ the ideal design and all the controls. How, then, will you choose between alternative controls or design features to best suit your circumstances? This question is addressed in the next chapter, in which we also illustrate the designs with more examples from actual evaluations of health education.

Chapter 9

SELECTING AND IMPLEMENTING DESIGNS FOR EVALUATION

In this chapter we return to the distinctions made in previous chapters among three objectives of measurement and evaluation designs—internal validity, external validity, and practical evaluation. These objectives are not always compatible in health education. Two of them—internal validity and external validity—are essentially scientific. Nevertheless, they are not entirely compatible with each other because scientific method has several rules of evidence and rigid adherence to one rule often sacrifices adherence to another. The third objective—practical evaluation—is primarily practical. It focuses on how practitioners and administrators, whose responsibilities are not principally scientific, can incorporate measurement and evaluation into their programs and still be accountable for their expenditures and their primary mission, which is service, not research.

The design you select for your evaluation will depend on whether your primary purpose is scientific or practical and on whether the most important objective of your design is to ensure internal or external validity or to establish accountability. In this chapter we explain how to select the design most appropriate for your purpose. We describe five elements of design that you need to weigh. We give some examples of how these elements have appeared in past evaluations of health education, and we present three hierarchies of techniques to maximize internal validity, external validity, and accountability. In order to show that practical evaluation of health education programs can be implemented effectively, we illustrate the hierarchy for accountability with evaluations actually carried out in sexually transmitted disease (STD) educational programs. This subject allows us to range across school, clinical, and community settings for examples of practical evaluation designs.

PURPOSES OF MEASUREMENT AND EVALUATION

Measurement and evaluation typically have a scientific purpose or a practical purpose. If the purpose of a design is scientific, the results should be useful or meaningful beyond the immediate circumstances in which the measurement or evaluation is done. Scientific results should be useful for (1) assessing the true character or efficacy of the object under study (regardless of the practicality of replicating the study circumstances elsewhere) or (2) estimating the probable value or effectiveness of the object if and when the study is replicated elsewhere. For the first, internal validity is required: You must have an accurate estimate of how well the program or method would perform under *optimum* circumstances. For the second, external validity is required: you need to know how the program or method would perform elsewhere under *typical* circumstances.

If the purpose of a design is practical, your primary concern is the usefulness of the data for pinpointing accountability or indicating how well a program or method is working. You are not particularly interested in certainty or replicability. Your concern is performance and the allocation of resources.

Two hard realities impinge upon the scientific and practical purposes of evaluation. First, internal validity in most programs is an elusive goal that cannot be reached without sacrificing some generalizability of results. The laboratory conditions necessary for complete experimental control may create such artificial conditions on methods or programs that the results cannot be generalized to most operating situations. Studies conducted in this manner thus may achieve internal validity at the expense of external validity. The way to reconcile yourself to this tradeoff is to say that you can improve external validity by sacrificing some internal validity. You can improve both by sacrificing some existing allocation of services or convenience to consumers (Fisher & Carlaw, 1983).

The second reality that must be faced is that *neither* internal validity *nor* external validity of research and evaluation can be maximized in most programs without sacrificing some attention or resources that otherwise would have gone toward service. For the practitioner or administrator, this sacrifice sometimes makes evaluative research seem counterproductive. You are left, then, to seek a level of evaluation that gives the answers you need immediately while requiring minimal intrusiveness and demands on staff and clients.

Later in this chapter we present a series of three hierarchies of design and sampling techniques that respectively maximize internal validity, or external validity, or accountability. Depending on which of these three factors is central to a given evaluation project, the selected hierarchy suggests an order of preference for various designs and sampling procedures.

THE FIVE ELEMENTS OF EVALUATION DESIGN

The ideal design for the evaluation of anything, including health education, is the true experimental design. The true experimental design consists of five elements:

1. Representative sample of target population or program recipients
2. One or more pretests (measures preceding the educational intervention)
3. Unexposed group for comparison
4. Random assignment of the sample to experimental and control groups[1]
5. One or more posttests to measure effects after the experimental intervention

The options for economizing or simplifying evaluation procedures consist of discretionary compromises on the ideal experimental design. By giving up any of the first four elements of the true experimental design, you can realize certain economies, avoid some sacrifices of services, or overcome some complications. In a pretest-posttest design, for example, you could eliminate the pretests and cut the cost of evaluation in half, as shown in the previous chapter.

The first four elements of the true experimental design can be compromised without a total loss of validity. The fifth element—at least one posttest or observation of educational effects after the experimental program—is essential to any evaluation and cannot be eliminated. Thus, we have at the *maximum* extreme of the proposed hierarchies of options the true experimental design containing all five of these elements. At the bare *minimum* end of the hierarchies of options is the design containing only a posttest following an experimental program and containing none of the other four elements.

The question for both evaluators and practitioners is "Which of the four dispensable elements can you compromise with the greatest gains and least loss?" This question has three answers, depending on the purpose your evaluation is to serve.

Before considering the optional hierarchies, let us understand more sharply how some typical designs for evaluation take shape as they combine various configurations of the five elements.

1. Technically, the requirement for an experimental design is experimenter control over all the other things that could influence the outcome of the experiment besides the independent variable or intervention. The best way to approximate such control when the experimental subjects are human beings is to assign them randomly to equivalent experimental and "control" groups.

EXAMPLES OF EARLY EVALUATIONS

Appendix D presents a summary of the authors, the year of publication, the educational targets, the evaluative designs, and the outcomes measured in various health education studies. These studies covered a variety of educational approaches, settings, program objectives, and eras. The objective of a program was often broader than the objective that the evaluation set out to measure. The educational goal is often only one component of a health program, and evaluation often must limit the number of outcomes measured, even within the educational component.

In an analysis of some early (1960–1966) evaluations in health education (Green & Figa-Talamanca, 1974), nearly half the studies used the single-group pretest-posttest design ($O_1\ X\ O_2$). This design tended to be preferred by many as superior to posttest-only designs with two groups. In fact, as we showed in the last chapter, the pretest-posttest design invites more threats to internal validity than the posttest-only design with a control group. These threats include the problems of extraneous historical events, maturation of the subjects, and the educational effect of the pretest. Each of these threats to validity in the pretest-posttest design could be ruled out with a control group that is identical in every way except that it does not receive the experimental educational program. In short, a single-group pretest-posttest design does not exclude rival hypotheses that might explain the observed changes following the health education program and that may be unrelated to the program. It fails to offer a firm base for any conclusion about the effect of the health education or health promotion program.

The other half of the early (1960–1966) studies used a "pre-post 2" design

$$\begin{array}{ccc} O_1 & X & O_2 \\ O_3 & & O_4 \end{array}$$

with a control group receiving observations O_3 and O_4 simultaneously with the pretest (O_1) and posttest (O_2) in the experimental group. "Pre-post 3" would refer to a similar design with three groups. This design attempts to control the possible effects of history, the effects of maturation, and the effect of the pretest. It has the weakness, however, of assuming that the experimental and the control groups were initially identical on all variables not measured by the pretest. In general, this assumption can only be made when the people have been assigned to the groups by a randomization procedure and when the sample allocated to each group is large. Random assignment was not used in many early studies shown in Appendix D, but has been used increasingly in more recent evaluations.

Of the thirteen earlier published evaluations (Green & Figa-Talamanca, 1974), three reported failure to meet their objectives, seven reported partial success in the aims of the program, and the results of the other three were inconclusive. Most practitioners recognize that some health education programs, by their voluntary nature, do not lend themselves easily to tighter designs with random assignment of subjects to experimental and control groups.

The more recent evaluations of health education, especially in patient care settings where randomization is easier, have included more frequent instances of true experimental designs with all five elements, as seen in Appendix D (Devine & Cook, 1983; Mullen, Green, & Persinger, 1986).

IMPLEMENTING COMMON DESIGNS IN HEALTH EDUCATION

The strengths and weaknesses of various design options for evaluating health education lie partly in the threats to validity that they cover or leave uncovered. They also lie partly in the demands some designs make on the normal flow of health education activities—potentially compromising the very effectiveness of health education that they are intended to test.

In the following evaluation designs, as in the preceding chapter, we use the symbol *X* to represent the independent variable of educational input, and *O* to represent observations on dependent variables collected before (to the left of *X*) or after (to the right of *X*). These pretest and posttest observations may have been collected from a variety of sources (e.g., service statistics, interviews, or other records available to measure the dependent variables). The subscripts from left to right indicate points in time when the observation or the educational interventions were made. Each row of *X* and/or *O* represents a different experimental (educated) or control (usual treatment) group. If R precedes a line, it means that eligible recipients of the health education were randomly assigned to that group.

True Experimental Design with Posttests Only

Experimental group:	R	X	O_1
Control group:	R		O_2

In this simple but powerful design, the differences between the posttest results for experimental and control groups (O_1 versus O_2) can be attributed almost unequivocally to the educational treatment given to the experimental group, assuming that your randomization procedure has achieved equality of the two groups prior to the participation of one group in the program. Note from the more recent studies in Appendix D that randomization has become increasingly common as the chosen method of equalizing experimental and control groups, but remains uncommon in community and school health education evaluations for logistical reasons. This design requires a sufficiently large pool of patients, students, workers, or other eligible people interested in the educational program so that you can randomly assign them to experimental and control groups. Consult a statistician or statistics book for sample size requirements after you have selected your dependent impact or outcome variables.

To illustrate this design, the specific steps in implementing such an experiment for a diabetic patient education program are outlined as follows:

1. Decide what will be the criteria of success; that is, the specific knowledge, attitudinal, behavioral, and medical indices and levels that will be accepted as indicators of educational impact—the dependent variables.
2. Determine how you will be able to obtain these measures from existing records and, where they are not available from records, what questionnaires, interviews, or other observations must be developed and pretested before conducting the experiment.
3. Decide what intervening variables would preclude the impact of education on these measures; for example, selected disabilities and handicaps, including learning disabilities, visual handicaps, and so on. Set these variables as screening criteria. (With diabetes, for example, nonstable diabetics should be screened from experimental and control groups.)
4. Obtain the total pool of subjects (e.g., stable adult diabetics) who are interested in participating in the educational program, screening out those not eligible according to criteria decided on in Step 3.
5. Assign each name randomly to experimental or control group by flipping a coin for each; or, better, use a random number table.
6. Schedule the educational programs at times convenient to all people in the experimental group. It is essential that virtually every person assigned to the experimental group has an equal opportunity to participate. The smaller the sample, the more important this equality is. If opportunity to be exposed to the educational program varies markedly within the experimental group, then the

results must be interpreted cautiously, because the effect of a program on any other population in which exposure also varies will depend on the attributes of *that* population. (A later date can be set for the control group members, so that they are not deprived of an educational program, but this date should be after the "posttest" measures are taken in both the experimental and control groups. (See our discussion of the next design.)

7. Conduct the educational program. If participants are divided into subgroups, as in classrooms, be sure that the educational treatment is similar for all subgroups. This equality can be best ensured by a strict protocol; careful training of the teachers, counselors, or educational leaders; and at least periodic monitoring of their adherence to the educational protocol. Variability may occur, within tolerable limits, but should be systematically documented.
8. Obtain the posttest measures simultaneously in the experimental and control groups. Some of these measures may be taken over a period of time, in which case the period should be the same for both groups.
9. The experiment applying this design is now completed, except for the data analysis and interpretation. The control group can now receive an educational program independent of the experimental constraints, or they may be given an identical educational program and posttests, extending this design to the next.

Staggered Experimental Treatments

	Time			
	T_1	T_2	T_3	T_4
R	X_1	O_1		O_2
R		O_3	X_2	O_4

In this design, O_1 versus O_3 is the same as in the previous design, but the extended time frame allows additional data to be collected on the sustained or diminished effects of the educational program (O_1 versus O_2), and on the effect of a pretest (O_1 versus O_4). If O_4 is greater than O_1, the difference can be roughly attributed to the effect of the pretest (O_3). This effect was referred to in the previous chapter as the "testing effect." The major advantage of posttest-only experimental designs over pretest-posttest experimental designs is that the former avoids the effects attributable to testing the program participants.

If the initial pool of patients, students, or other subjects interested in participating is large enough, this design can be extended to multiple groups to assure that all eventually receive the health education program:

	Time							
	T_1	T_2	T_3	T_4	T_5	T_6	T_7	T_8
R	X_1	O_1		O_2		O_3		O_4
R		O_5	X_2	O_6		O_7		O_8
R				O_9	X_3	O_{10}		O_{11}
R							X_4	O_{12}

The continued observations in Groups 1 and 2 are not necessary, but O_3, O_4, O_7, O_8, and O_{11} provide additional data on the retention of knowledge, attitudes, and behavioral changes over time. If it is convenient to administer the tests or conduct the observations with all subjects at each point in time, the additional data on maintenance of changes over time is of considerable value in health education.

Note that the use of multiple groups in this design requires that the initial pool of subjects must be large enough to allow the random assignment to multiple groups at the outset (e.g., by rolling a die rather than flipping a coin). You cannot achieve this design by merely adding new patients to new groups as they come along. Random assignment to groups is the key strength of both these first two designs.

If random assignment of patients into experimental and control groups is not possible, then we must assume that the groups are not equivalent. We must therefore have pretests in addition to posttests to adjust for any initial differences between the groups when comparing their posttest scores.

One-Group, Pretest-Posttest Design

$$O_1 \quad X \quad O_2$$

The major weaknesses of this simple design, as seen in the previous chapter and in our discussion of the early evaluations of health education, are that we cannot be sure that the results observed in O_2 could not have been caused by factors other than the program itself, such as the following:

1. *History*—that is, extraneous events such as a television program aired between O_1 and O_2
2. *Maturation*—that is, the growth and development of subjects that occurs with the mere passage of time between O_1 and O_2
3. *Testing*—that is, the effect of O_1 on O_2 (e.g., experience with the test)
4. *Instrumentation*—that is, changes in the measurement tools or procedures between O_1 and O_2
5. *Interaction* between the pretest and the educational program

Having a comparison group, even if it is not a randomly or otherwise matched group, can help respond to all these threats to internal validity. As for Problem 5, the interaction between O_1 and X is usually a legitimate part of health education programs. Insofar as we conduct pretest surveys for purposes of educational diagnosis, we should probably consider the direct and indirect educational effects of pretests as part of the educational program.

Nonequivalent Comparison Group, Pretest-Posttest Design

$$\begin{array}{ccc} O_1 & X & O_2 \\ O_3 & & O_4 \end{array}$$

This design can be extended in the same way as the staggered designs, adding additional posttests for the two groups, or adding additional experimental groups (X_2, X_3, etc.) to examine variations in the educational program, or both. The additional groups may be added (1) with simultaneous educational programs (if you have sufficient educational personnel and facilities), or (2) on a staggered basis.

1.
$$\begin{array}{ccc} O_1 & X_1 & O_2 \\ O_3 & X_2 & O_4 \\ O_5 & X_3 & O_6 \\ \text{etc.} & & \end{array} \quad \text{or} \quad \begin{array}{ccc} O_1 & X_1 & O_2 \\ O_3 & & O_4 \\ O_5 & X_2 & O_6 \\ \text{etc.} & & \end{array}$$

2.
$$\begin{array}{ccccccc} O_1 & X_1 & O_2 & & & & \\ & & O_3 & X_2 & O_4 & & \\ & & & & O_5 & X_3 & O_6 \end{array}$$

It might be advisable to use the simultaneous designs (1) rather than the staggered (2) for specific experiments, for two reasons. First, the pretests and posttests can be administered simultaneously for all groups, thus reducing the possibility of subtle changes in the administration of pretests and posttests or other observation methods. Second, with the staggered design, extraneous historical events may affect the groups differently. For example, if a television special on diabetes appeared on the air during the time period between pretest and posttests, it would affect simultaneous groups equally, whereas it would affect staggered groups unequally. This threat of "history" applies also to the staggered experimental design. Randomization cannot protect the staggered design against exposure to different periods of history.

Time-Series Trend Analysis on One Group

$$O_1 \quad O_2 \quad O_3 \quad O_4 \quad X \quad O_5 \quad O_6 \quad O_7 \quad O_8$$

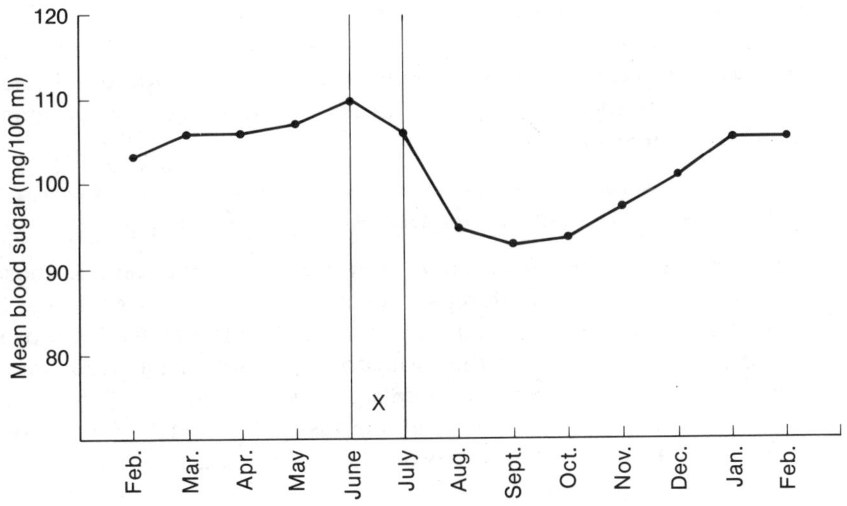

Figure 9-1 *A hypothetical trend analysis to evaluate a diabetes education program.* Source: *Green & Figa-Talamanca (1974), p. 66.*

In this design, some statistic would be routinely monitored from routine records over a period of time before the educational program, and then followed for a period of time after the program. A change in the trend line from before the program to after the program should be expected. In a diabetic program, for example, the percentage of diabetics examined with abnormal blood sugar levels should drop after a program. A trend line might be expected to appear as in Figure 9-1.

Statistics exist for testing the significance of a drop in the trend line such as that illustrated. The problem in interpreting the practical significance, however, is the same as that in the simple pretest-posttest design: the change may be attributed to some cause other than the educational program. Two competing explanations in the illustrated case might be (1) that the drop is a seasonal phenomenon that would have occurred in the summer even without an educational program, or (2) that something else happened in June (such as the television special, in the earlier example) that could account for the drop. Both problems could be met with the addition of a control group, adding a second trend line on the same chart. This solution is discussed in the next section and illustrated in Figure 9-3 (see page 216).

The other technique for dealing with the first competing explanation (seasonality) is to extend the observations another year prior to and/or after the year surrounding the educational program. Additional lines can be added to the same graph, one labeled "1984" (the year before the program), one labeled "1985" (the year of the program), and a third labeled "1986" (the year after the program). Comparisons of the trend lines will determine whether the observed peaks or troughs in the program year are consistent seasonal phenomena.

Time-Series Trend Analysis on Multiple Groups

The issues and techniques in this kind of evaluation are the same as those in previous designs. The only thing special about the time series design is that more observations are made before and/or after the educational program. This augmentation helps the evaluator rule out secular trends and seasonal variations as competing explanations for changes observed. Groups to be compared can be randomly assigned, matched on some other basis, or self-selected, in that order of decreased desirability for scientific purposes.

Longitudinal analysis is a special class of time-series analysis in which the same data are collected on the same people at each point in time. It is made most feasible with existing record systems in which you can select a single measure that is available on all consumers, students, or patients. You can then plot the mean or percentage for all or for a random sample of all subjects each day, week, month, or year. This plot can then serve as a baseline or control for comparison with health education groups. Any longitudinal group may be referred to as a "panel." Out of a large panel, if it is a representative sample, subgroup plots can be drawn for specific age groups, socioeconomic groups, and so on, for comparison with specific health education groups.

Although this historical, record-based design has the advantages of large numbers and the availability of data without special interviews or questionnaires, it has major disadvantages. One disadvantage is the poor quality of many routinely collected records in terms of their reliability and validity. If the bias is systematic, a statistical adjustment may suffice to correct the error, assuming that its direction and magnitude are known.

A second disadvantage is the inappropriateness of most medical or administrative record items as criteria of *educational* effectiveness. Blood pressure and blood sugar levels, for example, are routinely recorded in medical records, but they have such large variances and are subject to so many circumstantial influences that they are difficult to relate to specific behavioral changes without large numbers of patients in experimental and control groups. Medical records have few, if any, consistent behavioral measures. In short, medical and administrative records tend to measure record-keeping behavior as much as the behavior of the subjects observed.

Resolving the second disadvantage requires either (1) adding of specific behavioral questions to the routine records or (2) supplementing routine records with special interviews, questionnaires, or diaries to be kept by the subjects or their families. If the routine records must be supplemented, you might as well use one of the previous experimental or quasi-experimental designs with pretest and posttest questionnaires.

Using the five elements of evaluation design listed earlier in this chapter, let us now consider the optimum combination of elements for the various purposes of evaluation.

HIERARCHY OF OPTIONS TO MAXIMIZE INTERNAL VALIDITY

Often your primary purpose for evaluation will be to determine whether something works at all (efficacy), whether it achieves a certain standard (quality control), or how it compares with alternative methods (comparative evaluation or cost-effectiveness studies). If your purpose in such instances is not to generalize the results to other populations, you can conduct the test with an unrepresentative sample. The issues of internal validity in correctly relating the program elements to their desired outcomes, in this case, are more important than the external validity of whether the results can be replicated or generalized elsewhere.

When the purpose of the evaluation is to determine the efficacy of a health education method, to ensure a given level of achievement, or to compare the relative effectiveness of two or more methods in a given population of consumers, generalizability is not of paramount importance. The hierarchy of options to maximize economy and to minimize threats to internal validity is as follows:

Choice 1: True experimental design with all five elements.

Choice 2: Experimental design in a convenience (nonrepresentative) sample.

Choice 3: Experimental design minus pretests. See the first two examples in the previous section. This choice may be preferred over Choices 1 or 2 if the pretest is not a normal part of the program and if its application in the evaluation causes the subjects to pay more attention to the education than they normally would (reactive effects, or interaction of O_1 with X), or to perform better on the posttest because they learned from the pretest (testing effect); or if the cost of pretesting is so high that you cannot justify it on the basis of the small advantage it gives to your analysis.

Choice 4: Experimental design minus pretests in a convenience sample.

Choice 5: Quasi-experimental design with matched comparison group rather than random assignment to obtain a true control group. See the fourth and last examples in the preceding section.

Choice 6: Quasi-experimental design with matched comparison group without pretests.

Choice 7: Quasi-experimental design with pretest but no control group. See previous sections: one-group, pretest-posttest design; and time-series trend analysis on one group.

Choice 8: Choice 7 in a convenience sample.

Choice 9: Quasi-experimental design with no pretests and no control group. This design can only be justified if pretests and comparison groups are impossible and if the posttest is thorough enough to develop a retrospective estimate of preintervention status on the dependent variables.

Choice 10: Choice 9 in a convenience sample.

The notion of a convenience sample in this hierarchy is a way of reducing the costs or inconvenience of interrupting the usual management of consumers or clients in the program. The rule here also is the larger the sample, the better, because larger numbers allow subgroup analyses to control for the consumer variables that might account for results apart from or in addition to educational effects. The more heterogeneous the sample, the more subgroups (for example, age groups, males versus females, or socioeconomic groups) are available for analysis of group-specific effectiveness. But apart from these general rules, you can maximize internal validity without necessarily sampling from all consumers eligible for the program service. The only requirement of a convenience sample is that you thoroughly describe it in the evaluation report so that generalization can be limited to similarly defined consumers.

HIERARCHY OF OPTIONS TO MAXIMIZE EXTERNAL VALIDITY

If the evaluation is intended to provide evidence for the general effectiveness of a program or educational method, then external validity or generalizability of the results is paramount. If, for example, you want to know whether to continue using a given educational technique in a program or whether to recommend it to others, then you must test the technique on a representative sample of the people with whom the technique will be used. They must be similar to people in a variety of settings in which you might recommend the technique. This approach is equivalent to field-testing or the clinical testing of drugs or medical procedures, as distinct from the more basic testing on animals or nonrepresentative samples of human volunteers that usually precedes field-tests or clinical trials.

Evaluation for the purpose of recommending an educational strategy, method, technique, or medium for general adoption, then, requires generalizability, also called *external validity.* Under these circumstances, the element other than posttests that cannot be sacrificed is representativeness of the subject sample. A general rule is that the larger and more heterogeneous the sample, the more it can serve as a valid case from which to generalize to other settings. The hierarchy of options recommended for selecting an evaluation design is as follows:

Choice 1: True experimental design with all five elements.
Choice 2: Experimental design with no pretests.
Choice 3: Quasi-experimental design with matched control group(s).
Choice 4: Pretest-posttest design with no control group.
Choice 5: Quasi-experimental design with no pretest and no control group. (The same comments regarding the limited acceptability of this design apply here as in Choice 9 in the preceding section.)
Choices 6–10: The foregoing choices without representative samples of patients or target populations.

EVALUATING FOR ACCOUNTABILITY

When your primary purpose for evaluation is accountability for services rendered, then the scientific rules of evidence are less important than the integrity of the program. If you have been responsible for the expenditure of funds allocated for a specific service, then you need to show that some service has been delivered, or that some goal or objective has been achieved, but you are not required to "prove" that the service was solely responsible for a given effect. We defined evaluation as "the comparison of an object of interest against a standard of acceptability." Health education programs can be evaluated for accountability at three levels: formative, impact, and outcome. These levels have been discussed in previous chapters and are illustrated with examples from STD education in this section (see Table 9-1).

Formative Evaluation

In a formative evaluation, the object of interest is the "input" of programs or professional practice. These inputs or processes of health education differ most significantly by setting (school, clinic, community agency,

TABLE 9-1 Illustration of formative, impact, and outcome evaluation levels to assess the effects of STD education efforts

Education Effort's Target Population	Formative Objectives and Measures	Impact Objectives and Measures	Outcome Objectives and Measures
Adolescent students	Provision of accurate education about STDs to all junior and senior high school students by 1990. Implementation of school-based STD education programs for all junior and senior high school-aged students in the school district (local).	What percentage of students are able to recognize STDs, know how to protect against infection, and express intentions to use preventive measures?	Improve health status: By 1990, reported gonorrhea incidence should be reduced to a rate of 280 cases per 100,000. By 1990, reported incidence of pelvic inflammatory disease should be reduced to a rate of 60 cases per 100,000 women.
High-risk groups in the community	Identification of the establishment of contact with all high-risk groups (e.g., gays, adolescents) in the community through hotlines and other outreach programs contact.	Increase in self-referrals and referral of sexual contacts for STD screening and treatment at an earlier stage; increase in general knowledge and practice of behaviors that decrease risk of STD contact.	By 1990, reported incidence of primary and secondary syphilis should be reduced to a rate of 7 cases per 100,000 population per year, with a reduction in congenital syphilis to 1.5 cases per 100,000 children less than 1 year of age.
General population; subgroups within total populations	Provision of government funds and assistance for demonstration projects of community-based STD prevention.	Data on what types of STD education approaches are most effective for particular organizational settings.	

Health care professionals	Completion of the development and distribution, and assistance in the implementation, of the quality assurance guidelines for STD clinical care; provision of statewide continuing education workshops for health care professionals on how to identify high-risk individuals and how to educate patients for STD prevention (local).	By 1985, at least 95 percent of health care providers seeing suspected cases of STD should be capable of diagnosing and treating all recognized STDs. Increase in early referrals among private patients; increase in knowledge of STD prevention measures (local).

worksite, or mass media). The standard of acceptability in formative evaluation is appropriate content, methods, and performance. The *quality* of content, methods, or performance is monitored by various means, including audit, peer review, accreditation, certification, and government or administrative surveillance of services, contracts, and grants. Standards of acceptability for educational content, methods, and procedures are established both professionally and administratively and are derived chiefly by means of consensus among health education specialists and other experts. We have outlined methods of formative evaluation in Chapter 2.

Impact Evaluation

The second level at which you might compare your program against some standard of acceptability is impact evaluation. Evaluation here focuses on the immediate impact the program (or some aspect of it) has on one or more of the dependent variables of education, including knowledge, beliefs, attitudes, skills, social supports, and behavior. These variables are understood to be the determinants of longer-range goals for health promotion, disease prevention, or medical improvement. Have the predisposing, enabling, and reinforcing factors that influence the health-related behavior been altered? Have the short-term goals of a program been met? The planner will ask such behavioral questions as "Does it take as long for members of the target population to seek diagnosis and medical care as before the program? Has health-enhancing behavior increased? Are symptoms being diagnosed and treated earlier? Has exposure to risk been reduced?"

Cost-effectiveness is the most succinct standard of acceptability for most administrators in impact evaluation. Cost-effectiveness may be expressed as a simple ratio of cost per unit of impact; for example, as cost in dollars per new STD case disclosed or cost per reinfection averted following a patient education program; cost per case appearing at an STD clinic following community education; or cost per ten-point increase in mean scores on a knowledge test following a school, clinic, or worksite health education program.

Outcome Evaluation

At the third level, the objects of interest in health education are incidence and prevalence of risk factors, morbidity, and mortality. Have the incidence and prevalence of STDs been affected by a program? Has the average time of reinfection following detection and treatment changed? Again, cost-effectiveness is one standard of acceptability. Does the cost per case of STD averted by one strategy of education exceed the cost per case by another strategy? At this level, cost-effectiveness loses favor to measures of outcome expressed more humanely and simply in number of lives saved or improved. Outcome evaluation expressed in such terms is a long-term undertaking requiring a larger sample than impact evaluation. Ultimately, medical outcomes and public health criteria or standards must be related to social definitions of health problems and the quality of life.

Which Level to Emphasize

Table 9-1 illustrates the different objectives of each of the three levels of evaluation for various types of STD education efforts. It has not yet been possible to translate standards of educational practice in many school, clinical, and community settings into hard criteria or standards of acceptability for purposes of process evaluation. In STD education, for example, some attempt is being made to evaluate the match of language and concepts used in printed educational material with the comprehension levels and concerns of the populations served (Kroger, 1980; Kroger & Yarber, 1984).

In addition to the problem of defining criteria, a number of practitioners, including teachers and physicians, feel burdened and sometimes threatened in their academic freedom or confidentiality of practice by peer review and government surveillance. In community and patient education, then, formative evaluation is needed but may not always be the most fruitful pursuit if a choice must be made. In school health education, a stronger data base exists for the assessment of communication behavior. Classroom teaching practices customarily have been subjected to intense scrutiny. Some topics such as alcohol, drug abuse, sex, and STD education in the classroom, however, may require greater circumspection in attempts to observe teaching in process for purposes of evaluation.

In most community and school programs, outcome evaluation cannot be done efficiently within a normal program context (Kolbe, 1979, 1982). Health outcomes and social benefits often do not appear for long periods of time, and populations rarely remain stable. An evaluation of education and community organization efforts directed toward STD control in terms of reduced morbidity, for example, would require greater resources, larger populations, and more follow-up time than are likely to be available in those programs. Any attempt to relate STD education to subsequent prevalence or incidence rates will require unusual control over extraneous events and program elements besides education that might account for secular trends in STD rates.

Given the current development (or underdevelopment) of some areas of health education, impact evaluation—the assessment of changes in critical comprehension, attitudes, beliefs, and behavior that come about as a result of health education programs—is the level of evaluation most likely to produce the greatest improvements in such programs.

A Hierarchy of Evaluation Designs for Accountability

A variety of quasi-experimental designs, ranging from the simple but often neglected use of data collected as part of routine administrative procedures (see "Time-Series Trend Analysis on Multiple Groups") to data collection in highly controlled circumstances, are available for evaluation of health education before you need to resort to the more expensive and sometimes intrusive methods recommended as first choices in the other two hierarchies. The historical, record-keeping approach is the simplest and is applicable to most programs. The controlled experimental research approach is usually impractical in most service programs unless some sacrifice of service is allowed. Each design has its own utility. You will make your selections according to the kinds of data needed and the uses to which the data will be put, and according to the feasibility, cost, and intrusiveness of alternative designs. All the designs that follow can be implemented in two or three major steps. Each is illustrated from the literature on evaluation of STD education programs.

We list the design hierarchy here, not in order of the design strength, but rather in the order of feasibility and frequency of choice for ongoing programs.

Choice 1: The Historical, Record-Keeping Approach. The simple tabulation and charting of routinely collected records, as illustrated in Figure 9-2, can yield graphs that effectively demonstrate changes in a person, a group, a program, or a community. Historical designs are variations on Choices 7–10 in the first hierarchy and on Choices 4, 5, 9, and 10 in the second hierarchy. The procedure is simply to set up record-keeping procedures in order to accumulate data on the impact or outcome variables to be compared with standards of acceptability expressed by the objectives of the program. Periodically, you can tabulate the data on graph paper by plotting the direction and magnitude of change taking place over time. How often you tabulate and chart the data depends on the frequency of events being tabulated, which is partly related to the size and demographic composition of the population, and partly to whether the events being tabulated are rare or common.

For example, Atwater (1974) demonstrated the separate and cumulative benefits of three educational components of an STD education program designed to affect the number and composition of STD patients using a clinic over a two-year period. The impact of each educational strategy could be inferred from the trend lines in a simple graph showing changes in the absolute number of patients appearing at the clinic and in the sex and racial composition of the patient population (see Figure 9-2). Schuurman and de Haes (1980) similarly measured the impact of mass media exposure (see Figure 9-3, page 216).

Figure 9-2 *Illustration of results from a simple record-keeping evaluation: Visits to a venereal disease clinic, by month.* Source: *Atwater (1974), p. 435. Used by permission of the American Public Health Association.*

Bryant and her colleagues (1976) used a simple record-keeping approach to undertake a cost-benefit analysis of an STD information hotline. Records were kept of the number of calls handled by hotline operators during one year (process) and the number of clinic and emergency room visits for STD screening and treatment for the six months following the start of the hotline operation (impact). Results showed that emergency room and clinic visits for STD care were 53 percent greater than during the same period of the year before the hotline's existence. The cost per call in operating the hotline was calculated (process measure). A cost-effectiveness evaluation was hampered by an absence of information about financial and person-power outlays for hotline publicity by the medical center, and by lack of data about additional costs that resulted from the increased number of STD patients. Also, the investigators had no data to

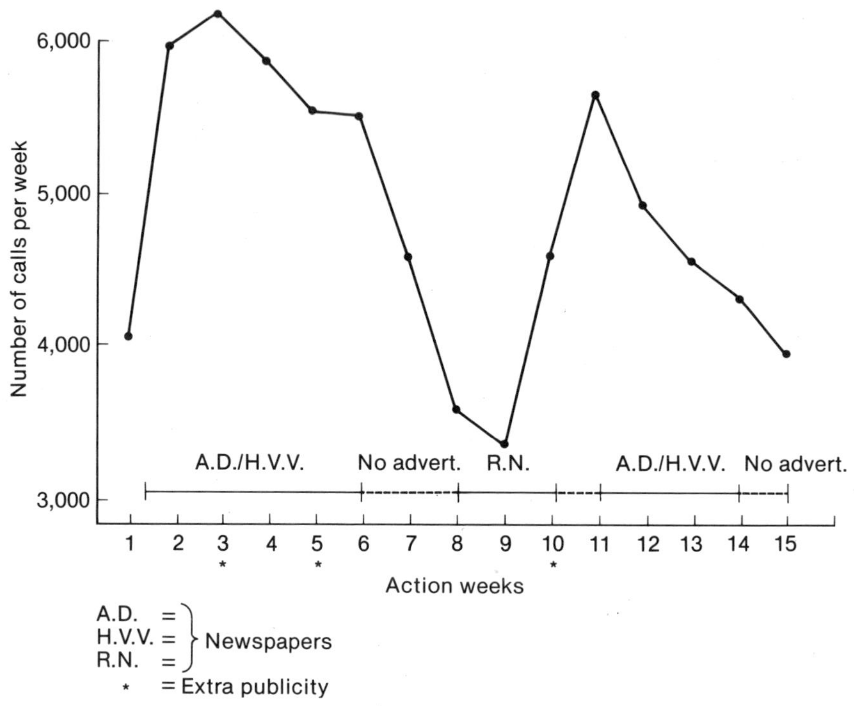

Figure 9-3 *Graphic representation of a record-keeping system showing results of an advertising campaign: Number of telephone calls received per week to evaluate the response to advertisements in two newspapers (*A.D. *and* H.V.V.*), then no advertising for two weeks, then two weeks of advertising in another newspaper (*R.N.*), etc., over a 15-week period.* Source: *Schuurman & de Haes (1980), p. 96.*

determine whether patients' decisions to seek care were influenced by the hotline.

The last example illustrates the importance of building interagency cooperation for coordinated record keeping into an evaluation plan in order to obtain the data necessary for process and impact evaluations. The several examples illustrate how informative and persuasive even this "routine" method of evaluation can be if the results are charted or graphed in a communicative way.

Choice 2: The Periodic Survey Approach. The survey or inventory approach requires that you periodically make a special effort to collect new data. Sometimes the prevailing record-keeping system does not incorporate the data required, and changing or expanding the system would be disruptive to the service program. Rather than accumulating the more obtrusive data on an ongoing basis, as is done with Choice 1, you can obtain the needed additional data by conducting special surveys. A combination of record keeping and periodic spot surveys or sample surveys is recommended for most evaluations of ongoing health education programs. This combination approach is illustrated for STD education in a two-volume report on *Communicating to Combat VD: The Los Angeles Experiment* (Bogue, Burs, & Mayo, 1979) and in a variety of other evaluations of health education in family-planning, immunization, nutrition, and hypertension control programs (e.g., Back & Stycos, 1959; Corsa, 1964; Dillman, 1978; Flay & Cook, 1981; Stahl et al., 1977).

The procedure for Choice 2 consists simply of setting target dates for the assessments, identifying the expected outcomes, and then conducting the periodic surveys as a way of estimating the outcome levels achieved at the selected points in time.

For most health education programs, some of the critical points for measuring behavior or reinfection rates are highly standardized by medical protocols. Your review of the current literature will suggest the times at which people are most likely to drop out or backslide in programs that address such behaviors as compliance with antibiotic therapy, contraceptive use, and temporary abstinence. In order to obtain more meaningful data on program impact, it is important to take these critical relapse or dropout periods into consideration when setting short- and long-term evaluation target dates (e.g., Hunt & Bespalec, 1974; Wang et al., 1975).

Comparisons in Choice 2 are "historical" in that success is defined in relation to a prior period of performance in the same program or population. Choice 2 is frequently used to assess pre-post knowledge gain or behavior change following a formal, time-limited health education program in school and clinic settings (Franz & Weisser, 1978). Rosenblatt and Kabaskalian (1966) used a Choice 2 approach to evaluate a community-based STD information campaign for adolescents. Through a set of surveys one year apart, they were able to assess the extent, intensity, and types of exposure received by subgroups of their sample population (process), and evaluate changes in STD knowledge levels (impact) in the population between 1962 (precampaign) and 1963 (postcampaign) in relation to the extent of exposure.

Choice 3: The Normative Approach. The normative approach to evaluation is an extension of the inventory or record-keeping approach. The same procedures for internal data collection are followed, but now external data from other similar programs are introduced for additional comparisons. The steps are (1) identify similar data on programs in other places; (2) borrow or copy the data or the record forms used in these programs or negotiate a common, standardized format for collecting data or keeping records on the similar programs; and (3) conduct periodic comparisons between the programs on the same basis as Choice 1 or Choice 2 designs. This approach allows for both a historical comparison over time within programs and normative comparison with other programs or with regional or national averages.

Various local and national data are generally available for normative comparisons. We reviewed the existing data bases in Chapter 6. National health surveys provide data derived from standardized questionnaires that can be compared with data collected in local programs. National norms suggest what health educators can expect on the average, for example, about age of first intercourse, frequency of sexual intercourse, number of sexual partners, use of condoms, and other health behaviors relevant to evaluation of a local STD education program. In many countries you can obtain reliable morbidity data at several levels of government insofar as private physicians and clinics are required to report new communicable disease cases to official agencies such as local public health departments. The Centers for Disease Control in Atlanta, for example, publish weekly and monthly statistical newsletters reporting on nationwide surveillance of incidence and prevalence of morbidity and mortality.

The extent of underreporting cases is of concern in evaluation research. Program evaluators often attempt more rigorous surveillance or reporting procedures for their program than government agencies are capable of providing. This attempt can result in making the evaluated program appear to have higher morbidity than the norm.

Comparability is an essential feature of cumulative evaluation or "time series" techniques. For this reason, we recommend using standardized formats for collecting data rather than developing original questionnaires for each separate evaluation. An example of a normative approach for evaluation of STD education can be found in a report by Franz and Weisser (1978). A variety of other examples for this design may be found in family planning, hypertension, driver education, and smoking. It is most common in evaluations of mass media campaigns (Dumbauld, 1981; Green & Krotki, 1968; Neill & Bond, 1964; Wilkenson et al., 1977).

Choice 4: The Controlled-Comparison, Quasi-Experimental Approach. In the controlled-comparison approach, you first find a community or population similar to your target population, but one not receiving the program. You then apply Choice 1 or Choice 2 in both the program being evaluated and the comparison program, and periodically compare the two communities. You might want to compare the effects of various kinds of interventions in similar populations: in schools, for example, or in communities. The Minnesota and Stanford Community studies are the most notable contemporary examples of the latter application

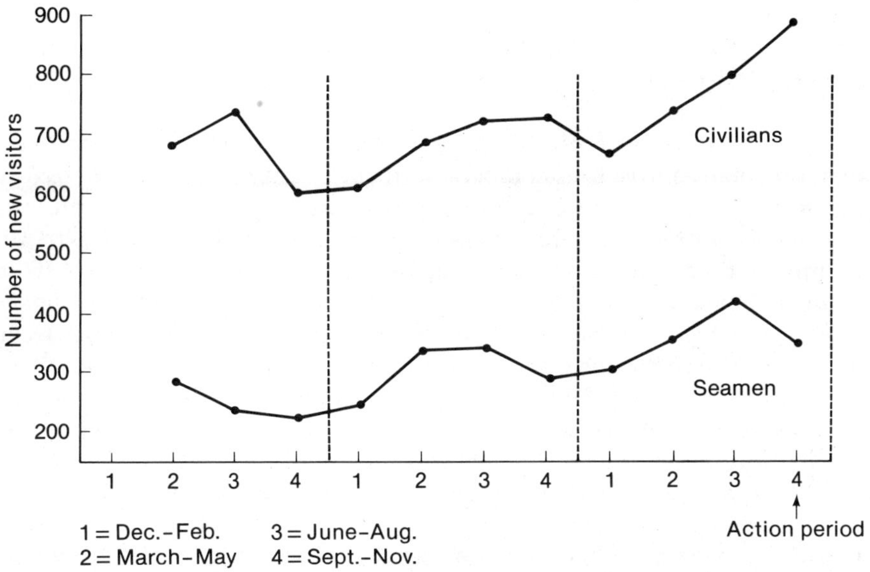

Figure 9-4 *Example of a normative comparison of a population exposed to an advertising campaign (civilians) with an unexposed control population (seamen).* Source: *Schuurman & de Haes (1980), p. 99.*

(Blackburn, 1983; Maccoby, Farquhar, Wood, & Alexander, 1977; Farquhar, Maccoby, & Solomon, 1984). The Stanford group studied three communities: one in which an intensive all-out education effort was made, another in which only a mass media effort was made, and another in which neither effort was made. Comparable resources and facilities were available to the populations in all three communities. The effectiveness of the strategies used in each of the three experimental communities and among their various subpopulations was compared, using impact and outcome data from surveys.

Schuurman and de Haes (1980) evaluated the impact of a media and hotline campaign on STD in Rotterdam by comparing trends in new visits to the STD clinic during the intervention for civilians with those of seamen who were not likely to have been exposed to the campaigns and were thus a "control" group (see Figure 9-4). The Rotterdam evaluation, if you study the trend lines in Figure 9-4, points out the importance of controlling for seasonal fluctuations or possible changes in the demographics of the population sampled when analyzing patterns of incidence and prevalence over long time periods.

Other examples of the controlled comparison or quasi-experimental design in health education evaluations are found in family planning, hypertension, cancer control, and American Indian health programs. It is most common in evaluations of school health curricula and mass media. (See Appendix D.)

Choice 5: The Controlled-Experimental Approach. The controlled-experimental approach is comparable to the randomized clinical trial in medical studies. It requires a formal procedure for random assignment of individuals *within* the target population to two (and sometimes more) groups. If there are two, one group will receive the educational treatment and one will not. Note that in this approach you must be in an ethical and legal position to deny certain people the educational treatment, or at least to delay their access to the educational program. Once the groups are set up and the program is under way, the evaluator uses records (Choice 1) or surveys (Choice 2) for measures of dependent variables in both the experimental and the control groups.

You may wish to collect baseline data on all groups prior to the program, but such collection is not essential, because randomization assures that the groups are equivalent on baseline characteristics if the samples are large enough. Records or survey data over time then are graphed to see how the groups compare at various points in the treatment. Relatively few health education programs outside clinical settings have been evaluated using controlled-experimental designs with all the elements in Choice 1 of the first two hierarchies described. This scarcity is largely because the requirements of random assignment generally are regarded as antithetical to the purposes of service programs.

Alkhateeb, Lukeroth, and Riggs (1975) used random assignment to treatment and control conditions to evaluate three methods of health (STD) education delivery in a clinic setting. (The investigators even controlled for the sensitizing effect of the pretesting procedure.) Potterat and Rothenberg (1977) used this experimental approach to compare the effectiveness of a standard fifteen- to twenty-minute "interrogation" procedure with a shorter experimental educational intervention that discussed the nature and implications of STDs and the importance of self-referral of sexual contacts. Both procedures yielded the same number of elicited names and referrals of sexual contacts; but because the new procedure was less expensive, the cost-effectiveness of the experimental procedure was much greater.

The only mass media evaluation using a randomized control design was an unusual opportunity provided by a community in which the cables for a cable television station were connected in such a way that the broadcast of seat belt messages could be randomly distributed to households. Actual observations of subsequent seat belt usage avoided the validity problem of self-reports by posting observers on street corners and identifying seat belt wearers and nonwearers by their license plate numbers. These numbers in turn could be traced to addresses where the television messages had been cabled (experimental) or not cabled (control). Note that the experimental treatment was guaranteed *access* to the messages, not guaranteed *exposure.* Not all the people in the experimental households saw the messages, but we may assume that the level of exposure *for a group* was similar to what might be expected in a random sample of households exposed to a similar broadcasted message. Thus, the design gets high marks on both internal and external validity (Robertson, Kelley, O'Neill, Wixom, Eisworth, & Haddon, 1974).

Choice 6: The Evaluative Research Project. The most complex evaluation designs, which might be described as full-scale evaluative research projects, are unlikely to be feasible in most community, worksite, and school programs, but are more feasible in clinical settings. Procedures are similar to those for Choice 5, the controlled-experimental approach, except that subjects are randomized to multiple groups with systematically varied "dose levels" or combinations of the experimental educational treatment. Multiple measures are obtained on intermediate impact variables such as changes in knowledge, attitudes, skills, and behaviors, as well as outcome variables such as improvements in health and even reductions in mortality. Group tendencies are analyzed, as are intragroup effects. The design can accommodate many refinements. Programs consisting of as many as six different treatments applied to various subgroups within randomized groups can be evaluated by means of this design (Green et al., 1975; Kirscht et al., 1981; Levine et al., 1979; Maiman et al., 1979; Morisky et al., 1983).

Somewhere between the simplicity of Choice 1 (with its inconclusive but helpful findings) and the complexity of Choice 6 (with its infringements on service functions), you will be able to find, for any specific health education program, a level of evaluation that is feasible and practicable as well as more rigorous than Choice 1. The problem with the more complicated designs is that they usually have to be carried out under more highly controlled conditions, which makes the behavioral circumstances unusual or unnatural. Often you must remove people from their social milieu, the ordinary context for their health behavior. Finding willing participants for controlled randomized experiments is sometimes difficult. Furthermore, such designs require informed consent, and the very act of achieving informed consent in a control group requires health education similar to that intended only for the experimental group.

In short, what you gain in internal validity through the more rigorous control and randomized procedures you may sacrifice in generalizability of findings (external validity) and in service (accountability). Can data from highly controlled classroom or clinical facilities be generalized to private practice and community-based programs? The only way to answer this question is to continue to accumulate data in different settings, documenting programs and methods as they are developed according to careful educational diagnoses, and applying the designs from among the foregoing choices that best fit the purposes of your evaluation.

SUMMARY

Evaluation designs have particular utility in the evaluation of health education, depending on which of two primary purposes the evaluator may have for conducting the evaluation. If the primary purpose is scientific, the evaluator chooses among designs that maximize the internal or the external validity of the study. Designs that maximize internal validity emphasize strategies that provide convincing evidence that the educational intervention, not other sources, produced the observed results. Designs that maximize external validity emphasize strategies that allow for the generalizability of the obtained results to similar populations. If the primary purpose of the evaluation is practical, evaluators choose designs and measurement strategies that allow them to demonstrate accountability for their activities and expenditures. Practical evaluation is less concerned with replicable results than with the quality of the current program's immediate performance or effects.

The five elements of the true experimental design provide the theoretical ideal against which alternatives between evaluation designs can be judged. These elements are (1) a representative sample, (2) pretest(s), (3) unexposed comparison group, (4) random assignment to experimental and control group(s), and (5) posttest(s). The alternatives for evaluation designs in any particular evaluation consist of discretionary compromises on the ideal experimental design. The key question for the evaluator is which of the dispensable elements of the ideal evaluation design can be compromised with the greatest gain and the least loss. Design hierarchies are identified that maximize internal validity, external validity, or accountability. Recent evaluation studies in socially transmitted diseases (STD) and other program areas (see Appendix D) provide examples of alternative designs that maximize one of these perspectives, and six common designs in health education evaluation are analyzed in terms of their ability to maximize internal and external validity.

The design hierarchies and examples can serve as a guide to the advantages and disadvantages of alternative designs for evaluation in health education. Depending on which of the three criteria of productivity or utility for which your evaluation is accountable, you can move up or down the three hierarchies to find the design that best suits both your purpose and your circumstances.

Chapter 10

SAMPLING

Early in the planning stage of any program, you will face the questions of whom to count as eligible for the program, whom to count as exposed to it, and whom to count as affected by it. Although the questions entail administrative, economic, ethical, and political considerations, they also pertain to the sampling problems of measurement and evaluation. You will need to consider samples because it is seldom possible to get measurements on *all* people in the population. If you want to generalize the estimates or the results obtained in the study sample to the total population or to other similar populations, you will need to question the representativeness of the sample. In this chapter we tackle sample representativeness from two approaches: probability samples and nonprobability samples. Before proceeding to these two sampling conditions, we introduce basic terminology and the logic of representative sampling. We also consider special cases justifying the use of nonprobability samples.

BASIC TERMINOLOGY

Levels of Sampling

Your need for sampling may arise at any of several points in a program development and evaluation process. First, in the diagnostic phase of planning a program, you can measure the *health education needs* of a population more efficiently and expediently from a sample than from the total population of potentially eligible participants or recipients of the program. Although it seems to contradict common sense, a *sample* survey of the needs of the population can give you an estimate that is possibly more accurate than if you attempted to survey the *entire* population. It is likely to be more accurate than a "census" of the entire population if the resources saved by pursuing a smaller number of interviews, questionnaires, or observations can be used to obtain more thorough measures on each person, and can be used to assure that each person sampled is included in the measures taken. In a census of a large population, some people will not respond to your first request for their participation. Some even will not respond to a second or third request. This nonresponse arises in a smaller sample too, but such a sample has fewer people to be pursued with second and third requests. This characteristic allows a population to be more fully represented in the sample than in a complete census. The accuracy of population estimates is impaired by the fact that the people who refuse interviews or questionnaires are usually not typical of the population, so their exclusion or underrepresentation creates a significant bias.

A second level of sampling may occur when the program has only enough resources to reach a proportion of the population at one time. Additional resources are expected later to reach the remaining people, but a decision is required on who shall be first and who shall wait for the services or benefits of the program. Political, ethical, and various criteria of relative needs may dictate priorities. "High-risk" groups are the usual priority of public health programs; "high-income" groups, of commercial programs. Sometimes the decision is to make the service available on a "first-come, first-serve" basis, but the location, hours, and financial conditions of the service may create barriers or incentives that produce a *de facto* bias (like *de facto* segregation) by overrepresenting the part of the population exposed in a "first-come, first-served" program. If your evaluation question is whether the program is effective for the population at large, then sampling may be necessary in the selection of subjects for the program in order to avoid the self-selection bias or the *de facto* bias.

Finally, a level of sampling or subsampling may be employed within the foregoing samples if you decide that components of the program (specific health education methods or messages) need to be compared for their relative effectiveness. You may decide that the program or evaluation budget can only support more intensive interventions or measurements for a limited number of people exposed to the broader program or survey. In both instances, comparisons can be made within a program and more detailed data can be obtained by sampling the sample, or by subsampling.

Population and Sample

Let us say that as senior health educator on the Brisbane Indian Reservation you are interested in the potential impact of a preventive dentistry health education program on all the teenagers on the reservation. Representatives from the community have worked with you and have identified the importance of a preventive health education program in this area. Your target population or population of interest includes all the adolescents who live on the reservation. Increasing the specificity of the population description, the focus is narrowed to youths between the ages of twelve and seventeen whose sole legal residence has been and currently is on the reservation and whose Native American parentage through both parents is determined. The population thus is all people who meet this set of eligibility criteria.

Your health education program has limited resources and can only reach approximately 25 percent of this target population of adolescents. You will request more funds for the total population if the program achieves its standards of acceptability, but you must now decide who will make up the initial 25 percent of the target population to be exposed to the program. This question is "Who should be in the sample, taking into consideration political or ethical constraints?" A sample is ideally a miniature of a population. A population is the larger set of all possible cases that meet a designated set of specifications.

Sampling is the process by which a portion of the population is selected. The ultimate goal of sampling is to represent the population as closely as possible; that is, with the least amount of bias. Data obtained from the sample can be used to describe the population. This goal immediately confronts the health educator: "How should you sample the adolescents so that the chosen 25 percent are representative of the larger population of all the adolescents residing on the reservation?" To the extent that you want the 25 percent sample to truly represent the larger adolescent population, you must consider a probability sample.

Probability Sample

A probability sample is a sample in which all elements of a population have a known probability of being selected. In a *simple random sample,* each individual has an equal chance or probability of being selected. In our preventive dentistry example, a simple random sample implies that each adolescent Native American from the target population has an equal chance of being selected to participate in the voluntary program. Other probability samples might purposefully give some individuals a greater chance of being included in the sample. A probability sample is important because it is the only type of sample that allows the evaluator to treat the sample as technically representative of the larger population. Only in probability samples can the health educator rely on the statistical theory of sampling distributions to specify how well the values (statistics) obtained in the study approximate the true values (parameters) of the population (Chein, 1976, p. 516). For example, probability sampling allows you to calculate estimates of the population means and proportions, as well as to calculate the precision of these estimates.

These precision calculations derive from two mathematical laws, the *law of large numbers* and the *central limit theorem* (Mendenhall, Ott, & Scheaffer, 1971; Lazerwitz, 1968). Simply stated, these laws claim that the properties of large samples assume a normal distribution around the values of their population equivalents. This characteristic of the sample allows you to calculate, around the sample estimates, confidence intervals that will include the range of possible population values with a known amount of sampling error. The amount of error is the calculated probability that the confidence interval fails to include the actual population value. For example, the evaluator could claim that a mean score of 145 on a self-report measure of preventive oral dental care, plus or minus 15 points, on a sample of program participants will include the true population value 95 percent of the time over the long run. (It is more precise to claim that the 95 percent level of precision is a range of possible values around the sample mean up to 1.96 times the standard error of the sample mean rather than claim 95 percent of the time.) Probability sampling has these advantages:

- Provides the only technically legitimate basis by which you can generalize information obtained from the sample to the larger population
- Allows calculation of sample size needed to stay within an established error bound
- Allows specification of confidence interval around sample estimates
- Provides basis for legitimate use of inferential statistics

The special case of random probability sampling in which each individual does not have an equal chance of appearing in the sample (i.e., not a simple random sample) but does have a known probability, is a *weighted random sample*. In a weighted sample, the probabilities are fixed in advance to assure overrepresentation of some types of people in the sample so that you will have enough of those people to carry out detailed analyses on them. If a simple random sample, for example, would yield only a few individuals of a given race, ethnic origin, or age because such people are a small proportion of the total population, then the evaluator may wish to double-sample or triple-sample that category of people in order to ensure more accurate estimates of their responses to the program. A weighted sample can be made representative of the total population either by eliminating the excess cases in the aggregate analysis or, better, by mathematically weighting (multiplying) the values of their total scores by the inverse of their sampling proportion. For example, if blacks are double-sampled, multiply their totals by 1/2; if they are triple-sampled, multiply their values by 1/3 in the total sample estimates.

For example, women generally make up a little more than half the adult population of a neighborhood. If you want to get more detailed and accurate estimates of female knowledge, attitudes, and behavior because your program is designed to prevent birth defects, then you might over-sample the female adults in a household or telephone survey. Rather than interviewing 50 women and 50 men, you might interview 75 women and 25 men. The sampling ratio for women then is 75/50 or 3/2. In calculating total population estimates for all adults in the neighborhood, you would multiply the female scores by 2/3 and the male scores by 2 (50/25).

Sampling Bias

Sampling error concerns the amount of bias introduced as a result of the sampling procedure. Sampling bias distorts your estimates of the true population values on your diagnostic or evaluation measures. Bias is introduced to the extent that the measures you obtain from the sample do not reflect the actual underlying population values. For example, the average or mean scores you obtain on a set of knowledge and attitude tests may not reflect the true knowledge and attitudes of the population if some bias has crept into the sampling or measurement procedures.

Sampling bias is the difference between the average of the sample estimates of a population value computed from a large number of identical samples and the actual population value. Stated in theoretical terms, sampling bias refers to the extent to which the operation of the law of large numbers yields a distribution of the evaluation measures whose sample mean is different from the value of the population mean being estimated. If the mean value of the normal curve obtained from the sample is not the same value as the true population mean, then the difference between the sample estimate and the population value is labeled *sampling bias.* In essence, an unbiased estimator of the true population value is an estimator whose long-range average—the average obtained from many repeated samples using the same procedures—centers around the true value of the population value being estimated. Unfortunately, we seldom know the true population value except where there has been a recent census. And a census is unlikely to include the exact items on which you need diagnostic or evaluation measures.

TYPES OF PROBABILITY SAMPLES

In the absence of true population scores, you can only hope to control bias from sampling error by controlling the sampling procedures. Continuing our earlier example, you want to be able to generalize your results to the total population of adolescents residing on the reservation. You will consider four types of probability sampling procedures: simple random sampling, stratified random sampling, systematic sampling, and cluster sampling. An overview of each type is presented in Table 10-1.

Simple Random Sample

A *simple random sample* is a probability sample in which every possible unit has an *equal chance* of being selected. This type of sample requires that all adolescents (the target population) have an equal probability of being selected for participation in the program. Given a complete and current list of adolescents registered as residents on the reservation, you could use a table of random numbers to select the potential participants.

Stratified Random Sample

Sex is a major factor (correlate or covariate) in dental health behavior, and both males and females comprise the adolescent population. So you may be concerned in a small sample that males and females might not be

TABLE 10-1 Summary characteristics of four types of probability samples

Type of Sample	Characteristic
Simple random sample	All sampling units have an equal probability of being selected. Sampling units are chosen through random numbers.
Systematic sample	Sampling unit is obtained by taking every *K*th case from a list of the population beginning with a number $X < K$, randomly selected.
Stratified random sample	Sampling units are randomly selected from each mutually exclusive stratum; may involve proportional or disproportional allocation.
Cluster sample	Sampling units are obtained by successive random sampling of superordinate and increasingly subordinate units, sets, or subsets that are heterogeneous with respect to population characteristics.

proportionately sampled, or you may wish to have a larger number of females sampled, to analyze their results in more detail. Stratified random sampling may be desirable for either of these two reasons.

A ***stratified random sample*** is a probability sample obtained by separating the population elements into discrete (nonoverlapping) groups, called *strata,* and then selecting a simple random sample, or a systematic sample, from each stratum. In our example, males and females would comprise the strata, and you could select a simple random sample, or systematic sample, of female adolescents and male adolescents. You would then have a stratified random sample.

Stratified random samples often have advantages over simple random samples. In general, there are three reasons why stratified random samples have a greater amount of information for a given cost: (1) data are usually more homogeneous within each stratum than within the population; (2) because of administrative convenience, the cost of conducting stratified random sampling is sometimes less than for random sampling; and (3) separate estimates can be obtained for each stratum without additional sampling (Mendenhall et al., 1971, p. 54). In short, stratified random sampling can be used to achieve greater accuracy for the same cost or less cost for the same degree of accuracy (Blalock, 1972, p. 516).

In order to carry out stratified random sampling it is important to define the strata so that each unit of the population appears in one and only one stratum.

Systematic Sample

Now let us assume that 1,200 adolescents reside on the Indian reservation, of whom 624 are boys and 576 are girls. If a random number table is used, it may be difficult to locate or define the 512th case or the 615th case by residential location, for example. You are concerned about this potential problem in a situation where the homes are not lined up on streets, and you wonder if there is a simpler way to draw a probability sample. You can consider a systematic sample for this kind of situation.

A *systematic sample* is a probability sample obtained by selecting at random one element from the first *K* elements and every *K*th element thereafter. Instead of using a random number table, or other methods of generating random numbers such as computers, you may simply generate or use an existing list of potential program participants and take every *K*th case, starting with a randomly selected individual. The random start for identifying the first individual to include is essential to meeting the technical requirements of a probability sample. If you wanted to select a sample of 60 subjects in the total population of 1,200, you would take every twentieth person encountered in the sample survey or program.

If the ordering used in compiling the list of adolescents or the order of encounter is random with respect to the variables of interest, a systematic sample is equivalent to a simple random sample. Under two conditions, however, systematic sampling may result in serious biases. First, the subjects to be selected may have been ordered so that a trend occurs (Blalock, 1972, p. 515). For example, if on the list of adolescents, adolescents with higher IQ scores are listed first, the position of the random start may affect the results. If the list is alphabetical, a systematic sampling of every *K*th name could result in an oversampling of Hispanics because of the clustering of Hispanic surnames around certain letters of the alphabet. Similarly, if the list is compiled as subjects appear at a sign-up site or at a clinic on their own initiative, then sampling only from an early period or only from a late period could result in an unrepresentatively motivated sample.

The second condition causing bias with a systematic sample occurs when the list from which the subjects are to be selected has some periodic or cyclical characteristic that corresponds to the sampling fraction generated by the *K*th case. For example, let us suggest that the list has been developed from classroom rosters organized according to academic standing of the students in each classroom, with an average of twenty students per class. If the sampling fraction also happens to be 1/20, you would generate a biased sample of high or low achievers, depending on the random starting point. To avoid this problem, you could slightly modify the sampling fraction—for example, to 1/21 or 1/19, shuffle the list, or use several separate random starts. For example, select ten people after the first random start, then choose another random number and select an additional ten people.

Cluster Sample

The fourth method of probability sampling starts with samples of groupings or "clusters" of people, patients, or beds randomly from the total population, rather than starting with individuals as the sampling units. In the *cluster method,* the total population is divided into clusters based on a natural or geographical grouping (i.e., classrooms, wards, clinics, clinic days, census tracts, neighborhoods, blocks, cities, counties), and then a predetermined number of clusters is randomly selected. All or some of the cases in the clusters may be used, depending on the needs of the evaluators. Elements (e.g., people) within a cluster are often contiguous or physically close together. Ideally, clusters are themselves heterogeneous so that you get the variability within each cluster. This approach contrasts with stratified random sampling, in which strata are internally homogeneous. With cluster sampling, subjects are chosen only from each randomly selected cluster, not from each population cluster identified.

If each cluster is subdivided into smaller clusters (e.g., states into cities, cities into hospitals), with random selections made from each subcluster, then this method is termed ***multistage cluster sampling***. Although usually less costly than other probability methods for large-scale surveys, cluster sampling is more prone to sampling errors than is the stratified random method, and usually is more difficult to treat statistically.

USING NONPROBABILITY SAMPLES

Up to now we have considered the situation in which a probability sample of adolescent residents is both desirable, from the scientific perspective of estimable sampling error, and feasible, from the administrative perspective of the people to be measured or the program to be evaluated. But what about those situations in which you are unable to obtain a probability sample?

Nonprobability samples are purposive samples obtained by sampling on a particular set of variables in the population. Sampling units are selected to obtain assumed target cases in the population. You seek to include certain subjects within the sampling frame that you think represent the various important elements, strata, or factions of the population. To obtain a homogeneous purposive sample, you sample on a narrow range of one selected variable—for example, women aged forty-five to fifty-five who obtained their annual Pap smears within the last six months. To obtain a heterogeneous purposive sample, you sample within a broader range on one variable represented—for example, adult women who obtained a Pap smear within the last six months. Samples obtained from purposive sampling have probabilities equal to 0 or 100 percent of being selected, or they have unknown probabilities of being selected.

Nonprobability samples are justified under five conditions:

1. When all the sampling units are not known or identifiable
2. When probability sampling may not yield the most sensitive results
3. When resources are restricted and the decision is between a nonprobability sample or no data at all
4. When the goal is to describe only the sample, not to generalize from the sample to a larger population
5. When the integrity of the randomly generated sampling units cannot be protected

These conditions are to be evaluated within each study; they are not to be accepted as imperative guidelines.

When a Complete Listing Is Unavailable

Probability sampling is not possible when all the elements to be sampled from the population are neither currently nor potentially identifiable. The sampling units must be identified in advance in order to generate a random list from these elements. For example, you may wish to sample health education experts in order to obtain their perceptions and projections about the future of health promotion in the next twenty years in the United States. You narrow further and select only those experts who are employed by federal or regional agencies. Let us assume that no list of such experts exists, nor can it be generated with any reasonable sense of inclusiveness or accuracy. Under these conditions, a probability sample is not feasible. Instead, you decide to sample federal and regional health education experts whose names you can readily obtain. If the elements of the population are amorphous, or extremely transient or unstable, it is also extremely difficult to enumerate or identify the elements of the population from which to draw the sample. In such instances of nonprobability sampling, the sampling procedure should be fully described so that the reader can discern the likely biases inherent in the data.

When Sensitive Measurement Is Wanted

Sometimes a probability sample does not yield the most sensitive measurements. As Chein (1976) pointed out, the choice may be between gathering more adequate information from a nonrepresentative sample, or less adequate information from a probability sample. Let us suppose you want to identify the attitudes toward cocaine held by local junior high students who use the drug. You realize that a small group of counselors have worked with many of the students who claim to use cocaine actively and have gained their trust. Through these counselors, you could obtain access to this subpopulation of junior high students. Admittedly, obtaining information on drug use from this subgroup of junior high students would not permit you to generalize your results to the population of local junior high students, nor to all users of cocaine in this age group. But the choice may be to collect superficial information from a probability sample of local students, or to collect more useful information from this subset of individuals.

When Resources Are Limited

Most often health education evaluation is carried out under restricted resources. You may not have time, staff, money, or access to program recruits to generate a probability sample in other than convenience samples. You must be wary of too passively accepting a nonprobability sample for your study, but your choice sometimes is between obtaining information that does not allow generalizability, or not obtaining information at all. The pressures toward nonprobability samples are particularly high when you are dealing with captive audiences, such as professional attendees at annual conferences, clinic patients waiting for their appointments, or schoolchildren visiting health fairs.

When the Purpose Is Not to Generalize the Results

Sometimes the evaluator does not want nor intend to generalize the obtained results to a larger population. The sample itself is considered the total population of interest. Information obtained from the study sample is limited to describing the current study sample. No reference is therefore made either to tests of statistical significance—that is, generalizing sample results to a larger population, nor to other hypothetical populations of which the sample is seen as a proxy. In such cases you describe the obtained results for the sample. This situation sometimes arises in agencies in which progress or status reports on program participants are written. No goal exists of generalizing the measures to anyone except those from whom the measures were obtained. The usual evaluation questions in such instances are whether the people received a specific service, and whether they demonstrated specific change or benefits from it.

When the Integrity of a Random Sample Is at Risk

Sometimes you have the resources as well as the list of sampling units needed to carry out a probability sample. But implementing a random sampling design demands attention to detail and precision throughout the entire process of assessing the sampling units and obtaining information from them. Errors can occur, and an initially well-conceived probability sampling procedure can thus lose its integrity. Random numbers may be incorrectly drawn; individual cases may be incorrectly substituted by staff for subjects who were supposed to be selected. Such field errors result in nonprobability samples for which level of precision or bias cannot be calculated. A carefully implemented quality control plan for the sampling procedure can maintain the sample's integrity. The availability of resources to implement a quality control plan can readily overcome the integrity problem as long as you believe in the ongoing need for both surveillance of and support for the staff who are implementing the sampling design. However, when the integrity of the sampling procedure cannot be protected you may prefer to abandon the attempt at probability sampling and instead choose a nonprobability sample.

TYPES OF NONPROBABILITY SAMPLES

Three models of nonprobability samples are relevant to the health education evaluator: (1) haphazard (convenience); (2) homogeneous, including rare element, extreme case, and strategic informant; and (3) heterogeneous, including quota, "representative," and modified systematic samples (see Figure 10-1).[1]

Haphazard Samples

Haphazard samples are samples selected fortuitously from whoever comes to hand. Sampling units are the available subjects most easily accessed by the evaluator. This type of sample is also known as a convenience or accidental sample.

Homogeneous Samples

Homogeneous samples focus on a narrow range of a variable and are of three types: extreme case, rare element, and strategic informant samples. Extreme case samples sample only extreme values of the variable under study, such as patients with very high blood pressure. Rare element samples sample variable values with low frequencies, such as patients with AIDS. They are also known as deviant case samples.

Strategic informant samples sample individuals in key positions or roles who are assumed to be exceptionally knowledgeable about the phenomena under study. This situation was described in the earlier example in which someone wanted to sample health education experts for their perceptions and projections about the future of health promotion in the United States.

Heterogeneous Samples

Heterogeneous samples focus on a broad range of a variable and are of three types: nontechnical "representative" samples, quota samples, and modified systematic samples. Nontechnical "representative" samples are those in which you attempt to select the broadest possible range of participants who are thought to reflect the underlying population. Because this type is not a probability sample in the technical sense of the term, you cannot claim it as a technically representative sample. "Representative" samples are typically referred to as "cross section" or "person on the street" samples and are used commonly by marketing firms.

1. See Smith (1975) for more models of nonprobability samples.

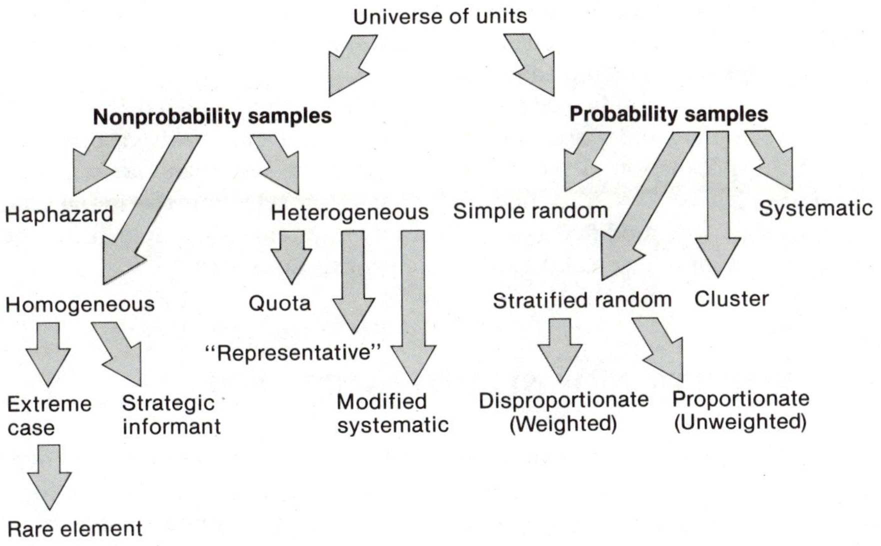

Figure 10-1 *Types of probability and nonprobability samples.*
Source: *Adapted from Smith (1975), p. 129. Originally adapted from Galtung (1967), p. 56.*

A quota sample is a subtype of the nonprobability "representative" heterogeneous sample. This subtype is sometimes identified as a stratified nonrandom sample. In quota sampling, the sampling units are chosen on the basis of the evaluator's knowledge of the salient population strata. The goal is to obtain certain proportions of "typical" people within each stratum. In other words, you sample a proportionate amount on either a single variable or on a combination of variables. When using the quota method, you divide the population into groupings on the basis of predetermined criteria or variables and then select a quota of cases from each grouping. The cases are not selected randomly and are frequently chosen on the basis of how convenient or available they are.

An example of the quota method is a study that assigns an interviewer a quota of patients to contact but allows the interviewer to select the number of patients in each of two or three symptom categories or the number per day. In household surveys, for example, each interviewer may be assigned a census tract and is allowed to visit the households in any order until he or she has interviewed twenty people with arthritis.

Historically quota samples evolved because interviewers were directed to obtain certain "quotas"—for example, so many subjects under forty years of age and unemployed; so many with education beyond the high school diploma. It is left to the discretion of the interviewer exactly which people are selected to fill the quota.

Another type of heterogeneous sample is the modified systematic sample. Sampling units are obtained by selecting every *K*th case from a list of the population beginning with a number less than the sampling fraction—that is, $X < K$. A nonrandom start on selecting the initial case distinguishes the modified (nonprobability) systematic sample from the systematic sample discussed earlier as a probability sample.

DETERMINATION OF NEEDED SAMPLE SIZE

Early in the design of the study you need to consider how many subjects to include in the sample in order to place a certain degree of confidence in the obtained results. The major objective in designing a sample is to obtain the highest level of precision for a given cost or to obtain a required level of precision for the lowest cost. This objective is accomplished first by selecting a particular type of sampling procedure and then determining the number of sampling units, most commonly individual respondents, to include in the sample. The sampling procedures were described earlier. Attention is now on selected factors that affect your decision about the necessary sample size. Five factors affect the needed sample size:

- Desired level of precision
- Variability in the most important outcome variable
- Sampling method used
- Subclass analyses
- Cost

Formulas and tables to determine the necessary sample size may be found in most statistics and research methodology texts (e.g., Mendenhall et al., 1971; Lazerwitz, 1968; Hays & Winkler, 1970; Dillman, 1978; Cochran, 1963; Kish, 1965; Sudman, 1976; Alwin, 1978). These formulas and tables are based on your prior decision about each of the factors just listed. Our comments will be restricted here to some general guidelines and issues surrounding the evaluator's decision about sample size.

Precision

Precision is the degree to which the values obtained from the sample mirror the actual existing values in the population. If data were available on the entire population measured by the same procedures, you would not need a sample, so precision is obviously a matter of statistical theory. Stated in another way, precision is the degree to which the values obtained from the sample approximate the value that would be obtained from a 100 percent count of the population. Precision is a measure of sampling reliability (Smith, 1975).

With probability samples, you can establish the degree of precision needed from the sample estimate in advance of actually collecting any data. You do so by deciding how wide or narrow the confidence interval should be around the sample estimate (e.g., plus or minus 200 calories) at a specified confidence level, typically 90 or 95 percent. This estimate, together with the considerations in the following paragraphs, affects the desirable sample size needed in order to obtain a sample estimate that stays within that preestablished confidence interval. Power analyses can also be calculated (Cohen, 1969). Lazerwitz (1968, p. 285) offers a clear example of calculating conservative sample sizes for simple random sampling.

Data Variability

In general, the more heterogeneous the population, the larger the sample needed in order to reflect the population more precisely. The formula for calculating the needed sample size for each sampling method is composed of an estimate of the variance in the outcome variable of greatest importance to the evaluation, as well as the preestablished levels for the desired confidence intervals. Sometimes, a homogeneous sample with respect to demographic characteristics such as age, sex, and income will nevertheless have a large variance in an outcome variable such as knowledge, attitude, behavior, or health variables. This characteristic will call either for a larger sample size or for a more restrictive definition or measure of the outcome variable.

Although greater variability increases the need for a larger sample, the discrepancy between sample estimates and the population values is not a simple linear (one-to-one) relationship. Rather, the discrepancy between values obtained from the sample and the precise population values is a function of the square root of the sample size (Waltz & Bausell, 1981).

Sampling Method

Each sampling plan has advantages. If homogeneous strata can be identified, stratified random sampling may offer the greatest level of precision for a given cost or the least cost for an established level of precision. Cluster sampling can be useful and cost-effective if the heterogeneity within clusters adequately reflects the variability in the population. Collecting data from large samples within a few of the randomly selected clusters is often less expensive than drawing a simple random sample from the entire population. Caution is in order; cluster sampling may inflate the standard error of the measures. This concern is best resolved with the help of a statistical consultant.

Subclass Analyses

So far our calculations of the needed sample size have assumed calculation of a total sample size. You also need to ask about sample size calculation for sample subclasses, such as cities or towns within a regional sample, neighborhoods within a city sample, males or females, age groups, or people exposed to alternative health education programs. If subclass analysis is important to the evaluation, then formulas for calculating total sample sizes should be applied to the desired subclass.

Cost Considerations

Once the sample size calculations are completed, you can translate the number of cases to be sampled into cost estimates. Total person-hours per interview plus travel, mailing costs or telephone costs, duration of data collection per case, and data coding and processing rates all need to be considered.

A one-hour period of data collection, including self-administered questionnaires, can often cost $50 per subject or more. Such cost considerations can help you decide whether you can afford the desired sample size. "Survey quality must not be permitted to suffer through such things as permitting a higher rate of interview refusals or poorer interviewer training" (Lazerwitz, 1968, p. 286). Recall that the objective of designing a sample is to obtain the highest level of precision for a given cost.

Additional Considerations

Unless you are working with a skilled statistician, your safest approach is to calculate sample size conservatively. A minimum sample size requirement can be set conservatively higher by assuming that the variance in your dependent variable is the maximum variance found in other studies of the variable.

You can also set your total sample size safely high by assuming that a sample size of 100 is needed before any sample mean or proportion can be considered to have an approximately normal distribution. When analyses are to be done by subclass, the same requirement of 100 cases for each subclass is needed. This situation occurs, for example, when you want meaningful cell sizes for breakdowns—for example, blood pressure by age by sex by ethnic group.

In general, the more heterogeneous the population, the larger will be the sample required to mirror accurately the population from which the sample is drawn or to detect a significant change or difference. This guide is true when the variables on which the population heterogeneity occurs, such as economic status or educational level, systematically covary with the variables under study, such as motivation to seek medical treatment.

DESCRIBING THE SAMPLE AND THE POPULATION

Whether using a probability or nonprobability sample, you are obliged to describe the characteristics of both the target population and the accessed sample. This description is done in order to know for whom the measures and the relationships obtain. First, summarize the defining properties of the population. Typically, these properties include salient demographic or background characteristics of the program participants or potential recruits. Of particular importance are those characteristics that are correlated with the evaluation's outcomes. Determining these relevant characteristics is neither easy nor obvious. A single table summarizing the age, sex, marital status, income, and education distribution of the sample and of the population is the usual method of description. Second, describe the sample so that when an area sample is drawn, the description includes the geographic boundaries enclosing the population.

Third, describe the procedures by which you did the randomization or other systematic sampling. These procedures may include coin tosses, random number tables, or computer-generated random numbers or assignments. You should also indicate whether the providers, recipients, and investigators of the education knew of the random assignment. This indication refers to "blinding" procedures. If both recipients and providers or investigators were blinded to whether subjects were in the experimental or control group, the study may be labeled a "double-blind" evaluation.

Your description of either the sample or the target population should be inclusive enough to permit others to judge the relevance of your findings to other populations or samples. Regardless of the sample's technical representativeness, it is always possible that other health educators and other evaluators may ask to what extent do the obtained results or measures potentially relate to their own settings.

SUMMARY

Early in the evaluation planning process you must decide whom to count as eligible for the program and whom to count as affected by it. These factors are relevant to sampling decisions. Before deciding, you can consider the potential contributions of the different types of probability and nonprobability samples that are your options.

Four types of probability samples and three types of nonprobability samples offer you a range of choices. The probability samples provide the only technically legitimate basis by which you can generalize information obtained from the sample to the larger population within a specified level of confidence. Probability samples are also the only legitimate basis for using inferential statistics. Simple random samples, stratified random samples, systematic samples, and cluster samples are examples of common probability samples used in health education studies. Despite their advantages, probability samples also have limitations. For example, simple random samples rely on a complete list of all potential study recruits that may not always be available. Systematic samples may inadvertently result in biased sampling if an ordering or periodicity occurs in the list or file from which subjects are drawn. Probability samples may not always yield the most sensitive measurements.

Nonprobability samples offer an alternative to probability sampling provided the health educator is knowledgeable about their limitations. Three types of nonprobability samples are relevant to the health education evaluator: haphazard (convenience); homogeneous, including rare element, strategic informant, and extreme case; and heterogeneous, including quota, "representative," and modified systematic. Nonprobability samples may be justified when all the sampling units are not known or identifiable; when probability sampling may not produce the most sensitive data; when resources are severely restricted; when there is no goal to generalize results beyond the sample; and when you cannot protect the integrity of a random sampling plan.

Factors that determine the needed sample size for any particular health education evaluation include the degree of precision required; the degree of variability in key variables to be measured; the magnitude of change considered "significant" for practical or policy decisions; and the number of subgroups on which the foregoing considerations need to apply.

PART FOUR

ANALYSIS AND INTERPRETATION

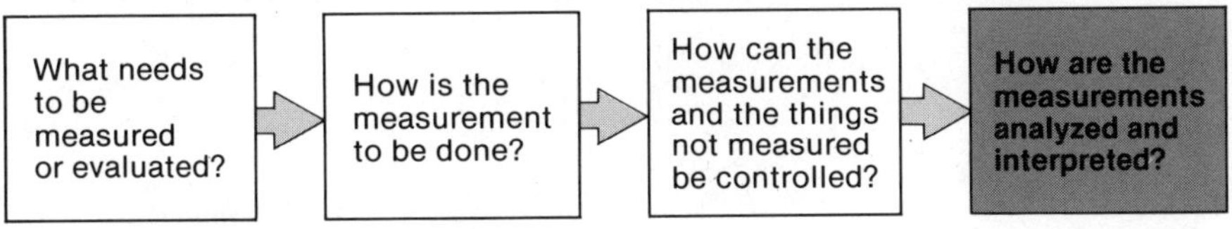

Analytic considerations bring us to the final chapters of this book. Analysis is the payoff for all your hard work in measurement, design, and sampling. Some see analysis as the most technical (and hence most important) aspect of research and evaluation, but no amount of statistical wizardry can substitute for a well-conceived, well-designed, validly and reliably measured, correctly sampled study.

If the tasks of conceptualization, measurement, design, and sampling from previous sections could meet the "highest" scientific standards, then analysis and interpretation would be a mere mechanical task of grinding out the data in tables and charts with a minimum of explanation. The reality of data collection in most health education and health promotion programs in democratic societies makes the highest standards something more than just scientific. They are also ethical, usually noninvasive, and they require voluntary participation of the subjects. These conditions, combined with some of the particular ways in which health education interacts with measurement and evaluation activities, complicate analysis and interpretation. In Chapter 11 we present some of the complexities. In Chapter 12 we conclude with a recommended sequence of computations or steps in analysis and interpretation that will answer most of the important questions to be asked of an evaluation.

Chapter 11

INTRODUCTION TO ANALYSIS AND INTERPRETATION

The most intimidating part of measurement and evaluation for most health professionals is facing the data and wondering what should be done with them. Analysis paralysis! How should the data be coded, processed, analyzed, and presented? Mathematics and statistics, especially in conjunction with computers, are the Waterloo of many health and social service workers who decided earlier not to pursue careers in engineering or basic sciences precisely because they disliked computational work. We hope to help overcome some of that disdain in this chapter by presenting concepts and procedures for analysis in verbal and graphic rather than numeric terms. This presentation cannot substitute for preparation in statistics, but you may be able to put statistics in clearer perspective after grasping the applications to analysis of health education measurements and evaluations presented in this chapter.

Even more onerous than analysis is interpretation. Unfortunately, most studies and evaluations in health education are short on analysis and long on interpretation. It is all too tempting to leap to conclusions from the first sign of light from the data produced by a superficial analysis, especially if the results are positive. Too frequently the interpretation goes far beyond what the data will support, inflating the meaning of weak relationships and explaining away contradictory evidence. The professional journals are filled with puffery, amounting to unfounded claims for health education and health promotion methods or materials.

The approaches to analysis and interpretation we present in this chapter, then, are not primarily concerned with better statistical technique, although that is sometimes needed. We emphasize more cautious and systematic interpretation. You will develop caution as you learn to recognize a number of pitfalls and fallacies that often result in misinterpretation of health education and health promotion outcomes. More systematic analysis and interpretation can come from the application of a

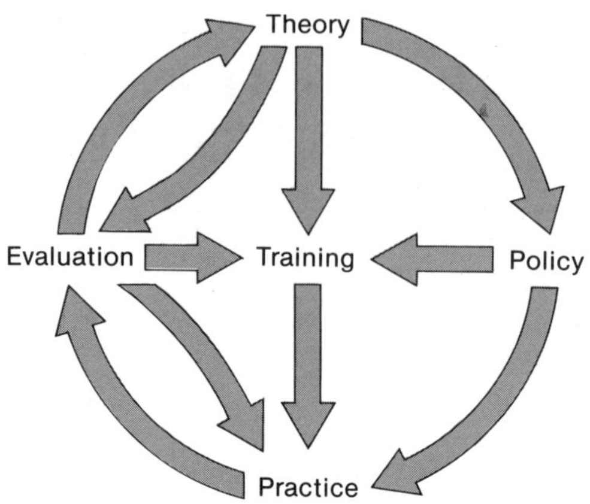

Figure 11-1 *The major paths of influence of evaluation, theory, policy, practice, and professional training.* Source: *Green (1980), p. 143.*

series of steps, definitions, and measures that we propose in the next chapter, including cost-effectiveness and cost-benefit analyses.

Few hard and fast rules of interpretation exist—only different ways of looking at data as evidence. Some are neither correct nor incorrect; some are sometimes purely a matter of interpretation. But you can avoid certain common errors, and learn some more direct and straightforward ways of getting answers to health education questions than are often applied in analyses of measures and evaluations.

ANALYSIS AND INTERPRETATION FOR WHAT?

Where are your results going to be useful or influential? This question—how and with whom your data might be used—is a primary guide to the level or extent of analysis required. The three main targets of most analyses are practice, theory, and policy. A secondary target influenced by data when any of the first three changes is professional training. Sometimes, especially when the evaluation or research is conducted by faculty of professional schools, the results will be applied first in professional training; later in practice, as the trainees go into the field; and much later, in theory and policy, as the professor's published results merge with others on the topic.

As seen in Figure 11-1, the prospects of influencing practice, theory, and training are direct, although by no means does this mean that the influence is simple. Policy, however, is a more distant target, which gen-

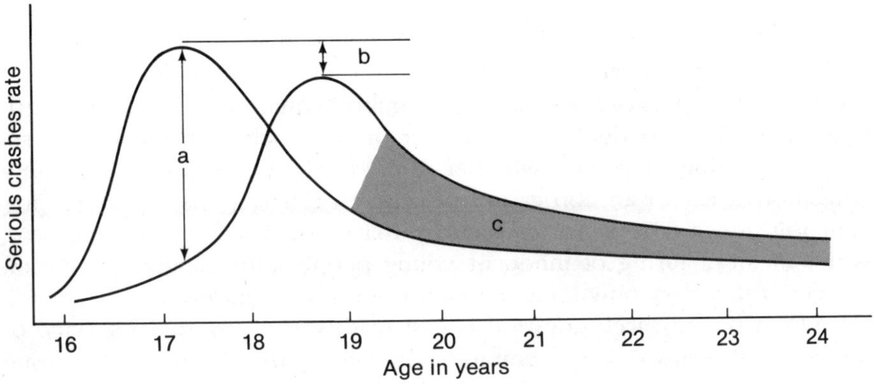

Figure 11-2 *Serious crashes rates by age for those receiving and not receiving high school driver education.* Source: *Green (1980b), p. 626.*

erally yields to the cumulative weight of evidence only after theory has been tested. For example, the evaluation of driver education has only recently revealed the limitations and even hazards of such education: It leads to earlier licensing of teenage drivers and consequently to more years of exposure to crashes, injury, and death (see Figure 11-2). Policy in some states has responded by eliminating driver training in high schools and in other states by raising the age of licensing (Robertson, 1980; Green, 1980b).

A CASE EXAMPLE: SCHOOL HEALTH EDUCATION*

The context, design, analysis, and interpretation of the evaluation study reported by Robertson (1980) can be understood best as part of a larger school of research and theory on injury control (Haddon, 1974; Haddon & Baker, 1978). The general position of this school of researchers is as follows:

> The tendency to attribute injuries to "human error" has nourished false hopes that they can be prevented through education. Neither public education campaigns nor driver education programs have yet been shown by scientific evaluation to justify the veneration and large budgets accorded them. Many injuries (including highway injuries) result less from lack of knowledge than from failure to apply what is known. (Baker & Dietz, 1979, pp. 58–59).

*This section was first published by Lawrence W. Green as "To Educate or Not to Educate: Is That the Question?" in the *American Journal of Public Health* 70(6): 625–626, 1980.

From this perspective, the research question in such studies is not whether health education, safety education, or driver education achieve their primary purpose—namely, the improvement of knowledge, attitudes, and skills conducive to healthier or safer behavior. Rather, the research question becomes whether the social act of providing safety education leads to an abrogation of other social responsibilities to prevent injuries; a false sense of security that enough has been done; and, worst of all, a luring of innocent young people into dangerous acts on the belief that they now know enough to protect themselves.

When the research question is cast in this way, any social service or humane intervention is vulnerable to the finding that, by itself, it is insufficient to achieve any lasting benefit. Without attending to the social, economic, organizational, and environmental circumstances surrounding a given health problem, any single intervention designed to contribute toward the reduction of the problem will fail by that criterion. It is possible, then, to call any social program into question on the grounds that it does not solve the ultimate social problem to which it is addressed, especially if the existence of the program precludes, discourages, or detracts from some other program or component of a comprehensive program that would be more effective.

In Robertson's analysis, the program in question is driver education for high school students. The complementary strategy from which the existence of driver education detracts is the restriction of teenage driving by delayed licensure of sixteen- to seventeen-year-olds. Robertson advocates the abolition of driver education in high schools on the grounds that its existence encourages early licensure and discourages the legal restriction of teenage driving. The same reasoning could advocate the abolition of sex education in schools if it were found that teenage pregnancies increased in the absence of family planning services for teenagers. The opponents of sex education and drug education have used this line of reasoning to resist the introduction of these subjects in schools and have pointed to trend data on teenage pregnancies and drug use similar to the "serious crashes" reported by Robertson.

The response to such arguments and data cannot be to deny the potential short-range effect of driver education, sex education, or drug education leading to an interest and often an attempt to experiment with driving, sex, or drugs. Education of any kind in schools seldom can be defended or promoted entirely on the basis of its short-range effects on behavior, except as necessary preparation for the next phase of education and experience. Age-graded experiences in school and in society must be anticipated by the educational system and appropriate steps taken within that system to prepare children with the knowledge and skills necessary for their informed and responsible coping with those experiences (Green,

Heit, Iverson, Kolbe, & Kreuter, 1980). If the critical age of intensified peer pressure for smoking, for example, is thirteen, then schools should include some education on peer pressure and smoking at age twelve or earlier to predispose and enable most students to resist peer pressure for smoking and to reinforce the decisions of some not to smoke. An increase in smoking at age thirteen is inevitable, some of it possibly caused by the interest in experimenting with smoking aroused by the education. But the schools cannot abrogate their responsibility to fulfill their role in providing students with the knowledge and skills they need to face the decisions and experiences that will confront them in the year ahead, and in laying the educational foundation on which longer-term learning and experiences can build (Green, Kreuter, Deeds, & Partridge, 1980).

The question, then, is not *whether* the schools should educate, but rather how to supplement the classroom experiences with the appropriate services and safeguards in the community to reinforce and support the positive effects of the education and to offset some of the inevitable negative effects. For driver education, the community must coordinate the timing and enforcement of educational services and legal restrictions. If it is the judgment of a community that it must permit sixteen- to seventeen-year-olds to drive, for economic or other reasons, then that community must strengthen its high school driver education and its supplementary testing and enforcement procedures. If it is decided by a community that it can afford not to permit sixteen- to seventeen-year-olds to drive, then driver education can be deferred to age eighteen and the laws restricting licensure and driving must be modified or enforced. Either way, the community has no choice but to educate its young citizens in matters critical to their survival and development as responsible and competent participants in society.

Finally, the case for or against a particular component of high school education cannot be made entirely on the basis of its short-range effects, even if the community can offset the negative short-range effects with added health services and legal enforcement. The case must consider also the longer-range implications of including or excluding a subject in the high school curriculum. In the case of driver education, short-range evaluations such as Robertson's indicate clearly that the community should delay the licensure of teenage drivers. They do not show how the private market for driver education will adjust in the longer term to the change in supply and demand, nor do they show how the "serious crash" rates will evolve over time for those who receive earlier driver education and those who are licensed after age eighteen without a high school course in driver education. It is a reasonable assumption that long-range curves for those who do or do not receive high school driver education might follow the two plots projected in Figure 11-2.

The first curve, which rises sharply in serious crash involvement at ages sixteen and seventeen, is attributable to high school driver education *and* earlier licensure that it permits. The second curve is the expected curve for people who do not receive high school driver education, more of whom will obtain licenses at ages eighteen and nineteen than at sixteen and seventeen, so their relative inexperience and possible lack of training show up with higher crash involvement at age nineteen and onward. The data reported by Robertson show us only the difference represented by *a* in the figure. He refers to this as the "total effect" of high school driver education on serious crash involvement. In fact, the net effect two years later might actually be no more than the difference represented by *b* in the hypothetical plot.

But in the long run, the more experienced and presumably better trained drivers who received formal preparation in high school might be expected to have slightly lower rates until the cumulative difference represented by *c* would eventually exceed *b,* leaving a net benefit from high school driver education. The important lesson from Robertson, then, is not that we should eradicate driver education in high school, but that we could prevent some of *a* by disallowing licensure at ages sixteen and seventeen.

As health professionals we are limited in our perspective on the role of education in society when we attempt to use the schools as an isolated tool in our clumsy attempts to solve social problems. The schools will continue to perform their function of educating young people. Communities must coordinate that function with other interventions—some educational, some legal, and some economic—to solve social and health problems.

DECISION LEVELS

Evaluation usually seeks to estimate both the effectiveness of a particular program and the applicability of the results to other potential beneficiaries or consumers of the program. As such, evaluation research concerned with external validity attempts to move beyond description to a higher level of inference; it moves away from (1) summary measures (e.g., average weight loss) relevant to an isolated or unique audience toward (2) the application of inferential statistics that allow the obtained results to be generalized to a larger population of potential treatment subjects. "Unless inference can be generalized beyond the data at hand, a study is of little value to others" (Houston, 1972). At this level, evaluation is no longer viewed as a benign social science activity but as a politically supported and motivated endeavor geared eventually to influencing rational policy making and social planning (Freeman, 1974).

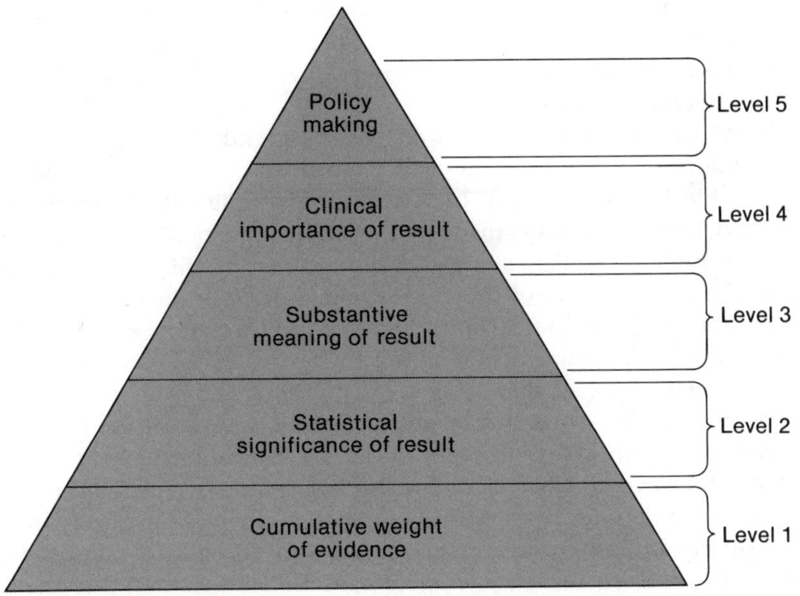

Figure 11-3 *A hierarchy of decision levels in health education evaluation.* Source: *Green & Lewis (1981), p. 52.*

If we accept this framework in health education evaluation, a hierarchy of decision levels emerges (see Figure 11-3). At the base of all recommendations or decisions, the health education evaluator might initially be persuaded by the weight of similar evidence that accumulates from a number of studies (Green & Lewis, 1981). These studies may suffer from designs that do not permit statistical inference, but the collective results do permit the formation of a general hypothesis that relates program components to behavioral changes or health outcomes.

At the second level, the evaluator would like to have a *statistically* significant association between the proposed intervention and the expected outcomes. At the next level of decision making, the evaluator derives *substantive meaning* from the obtained statistical result. Meaning comes from two sources: (1) a theoretical understanding of the process by which the result was obtained and (2) an understanding of the numbers reported in the statistical results. A correlation of .25 may be statistically significant with a large enough sample but may not be substantively meaningful. At an even higher level of decision making, the evaluator must question whether the result has practical significance: "Is the result *clinically* important?" At this point a catalog of implicit and explicit standards of acceptability exists for making this decision. Lastly, at the most onerous level, the question becomes "What social program policies should be recommended on the basis of the observed effect or impact?" This question taps *social* significance.

The decision levels in this hierarchy are intended to be cumulative—that is, built on decisions made at the more basic levels. This cumulativity is the ideal state, however. In actuality, most policy decisions in health education have had to be made without the statistical base. Policy has also been built on statistically significant results in which little or no assessment has been made of the clinical importance of these results, much less the social significance. The evaluator's interpretation of the data can and should include comments on all five levels identified in the hierarchy.

Our perspective is that advice on policy requires evidence of the clinical significance or the social and economic impact of the changes in behavior or health status brought about by educational programs. One must be clear about what is valued by society or by the consumers of our recommendations. Even with documented changes in socially or clinically significant outcomes, asserting that interventions caused those changes requires an understanding of causal chains linking the interventions with the changes. Finally, theoretically plausible linkages must be backed by empirical evidence that those linkages are not based on statistical chance, historical fluke, or regional idiosyncracy. Here the scientific rules of evidence must be weighed against the realities of programmatic and measurement difficulties in evaluation research. Ideally, the process is not antagonistic, but addresses the dilemma of obtaining valid data with sensitivity to the constraints of practice.

ANALYSIS AS DETECTIVE WORK

Evaluation research is seldom equivalent to null hypothesis research. Null hypotheses are characteristic of more basic educational research in which a single or small number of definitive tests are made on the experimental effect of an educational technique or method. In such studies, random assignment to treatment or control groups often allows the investigator to assume pretreatment equality of the two groups. The experimental treatment and the intrasession history have both been tightly controlled. Data analysis in such studies is thereby reduced to a small set of tests of selected null hypotheses. For example, knowledge gain scores will show no difference for treatment as compared to control groups.

An evaluator's task in more complex health education or health promotion programs is not so easy as calculating statistical tests associated with a single or small number of null hypotheses. The conditions under which you are able to assign individuals to treatment and control or comparison groups often cannot be blindly relied on to equate the treatment and the control groups. One of the first tasks under such conditions is to examine the equivalence of the treatment and comparison or control groups on the preintervention levels of the outcome or impact variable. If pretest measures are available on both groups, you need to determine how the groups compare on their distributional properties, including measures of central tendency. Recall that the goal of experimental or quasi-experimental designs is to equate the treatment and control or comparison groups as much as possible at the outset, especially on the outcome or impact variable of greatest interest. Covariate analysis may need to be used to manage nonequivalent treatment and control or comparison groups (Elashoff, 1969).

When process evaluation data are available, the evaluator examines the level of program implementation for all participants. If every participant received (or at least had an equal opportunity to receive) every part of the program, the detective work is simplified. If, however, different participants were offered different parts—but not all—of the program, the evaluator needs to consider either (1) making subsample analyses for groups receiving different parts of the program or (2) developing an indicator of the level of program implementation for use in the data analyses and interpretation.

Despite the known heterogeneity of our health education program participants, evaluators are often inclined to examine the total group's response to the program rather than the response of systematically identified subgroups. This inclination may have unfortunate consequences. Total group scores used as the outcome or impact measure may camouflage the differences in program effect achieved in subsamples of the program participants. Adolescent boys, for example, may be expected to respond very differently to a general nutrition program than do adolescent girls. Tests can be made to examine the degree of similarity or differences in the outcome or impact variables for such subsamples. The t-test for independent samples can be calculated or tests of statistical independence can be computed for the subsamples—for example, the Mann-Whitney U test.[1] Sometimes physical inspection of the data in the absence of statistical calculation reveals differential effects between the subsamples of program recipients.

1. Statistical tests are offered merely as examples, not as exhaustive options. Clearly, you will examine the assumptions of any statistical test to see if the data from any particular study are able to meet those assumptions and, if not, that the statistical test is robust enough to handle the violations of the assumptions.

Throughout the analyses, the evaluator is guided by the sympathetic critic stance introduced earlier, in Chapter 1. Rather than trying to prove that the program worked or did not work, the evaluator is looking to see what happened, to whom it happened, and how it happened. These questions ultimately force the evaluator into a veritable Socratic debate. Initially, molar-level questions are raised about the broadstroke impact of the health education program. These broadstroke questions are eventually supplemented by more refined or conditionalized questions. Let us take an example. Young adolescents from ten urban junior high schools participate in five 1½-hour sessions on healthy nutritional intake with particular attention on low salt, low saturated fat, and low cholesterol intake. Five comparison group junior high schools received the pretest and posttest scores over a five-day interval. The program is completed, and the evaluators want to know if their program "worked." Initially they examine the pretest knowledge and behavior scores of the treatment and the comparison groups. They want to see if the two groups are similar on the scores. They further examine the scores for boys versus girls (to detect gender-specific differences), by school district (to detect potential regional influence), and by grade-point average (to detect achievement-related differences). If differences are found in these subsamples, the evaluators can analyze the data for each subsample, thereby statistically separating subjects for the analyses. The evaluators may also choose to use gender, school district, or grades as covariates in subsequent analyses, thereby controlling for the potential effects of these covariates on the outcome or impact variables of interest.

REASONS FOR FAILING TO ACHIEVE THE STANDARD OF ACCEPTABILITY

An evaluation may fail to detect the acceptable level of change (see Figure 11-4) for three possible reasons. First, the performance of the program may be inadequate to set into motion the causal chain that links program characteristics to outcomes or impact. In this case, the program may or may not be sound in theory or concept, but we observe no effect or an inadequate effect, because the program was poorly administered or poorly implemented. The second possibility is that the theory on which the program was based is inadequate, in which case we may have conducted the program properly but failed to set the necessary determinants into motion. We may have aimed at the wrong determinants or designed the wrong interventions to influence them. The third possibility is a measurement failure. In this failure to detect effects, the program might have been adequately conducted and appropriately targeted, and may even have

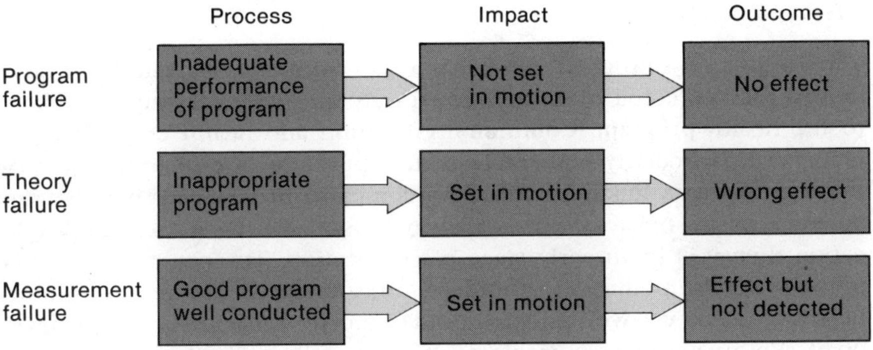

Figure 11-4 *Three ways in which program effect may fail to be detected in a program evaluation.* Source: *Extended from Weiss (1972), p. 38. Copyright © 1972 by Prentice-Hall, Inc. Used with permission.*

achieved the expected results, but we have inadequate measures, or insufficient sample size, to detect the changes sought. Details of these three types of failures in evaluation follow.

Program Failure

Sometimes the program was not fully delivered or, if delivered, did not adhere to the protocol specified by the program planners. Program failure of this nature includes misappropriation of resources necessary to carry out the program, implementation of only part of the program, poor implementation because of inadequate staff efforts or poor staff qualifications, subversion of the program at the site, failure to deliver enough effort to reach a threshold level necessary for change, and program implementation to fewer than the total of the projected recipients. Poor training, supervisor support, or morale of the staff responsible for delivering a program usually results in program failure.

The program evaluator could claim with authority that the lack of effect was *not* the fault of the program. In this case the program was not technically implemented. However, the evaluator would *not* be free to claim or project actual positive effects as if the program had been properly implemented. Program effect could be estimated for the case in which only part of the target population received the projected program. Potential sampling bias would then have to be assessed. The program, while theoretically valid, may not be practical. It is important to give program personnel or administrators information on the factors that caused the faulty program implementation.

Theory Failure

The absence of a program effect may result from "theory failure." In other words, the projected or hypothesized outcomes are not causally related to the health program. Continuing education and health education programs are particularly vulnerable to this problem of evaluation, because the logic or data linking medical outcomes to professional practice and personal health behavior are not always sound. Furthermore, health education theory is in an early stage of codification. The nature of the relationship between educational interventions and professional or consumer behavior is not yet well understood. Diagnostic tools are not well developed. We further discuss problems of theory failure in a later section.

Measurement Failure

The failure to detect a program effect may be a measurement failure. Here, the health education program may have been effectively implemented, the theory relating program to outcome is reasonably sound, but no acceptable level of effect is documented.

Evaluation research seldom documents a "slam-bang" or landslide effect. The evaluator therefore almost always faces the problem of specifying what could have interfered with success, in cases of modest success or failure. In attributing the absence of a program effect to one of the three sources (program failure, theory failure, or measurement failure), the evaluator is actually noting areas where further research and evaluation are needed, as well as indicating guidelines for interim policy and management decisions.

Evaluators can claim with authority either that they *observed* no effect or that they *observed* a specific amount of effect. They may also discuss with authority the level of confidence they have in their observation instruments and their measurement and sampling procedures. Such a discussion should include the psychometric properties of the instruments, the adequacy of the sampling design and sample size, the limitations of the data collection procedures themselves, and other related issues that constrain the firmness of conclusions and recommendations.

However, they cannot claim categorically that a program should be rejected unless they have clearly ruled out measurement failure. The absence of effect in the case of measurement error is not a case of program or theory failure. It is related to the classical Type II error problem—failure to reject the null hypothesis when it is false or, to put it more positively, failure to detect a true difference. Later in this chapter we reconsider this problem of failing to detect a true difference.

If measurement error is suspected, the program evaluator may speculate about a "missed" effect. The failure may in fact be spurious. The measurements may not have been sensitive enough to document the impact. Investigator bias in measurement or subject bias in nonrandom assignment to experimental and control groups may have interfered.

Sometimes applicable and reliable instruments do not exist. Sometimes, as Weiss (1972) points out, "for all the assiduity of his research, the evaluator finds no measures directly relevant to the subjects he wants to study." As Houston (1972) elaborates, variation among units and unreliability of measurement obscure the detection of large changes; large increments themselves are difficult to achieve.

In a composite index of multiple measures, upward and downward movement of the separate indicators may cancel each other out, producing a net effect of zero, when in fact considerable movement has occurred. Measurement error may occur as a result of timing: long-term effects are affected by decay; short-term effects may not allow sufficient time for impact to occur. Reliance on single measures is weak because each is measuring only a fraction of the larger construct (e.g., Etzioni & Lehman, 1967), such as patient adherence, preventive health behavior, or lifestyle.

Although the danger just discusssed (of measurement error confounding results) concerns reporting unfavorably on socially useful programs, the evaluator is not free to report *favorably* on the health program unless the evaluation results unequivocally reach at least one of the standards of acceptability set down by the program objectives. The absence of an effect precludes this attainment. Then one can only discuss—with qualifications—why the potentially useful program might justify further consideration and testing.

HOW MUCH CHANGE IS ENOUGH?

The results of measurement and evaluation do not automatically influence theory, policy, or practice. The practitioner would be naive to believe they do; the researcher would be irresponsible to claim that they should. Results of diagnostic studies merely document the extent and distribution of needs and suggest targets for intervention. Results of formative evaluations merely document quality and progress of interventions. And results of summative evaluation studies merely document the amount of change, if any, that is observed or inferred as a result of the program. This documented level of need or change—or the absence of it—demands systematic critique before theory, policy, and practice can build on the results.

How much change is enough depends, first, on the willingness to wait for change. That willingness is a matter of patience, urgency, and sample size. Second, adequate change depends on the amount required to satisfy a specific need or expectation, which is a matter of acceptability. And third, how much change is enough depends on how much confidence can be placed in the observed change, which is a matter of measurement.

Besides the amount of change, the other determinants of the applicability of evaluation findings to theory and practice are the usual rules of evidence and the circumstances that make the findings more or less generalizable to other situations. Evaluation studies carried out under highly controlled, heavily financed, or highly talented staffing circumstances, including expensive clinical trials, often have less credibility with most practitioners and policymakers than do studies that emerge from the circumstances of normal educational practice. Such circumstances may suppress the magnitude of effects, so we are left again with concern over the amount of change. This section, then, addresses the question "How much change is enough?"

The Fallacy of Equating Statistical Significance with Practical Significance

At the most basic level, analysis of statistical data seeks to establish statistical significance. Let's examine significance first in simple descriptive statistics, then in evaluative data.

With descriptive measures from a sample of patients, students, or other subjects, the term *statistical significance* refers to the range of possible average or percentage scores around the obtained average or percentage that might be the real average or percentage for the population from which the sample was drawn. If the variance of scores obtained in the sample was great, then the statistical confidence interval or range will be great, leaving the statistic with little *practical* significance.

For example, if a sample of only two diabetic patients were drawn from a clinic population and you gave both of them a test of knowledge about diabetes, one might score high (say 50 correct answers) and the other might score low (say 10 correct answers). The mean score would be 30, but can you make any practical use of this statistic? Because the two scores were so divergent, the variance and standard deviation (square root of the variance) will be high. Thus the confidence interval or range of probable mean scores for the population will be so large that you cannot generalize the mean score of 30 to the clinic's population of diabetics. So you cannot say with any confidence that the average diabetic patient in this clinic will score 30 on this knowledge test.

The most efficient way to reduce the variance in scores, and thereby narrow the confidence interval for any statistic such as a mean score, is to increase the sample size. This increase gives you a more confident statistic. Then your mean score for the sample can be ascribed to the population, "give or take" a smaller margin of error. This margin of error is

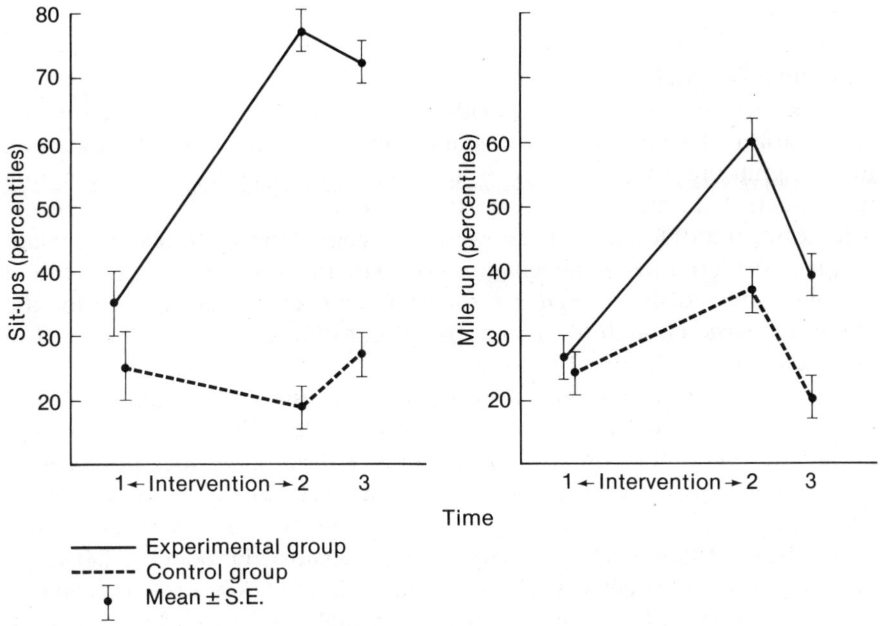

Figure 11-5 *Sit-up and mile run scores for experimental and control groups at Times 1–3.* Source: *Duncan, Boyce, Itami, & Puffenbarger (1983), p. 470. Used by permission of the American School Health Association.*

called the *standard error of the mean* and is usually expressed as a number for the mean followed by plus or minus its S.E., or standard error ($\overline{X} \pm S.E.$).

The smaller the confidence interval, the better. A wide margin of error makes the mean score of 30 virtually meaningless. If you increase the size of the sample, the result could become as "significant" as 30 ± 1.

The other way in which a standard error may be usefully expressed is in a graph with a band around the mean scores on a trend line or frequency polygon, as illustrated in Figure 11-5. This figure shows two lines, one for the experimental group and one for the control groups. If the confidence intervals overlapped, we could not be confident about the significance of the differences between them.

Now let us consider another problem, that of statistical significance versus practical significance. This problem plagues evaluations. It is possible to make the standard error so small with a large sample in both experimental and control groups that the confidence intervals would not overlap even for a very small real difference between the two groups.

Therefore, it is possible to get a statistically significant difference between two groups even when the practical or clinical importance of the difference is trivial.

The best safeguard against both the expense and the possible misinterpretation of such excessive sample sizes leading to results that look more significant than they are is to decide in advance of the sampling how much difference will be considered socially, clinically, or practically significant. If a difference of ten points on your knowledge test, for example, is considered just sufficient to make patients safer or more capable of following their diabetic regimen, then you can set the sample size for the study just large enough to detect a ten-point difference at a given level of confidence (see Chapter 10, on sampling).

Your sample size, however, must be set on the basis of only one outcome variable. At the analysis stage of most evaluations, you will be looking at the differences on several variables. So sampling does not protect you from the possible error of reading practical significance into statistical significance on those other variables. Your best defense against this fallacy is good judgment. Your best defense against the possible fallacy of equating *your* judgment with good judgment is to seek a consensus among several experts on how much change is enough. Once you have this consensus, you can then analyze the results of an evaluation with confidence that those results achieving both practical and statistical significance are indeed meaningful.

The Fallacy of Equating Effectiveness with Efficiency

One further extension of the "good judgment" fallacy may occur if you read policy significance into practical significance or clinical significance. In health education what works best for some students, patients, or other learners in a controlled situation often is not appropriate for larger populations because it costs too much. You can demonstrate change in almost any attitude or behavior if you spend enough time and effort with the learner, but such time and effort are not available in the usual classroom, clinic, worksite, or community situation where health education and health promotion normally take place.

In addition to effectiveness, you must also consider cost in most evaluations if your results are to be useful for others. The combination of effectiveness measures with cost measures leads to cost-effectiveness analysis, or efficiency analysis. The term *cost-effectiveness* applies to those analyses in which costs are measured in monetary terms. The more generic term is *efficiency analysis*. It applies to any measure of input, including monetary cost, time, number of personnel required to get the job done or to achieve the effect, equipment or materials required, and other resources consumed by the program. All these resources, of course, cost money in one way or another, but it is sometimes difficult to measure all the inputs in monetary terms. Efficiency analysis allows you to state results in terms of hours per service delivered, or number of contacts per outcome achieved. Cost-effectiveness analysis expresses these results in dollars (or francs, or yen) per effect.

We discuss these distinctions and procedures to calculate effectiveness, efficiency, and cost-effectiveness more concretely in the next chapter. Here we are concerned with understanding how the concepts of effectiveness and efficiency or cost-effectiveness can help you analyze and interpret evaluation results.

By aggregating and standardizing health education, rather than individualizing and tailoring it for each potential learner, health educators can achieve economies of scale at the expense of some effectiveness at the individual level. This idea is the implicit theory behind public health education. The cost per unit of production per person educated, or per message disseminated, can be reduced through aggregation (e.g., by using the mass media, rather than by counseling). The goal in educational innovation is to design standardized materials, methods, and procedures that can be produced or implemented on a larger scale (and therefore at lower unit prices) without sacrificing a proportionate amount of effectiveness inherent in more individualized, personalized, and flexible methods and procedures.

The usual form of the economy of scale curve is illustrated in Figure 11-6. The vertical axis represents the cost per unit of education. The horizontal axis represents various ways of increasing the scale of educational production, all three of which usually result in reduced effectiveness in terms of behavioral change achieved. Effectiveness is not represented in Figure 11-6 except as it tends to be greater at the individualized rather than at the aggregated end of educational methods.

Aggregating Learners. An example of an educational innovation with adults that achieved the economy of scale represented by the difference between the two curves in Figure 11-6 was group discussion and decision. This innovation was first demonstrated in nutrition education by Lewin (1947), in breast cancer self-examination by Bond (1956), and more recently in reducing asthmatics' emergency room use and dependency (Green et al., 1977). The beauty of this approach was that it achieved economy of scale through aggregation while *increasing* rather than decreasing effectiveness. The group, if properly constituted and guided, proved to be more powerful as an agent of change in health behavior than were the individualized exhortations of doctors and nurses. Such groups were also more effective than similarly aggregated education delivered through lectures.

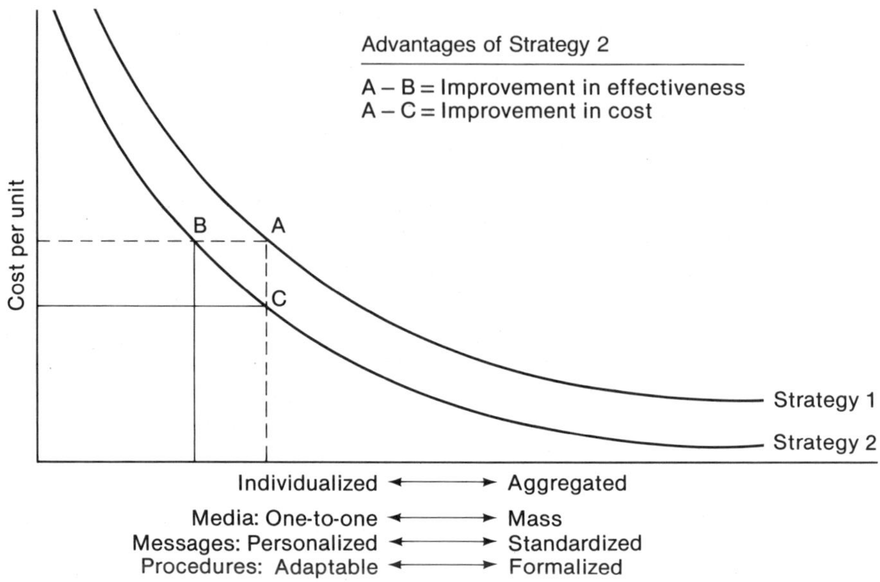

Figure 11-6 *Economy of scale as applied to health education program components.* Source: *Adapted in part from Oettinger & Zapol (1972), p. 157. Used by permission of* Teachers College Record.

Types of Educational Personnel. Another example of an educational innovation that might fit the curve of Figure 11-6 for educational strategy 2, relative to the curve for educational strategy 1, is the introduction of indigenous health education aides to carry out health education (Strategy 2) in place of health professionals (Strategy 1). The cost would be lower at any level of aggregation (A–C), and the effectiveness might be improved at any level of cost (A–B) because the indigenous aide would be able to communicate more personalized messages (Green, 1975, 1979a). For example, Cuskey and Premkumar (1973) demonstrated that a medium-size drug treatment center serving about 1,000 addicts could save up to $100,000 annually if ex-addict counselors were used in place of professional counselors with graduate-level training. Even better than paid indigenous workers for some educational purposes are patients themselves as counselors, recruiters, or reinforcers of other patients. Fisher (1974) experimentally demonstrated that family-planning patients given postcards to pass on to friends achieve recruitment rates at approximately one-third the cost per new appointment in comparison with the next most cost-effective method. Fletcher (1973) demonstrated the cost-effectiveness of a clerk in the emergency room assigned to call and remind patients of their return appointments. Any strategy that is successful in reducing broken appointments must have considerable appeal to hospital administrators, and to staff concerned with continuity of care.

Technologies and Specialized Personnel. Other educational technologies that might be expected to meet the criteria of a cost-effective innovation as defined by the difference between the two curves in Figure 11-6 are (1) programmed instruction and (2) cable television. Teaching machines, or "computer-assisted education," as one kind of programmed instruction, can achieve an economy of scale in production while preserving the effectiveness of personalized and adaptable messages and procedures. The marketing problems associated with these technologies are beginning to be overcome with microcomputers, which should allow the unit cost to be low enough to achieve the promised economies of scale (Oettinger, 1969; Deeds, 1973).

However, the tendency of some health administrators to invest in expensive hardware rather than in salaries of educational personnel has been based on the sincere but misguided assumption that audiovisual technology is as effective educationally as it is attractive. As concluded by Campeau (1974, p. 31) from her extensive and scholarly review of experimental studies evaluating audiovisual media in adult education:

> What is most impressive about the formidable body of literature surveyed for this review is that it shows that instructional media are being used extensively, under many diverse conditions, and that enormous amounts of money are being spent for the installation of very expensive equipment. All indications are that decisions as to which audiovisual to purchase, install, and use have been based on administrative and organizational requirements and on considerations of cost, availability, and user preference, not on evidence of instructional effectiveness.

The use of expensive hardware in patient education can be approached on the same purchasing basis as other overpriced medical hardware such as kidney dialysis units—that is, on the basis of regionalization of resources. Health education centers could be established to serve several schools, worksites, hospitals, and clinics through the pooling of their resources. Under these circumstances, a total decrease in training time and in provider-patient ratios or teacher-student ratios for all the hospitals, schools, or worksites can be translated into cost savings to the system (Thompson, 1973). This situation obtains when computer-assisted instruction (CAI) or other specialized educational resources can be used for the education and training of professionals as well as patients or students whose special learning needs cannot be met by routine clinical or classroom procedures. Evaluation of CAI and other educational technologies in schools has led to essentially the same conclusions (Butman, 1973; Kreuter & Green, 1978).

Variety in Educational Approach. Another aspect of the economy of scale concept in analysis and interpretation is that what works for some learners or patients does not work for all. The educational strategy, medium, or message that supports behavior conducive to health in some people may fail with others. As with prescribing drugs, different "dose" responses and side effects also arise with health education. This variability poses a specific set of problems for evaluation of health education programs, and calls for a degree of skill in educational planning that is not to be expected of every teacher, doctor, and nurse. We generally recommend, therefore, that the person assigned overall responsibility for educational planning have graduate training, preferably in health education. As with expensive hardware, this recommendation often requires the sharing of a specialist on a regional or multihospital basis.

In addition to the principle of "different strokes for different folks," health education programming also calls for shifting emphasis and technique within a group or population over time. These principles can be seen in terms of benefits in programs requiring sustained behavior over time (e.g., Mullen & Culjat, 1980).

The Fallacy of Assuming a Constant Rate of Progress

A third mistake you can avoid in analyzing and interpreting evaluation results is expecting the rate of change to be the same at all points during and after the program. Common sense tells you a steady change rate is not likely in health education, yet this assumption is implicit in many analyses and in most interpretations of health education results. The mistake takes the form of measuring the impact or outcomes of a program at one point in time and concluding that the program failed because the result was not as high as expected. It also takes the form of concluding that the program succeeded because the result *was* as high as expected. Both interpretations can be wrong if the timing of the impact or outcome measure was too soon or too late.

Workers in a variety of fields widely acknowledge that the rate at which innovations are adopted varies with the time from the first introduction of the innovation to its ultimate diffusion in a population. In the early stages of its introduction, a new idea or practice will catch on slowly. During this phase, innovators and early adopters gradually endorse the new idea or product and begin to influence others to do so. As more and more people accept the innovation, more and more people are available

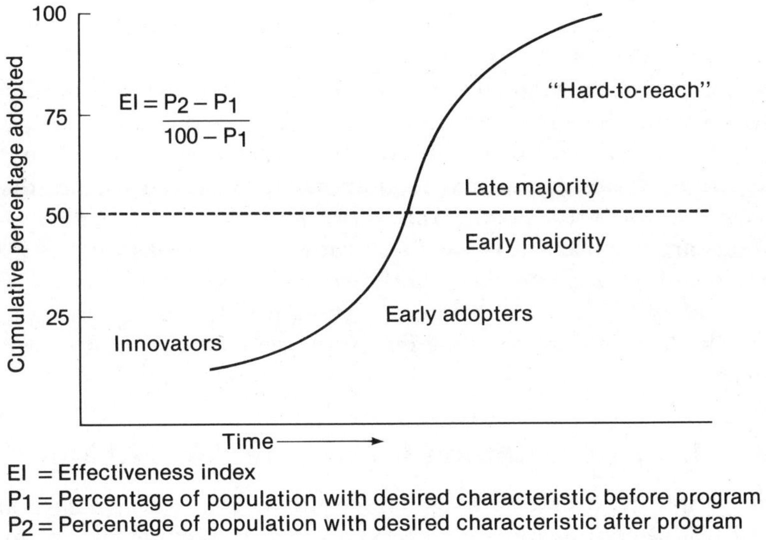

Figure 11-7 *The diffusion adoption curve and the effectiveness index.* Source: *Green & Lewis (1981), p. 53.*

to influence others to do so, and the rate of adoption gains momentum. This well-documented pattern of cumulative diffusion is described in the S-shaped curve in Figure 11-7. The major categories of adopters are identified by the standard deviations from the mean time of adoption.

One might expect that this curve could define projected rates of adoption more accurately than the usual straight line implied by most evaluations in projecting the estimated number or percentage of adopters in prospective studies. The tendency to use simple differences in percentage of adopters before and after programs leads evaluators to overestimate the impact of programs during their early stages and to underestimate the value of program activities during their later stages. In later stages, it becomes more and more difficult to achieve an increment of change.

This fallacy of equal-appearing increments has been repaired by an effectiveness index in studies of health education impact (Green, 1974; Levine et al., 1979). This index, which was first developed by Hovland (1949) in the early studies on persuasion, was an attempt to control the ceiling effect observed in communication studies. The index, which Hovland called the Effectiveness Index (EI), merely calculates the actual change as a ratio of potential change. This approach gives greater weight to changes at the later stages of the diffusion of an innovation than to equal increments at the earlier stages. This Effectiveness Index is particularly appropriate in evaluating public health efforts and patient education activities with indigent populations. In indigent populations, the problem is usually handed over to health educators after the innovators and early acceptors have already adopted the innovation. What remains are the hard-to-reach and high-risk populations. More intensive and less cost-effective methods are required to reach these patients or populations. As a result, public health efforts compare poorly when contrasted on a cost-effectiveness basis with "Madison Avenue" techniques. The latter are not much more effective, but are reaching out to the populations most receptive to innovations.

The Fallacy of Assuming Inexorable Forward Movement

Many people who enter a program do not remain permanent converts. Patterns of discontinuation and dropout rates are well developed in some areas of programming, such as family planning and smoking cessation. The relapse rates or discontinuation rates are remarkably similar when plotted on simple frequency polygons. The curves look surprisingly similar to learning curves or memory curves. Rapid decline appears in the number of participants who continue during the early period following adoption, and then a gradual leveling off appears in the number of dropouts (Hunt & Bespalec, 1974). Plots of average rates of smoking relapse in a large number of studies yields a curve similar to those derived from studies of memory failure following the learning of new information (Ley, 1978).

The implication for public health education is to recognize that a disappointing increase in acceptors or users of the innovation may not be due to the "apathy" or resistance of people to try the innovation, but rather to the inadequate follow-up and reinforcement necessary to sustain the adoption (Wallack, 1981). Booster education and reinforcement could be offered at critical times following the acceptance of an innovation or health practice.

In assessing program effectiveness and benefits, you must take into account these and other time-dependent problems of behavioral change. Most have to do with timing measurement of outcomes after the educational inputs. Some effects of health education are immediate and temporary; others are slower in developing but are longer lasting. These variations and others are illustrated in Figure 11-8.

Delay of Impact. The first curve (A) illustrates the error that would be made in understanding the impact of an educational program if the effect were measured as the difference between Observation 1 before the program and Observation 2 after the program ($O_2 - O_1$). The so-called

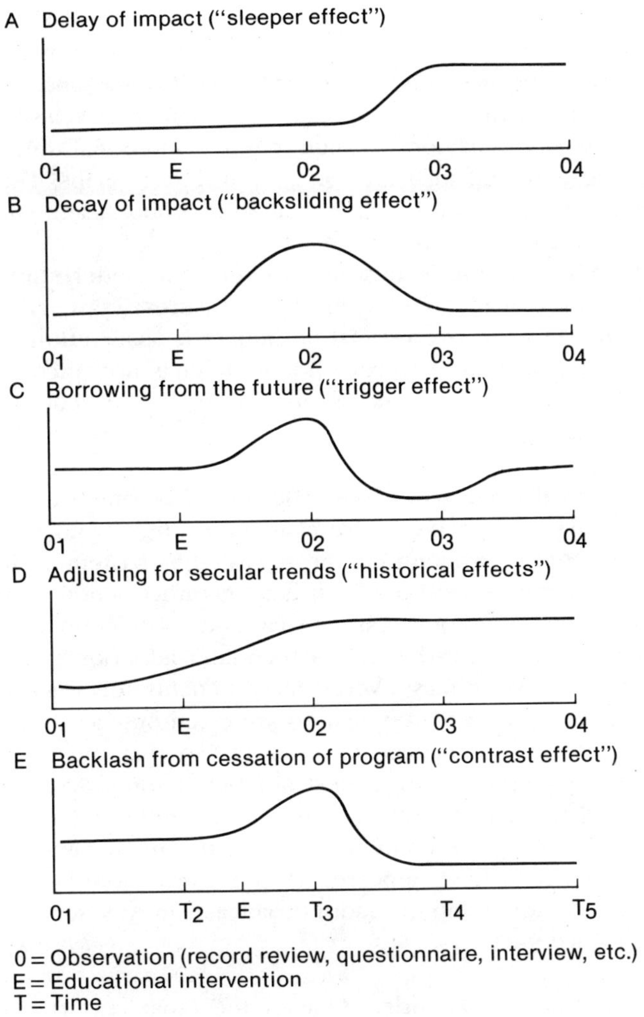

Figure 11-8 *Points of observation* (O) *relative to different educational* (E) *inputs, where time* (T) *elapsed following the first observation* (O_1) *can result in widely varying conclusions.* Source: *Green (1977), p. 159. Used by permission of the American Public Health Association.*

sleeper effect in much behavior change occurs when the audience must go through a process of attitude change or skill development between the educational exposure and the actual internalization and adoption of behavior that yields the health benefits. This effect may also be found where an immediate behavioral change requires additional time before its benefits can be detected in health or administrative terms. The "sleeper effect" is especially important in the evaluation of school health education.

Decay of Impact. Curve B illustrates the error in underestimating benefits that might be made if comparative measures were taken only at Time 4 or Time 5; or in overestimating impact if observations at Time 3 were taken as permanent. The backsliding effect is not uncommon with complex behavioral changes such as smoking cessation, diet change, and complicated drug regimens.

Borrowing from the Future. Some educational programs are really only triggers to behavior that would have changed eventually anyway. In such cases, the educational program can be regarded as hastening the inevitable. Real benefits may be realized from getting earlier action, as with early diagnosis of cancer symptoms, earlier treatment of infections or injuries, earlier prenatal care, and earlier rather than later adoption of healthy lifestyles. But the evaluator may overestimate benefits for some health actions if the observations on a population are taken only at O_1 and O_2. The population's gains at O_2 may be offset at O_3, so that the net long-term gain is zero. This phenomenon is most notable in some mass media campaigns designed to recruit new patients to a screening clinic or smoking cessation clinic. The gains immediately after the broadcasts turn out to be people who would have appeared within a few months anyway. This effect can be seen following the radio broadcasts in Atwater's data on the STD clinic (Figure 9-2).

Adjusting for Secular Trends. One of the most important purposes served by having a control group in the evaluation of program impact is that the apparent gains following the program can be partitioned into gains resulting from the program and gains that were occurring as part of general trends or extraneous events. Curve D in Figure 11-8 applies to an "experimental group" of patients exposed to an educational intervention of some kind. If another curve existed, for a control group of patients not exposed to the education, it would probably parallel D, because the gains were actually developing and heading toward the O_2 level *before* the educational intervention. In this case the error (if adjustment were not made for secular trends) would be that of overestimating the program benefits (Bertera & Green, 1979; Campbell, 1969; Morisky et al., 1980).

The secular trend, however, may be negative (expressed as a downward sloping curve prior to or simultaneous with the health education program). In this case, the error would be a false-negative underestimation of the program's impact. In every case, carefully plotting trend lines or using a control group not exposed to the program is essential to accurate estimation of the true program benefits.

Contrast Effect. Another dilemma posed by short-term evaluation is illustrated by Graph E in Figure 11-8. Here, premature termination of the educational treatment may induce a contrast that demoralizes or embitters the experimental group, causing a backlash, a definite reduction or reversal of the behavior advocated. Self-care programs, smoking and diet programs, and family-planning programs have experienced such contrast effects when the educational activities were insufficiently developed, creating expectations that were not met.

The Fallacy of Underestimating the Complexity of Change Processes

The biomedical tradition of research tends to oversimplify the cause-and-effect relationships between (1) educational interventions and (2) health or medical outcomes expected to result from such interventions. Clinical trials in which we designed patient education interventions to improve compliance with medical regimens and thereby reduce blood pressure or increase blood pressure control illustrate this problem (Green et al., 1975, 1979; Green, Lewis, & Levine, 1980; Levine et al., 1979; Morisky et al., 1983). We began with the understanding that evidence linking any *single* patient behavior with blood pressure control was somewhat tenuous. Therefore, we chose a variety of patient behaviors as our primary dependent variables. The program achieved some significant but modest changes in each of the behavioral variables—for example, medication compliance; self-reported restriction of salt in the diet; weight gained, reduced, or stabilized; and reduction in broken appointments (Chwalow et al., 1978; Fass et al., 1977; Levine et al., 1979). Despite the modest changes in each of the behavioral variables, a considerably greater impact on blood pressure was obtained. Rather than "washing out" in their effect on blood pressure, the various patient behaviors had a cumulative or additive effect in achieving long-term blood pressure control as well as mortality reductions (Morisky et al., 1983).

One lesson from this experience was that the measurement of differences or magnitude of effects is highly sensitive to the placement and relative importance of the variables selected within a complex causal chain. The chronic diseases and degenerative diseases are particularly responsive to a variety of interventions, no one of which by itself would be expected to yield an immediate or sufficient impact on the health indicator. Together these multiple indicators may constitute a lifestyle (a configuration of behaviors that are cumulative in their effect), yielding a greater change in the ultimate health outcome than in any of the more immediate behaviors.

A second lesson from this experience was that certain characteristics of the patients were highly influential in determining which patient behaviors were most likely to change and which interventions were most likely to work. Different patients changed different behaviors at different rates. This approach also resulted in a rather modest showing for each behavior in the aggregate, but had a more impressive cumulative or aggregate impact on blood pressure.

The fallacy of causal simplicity works the opposite way in some instances. Blackwell (1976) reports a study in which a mechanical method of dispensing antihypertensive medication resulted in a larger improvement in pill-taking *compliance* than did a patient-counseling intervention alone. However, when the *blood pressure improvements* were observed, the counseling only, and the counseling combined with the mechanical device, both resulted in better control of blood pressure than did the mechanical device alone. This study reminds us of the importance of interpersonal factors above and beyond the pharmacological or therapeutic maneuvers themselves. The so-called placebo effect in medicine is considered to account for approximately 35 percent of all therapeutic effects (Shapiro & Shapiro, 1984). This estimate calls for more complex causal modeling than even the multiple behavior model required in the previously described hypertension study.

The lesson for health education from these kinds of examples is that causal models are not well developed. Many possible educational treatments exist. And often the differential effects of treatments are quite small. Rubin (1974) therefore recommends that the trial-and-error approach to experimentation in education and social programs should await a search for treatments with large effects, using well-controlled, nonrandomized studies when experiments are impractical. Further experimental study could supply more refined estimates of the effects of those treatments that appear important.

This approach has been natural in the medical sciences where extensive laboratory tests could be concluded before clinical trials were mounted to test new therapeutic strategies. But with the increasing number of conditions for which multiple interventions are required, each of which can expect to achieve only small effects by itself, we cannot await the randomized clinical trials approach to investigation in all human services.

Sampling Failure

The large number of randomized clinical trials resulting in negative findings is partly a function of the fallacy of causal simplicity, discussed earlier. But, beyond that, the number is also a function of failing to provide adequate sample sizes to detect the amount of change expected or defined as the standard of acceptability. The provision of an adequate sample size is one way to minimize the classical Type II error problem—the problem of failing to detect an actual effect. An analysis of the situation is provided by Frieman, Smith, and Chalmers (1977). They inspected 100 randomized clinical trials characterized by their authors as negative or having no statistically significant results ($p < .05$). Their objective was to determine whether the results were truly negative. Frieman's team found that all the papers measured Alpha (the probability of a Type I or false positive error) but only one discussed Beta (the probability of a Type II or false negative error). The Beta error and the power or true positive (1-Beta) were calculated in 81 of the 100 studies. In all but one of the studies, the power was *inadequate* to demonstrate a true effect favoring the treatments. None of the studies achieved the 90 percent level of power or even the conventionally acceptable 80 percent level. The range of power in these clinical trials ranged from 3 to 60 percent.

Frieman, Smith, and Chalmers (1977) further inspected the thirty-eight clinical trials that used case fatality rates (CFR) as the outcome. Of the thirty-eight studies showing a trend that favored the experimental therapy, although not statistically significant, only seven had a power sufficient to detect a 50 percent reduction in CFR, defined as a clinically meaningful therapeutic effect. Only one study detected a 25 percent reduction in CFR.

One problem of inadequate power was the nonparticipation rate of the patients. On the average, only 34 percent of the sample patients participated in the trials for the studies defining a 50 percent reduction in the CFR as the standard of acceptability. On the average, a mean of only 17 percent participated in those seeking a 25 percent reduction in CFR.

Frieman's study raises doubts about the efficiency and the sensitivity of randomized clinical trials to detect the magnitude and types of change expected of educational and therapeutic interventions with chronic and degenerative diseases. We strongly recommend, at the very least, that the sample size in randomized trials be based on a calculation of the requisite power to detect differences of a magnitude defined as acceptable or clinically significant.

Adequate sample size alone does not justify the use of clinical trials. The multivariate nature of most health problems demands more complex factorial designs for experiments, and we consider the state of the art to demand more extensive piloting and descriptive and qualitative analysis of the interventions and the behavior before the investments in large-scale, multifactorial clinical trials can be justified.

SUMMARY

Theory and "facts" in health education do not automatically emerge from measurement and evaluation. Results—or the failure to detect them—require careful scrutiny by both the consumer and the researcher. Acceptable levels or standards of health outcomes should be predetermined, and results compared to these standards. These targeted levels of effect are influenced by historical, normative, theoretical, and absolute standards. Choices are made to measure intermediate or ultimate effects, or both.

When evaluation research fails to document a "slam-bang" effect, we must ask three questions: (1) "What can be said with authority? (2) What can be said with qualification? (3) What things are important for the system to know?" The absence of a significant program effect can result from program failure, theory failure, or measurement failure.

Differentiation is made between statistically significant results, meaningful results, and clinically important results. Merely documenting effects is not enough to influence theory and practice in health education. Results need to be screened through a series of questions before major practice or policy decisions are justified.

Theory failure can cause problems in measurement and lead to the misinterpretation of results. Three common errors of this type are (1) the fallacy of equal-appearing increments, (2) the fallacy of inexorable forward movement, and (3) the fallacy of causal simplicity.

The reliance on clinical trials in health education to expose the "truth" may be premature. A review of 100 clinical trials revealed that most had insufficient power to detect a true effect. False negative results could be the price of misplaced emphasis on clinical trials research when sample size is inadequate.

Evaluation research can provide the data for building theory and developing policy and practice in health education. The building process requires active engagement by the practitioner and the researcher. It would help if practitioners were more conversant with theory and evaluation research methods, but even more urgent is the development of researchers and theorists who have had clinical or field experience as practitioners and who can ground their theory and research in practice settings.

Chapter 12

STEPS IN ANALYSIS AND INTERPRETATION

You are now on the brink of "cashing in" on all your hard work in designing and implementing measurements for diagnosis or evaluation. The toil of implementing your protocol can be converted into useful information only if you carry out the step-by-step procedures for assessing your data. These procedures include a cumulative series of estimates and calculations that build up to analyses of cost-effectiveness and cost-benefit potentials or achievements of your proposed or actual program.

We have saved these subjects until this late point in the book because they tend to discourage health educators, even those willing to tackle most other aspects of measurement and evaluation. Some people recoil at these terms because they connote a combination of tedious statistics and economics, which they think of as "the dismal science." Others express more philosophical objections to imposing these criteria of success on health education, arguing that other social service fields have not been subjected to such crass indignities. Indeed, until recently medicine seemed to defy all the laws of economics as the only U.S. industry subject neither to government regulation nor to the rules of the marketplace. That feat has changed in recent years.

Even if health education should not have to be justified in economic terms, it *can* be so justified; and in these times, unfortunately, it apparently must be in order to gain policy and administrative support (Banta & Luce, 1983). In opening health education to such economic accountability, we are exposing it to criteria of success that were previously unnecessary, when health education could be defended on philosophical grounds alone. Differing philosophies now compete for scarce resources, and the only common yardstick besides humanism—which they all profess—by which their claims can be compared is cost relative to effectiveness (if they claim the same outcomes) or relative to benefits (if they claim different benefits).

The essential difference between cost-effectiveness and cost-benefit analyses is that one is concerned with the cost to achieve a specific effect; the other is concerned with any and all the benefits that can be reasonably commensurated as the yield for a given program cost. Cost-effectiveness will be expressed as dollars per unit of effect—for example, $10 for every new patient recruited for treatment in a sexually transmitted disease program. Cost-benefit will be expressed as a ratio of total benefits accrued per dollar spent on a program—for example, $20 saved in emergency room visits and lost work time for every dollar spent on a self-care program for adult asthmatic patients.

In this chapter, a simple example illustrates how you can go about the basic calculations to evaluate the relative costs, reach, impact, benefits, and ongoing cost-effectiveness of two health education alternatives.

COMPUTING THE INPUTS AND THE OUTPUTS OF HEALTH EDUCATION

To avoid straying too far from our promise to introduce evaluation with a minimum of number crunching, we have stripped the following example down to sixteen calculations that would provide a comprehensive analysis and interpretation of a health education program. Table 12-1 lists

TABLE 12-1 Process, impact, efficacy, effectiveness, cost-effectiveness, and cost-benefit computations

	Line	Program 1	Program 2
A.	Need (estimated population eligible)	10,000 M.D.s	100 R.N.s
B.	Reached (attended)	1,000 M.D.s	50 R.N.s
C.	Coverage [(B/A) × 100]	10%	50%
D.	Impact (immediate effects)	100	40
E.	Efficacy [(D/B) × 100]	10%	80%
F.	Effectiveness [(D/A) × 100]	1%	40%
G.	Program cost ($)	$10,000	$200
H.	Efficiency (G/B)	$10/M.D.	$4/R.N.
I.	Cost-effectiveness (G/D)	$100/effect	$5/effect
J.	Benefits (D × value)	$100,000	$4,000
K.	Cost-benefit (J/G, expressed as ratio)	10/1	20/1
L.	Income	$6,000	0
M.	Net gain (or loss) (L − G)	(−4,000)	(−200)
N.	Start-up costs (planning)	$1,000	$100
O.	Operating cost (G − L − N)	$3,000	$100
P.	Operating cost-effectiveness (O/D)	$30.00/effect	$2.50/effect

the sixteen calculations in the order in which they would likely be performed. Lines A to C represent process measures, Lines D to F measure actual effects of the program or method, Lines G to K build the econometric analysis, and Lines L to P provide the financial balance sheet for projecting the ongoing requirements to maintain the program.

The examples presented in the two columns of figures in Table 12-1 are hypothetical continuing education programs, both intended to get hospitals to adopt a method of behavioral and educational diagnosis for self-care evaluation of patients to prepare them for earlier discharge and home care. The questions for evaluation are "Which program will get the best coverage of the 100 hospitals? Which will achieve a greater adoption of the educational diagnostic procedure? What are their relative costs and cost-effectiveness? What are their relative benefits and cost-benefit ratios? If they can generate any revenue, what are the net proceeds or costs? Considering all the answers to the foregoing questions, what will it take to maintain the preferred program in the future?" These are the questions that decision makers, legislators, or consumers will want you to answer, even if they don't ask them in exactly this way.

Administrative and Process Analyses

The first few steps in analysis, whether for planning or for evaluation, usually entail determining the population in need, the population eligible, and the population reached. These steps are essential to learning the scope of the program and to mapping and staking out the territory for further analysis. Some health programs never get beyond this level of analysis because they are accountable only for the number of services rendered or for the percentage of the population reached.

A. Need. The first statistic or estimate to be established in most analyses, whether for planning or for evaluation, is the population in need or the population eligible for the program or service. This number becomes the denominator for subsequent calculations (1) of the proportion of the population reached by the progam and (2) of the overall effectiveness of the program. The population in need is usually estimated from census data or from previous counts of the number of people passing through a health facility monthly, the number of students in a grade level, the number of workers in a plant or office building, or the number of people who have enrolled in a program, a health insurance plan, or an HMO. Any of these numbers probably needs to be qualified by certain screening or exclusion criteria. For example, some public health programs might only admit people below a certain income level, only those women who are pregnant, or only those teenagers who have an admitted alcohol problem.

Such eligibility criteria complicate the estimation of need because the data on such parameters are less likely to be available on your population. Estimates then must be interpolated from national or state data. You simply apply the national average for the proportion of people below an income level, or the national pregnancy rate, for example, to the total number of people or women in your population. This method produces a "synthetic estimate," so-called because it synthesizes data from local and other sources.

In the example in Table 12-1, we are analyzing two programs, both designed to accomplish the same objective; that is, to meet the same need. Broadly defined, the need could be expressed in terms of the number of patients who might benefit from new hospital practices in educating patients, but this quantity is unknown and potentially infinite. Therefore, we define need in terms of the populations eligible to receive the alternative programs. These populations are the 10,000 physicians affiliated with the 100 hospitals in our region, for Program 1, and the 100 head nurses for these same 100 hospitals, for Program 2. The rationale for these hypothetical populations is that the physicians function independently with respect to patient education, so each of them needs to be individually exposed to our continuing education program. The nurses, however, perform patient education under the direction of their head nurse or the physician in charge of a given patient. We can assume that these staff nurses will be reached either through the physicians enlightened by our Program 1, or by their head nurses if we select continuing education Program 2.

B. Reach. The second statistic you need in most analyses is the number of the eligible population who would be or were actually exposed to the program, method, or service in question. If your analysis is for policy or planning purposes, you may have to estimate this figure on the basis of (1) previous experience with such programs, (2) the rules and regulations that might be invoked to get people into the program, and (3) some "market analysis" of the product, the price, the demand (awareness, interest, motivation), and the distribution system and resources available to make the program accessible. If your analysis is made after the program has been carried out, you need only count the number of people who enrolled, attended, or otherwise participated. If the program is a broadcast media program, the estimation of reach is more difficult because exposure to the broadcasts is private and largely unobservable.

In our example in Table 12-1, the reach of Program 1 is expected or observed to be 1,000 physicians. Program 2 has the advantage of being more accessible to the head nurses because it is conducted in the same hospitals where some of them work. We estimate, or we find in our evaluation, that 50 head nurses attend the continuing education program for them.

You have noted by now that we refer in our example to both estimating and evaluating to arrive at the figures. We do so because we want to illustrate that these analytic procedures apply both to policy analysis, which usually takes place before a commitment to a program has been made, and to analysis of an evaluation, which always occurs after a program has begun. Thus, in policy analysis, the choice between Program 1 or Program 2 may hinge on the accuracy of your projections, predictions, interpolations, and generalizations from previous experience in similar and dissimilar situations—in short, your estimates. The same analytic procedures apply to evaluative data. The only difference is that you have actual data rather than hypothetical data. Nevertheless, Table 12-1 applies to both stages of analysis.

C. Coverage. Like most raw numbers, those numbers generated for Lines A and B in Table 12-1, namely need and reach, have little meaning in their absolute form. The question almost inevitably asked of any absolute number in an analysis is "Relative to what?" or "Compared to what?" Recall that we defined evaluation as the comparison of an object of interest against a standard of acceptability. The statement that we reached 1,000 physicians in one program and 50 head nurses in another has no meaning by itself, even if we compare 1,000 with 50. We must first convert the absolute numbers to relative numbers before we can compare them. We need to know not the absolute reach of the program but rather the relative reach: "Relative to what?"

Relative numbers imply ratios, rates, fractions, proportions, or percentages, all of which have numerators and denominators. The standard of acceptability implied by a simple proportion or percentage is unity, which is 1 for a proportion, 100 for a percentage. Unity of the numerator and denominator means that the numerator equals the denominator. Anything less, by this absolute standard of acceptability, is short of total success. Total success by the coverage criterion is when reach equals need; that is, all the people eligible for the program were reached. In our example in Table 12-1, 10 percent of the eligible physicians and 50 percent of the eligible head nurses were reached.

Now that we have standardized the absolute numbers reached by converting them to percentages, we can apply other standards of acceptability. In Chapter 8 we defined several standards of acceptability in addition to absolute (100 percent) standards. These included normative standards, historical standards, theoretical standards, and negotiated or compromise standards. Table 12-1 provides one kind of normative comparison. The comparison of the 10 percent coverage by Program 1 with the 50 percent coverage of Program 2 is a simple normative comparison. Although Program 2 reached only 50 nurses compared to the 1,000 physicians reached by program 1, the relative coverage of the target population was 5 times greater in Program 2.

If we conducted an evaluation of another round of Program 1 or Program 2, we could apply a historical standard of acceptability, comparing the coverage by the same program before and after we improved the marketing or recruitment component. If we had a body of research literature on marketing such continuing education programs, we could derive from the literature a theoretical standard of acceptability, based on what we should expect to be the percentages attending a well-marketed program. If we had all these possible comparisons available to us, we might average them—giving more or less weight to the normative, the historical, or the theoretical—to arrive at a compromise standard of acceptability.

These considerations in the analysis of comparisons against standards of eligibility apply in all the standardized calculations that follow. The standardized objects of interest are those in which there is a divisor sign in Table 12-1, including coverage (Line C), efficacy (E), effectiveness (F), efficiency (H), cost-effectiveness (I), cost-benefit (K), and operating cost-effectiveness (P).

Impact Analysis

At the second phase or level of analysis, three measures can be generated to assess the *results* of the program, as distinct from assessing the *process* of delivering the program in the previous steps. Here, measures of impact, efficacy, and effectiveness provide a view of the short-range results considered necessary if the long-term benefits or objectives and goals of the program are to be realized.

D. Impact. The immediate effects of a program or intervention are referred to in health and medical fields as *impact,* or *short-term outcomes,* to distinguish them from the unadorned term *outcome,* which generally refers to changes in health status. In some other fields of evaluation, the terms *impact* and *outcome* are used in the opposite way.

The impact of a program or intervention usually consists of several variables or immediate effects expected to result from its implementation. Some of these immediate effects are considered essential *intermediate* variables in the causal chain linking the program or intervention to the ultimate objectives, goals, or benefits justifying the program. Thus, the rationale for most programs or interventions in the complex world of health education includes assumptions about the relationship between educational inputs and their impact on such intermediate variables as knowledge, attitudes, perceptions, skills, beliefs, access to resources, social support, and other predisposing, enabling, and reinforcing factors. These immediate impact variables, in turn, are expected to combine in their further impact on the intermediate behavioral variables, which in turn are expected to influence health, fitness, psychological well-being, and quality of life. These latter benefits might stand little chance of being measurable within the time frame of most evaluations, so you will be that much more thorough in measuring the more immediate and intermediate impact variables. You will then lean heavily on the scientific research literature to verify the further assumption that by changing these variables you can reasonably expect to improve health and quality of life.

With this logic, selecting the most important impact variables to be used as measures of success in your analysis is essential to the credibility of your evaluation. The most credible impact variables in health education, short of changes in health measures themselves, are behavioral variables. Demonstrated change or no change in behavior carries more weight for most potential readers of an evaluation report than demonstrated changes in predisposing, enabling, or reinforcing factors. We do not mean to say that these more immediate impact variables are trivial, but you will need a larger number and a greater magnitude of such changes to convince most reviewers that the program or intervention was successful.

In Table 12-1, we have merely shown numbers representing the impact of the two continuing education programs. If you assume that these are the numbers of physicians (100) and head nurses (40) who passed a test of knowledge about patient education procedures after their respective programs, you would not be too impressed. But if we tell you that these numbers represent the number of physicians and nurses who adopted the recommended patient education procedures in their own hospital practices, you would find the same numbers more impressive and more convincing evidence of the effectiveness of the programs. Before we can say anything about effectiveness, however, we must once again standardize the absolute numbers to make them relative numbers. All we can say from the figures of 100 and 40 is that the program appears to have had an impact on the behavior of this many physicians and nurses.

E. Efficacy. Even before we analyze effectiveness, another concept in evaluation describes the analysis of how effective a program or intervention method is for those who receive it under controlled circumstances. Recall that our program in Table 12-1 was designed for the entire population in need, yet only 1,000 (10 percent) of the physicians and 50 (50 percent) of the head nurses were actually reached or directly exposed to the interventions contained in the continuing education courses. The measure of efficacy applies only to those people actually exposed to the interventions within the controlled circumstances of the continuing education programs. To standardize this measure, then, we divide the impact number by the number reached (D/B) and multiply by 100 to convert the proportion to a percentage.

This analysis reveals that even though we had an impact on more physicians than nurses, the efficacy of the educational courses was eight times greater for the head nurses who enrolled than for the physicians who enrolled. A better test of efficacy would be a randomized trial in which the physicians who enrolled would be divided into equivalent educational and control groups; likewise for nurses who are enrolled.

What about those people who did not enroll but were part of the target population?

F. Effectiveness. When you claim that your program has been effective on the basis of its effects on those who came in to receive its educational services, the next question any discerning reader or administrator will ask is "Who were the people who came in?" By implication, this question suggests the possibility that (1) not many people came into the program, and (2) those who did come in were already highly motivated so you missed the people who needed the health education most. You can address the first part by distinguishing between efficacy and effectiveness with two separate calculations, both having the same numerator based on the number of people who successfully changed on an important impact or outcome variable. The denominators differ. As we have seen, the denominator for efficacy is the number of people actively exposed to the intervention. For effectiveness, especially in public health programs, we suggest that the denominator should include all people who were intended to receive the program.

Seldom is this distinction maintained in evaluation reports. The conventional practice is to evaluate programs or methods of education on "captive" audiences and volunteer subjects. This practice provides a fair-enough measure of the program's efficacy in achieving the desired impact or outcomes. It is even fair to call this effectiveness if the program is not intended for use outside such "captive audience" situations. But when a larger population of eligible people in need was identified at the outset as the target population for the program being evaluated, then it is only fair to include that larger population in the denominator of some measure of success.

The confusion on this distinction is most troublesome in patient education evaluations. The reason for the confusion there is that patient education tends to be evaluated, in the better studies, by using the true experimental designs of randomized clinical trials. Medicine has a rich tradition and understanding of the randomized clinical trial as the definitive test of the efficacy of drugs and medical or surgical procedures. The difference in patient education is that the patients are at greater liberty to participate and to accept or not accept the various components of the educational intervention than they are in clinical trials of medical interventions once they have given their consent and have been randomly assigned to experimental and control groups. When health educators report their evaluation results, the discrepancy between the number of people randomly assigned to each experimental group and the number who actually received the full health education intervention intended for that group is often much larger than in medical trials. The difference causes some eyebrows to rise. Is it a fair test of the intervention if some of the people randomized to receive it do not?

Our answer to this question is that it is not a fair test of the efficacy of the method, but it *is* a fair test of its effectiveness. Part of the effectiveness of an educational method lies in its ability to attract and to hold the attention of its learners. A written health education message, for example, might be extremely persuasive for those who read it, but it would be relatively ineffective in a population in which a large proportion of the people are illiterate, unable to read the language in which it is written, or in a very elderly population in which eyesight limits exposure to written material.

You cannot assume, however, that just because many people do not participate in one or more components of an educational program the program will necessarily fail. Indeed, the people who decline to participate in some parts of a health education program exempt themselves for good reasons. Often they already know the material, already accept the principles and attitudes emphasized in the "pep talk" component, and are just waiting for the skill development sessions. In such programs, effectiveness may equal efficacy.

In Table 12-1, the figures calculated for effectiveness suggest that few if any of those who did not attend the continuing education programs adopted the recommended practices of patient self-care education. Sometimes the impact figure will be greater than the number of people directly reached by the program. This result usually means that a diffusion effect has followed the introduction of the program.

Economic Analyses

Even if you have shown remarkable results in the preceding analytic steps, you will need to assure yourself and convince others that you achieved these results at reasonable costs. The remaining steps in analysis provide measures of cost, efficiency, cost-effectiveness, and cost relative to benefits.

G. Program Cost. The next calculation you would pursue if you have any need to go beyond the simple measures of efficacy and effectiveness is cost of the program. Why should you need to go beyond effectiveness measures? In many instances in health education and health promotion, two programs with the same objectives are equally effective in achieving those objectives, but one costs more than the other. In such instances, having just the additional data on cost is sufficient to advise policy or management on the preferred choice between the alternative programs or methods.

Cost analysis is essentially an accounting procedure, but it cannot be done properly unless the "books" or ledgers have been set up from the beginning of the program in such a way as to keep track of the actual expenditures. The major consideration for the evaluator is to be able to separate evaluation costs from program costs. If the expenditures associated with data collection and other evaluation functions are included in the program cost estimates, the analysis will result in an inflated figure that makes the program seem more expensive than it really needs to be. The one exception to this rule is when the evaluation procedures consist mainly of data collection procedures that are recommended as integral parts of the program, such as pretests and posttests, diagnostic or marketing surveys, and routine record-keeping functions. The costs of these components of the evaluation should be included in program costs only if they are essential to the ongoing maintenance and performance of the program.

The examples in Table 12-1 show estimated costs of $10,000 and $200 for the continuing education programs. Such nicely rounded figures do imply estimates rather than carefully totaled accounts. In the absence of full accounting of expenditures, such estimation is unavoidable. Even with full accounting, some revised estimates may be in order if, for example, the personnel used in the pilot project or first run of the program were people whose salaries or fees were higher or lower than the people who would normally operate such programs.

With all these variations on the ways in which costs might be calculated, you are all the more obliged to report your methods, assumptions, inclusions, and exclusions when presenting a cost analysis and final cost estimate. (For examples of the problems and issues in costing programs in smoking cessation, see Green, Rimer, & Bertera, 1978; in family planning, Bertera & Green, 1979; in hypertension patient education, Eastaugh & Hatcher, 1982).

H. Efficiency. Measures of efficiency may apply to the rate at which any particular resource is consumed in a program per unit of service delivered. For example, efficiency might be expressed as the number of personhours of professional or clerical time required to serve each patient in a clinic, as an answer to the question "How efficient are they?" Alternatively, efficiency might be expressed as the number of hours of computer time required per lesson in a computer-assisted instructional (CAI) program, as an answer to the question "How efficient is this software?" Efficiency might be expressed in units of media time, number of brochures, number of home visits, hours per counseling session, or any other measure of resources consumed. All these resources can be commensurated most conveniently in monetary terms. Time *is* money, as they say. So are materials. Thus, the numerator suggested for a composite measure of efficiency is the total cost of the program, just calculated in the previous step.

For the denominator, you will note that efficiency is a way of standardizing the ratio of resources to reach. Efficiency is not necessarily a measure of effectiveness unless reach and impact are the same. This situation might be the case in an immunization program, for example, where one person reached with a vaccination is equal to one person protected from the disease to be prevented. In the health education component of the immunization program, however, the term *reach* would likely refer to the number of people who receive the educational interventions designed to predispose, enable, and reinforce their actions to obtain immunization. Some, of course, will not avail themselves of the immunization after even the best health education, so reach is not equivalent to impact.

In Table 12-1, we have illustrated the calculation of efficiency as the result of program costs divided by the number of the respective target audiences reached. This ratio yields an efficiency quotient of $10 per physician reached by Continuing Education Program 1, and $4 per head nurse reached by Continuing Education Program 2.

Now, ask yourself what this calculation tells us that the previous measure of program cost did not tell us. Note that the "doctor" program at $10,000 was fifty times more expensive than the "nurse" program at $200. Yet the efficiency measure shows us that the program for physicians was only 2.5 times more expensive per professional reached than the program for head nurses. We see that the efficiency measure closes the gap between the raw cost measures in Step G. We have achieved an "economy of scale" by extending the doctor program to reach larger numbers. But has this extension of the program paid off in terms of outcomes?

From the perspective of the people paying for the program, efficiency is a measure of input, although from a managerial perspective it might be seen as a measure of output. The quality of management, including the control of waste, the containment of costs through prudent purchasing and time management decisions, and the control of quality through good training and supervisory arrangements all add up to efficiency. They do so by reducing the numerator (cost) and increasing the denominator (reach). Whether all these economies and increased reach pay off in terms of impact and benefits depends on the effectiveness of the interventions. An extremely efficient program sometimes accomplishes nothing because it was misguided in its design, not in its delivery.

I. Cost-Effectiveness. The measure that combines the gains from efficiency of input with the gains from strategic targeting and appropriate formulation of the input is cost-effectiveness. The two ways in which a highly efficient program can be misguided and result in a minimum of impact are (1) delivering a good program to the wrong people, or (2) delivering an inappropriate program to the right people. The best safeguard against these pitfalls of planning is a good diagnosis of who the people in the greatest need are (see Line A) and of what causes predispose, enable, and reinforce their actions (see Green, Kreuter, Deeds, & Partridge, 1980). At the analysis stage, however, the damage is done and we must reap the results and harvest the data. Cost-effectiveness standardizes a comparative measure of cost relative to a specific impact.

In Table 12-1, we have divided the program cost (Line G) by the number of physicians or head nurses who adopted the patient education practices recommended by the continuing education programs. The results are expressed as the ratio of dollar cost per unit of impact, in this case dollars per doctor or per head nurse who changed his or her behavior with respect to patient education of the kind recommended. We see that the calculations yield a ratio of $100 for every physician who adopted the self-care education program for patients, and $5 for every head nurse who adopted the program.

The "bottom line" seems to be that we can get the same effect twenty times cheaper with the continuing education program for head nurses than with the continuing education program for physicians serving the same hospitals.

We have come a long way from the first two rows of Table 12-1, which seemed to argue for the preferability of the program for physicians over the program for head nurses. Even Line D might have seemed to favor the physician program, but, like Lines A and B, it was not a "standardized" measure so it could not provide a true comparison. When we began standardizing the comparisons, first with percentages in Lines C, E, and F, and then with ratios in Lines H and I, we could compare the data between the two programs. Recalling our definition of evaluation as the comparison of an object of interest against a standard of acceptability, we have found several standards of acceptability on the basis of which either program could be compared with its own prior or subsequent history, with some national average of continuing education programs, or with objectives based on theory, politics, or some negotiated mix of these.

But have we in fact reached a bottom line? As we stated in the previous chapter, the level and extent of analysis required depend on how and with whom your data might be used. If we were using this hypothetical evaluation for commercial purposes, our purposes of evaluation might have been satisfied at the point that we established the extent of the "market" (A), or the number of doctors or nurses we could attract in that market with a single round of continuing education programs (B and C). If we intended to communicate our evaluation results to hospital administrators, rather than to commercial continuing education vendors, then we would need to carry out the additional analyses that provided evidence of the relative impact, efficacy, and effectiveness of the programs in affecting hospital practices of professional staff (D minus F).

If the evaluation were being conducted for the managers of the continuing education programs, a demand would arise for the additional data on cost and efficiency (G and H) so that they could know how to improve their managerial practices. Health educators themselves also want cost-effectiveness data to satisfy their own professional curiosity and to test their theories and hypotheses about the best ways to get a specific effect at the lowest cost. Such data would improve their future practice and contribute to the theories and training influencing the practice of other health educators.

J. Benefits. Two important constituencies for evaluation results remain, whose stakes lead us to yet further analyses. These constituencies include the ultimate beneficiaries and benefactors, whose interests are in the ultimate benefits—taxpayers, and their appointed or elected officials, and others who pay the bills for social programs. These consumers of evaluation cannot be satisfied with assurances that a program has efficiently and effectively achieved an effect, because there are more desirable effects to be sought than there is money to pay for all the programs necessary to achieve them. Therefore, some analyses may be called on to offer evidence that the program had a more profound effect on outcomes considered by society to be more basic to the quality of life than just the efficient transfer of resources into programs or the effective transfer of programs into behavioral changes.

Luckily, health is considered one such quality of life outcome. It is an egocentric error, however, for health professionals to assume that health is always an end in itself. For most people, most of the time, health is an instrumental value rather than a terminal value. When pressed to explain why health is important to them, people will tend to give reasons having to do with the importance of health to enable them to remain productive, independent, attractive, effective in their work, and financially solvent.

If health education, health behavior, and even health itself are instrumental values, how can the analysis of evaluational data go beyond measures of these effects to capture the ultimate value of programs? Unfortunately, the answers to this question lack much consensus among economists, health educators, other professionals, legislators, and the public at large. The only yardstick broadly applied with any consistency and standardization is monetary value, even though everyone readily concedes that many ultimate values to which health contributes cannot be commensurated in monetary terms. Nevertheless, people customarily express benefits, for purposes of analysis, in terms of dollars saved, costs averted, or medical insurance claims reduced.

Even morbidity and mortality are conventionally converted into disability days, lost productivity, absenteeism, hospital days, and similar counts on which price tags can be affixed. This approach allows many effects to be accumulated in a single register, and the stream of benefits variously flowing from improved health, reduced morbidity, and delayed mortality can be commensurated in a uniform dollar total.

This calculus of health and life is mystifying to most people, and offensive to some. When applied to the value of human life, the calculations are such that in traditional societies and in capitalist countries, the value of a male life comes out higher than that of a female life. Are we to conclude from such calculations that health priorities should be shifted away from women's health programs? Similarly, the employed in general and the professional and executive classes of employed people in particular turn up in econometric valuations as having greater monetary worth than the unemployed, the underemployed, and the elderly. To follow such analyses to their apparently logical conclusions would be to abrogate any social responsibility for investment in human resources and in social equality.

We prefer, therefore, an approach to the commensurating of benefits that concentrates on one or a few tangible outcomes beyond the strictly medical but not beyond the measurable near-future outcomes for which actual dollar savings can be tracked. This approach avoids many of the tenuous and controversial assumptions that must go into longer-range projections of benefit streams. It avoids as well the invidious comparisons of the worth of different types of human lives. Fortunately, health education and other disease prevention and health promotion strategies still come out ahead in such restricted short-term calculations of benefits.

The estimates of benefits in Line J of Table 12-1 illustrate this short-range approach. We have assumed that each physician who changes his or her patient education practice with regard to postoperative self-medication will have greater influence over the patients' learning and adoption of the regimen than will the head nurses. We make this assumption on the basis of the physician's more frequent personal contact with the patient both during and after hospitalization, plus the possibility that the physician can have at least as much influence over the staff nurses interacting with his or her patients as the head nurse can have. In addition, the physician can prescribe and order procedures in support of self-medication practices not only by staff nurses but also by pharmacy and other allied personnel such as respiratory therapists. All these power advantages for the physician can result in more effective self-medication and self-care by patients, which in turn can prevent more unnecessary rehospitalizations.

Based on previous research and evaluation (e.g., D'Altroy, Blissenbach, Lutz, Beardsley, Cain, Mardt, & Quarn, 1978), we can translate these relative advantages into values. The evidence from previous research shows that effective self-care education of patients can reduce subsequent hospital days by as much as an average of one day per patient in the first year. This approach allows us to calculate monetary values for the changes in physician and head nurse behavior. Applying the most conservative assumptions, which is always advisable in any cost-benefit analysis, we can estimate the benefits accruing from the two continuing education programs as follows:

1. Assume that each physician effectively educates ten patients per year to follow self-care procedures following their hospitalization.
2. Assume that each head nurse who adopted the continuing education program's recommendations effectively influences the self-care practices of one patient per year.
3. Assume that the savings in excess hospitalization is $100 per patient whose self-care practices are effectively influenced.

Now, multiplying the number of physicians (100) and head nurses (40) on whom the continuing education programs had an impact (D) by the value attached to each physician's change in practice ($1,000) and each head nurse's change in practice ($100), we get the figures shown as benefits (J) in Table 12-1.

K. Cost-Benefit. The figures just calculated are once again unstandardized in that they do not have a common denominator. As such they are not directly comparable for purposes of evaluation. To make them comparable, the convention in cost-benefit analysis is to reduce the common denominator to $1 of cost, so that the ratio is expressed as dollars of benefit expected for every dollar invested in the program.

As seen in Table 12-1, the calculations (K) for the two continuing education programs show that we still must recommend in favor of the program for head nurses. We can predict twice as much return for each dollar invested in that program than in the continuing education program for physicians. Some more caveats and qualifications are now in order, however.

First, recommending one program over another on the basis of any of the standardized measures so far (C, E, F, H, I, or K) assumes that a choice must be made. Often, the decision facing those people who might use the evaluation results is how to get the best mix of results, taking into account the administrative and political realities of giving all their resources to educate one group, or denying any one of several groups access to some part of the resources available for a commodity such as continuing education or health education. As with the stock market, you can only maximize your investment at some greater risk than you need to take to get a decent return on your investment. The risks in the stock market with the highest yielding stocks are purely financial. The risks of putting all your eggs in one basket in social services are ethical and political. Depending on the source of funds and the mandate for their allocation, you may not find it possible to allocate funds exclusively to one program.

Second, note that even the less favored program yields a substantial return on the investment. A 10-to-1 benefit-to-cost ratio could be likened to a 1000 percent interest on savings or a tenfold increment in the value of stocks, to carry that analogy a step further. Such a return in private market terms would be the stuff of which millionaires and the *nouveau riche* are made. In the public and nonprofit sectors, however, the benefactors of a program are not necessarily the same people who made the investment in the program. In our example, the investment in continuing education programs might be made by the federal government, the professional societies, the hospitals, the insurance industry, or the individual professionals attending the programs. Often some combination of revenues supports a program. In any case, the cost-benefit analysis does not necessarily take into account whose costs and whose benefits are being counted. Thus, even a highly favorable benefit-to-cost ratio such as 10/1 might not benefit those whose funds are used on the cost side.

Operational Questions, Theoretical Guidance

Having generated what might seem to be an airtight analysis of your proposal or your program, the question that will be asked now is "How will it play in Peoria?" Naturally, your innovative, experimental program performed magnificently. But how will it perform when it goes into routine operation without the grants or special administrative pampering you got in the pilot project, without the novelty effects, the limelight of the new program, the honeymoon with curious staff and patients, the most advanced students, or the most affluent consumers? Some of these questions can only be answered by taking the program into new settings, new populations, and new circumstances.

L. Income. This discussion brings us to one further round of calculations. These calculations are concerned with the question of whether the agency or organization considering a program or choice between programs can afford to operate the proposed programs. As we have just seen, it is one thing to know that an investment is a sure-fire winner; it is another to have the cash or other resources available to make the investment. This dilemma faces stock market investors and horse race gamblers alike, but the social service planner and health administrator face a further complication. They must consider not only the capital outlay but also the recurring costs of operating and maintaining the program once a commitment is made. This necessity raises the question "Where will the money come from?"

Sources of revenue for health and social service agencies include grants, contracts, donations, recurring or zero-based budgets from a parent organization (which could be a city council, a governor's office, or a legislative body), and fees for services rendered. Except for recurring budgets, which are increasingly rare, all these are unstable sources of revenue. Therefore agencies must ask how they can hope to maintain a program beyond their current budget cycle before they can commit themselves to it, no matter how well documented the need, the effectiveness, and the cost-benefit.

One of the most reassuring responses to this question, if such a response is possible, is that the program has the potential of being self-supporting. This answer usually applies to programs in which a fee for services can be levied on the participants. Government and nonprofit agencies, however, seldom expect to recover the full cost of their programs from fees. If they could, the program would quickly be taken up by the private sector, to turn a profit. The usual pattern is for the private sector to tap the most lucrative part of the market for a given sector, leaving government and charitable agencies to serve the remaining part of the population—people either unable to pay or unmotivated to seek the service, or both.

These realities of health and social service economics place two additional burdens on the health education evaluator. One need is to analyze revenue and operating cost components; the other need is to analyze and interpret the effectiveness of the programs evaluated, taking into account the economics of the diffusion curve. Let us consider the latter first, before it becomes a bugaboo.

The diffusion of any innovation or new service in a community or larger population follows a predictable pattern described by an S-shaped curve. Figures 12-1 and 12-2 reflect both the shape and some of the forces operating at various phases of the diffusion process. Note especially some of the marketing considerations that both drive and respond to the rate of adoption. When the rate is highest, during the inflection phase in the middle of the curve, the income-generating potential of the innovation is at its greatest and commercial firms will likely "skim" the demand for services and products during that period. During this phase

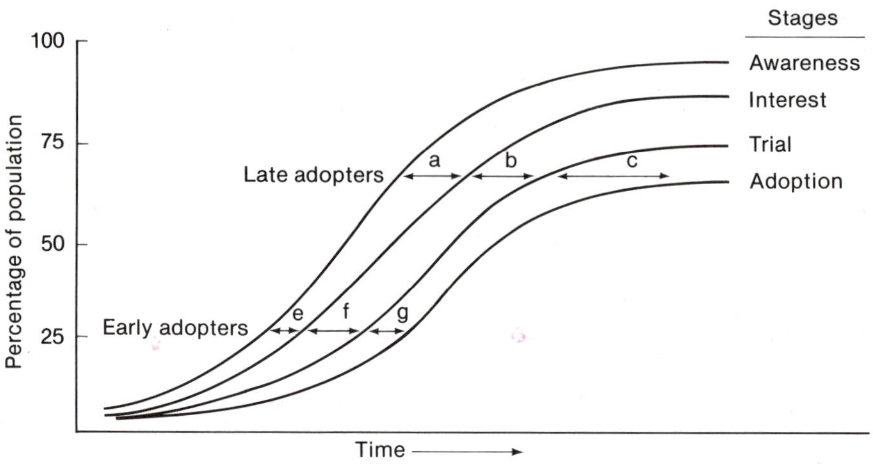

Figure 12-1 *The diffusion process. The gaps between stages of adoption are greater for late adopters (a, b, and c) than for early adopters (e, f, and g).* Source: *Green & McAlister (1984), pp. 323–339.*

the physical fitness and exercise boom in North America has recently fanned a proliferation of commercial fitness centers, products, and programs.

After the boom phase in which the middle majority of the population adopt the new practices, with minimal time between awareness, interest, trial, and adoption (in Figure 12-1, e, f, g), the gradual decline in the rate of diffusion and adoption leaves a residual population of people who are less interested (time a > e), less motivated (b > f), and less able to adopt for financial or other reasons (c > g in average time between trial and adoption). In the health field, these people are often at greatest risk of suffering the consequences of not adopting the health practices, but they are also the most socially or geographically isolated, so the cost of reaching them increases.

The appropriate correction for this difficulty in the analysis of evaluation data from health education programs is an index that standardizes measures of change in the percentage of people who have adopted. The standard in the denominator is the percentage of the population still left to adopt the practice. Let us say that P_1 is the percentage of the population who had already adopted the recommended practice before the program you are evaluating, and P_2 is the percentage who have adopted the practice by the end point of your evaluation. The measure of change that would permit you to compare this program's impact with any other program's impact on the same practices is the Effectiveness Index:

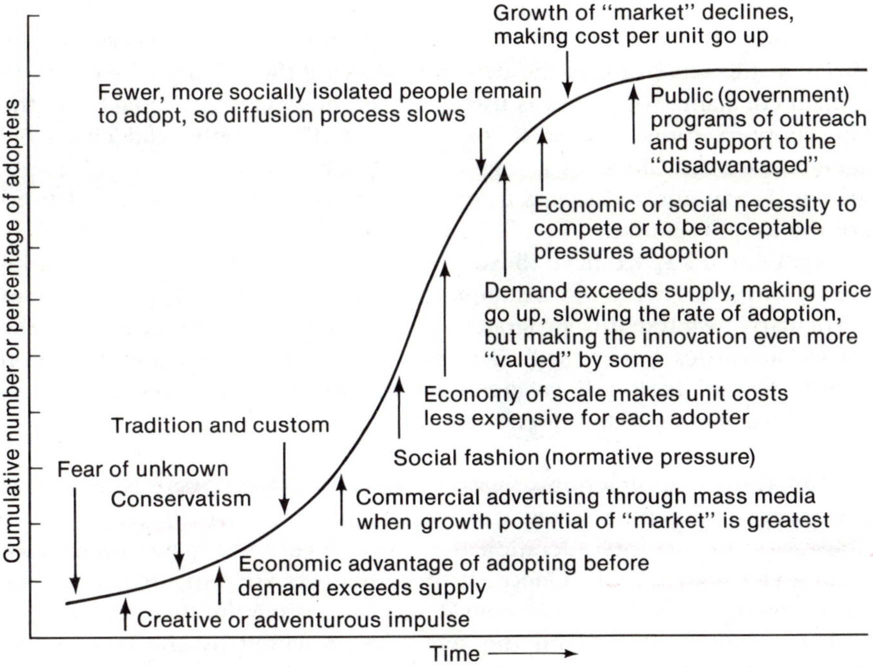

Figure 12-2 *Forces facilitating (arrows up) and retarding (arrows down) the diffusion process.* Source: *Green & McAlister (1984), pp. 323–339.*

$$EI = \frac{P_2 - P_1}{100 - P_1}$$

Try this formula with any two percentages for P_1 and P_2 where P_2 is larger than P_1. Then try it for any two equally distant values for P_1 and P_2. You will find that this index gives a higher score for change from a higher baseline (P_1) than for an equal amount of change from a lower baseline. This result is in keeping with the theory of diffusion, which would hold that it is more difficult to get an increment of change from 80 to 90 percent (EI = .50) than to get an equal number and percentage of people in the same population to adopt when only 20 percent had adopted—[(30 − 20)/(100 − 20) = .25]. The higher score for the change from 80 to 90 takes this "ceiling effect" into account.

All this discussion relates to the consideration of income for a program in that the prospects of generating fees for services decline as the diffusion curve reaches its point of diminishing rates of adoption. The simple reason for this decline is that the market or demand is shrinking.

If commercial vendors of continuing education or health promotion begin closing their businesses at this point, the supply of services may shrink at the same rate as the demand, allowing the pricing of services to remain constant. This effect is usually offset, however, by the fact that the late adopters cannot afford to pay the fees. Thus public and charitable agencies are left alone in a "market" of poor and "hard-to-reach" target groups. Donations and grants from government agencies and foundations are the usual recourse.

In Table 12-1, we have illustrated the income of the continuing education programs with the assumption neither the physicians nor nurses particularly wanted this program, so they had to be recruited. Yet the physicians, at least, were willing to pay $6 each for continuing education credits toward their relicensing requirements. This fee structure generated an income of $6,000 for Program 1.

M. Net Gain. Subtracting program costs (G) from income is all that is necessary to compute a net gain or net loss figure. This computation does not take into consideration the speculative future gains implied by the cost-benefit ratios in Line K. If those benefits are expected to accrue to the agency conducting (or considering) the program, then they can be added to future income on the schedule projected by the cost-benefit analysis. If all of the $100,000 benefit were expected to be savings to the agency sponsoring the continuing education program for physicians, for example, that agency's net gain at the end of one year might be $96,000 rather than the $4,000 loss shown in Table 12-1.

The more likely scenario is that some part of the savings represented in the cost-benefit analysis might accrue to the sponsoring agency, but not all of it.

Operational Projection Analysis

The cost analyses conducted in previous steps were likely calculated with the expenses of starting the program included. When you package and export the program for use elsewhere, or replicate it in the same agency, you can subtract some of those investment expenses. This will lead to a series of adjusted cost analyses.

N. Start-Up Costs. In calculating the program cost (G), we subtracted the costs of evaluation, but we did not subtract the costs of planning and capital outlays that represent one-time expenditures. In approaching an answer to the question of what it will cost the client agency to operate the program on a continuing basis, now is the time to remove any "front-end" expenditures that will not have to be repeated now that the program has been developed and evaluated.

One exception to the rule of subtracting start-up costs is if they were incurred by the same agency that is considering whether to continue operating the program on the basis of your evaluation. If that agency wishes to amortize the developmental as well as evaluation expenses, then these need to be divided by the number of years over which they want to spread these costs. This practice is not common in public or nonprofit agencies, but is quite common in the private sector, where the tax on future profits from a program or service can be reduced by carrying forward the expenses in producing it. This logic is the same that applies to depreciating equipment rather than taking a one-time deduction on taxes before the equipment has contributed to the production of goods or services.

O. Operating Cost. The bottom line on costs for purposes of deciding whether to continue a program that has been piloted and evaluated is the estimated recurring or operating cost. This cost is calculated, as seen in Table 12-1, by combining the original cost estimate in Line G with the income or net gain/loss figures and subtracting the start-up costs. For a commercial program, this balance would have to be a profit margin rather than an annual cost. For a public agency, the assumption of annual costs rather than gains is based on the notion that the gains are distributed to the public. Cost-benefit analyses of public programs attempt to assure that such gains are in fact forthcoming.

P. Operating Cost-Effectiveness. On the outcome side, the agency would like to know what it can expect to get for its effort and cost if it continues the program. The original cost-effectiveness measure (I) can be recalculated by using operating costs in the numerator. Using this standardized measure on two or more optional programs allows a more refined decision on the allocation of resources to the two programs.

These figures can be extended yet further to include other effects, and even to include a revised cost-benefit analysis (J/O), but by now you will have provided as much data as most decision makers can digest and more than most will request.

COVARIATE ANALYSES

In the samples up to this point, we have analyzed the results of two separate programs on their respective target groups. Analysis and interpretation usually require an additional level of subanalysis to understand the differential effects of a program on different types of people within the target population. Let us illustrate the importance of considering covariate analysis, using a fresh example. A health educator designed a short self-care program to decrease the number of clinic visits of children with simple viral upper respiratory infections (colds). The logic of the program was that parents who were knowledgeable about simple viral colds would be able to differentiate them from bacterial infections. The goal of the program was to decrease the frequency of unnecessary clinic visits for simple colds. Table 12-2 summarizes the results. Using a two-group, quasi-experimental design, 100 subjects each were nonrandomly assigned to the program or to a comparison group. The latter group did not receive the educational self-care program. The top portion of Table 12-2 might lead the evaluator to think that the program had a major effect in reducing clinic use for children with simple colds. The table shows that 80 percent of the treatment group, as contrasted with only 40 percent of the comparison group, had at least a 30 percent reduction in clinic visits. A 30 percent reduction was established as the standard of acceptability or criterion of success. On further inspection, however, it appears that age functioned as a covariate in this study. Referring to the bottom half of Table 12-2, we find that the numerically greater reduction in clinic use occurred in children over five years old.

The older children are simply not coming into the clinics as frequently as the preschoolers. As a result of not starting with randomized or equivalent groups, however, many more older children are in the program group than are in the comparison group. More children under five years of age are in the comparison group (68 percent) compared to the program group (35 percent). As a result, you are left to conclude that the child's age, and not the program, was probably the main source of differences in clinic use.

The most troublesome covariate in health education and health promotion evaluations is socioeconomic status, as variously measured with income, education, occupation, and ethnic or racial group. A procedure for the optimal combination of these measures in an index of socioeconomic status is offered in Green, 1970.[1]

Covariate analysis follows this logic and general approach to partitioning data according to the factors that might bias comparisons of experimental and control groups. More extensive statistical treatments of the data allow numerous covariates to be controlled and compared in sequence or simultaneously. Partial correlation coefficients, multiple-regression analysis, two-way and three-way analysis of variance, and analysis of covariance provide alternative ways to analyze or control covariates. And here we must leave the topic, to stay within the scope of our text and not presume to turn this into a statistics book.

1. A revised version of the Manual for Scoring Socioeconomic Status for Research on Health Behavior based on 1980 Census data is available for $3 from the University of Texas Center for Health Promotion Research and Development, P.O. Box 20186, Houston, TX 77225.

TABLE 12-2 Clinic use following self-care program, children aged 0 to 15 years (based on frequency of diagnostic visits for upper respiratory infections)

	At Least 30% Reduction	Less Than 30% Reduction
Program group ($N = 100$)	80%	20%
Comparison group ($N = 100$)	40%	60%

	No. of Children Under 5 Years of Age		No. of Children 5 or over 5 Years of Age	
Breakdown	**≥30% Reduction**	**<30% Reduction**	**≥30% Reduction**	**<30 Reduction**
Program group	25	10	55	10
Comparison group	10	58	30	2

META-EVALUATION AND META-ANALYSIS

Policy analysis and other uses of measurement and evaluation have depended heavily in the past on reviews of the literature in which a reviewer tries to draw conclusions from a large number of studies by reading each of them individually and weighing their conclusions mentally. This method runs considerable risk of biased interpretation and tendencies to remember the most unusual studies. Out of frustration with the increasingly cumbersome literature, and these problems of evaluating it, has developed a set of methods referred to variously as "evaluation of evaluations," "meta-evaluation" and "quantitative reviews of literature" (Green & Hall, 1984; Light & Pillemer, 1984). These methods consist of systematic procedures for standardizing the results from various studies so that they can be compared and summarized with a common yardstick.

Meta-evaluation can apply across the spectrum of evaluation including process and formative evaluations and even nonempirical evaluations, such as advocacy studies. The subset of procedures of interest here is sometimes referred to as "meta-analysis," in which the empirical findings from summative evaluations are standardized in a way that permits a single summative evaluation of their collective results (Glass, 1977; McGaw & Glass, 1980; Hedges, 1984).

The methods of standardization adjust the measures of change or differences between experimental and control groups by taking into account the sample size and standard deviation of the changes. This adjustment causes studies with small sample sizes and large variances to be given less weight than those with large sample sizes and small variances. The summary statistic for each measure of change in each study is referred to as an "effect size."

The standardization of effect sizes allows the magnitude of changes or differences resulting from various studies to be compared, but it does not let the reviewer ignore other methodological weaknesses in the various studies. Meta-evaluation and meta-analysis, then, represent great improvements over the usual narrative review of literature, but they do leave considerable room for critique and judgment on the relative merits of the designs and measurement procedures used in the studies reviewed. More than anything else, they force the reviewer to recognize the actual magnitude of effects rather than depending on the conclusions and abstracts written by the authors of the original studies. Insofar as the actual magnitude of effects is standardized by using the variance from the original study in combination with the measure of change, the procedure takes into account sample size and some problems of reliability and errors of measurement, all of which tend to show up in standard deviations.

These methods have been widely and increasingly adopted in various fields with some consistency of procedures in reviews of literature. Published meta-analyses in health education include Mazzuca (1982); Mullen & Green (1984; 1986); Mumford, Schlesinger, & Glass (1982); Posavac (1980); Devine & Cook (1983); Levy et al. (1980). Appendix D is based on these plus Bertram & Brooks-Bertram (1977); Eriksen & Geilen (1983); Green, Heit, Iverson, Kolbe, & Kreuter (1980); Lau, Kane, Berry, Ware, & Roy (1980); McLeroy, Green, Mullen, & Foshee (1984); and Ottoson (1981). There is increasing pressure on serious policy analysts to adopt some of these more systematic methods of review in place of the traditional professional judgment and narrative review.

SUMMARY

The analysis and reporting phase of measurement and evaluation can be broken into four levels of computation. The first level produces administrative or process data that establish the denominators for later analyses. Process data include population in need or eligible population reached or exposed, and the ratio of reach to need that we call *coverage.*

The second level of analysis measures impact, efficacy, and effectiveness. The third level measures costs, efficiency, cost-effectiveness, benefits, and cost-benefit. Each of these calculations builds on data generated in previous steps.

A final series of calculations take into account the future of the program by assessing the income it generates and the net gain or loss. It then partitions the one-time expenditures required to create or start the program, and subtracts these to produce an estimate of ongoing operating cost and operating cost-effectiveness to be expected if the program is adopted.

Methods of covariate analysis can be used to provide some statistical control at the analysis and reporting stage that was not possible in the design and data collection stages.

When evaluations accumulate, they can be subjected to another level of analysis called *meta-analysis* or *meta-evaluation.* These methods allow the results of several studies, each of which might have used somewhat different measures of impact and outcome, to be commensurate for purposes of arriving at statistical conclusions based on more than one study.

Postscript

The first few chapters in this book took great pains to cast the subjects of measurement and evaluation in the most practical and relevant terms for health education. The middle chapters grappled with some of the most difficult problems that health education and health promotion programs present as challenges to measurement and evaluation, including sampling and design problems. The final two chapters brought us full circle, back to the most practical questions you can ask for the improvement of programs: "What do the data mean? For whom should they have meaning? What can we say with certainty? How should we qualify our results to acknowledge the limitations of sampling, measurement, and design?"

Now that you have covered the suggested steps in analysis and interpretation, you will be in a stronger position to make more prudent decisions at the measurement, sampling, and design stages because you can anticipate more of the data requirements and analytic issues that hinge on good management, sampling, and design. The summary of these data requirements and analytic issues is most succinctly contained in our definition of evaluation: *the comparison of an object of interest against a standard of acceptability.* To compare, you need two or more measurements. To isolate an object of interest (a health education method or program), you need a design that allows you to partition the variations in measurement into (1) those attributable to the object and (2) those attributable to other sources of variation. To set up standards of acceptability, you need denominators for each of your measurements that allow you to compare them on equal or "standardized" terms. The steps from A to P in Chapter 12 build up from denominators to numerators to ratios, rates, and percentages; from needs to process to impact to outcomes.

This discussion brings us to a yet larger issue in health education and health promotion, one that puts measurement and evaluation in proper perspective. Insofar as our definition of needs is the starting point for the series of computations leading up to estimates of effectiveness and benefits, our measurement and evaluation efforts are only meaningful and useful if we have accurately assessed needs. This approach requires measurement at a pre-evaluation stage of program development. It also requires a logic and understanding of the art and science of health education and an appreciation of human needs that depends on the cumulative development and synthesis of previous measurement and evaluation.

Our responsibility as professionals is not merely to measure with accuracy and to evaluate with objectivity, but it is also, and as much, to develop our programs and to interpret and report our findings in the context of previous experience in the field. If we leave that development and synthesis of the cumulative body of knowledge in health education to scientists who have no experience in practice, we have only ourselves to blame when theory does not seem to fit reality. Practitioners can and should participate in measurement and evaluation.

Appendix A

CRITERIA FOR FORMATIVE EVALUATION

The following list of criteria for formative evaluation is offered as an example of explicit criteria that could be applied in self-evaluation and peer review of health education practice in a variety of programs.

These criteria were developed originally for a review of drug education programs in collaboration with Marjorie A. C. Young of Harvard University and Ralph Solad of Marco Systems, Inc., for the U.S. Department of Health, Education, and Welfare. They have since been applied in a variety of other programs. The corresponding rating scales (standards) may be found in Green, Kreuter, Deeds, and Partridge (1980), Appendix A. More extensive listings of criteria and standards have been published for health education and health promotion in HMOs (Mullen & Zapka, 1982) and reproductive care settings (Hirschhorn et al., 1984; Mullen, Ottoson, & Williams, 1981).

A. Problem Diagnosis
   1. Data from available sources (e.g., school district, health department, census) should be gathered, supplemented with new data, and consolidated for planning purposes (data on both the problems and the population).
   2. Existing literature on the specific problems identified should be reviewed before planning.
   3. Available resources should be surveyed in the community to avoid overlap and to identify individuals and groups with prior experience with the problem.
   4. Consultation from national or state health agencies should be used where specific data, literature, resources, or experience were lacking.

B. Planning

1. The specific target and transmitter populations should be identified (geographic, ethnic, socioeconomic status, age, etc.).
2. Representatives from the "target" and transmitter populations should be included from the beginning of the formal planning.
3. Representatives from each level and occupational category ultimately responsible for implementing the program should be included in the planning.
4. Objectives for the program should be stated from the consumer's perspective (i.e., in terms of *their* goals or expected benefits and with numerical targets).
5. Priorities should be established among objectives.
6. Participating agencies should be represented throughout the planning.
7. Participating personnel within each agency should be kept informed of progress on planning.
8. Planning sessions should be varied in format and location to provide opportunities for input from individuals and groups who are more or less responsive under different circumstances.
9. Planning should not end with submission of the grant proposal or receipt of the contract or budget.
10. Attention should be given to the knowledge, attitudes, values, and social relationships of the target population as related to their health behavior.
11. Referral sources and cooperating agencies should be designated and informed of the beginning date for the program.
12. Methods of recruiting clients or consumers should be specified.

C. Implementation

1. Publicity spread or promotion of the services should be limited initially to avoid creating more demand for services than can adequately be met at the outset.
2. High-priority cases or groups should be handled first. Satisfied clients should be a major goal of the initial services rendered.
3. Data collection and record-keeping procedures should be appropriately applied and monitored.
4. Examples of criteria for implementation of specific instructional methods—criteria for film, videotape, or slide-tape showing—are as follows:
   a. Films or videotapes should be previewed several days in advance of their scheduled showing, with representatives of the target audience reacting to the preview.

   b. Audiences should be small enough and homogeneous enough to allow discussion following showings.
   c. Verbal introduction of videotape showings should include a statement on the purpose of the videotape, reasons for selecting it, what to look for, and what aspects will be discussed following the showing.
5. Examples of criteria specific to training—criteria for teacher training workshops—are as follows:
   a. A normative ratio of dollars per teacher-day of training provided should be developed and used as one index of program support.
   b. The program should have the active support of school administrators, teachers' union (if any), and parent-teacher associations.
   c. Teachers should be allowed release time (with pay) or receive graduate credit or both.
6. Staff and supervisors should perform the functions specified in Items B4 and 5.
7. The program should make appropriate use of volunteers, audio and visual aids, cooperating agencies, and referral sources (see Items B3, 6, 7, and 11).
8. Communication and feedback should be maintained among personnel at all program levels (vertical) and among cooperating agencies or groups (horizontal).

Appendix B

THE DACCA FAMILY-PLANNING EXPERIMENT

This appendix provides excerpts from an extensive evaluation of a family-planning program (Green, Gustafson, Griffiths, & Yaukey, 1972). It represents a cross-cultural case study of the linkage between program objectives and program evaluation, the logic and methods (though not the statistical procedures described in Chapters 4, 5, and 6) of assessing the reliability and validity of measurements, and the steps one goes through in planning and implementing an evaluation, including the development of a survey questionnaire in another language.

This case study comes from one of the first large-scale community and clinic-based evaluations of a health education program, predating by more than a decade the Stanford Three-Community project in cardiovascular risk reduction. The project was sponsored by the Ford Foundation and the Population Council through the government of Pakistan and the University of California School of Public Health. The principal investigators were William Griffiths and Beryl Roberts. Harold C. Gustafson was the project field director, and David Yaukey was the field social scientist on the project, responsible for developing the design and survey instruments, along with his Bengali colleagues, S. Jahangir Haider, Akhtar Iqbal Begum, Nural Islam Khan, and A. B. M. Shafiullah.

The project was carried out in matched government housing colonies in the city of Dacca, East Pakistan, now Bangladesh. The purpose was to test the effectiveness of family-planning education in raising the consciousness of the population, increasing their use of contraceptives, and improving their pregnancy spacing and total fertility. The case material presented here is excerpted from Chapters 3 and 4 of the monograph reporting on the complete study (Green et al., 1972; see also Rossi & Freeman, 1982, pp. 225–227, for a summary).

EDUCATIONAL PROGRAM OBJECTIVES AND ASSOCIATED CRITERIA OF PROGRAM SUCCESS

Operational program objectives are spelled out below in relation to criteria of program success. The criteria of success are grouped into three broad areas of indicators or measures of change: knowledge, motivation, and behavior.

A. Knowledge Criteria	Educational Objectives
No. 1. Increase in knowledge of selected methods of birth control:	1. To learn that there are methods by which birth can be controlled or limited. 2. To learn that babies come from seeds planted inside a woman by a man at time of intercourse. 3. To learn that babies result from the male semen meeting with the female egg and that birth control methods stop the man's "seeds" from reaching the female egg. 4. To learn that specific contraceptive methods do not kill a life. 5. To learn that methods are not harmful to health. 6. To learn that use of contraceptive methods do not interfere with sexual pleasure. 7. To learn that many people in Pakistan and throughout the world use these methods. 8. To become acquainted with the specific methods that are available. 9. To hear how each method is used. 10. To discuss the advantages and disadvantages of each method in relation to self and spouse.

No. 2. Increase in knowledge of where to go to obtain birth control information.

1. To learn the location of the clinic.
2. To obtain information about clinic hours.
3. To obtain information on clinic costs of contraceptives and comparative prices in the market.
4. To learn about amount of supplies given and proper storage.
5. To know clinic personnel and what they will do.
6. To be assured that advice at the clinic is free.

B. Motivational Criteria

No. 3a. Increase in attitude toward general desirability of small families.

No. 3b. Increase in knowledge of spouse's desire for small families.

Educational Objectives

1. To believe that there are economic advantages of having a small family.
2. To believe that there is a relationship between size of family and mother's health.
3. To believe that there is a relationship between size of family and health of children.
4. To believe that children have a greater opportunity for education, thus, with job opportunities.
5. To believe that members of the family have more time to spend with one another, husband with wife, mother and father with children.
6. To believe that today in Pakistan and throughout the world, many families desire a small number of children.
7. To know that the Pakistan Government is encouraging small families.
8. To seek discussion with spouse of desirability for small families.

No. 4a. Increase in attitude toward spacing as a desirable practice. No. 4b. Increase in knowledge of spouse's desire for spacing.	1. To believe that spacing of children improves the mother's health. 2. To believe that spacing allows the mother to devote a longer period of time to her youngest baby and other children. 3. To believe that spacing allows the mother more free time for herself. 4. To believe that spacing results in fewer deliveries, thus, lower maternity costs. 5. To know that the Pakistan Government is encouraging spacing. 6. To seek discussion with spouse of desirability of spacing.
No. 5. Increase in acceptability for others to use contraceptives.	1. To believe that people who use contraceptive methods are acting wisely. a. They grasp the economic advantages of small families. b. They are showing concern for their health and the health of their children. 2. To believe that people who use contraceptive methods are to be praised by their relations and friends. 3. To believe that high officials in the Government are pleased when people use contraceptive methods.
No. 6. Increase in acceptability of self to use contraceptives.	1. To believe that using contraceptives is wise behavior. 2. To understand that the cost is very low.

	3. To believe that the methods are simple and easy to use. 4. To believe that the securing of contraceptives is very easy. 5. To believe that using contraceptives is good for oneself, one's family, and one's country.
No. 7. Increase own desire to learn more about contraceptive methods.	1. To believe that learning as much as possible about methods is desirable behavior. 2. To believe that the clinic staff is most willing and anxious to teach about the methods.
No. 8. Increase in willingness to meet with others.	1. To believe that family planning is an appropriate subject to discuss in small groups. 2. To know that people in other parts of the world discuss such matters, in groups. 3. To believe that by discussing in a small group, individuals can learn about family planning.

C. Behavioral Criteria

No. 9. Increase in reported use of non-clinical methods.	Educational objectives for Criteria 1 through 8 were all directed to Criteria 9 through 12. In addition, there were the following specific operational objectives:
No. 10. Increase in attendance at clinic.	1. To use all opportunities to urge people to attend the clinic.
No. 11. Increase in the taking of materials from the clinic.	2. To make specific clinic appointments.

No. 12. Meeting with others in small groups to discuss family planning.

3. To urge individuals at the clinic to try contraceptives.
4. To identify and correct blocks to clinic attendance or contraceptive procurement.

RELIABILITY AND VALIDITY OF THE INTERVIEW DATA

Most types of behavior can be measured more efficiently through interviews than by direct observation. For some aspects of marriage and birth control, verbal reports are the *only* measure obtainable. Smith (1965) warns us, however, that we are dealing in family planning surveys with "... sex and the marriage bed around which surely are woven some of the strongest and least rational motives, the most intimate and private relationships and the firmest institutional norms and taboos known to man."

The Problem of Quality

The emotional reaction to family planning surveys is compounded in cultures such as that of Bengal with relatively low literacy, little orientation to numbers and planning, perceptions at wide variance with those of the investigators, and with such crowded housing that interviews can seldom be held in private (e.g., Green and Jan, 1964; Corsa, 1964; and Choldin et al., 1967). These problems compelled us to investigate the reliability and validity of verbal reports in our Before and After surveys and to attempt to estimate the direction and magnitude of errors in our interview data. Such estimates should improve our interpretation of results of the experiment.

Four general approaches were used in this effort: (1) internal consistency of responses given by individuals within a given interview; (2) comparison of factual responses given by husbands and wives about characteristics of each other and of the couple; (3) comparison of responses to factual questions given by the same respondent in the Before and After surveys; and (4) comparison of After Survey responses concerning knowledge and use of contraceptives with clinic and education program records on the individuals and couples.

Previous Research. In his inventory of family planning studies, Berelson (1966:657) concluded that surveys are valid for indicating broad tendencies within groups, but "not for every specific item in each individual case, and that their substance can be taken seriously in administrative calculations." This would imply that errors at least partially cancel out; that is, the overreporting of events, time, attitudes, knowledge, and practices by some individuals would balance out with the underreporting of others to give small net errors for the group. Independently recorded check data on individuals are needed to determine the direction and the degree of misreporting.

The cumulative evidence from methodological studies done elsewhere suggested that the use of birth control methods would tend to be underreported, especially by women and especially in more traditional societies; and that reliability and validity in general would vary with certain characteristics of the respondents and the questions asked.

Back and Stycos (1959), for example, inferred underreporting in a Jamaica survey by asking the interviewers to estimate the accuracy of the interview data on the incidence of birth control practice. Of 15 interviewers, nine felt the data accurate, six felt that the use of contraceptives was underestimated, none felt that it was overestimated. Poti et al. (1962) detected female disavowals of contraceptive use in a Calcutta study by husband-wife comparisons and reinterview of husbands. Frequent reference was made to shyness among wives, often ascribed to lack of privacy in the household in which the interview was taking place.

In an urban Jamaica sample, the names of 60 interviewees who claimed to have secured contraceptives from a specific clinic were compared with clinic records. All but two of the names were found, confirming the relative absence of false-*positive* reports (Back and Stycos, 1959:28). This makes the possibility of false-*negative* reports all the more important, since underreporting of contraceptive use will not tend to be cancelled out by overreporting.

Family planning surveys typically also try to reconstruct fertility histories for couples. To do this, it is important that they get full reporting of fertility events and fertility determining practices. It also is important that they get accurate time reports to enable them to place these events and practices in the histories. Unfortunately, there has been little specific study of the accuracy of such time reports in fertility surveys. The Before and After surveys provided relevant data on reports of years spent in present marriage, of time since last live birth, and of months of separation in the last year, all of which will be inspected in this chapter.

General Quality of the Surveys. It is necessary that we cast modesty aside and state our confidence in the general quality of the Dacca survey procedures and interviewing if one is to try to generalize from our experience to others. We believe that the Before and After surveys did not encounter any more bias in the interviewing, recording, or coding of responses than would result from other careful KAP [knowledge, attitude, and practice] surveys in similar areas (cf. Westoff et al., 1961:68).

All of those responsible for the study were involved in the construction, translation, and pretesting of the interview schedules and other preparations for the survey. The four field supervisors were given a week of special training, including a thorough analysis of the interview schedule and the instructions for interviewers, principles and problems of interviewing, methods of supervising interviewers, demonstration and practice interviews in both English and Bengali, and the development of specific training procedures for the interviewers.

With four supervisors, we decided to employ 24 interviewers so that each supervisor would work with no more than six interviewers. Two interviewing teams were assigned to each supervisor, a team consisting of one female and two male interviewers.

Through newspaper advertising and the government employment exchange, about 100 applications for interviewers were obtained. A two-step selection process was used. One-third more than the actual number of interviewers needed were employed initially for the training period, so that elimination could be made on a merit basis during that time. All applicants were carefully interviewed, and rating procedures were worked out for the initial selection process.

Training of Interviewers. The staff developed an intensive and thorough program including a variety of role-playing experiences. Instructions were imparted as questions arose in the trainees' experiences rather than all at once. Each practice interview was critically observed by the four supervisors, the Bengali project director, and the Bengali research associate.

In the final selection fifteen male and seven female interviewers were employed on the basis of interview-recording tests and rankings by the trainers. Ages of the female interviewers ranged from 19 to 35; two were unmarried. Two of the women had passed the ninth grade; the others had completed the tenth grade. Four claimed some previous experience in interviewing. The males ranged in age from 19 to 30, with ten unmarried. For all but one, the tenth grade was the highest educational level achieved; the other had finished the ninth grade. Fourteen of the males stated that they had had previous interviewing experience.

Internal Consistency Checks

The responsibility for editing the completed interview schedules went to the supervisors. They were instructed to check each interview schedule for internal consistency and completeness of recording. The schedule had to be in such form that in the future another person could code the responses directly from the schedule. If further information was necessary to make the schedule complete, the supervisor insisted that the interviewer return to get the required information. Supervisors edited schedules immediately upon the daily reporting of the interviewers. After a schedule had been edited, and after the Supervisor had taken from it all information necessary for his own records, he turned it over to the Research Associate.

The Research Associate was instructed to start out by making a 100 percent check on the editing of the supervisors. This proved valuable, because some minor errors were located quickly and the supervisors were instructed accordingly. At the beginning of the third week of interviewing, the RA started making a 50 percent check, and at the beginning of the fourth week a 25 percent check, which he continued to the end of the interviewing.

Part of our faith in the interviews results from a quality check made possible by the fact that we were interviewing both husbands and wives on the same topics. We devised a male-female interview comparison form, unknown to interviewers, which would allow the quick comparison of responses to factual questions by husbands and wives of every couple interviewed. These forms were filled out by supervisors as soon as completed interview schedules were turned in by the male and female interviewers. From these forms, carefully employed, we had empirical evidence that at least no falsification of completed interviews took place. The husband-wife comparison forms also directed our attention, very early in the Before Survey, to items on which there were frequent inconsistencies so that we were able to clarify instructions to interviewers.

Another purpose of these forms was to locate discrepancies between responses so large that clearly not only memory failure was involved, but also misunderstanding of the question by either husband or wife. In such cases, reinterviews were made on those specific questions involved. It is important to mention this here because reinterviewing on this basis acted to eliminate extreme discrepancies between spouses' responses on some of the topics whose reliability we will report below. Specifically, reinterviews were assigned where (1) there was a discrepancy of more than seven years in the reported duration of present marriage, or (2) there was a discrepancy of more than ten years in the reported age at marriage of the wife, or (3) there was disagreement as to whether there had been any live births in the present marriage, or (4) there were discrepancies in number of living boys and girls by present marriage, or (5) there was more than two years' discrepancy in years and months since last live birth. In no case in which we were able to reinterview both spouses did we fail to get responses compatible within these limits. Of the total of 63 cases corrected on these topics through reinterview, 33 were based on errors in the original male interview and 30 were based on errors in the original female interview. The important thing to remember in the husband-wife comparisons and in the between-survey comparisons is that the range of discrepancies on topics listed above were curtailed by our quality-control procedure.

Between-Spouse Comparisons

After all interviews from the Before Survey were coded we analyzed the responses of husbands and wives to questions on the use of contraception, on the years spent in the present marriage, on the time since the last live birth, on the months of separation in the last year, on live births and unsuccessful pregnancies in the last year, and on the pregnancy status of the wife at the time of interview. The comparisons will be discussed in that order here, but for details on methods and data, the reader is referred to Yaukey et al. (1965) and Green (1969).

The basic data in all cases were paired comparisons between the male and female responses of individual couples. The simpler method of comparing frequency distributions of responses by all husbands with those of all wives was rejected on the basis of the experience of Westoff (1961), who repeatedly found that such distributions for initial interviews were quite similar to equivalent distributions for reinterviews of the same women, but that this apparent similarity masked considerable difference between initial interview and reinterview responses for particular women.

Knowledge and Use of Contraception. Our use of the term "contraception" in the Dacca study is made clear by the series of questions beginning with Q21a [See Green et al., 1972, pp. 145–156, for the interview instructions, questions, and precoded response categories]. Each time a respondent described a method, the interviewer classified the method according to an exhaustive list in the schedule. The interviewer then probed with: "Have you heard of any other methods?" Equipped now with a list of methods known, the interviewer proceeded to determine for each method known whether the couple had *ever* used the method, asking question 24a consecutively about each method known.

Of the 545 couples who answered the questions, 21 percent did not agree on whether they had ever used a method. These 115 disagreeing couples represented 54 percent of the 211 couples where at least one member admitted ever using any method. Of those 96 couples agreeing that they ever had used any method, 31 percent did not agree on whether they had used any method during the last year.

Disagreements tended to be larger for specific methods. The three most popular methods were condom or sheath, a male method, foam tablets, a female method, and safe period or rhythm, controllable by either spouse. For each class we determined the number of couples who disagreed on ever-use divided by the number of couples where either member claimed ever-use. The resulting percentages were 75 for the condom, 58 for foam tablets, and 89 for rhythm.

Wives tended to underreport contraceptive use relative to their husbands, and the reverse was not true for any of the methods. This was substantiated from individual comparisons of spouses' responses: of the 194 couples where the husband reported ever-use of any method, 50 percent of the wives reported never using any method. Of the 113 couples where the wife reported ever using any method, only 15 percent of the husbands reported never using any method. The nature of difference in reports is the same for each of the specific types of methods. For example, of the 136 couples where the husband reported ever using the condom or sheath, 48 percent of the wives reported never using that method; of the 89 couples where the wife reported ever using the condom or sheath, only 20 percent of the husbands reported never using that method (see Yaukey et al., 1965, for detailed results by method).

Differences of the nature described could be explained either by husbands overreporting contraceptive usage or by wives underreporting. Although this issue is taken up later in the comparison of After Survey responses with clinic records, there was considerable circumstantial evidence in the Before Survey alone that the wives were making the most errors of omission. Although husbands could have been boasting about use, they could not have been boasting about their knowledge of methods. The questions were asked in such a way that the respondent was supplied with no information, and had to supply all of it from memory. The husbands volunteered their possession of more knowledge, irrespective of use. Of the 545 husbands responding, 76 percent described one or more methods; of the 547 wives responding, only 69 percent described one or more methods.

Evidence will be presented later indicating that women were relatively underreporting even *knowledge* of methods. In the Before Survey, one would expect that when one spouse reported using a contraceptive the other spouse would at least know about that method. Of the 194 couples in the Before Survey where the husband reported ever using any method, 16 percent of the wives reported never hearing about any method. Similar results are found for each class of method of which there was substantial reported use. Which sex had to control the use of a particular method seemed to make no difference.

There was one additional source of circumstantial evidence from the Before Survey. Right after asking about all the methods heard about, the respondent was asked the following question (Q23b): "Do you think that your wife/husband has ever heard of any methods?" Interviewers were instructed to probe for the respondents' best guesses. Husbands perceived

376 of their wives as knowing about any method; only 322 of the wives perceived husbands as knowing about any methods. Thus the perceptions of the spouses were the reverse of the claims by the spouses themselves. It seems that the wives were relatively underreporting not only their own knowledge of contraception but also the knowledge of their husbands.

Duration of Marriage. The distribution of the 547 couples on the basis of years of differences between husband's and wife's report on duration of marriage revealed that only 39 percent of the couples gave exactly the same answer. Another 36 percent disagreed by one year; another 12 percent disagreed by two years. Of those couples who were not in complete agreement, 78 percent differed by one or two years only.

A reported difference of as much as two years could result from one spouse reporting precisely and the other rounding to the nearest year ending with zero or five. Class limits for the distribution of reports by each spouse were chosen to minimize the effect of rounding toward years ending in zero and five. No tendency was found for one sex to report more years spent in marriage. The interpolated median for both distributions was the same: 14.3 years.

Wives, however, did favor the modal and central categories more than did the husbands. There was a relative deficiency of husbands reporting between 9 and 18 years spent in present marriage. The effect of this is to limit the dispersion of wives' reports when compared with husbands'. The interquartile range of reports was 9.2 years for husbands and 8.3 years for wives.

We computed indexes of heaping on numbers ending in either zero or five (adapted from Barclay, 1958:69). The index of heaping for wives was more than twice as great as the index for husbands. The inference is that, although the husbands were not blameless, the wives were more guilty of imprecise reporting. This suspicion is reinforced by the observation, reported above, that the wives more favored the modal categories, a tendency which could be interpreted as an extreme form of rounding.

We have only partial evidence as to whether husbands or wives were less precise in their statements. Let us suppose that the sex giving more careless time reports will show this tendency by more frequently rounding to popular numbers. Inspection of the ungrouped distributions showed the most popular numbers for both husbands and wives to be those ending in a zero or a five. There also was some lesser heaping at numbers ending in two and six, by both sexes.

Time Since Last Live Birth. The degree of disagreement on years since last live birth (see Q15d) was relatively small. Whereas only 39 percent of the couples had agreed on years spent in present marriage, 78 percent agreed on the number of years since last live birth. Of those couples who did disagree, 78 percent differed by one or two years only on years spent in present marriage; the analogous figure for years since last live birth was 95 percent. The couples' superior precision in placing the last live birth in time is explained partially by the relative recency of the event; the median years spent in present marriage was about 14; the median years since last live birth was about 1.

On the other hand, demographers usually require more precision in reports on the time since live birth. For instance, this information is needed to determine periods of exposure to the risk of conception.

It was still important, therefore, to look for any apparent tendency of husbands or wives to differ systematically in reports when compared with their spouses. Of 114 couples where there was any disagreement in years since last live birth, 55 percent had wives reporting a longer period than the husbands and in 45 percent the husband reported a longer period than did the wife. The wives showed only a slight relative tendency to report longer periods since last live birth.

As to the relative accuracy of reports by spouses, again our main clue was the degree to which the sexes tended to round-off their reports. In this case we could analyze the tendency to round to popular numbers of *months* beyond reported years. Inspection of the distributions shows that both husbands and wives tended to report either zero months (reports rounded to years) or six months (reports rounded to half years). The indexes of heaping at zero or six months were high for both but slightly higher for wives.

Months of Separation in Last Year. All husbands and wives were asked to indicate the longest period, in months in the last year, during which the wife was not pregnant and the couple did not see each other (see Q20b). Interviewers were encouraged to get respondents' best guesses.

Of the total couples, 70 percent were in agreement. Of the disagreeing couples, only 36 percent differed by more than two months in their reports.

There seemed to be a very slight tendency for wives to underreport periods of absence when compared with their husbands. Whereas 460 husbands reported no separation of a month or more, 468 wives reported no such separation. Measured another way, husbands reported a total of 149 months of separation while wives reported a total of 142 months.

The slightly greater tendency of wives to report zero months of separation might be viewed as an expression of a greater tendency to round off numbers; that is, they were less likely to report slight deviations from zero. Support for this view is gained from the heaping of wives' reports at six months; seven wives, but only one husband, reported separations of six months even though more husbands reported any separations. In sum, 475 wives but only 461 husbands reported either zero or six months of separation. Though the difference is small, one could infer again that the wives tended toward less precise reporting.

Live Births During the Last Year. Given accurate time reporting, a precise pregnancy history still requires complete reporting of the existence of all pregnancies and their fates. We had data on reports of live births during the year before the interview, of abortions and still births during that year, and reports of pregnancy at the time of the interview (see Q16–17).

The degree of difference between husbands' and wives' reports were relatively small. Of the 526 couples of which both members had reported the wife ever giving live birth, less than 4 percent disagreed about whether or not the wife had had a live birth during the last year. Within this limited range, the women reported slightly more live births than did the husbands.

In sum, there was little disagreement among spouses as to live births in the last year and little pattern to the small differences that did exist. The same cannot be said of reports on unsuccessful pregnancies.

Abortions and Still Births in Past Year. Although we found no studies of the reliability of husbands' reports on unsuccessful pregnancies, two studies gave evidence on the unreliability of wives' reports. Back and Stycos (1959:28) reinterviewed 77 urban Jamaican women of low education about one year after their initial interviews. They found that, in reinterviews, only 77 percent of the women reported the same total number of pregnancies for the period before the first interview. However, 92 percent of the women reported the same total number of live births for that period. One might infer that reports of unsuccessful pregnancies were less reliable than those of successful pregnancies. Westoff (1961:68) reported considerable reinterview unreliability in reports on miscarriage by urban American women of low parity.

Of the 547 couples in the Dacca Before Survey, there were 35 where either husband or wife or both reported one or more unsuccessful pregnancies. Of these 35 couples, 63 percent had some difference between husbands' and wives' reports. The 22 differing couples were inspected individually to find any patterns of difference. The dominant pattern was that of the wife reporting a spontaneous abortion where the husband reported no unsuccessful pregnancy. In 15 of the 22 differing cases, only spontaneous abortions were reported by either spouse. In 14 of these 15 cases, the wife reported more spontaneous abortions than did the husband.

Of the 22 differing couples, 3 followed another pattern: abortions reported as spontaneous by wives were reported as induced by husbands. There were only three cases in which either spouse reported an induced abortion. In all three cases the pattern of difference was identical: a single unsuccessful pregnancy was reported by both husband and wife. The wife reported it as a spontaneous abortion; the husband reported it as an induced abortion.

Whose reports were the more accurate? We compared the rates of reported spontaneous abortion with those available elsewhere. Husbands reported a rate of 100 spontaneous abortions per thousand pregnancies ending in the year before the interview; the rate reported by the wives was 166. Unintentional abortion rates reported by the United Nations (1954:15) ranged from 51 to 129 per thousand, but these were all for western populations. Yaukey (1961:113–115) used essentially the same questions as those asked in Dacca in measuring pregnancy wastage on a population of Lebanese women. The spontaneous abortion rates reported by four types of Beirut wives (distinguished by husbands' education and by religion) were 104, 100, 111, and 148 per thousand pregnancy ends. Evaluation of the data made him guess that the first three of these rates were slight underestimates and the fourth was a slight overestimate. But Beirut can be considered a more modern city than Dacca, and probably had better health facilities.

Our exercise at trying to guess whether husbands' or wives' reports on spontaneous abortions were more plausible was inconclusive. On the one hand, husbands' reports result in a spontaneous abortion rate more like those reported from elsewhere. On the other hand, such other reports are from dissimilar populations.

Pregnancy at Time of Interview. Only five percent of the couples did not agree in their "yes" or "no" responses to whether the wife was pregnant at the time of the Before Survey (Q19). Let us suppose that all wives were in fact pregnant who were reported as such by either husband or wife or both. Of 95 such pregnancies, 26 percent were reported by only one member of the couple.

The wives reported more pregnancies than did their husbands. Of the 90 couples where wives reported themselves pregnant, 20 of their husbands did not; of the 70 couples where husbands reported pregnancies, only 5 of the wives did not.

We could only speculate as to whether women tended to overreport or men tended to underreport current pregnancies. One source of relevant information was question 18, asked of all couples who had reported a pregnancy ending in the last year. Of the 547 couples, 141 husbands and 150 wives reported the wife as pregnant exactly one year previous to the interview. Either of these figures is considerably above the 90 pregnancies reported by the same population of wives exactly one year later. In short, it seems that the main error on the part of both spouses was probably in the direction of underreporting, and that the husbands committed this error more frequently.

Interview-Clinic Record Comparisons

Having established that there was some underreporting of contraceptive knowledge and use, we wanted to determine the degree. We sought to obtain underreporting rates for men and women in the Dacca interviews. This required the establishment of independent behavioral criteria or measures of knowledge and use against which to compare verbal reports. The longitudinal data on the panel of 519 couples included both direct behavioral measures from the clinic and education program records, and verbal reports of behavior from the After Survey.

Method. The procedures used in this analysis have been described in some detail elsewhere (Green, 1969). They consisted essentially of an evaluation of the clinic and education experience of every individual male and female and a comparison with their subsequent interview responses. The clinic and education records on each individual included number of clinic visits, number of home visits by Project health educators, number of times the person attended small group meetings on family planning, and specific number of home visits by Project health educators, number of times the person attended small group meetings on family planning, and specific aspects of these experiences during the 18-month program between the Before and After surveys.

The individual experiences of husbands and wives were given a score based on the implications of each type of experience for the individual and for his spouse in terms of their knowledge and use of contraceptive methods. If an individual, for example, was ever exposed to one of the recorded educational experiences specified above, he most assuredly heard about contraceptives and should have known of at least one method, if only by name or description, at the time of the After Survey. If such a person claimed no knowledge of any method in the subsequent interview, he was regarded as underreporting his knowledge. A person taking contraceptives from the clinic even more assuredly should have known of a method when interviewed, and the probability of his spouse also learning should have increased with this experience. By extending this logic to cover the implications of different types of experiences in the clinic and education program for different levels of "expected" knowledge and use of contraceptives, we were able to establish a set of independent criteria against which to judge the validity of verbal reports in the After Survey.[1]

Actual verbal reports of husbands and wives in the After Survey were compared with the "expected" knowledge and use levels based on the couple experiences in the clinic and education program. This was accomplished by combining the responses to the series of questions on contraceptive history (see Q23a).[2]

When negative reports in interviews were compared with expected knowledge and use scores, it was possible to obtain three groups each of false-negative knowledge reports and false-negative use reports for husbands and for wives. The three groups consisted of the three levels of certainty for husbands and for wives that their reports were false. The levels (0 to 3) of "expected" knowledge and use were regarded as degrees of certainty that a negative verbal report on knowledge or use was invalid.

Verbal Reports of Knowledge and Use in the After Survey. In response to the question on knowledge, the majority of respondents named one or more contraceptive methods. Those who did were asked the additional questions regarding use, with their present spouse, of each method named. A cross-tabulation of these responses revealed considerable disagreement between husbands and wives in the panel. Inasmuch as the

1. In general the criteria for expected knowledge and use scores were (a) that if the individual took any action (attended the clinic, had a home visit, or attended a small group meeting) it was assumed that he should know of at least one temporary method of contraception (score 3 on expected knowledge) and there was considerable evidence that the spouse should know a method (score 2 on expected knowledge); (b) that if the individual took supplies from the clinic once, he must know of a method (score 3) and the probability that his spouse also learned of the method was high (score 2), and it was likely that they used the method (score 2 on expected use if wife took; score 1 if husband took, because husband is more likely to be able to take supplies without wife's knowledge); (c) if the individual took supplies from the clinic more than once it was considered highly probable (score 3 on both expected knowledge and expected use) that both spouses knew and used the method; (d) if both spouses took supplies from the clinic, the effect was assumed to be the same as one spouse taking supplies more than once.

2. The present analysis is concerned only with knowledge of any method and use of any method at any time, not with specific methods, number of methods, or recency of use. The interviewees are placed in one of three groups on the basis of their responses to questions 23–24: does not know of any method; knows of one or more methods but never used any method; and used one or more methods at any time. A respondent in the last category admits knowing *and* having used at least one contraceptive method other than sterilization. These are positive knowledge and positive use responses, the verity of which cannot be tested here, although it is certain by the open-ended nature of the question that there can be no false-positive *knowledge* responses (unless by coding or punching errors). Interviews in the second category, on the other hand, are positive knowledge responses but negative use responses. Those in the first category are negative knowledge and negative use reports. Only those in the first category, then, are negative knowledge reports, while the negative use reports consist of the cumulative total of those in the first and second categories.

519 husbands and wives are of the same 519 couples, the discrepancies in their distributions of responses were evidence either of (a) gross underreporting by females, (b) gross overreporting by males, (c) misreporting by both, but more by one than by the other, or (d) misreporting by both, but in opposite directions. We have presented the circumstantial evidence from the Before Survey that the first alternative would explain most of the discrepancy, i.e., that most of the underreporting was a function of the shyness of Bengali women.

The technique applied in the validity analysis allowed false-positive reporting to be partitioned out while the degree of false-negative reporting was measured. This was done by including in the numerator only those individuals whose couple experience indicated that they knew or had used contraceptives. The degree of underreporting, independent of overreporting, then became the proportion of those who said "no," of all those who should have said "yes." By this technique we were led to conclude the third alternative, that both husbands and wives underreported their knowledge and use but that women did so more than men.

Knowledge Underreporting. Unknowledgeable respondents were partitioned from those who probably knew of contraceptives but said they did not by cross-tabulating the degrees of certainty of knowledge based on observed behavior with the reported knowledge from the After Survey.

Expected knowledge levels were taken as degrees of certainty that negative responses were false. A conservative estimate of the number of men who knew of some contraceptive, out of the 519 couples, based on their clinic and education records, was 271. Of these 271 men, 42 said they knew of no methods when asked in the After Survey. This represented a conservative underreporting rate, f_3, of $42/271 = .155$, or approximately 16 percent. A slightly less conservative estimate, i.e., one based on slightly less conclusive evidence of contraceptive knowledge from the clinic and education program, was the sum of respondents who gave negative reports and whose clinic and education records placed them at the second and third levels of incriminating evidence as a proportion of the sum of all presumed knowledgeables at the second and third levels of evidence.

$$f_2 = \frac{(28 + 42)}{(120 + 271)} = \frac{70}{391} = .18$$

The most liberal estimate of knowledge underreporting by husbands was the sum of all three groups of negative reports as a proportion of all three groups of possibly knowledgeable men:

$$f_1 = \frac{(33 + 28 + 42)}{519} = \frac{103}{519} = .20$$

The female knowledge reports and behavior-derived expectations were partitioned in the same way and their three corresponding rates of false-negative reporting were 27 percent (liberal estimate), 25 percent, and 19 percent (conservative estimate).

Underreporting of Contraceptive Use. The "expected use" rates for husbands and wives were necessarily equal since the use of contraceptives, unlike knowledge, is a couple affair rather than an individual affair. The computations here followed the same procedure as the knowledge underreporting rates above. The liberal rate of underreported use for husbands was 22 percent; for wives, 35 percent. Intermediate (f_2) rates were 21 and 32 percent, respectively. Conservative estimates of underreporting use were 13 percent for men and 26 percent for women.

Wives underreported knowledge and use more than their husbands, and both males and females underreported their use of contraceptives more than they underreported their knowledge, i.e., they were less reluctant to admit knowledge of family planning methods than they were to admit that they had used the methods. The direction of these differentials was as expected, but the magnitudes were greater than expected even by field workers in the program.

The differences between male knowledge and use underreporting rates were less than the differences between female knowledge and use rates. This suggested that among males and females who admitted their knowledge of contraceptives, the males were more willing to admit using them. Therefore, in a given population of couples who have ever *used* contraceptives, the wives will be just as likely to admit *knowing* of any methods (94 percent of the female users vs. 95 percent of the male users admitted knowing of one or more methods) but the wives will be less likely to admit using any method (about one out of three wives who use contraceptives will deny use whereas only about one out of five user husbands will deny use).

Rates of underreporting by colony were somewhat less stable since the sample sizes were rather small in some colonies. These rates, however, did suggest that the nature of the program may have had some influence on the magnitude and sex differentials of false-negative reporting. In the colony in which the family planning program was directed at both men and women, the men had much lower underreporting rates on both knowledge and use of contraceptives. The female underreporting in this program, however, was not much different than in other programs. The highest female underreporting occurred where the program was directed at men only.

One exception to the usually high female underreporting rate was in the control colony. This suggests that when there is no intensive community educational program, women are less guarded with an interviewer in discussing what they know and do about family planning. It was noted in our home visiting reports, for example, that women sometimes became less cooperative when the family planning workers contacted them a third or fourth time. This suggested the possibility of a point of diminishing returns in home visits, probably because the women became concerned that neighbors may begin to gossip when the family planning workers are seen repeatedly at their apartment. A study in Karachi revealed a similar effect in that proximity of residence to a family planning clinic apparently tended to discourage attendance at that clinic (Green & Krotki, 1966).

Other Differentials in False-Negative Reporting. The two most certain false-negative groups were compared with positive reporting groups, those who admitted knowledge or use, on selected demographic and social characteristics. This constituted a comparison among all presumed knowledgeable respondents and all apparent users between those who admitted their knowledge or use and those who did not. Excluded from the comparison were those negative respondents who were not expected to have knowledge or to have used contraceptives and those on whom the evidence of knowing or using was least conclusive from clinic and education program records.

Urban-rural differentials that might be expected in underreporting were suggested by the social characteristics of the false-negatives as compared with the positives. The formal educational levels of false-negative respondents, male and female, were significantly lower than those of positive respondents (see Q12a). The literacy of false-negatives was also lower, in terms of wives being literate in any language (Q12b), and in terms of husbands being literate in more than one language (Q12c), usually Bengali and English.

The husband's class of governmental employment (Q8b) was significantly lower for false-negative men and women respondents. Among male knowledgeables, 33 percent of those not admitting knowledge were Class IV (lowest level employees), while only 15 percent of those who admitted their knowledge were Class IV.

We also anticipated differences in underreporting with age and other demographic variables. Roundtree and Pierce (1961:7) interpreted their lower reporting rates among older British couples as a function of lingering taboos from an earlier era. A similar phenomenon apparently was operating in the Bengali false-negative knowledge reports. Among twelve demographic variables, only five showed consistent differences between positive and false-negative respondents. These five were tentatively grouped into two sets: the age variables and the fertility variables. The age of the respondent was judged to be the most important of the five variables by noting first that the other variables were dependent on age, and second that if low fertility had been the cause of underreporting, larger differences should have been found in the mean number of children. Some independent effect of low fertility possibly occurred when a couple was exposed to family planning education, but because of their childlessness or their sub-fecundity, the salience of the message was minimized. When the personal importance of information is minimal, recall of the information tends to be lessened. This factor may apply to some older couples as well as to childless and sub-fecund couples.

Experience in the educational program supports the "lingering taboo" explanation and, therefore, the age variable more than the fertility variable. In general this experience revealed greater receptivity and more positive attitudes toward family planning education among younger couples than among older couples, regardless of parity.

Greater differences were found between positive and false-negative knowledge respondents than between positive and false-negative use respondents on thirteen variables on which the groups were compared. Thus, for both husbands and wives, the trait differences between positive and false-negative respondents were greater in reporting knowledge of contraceptives than in reporting their use.

Between-Survey Comparisons

The final methodological analysis performed on the Dacca data consisted of a comparison of responses given by individuals in the Before Survey with their corresponding responses in the After Survey. This analysis utilizes the 405 couples who were interviewed both in the Before Survey and in the After Survey.

We have presented the evidence of misreported survey data so far based on husband-wife comparisons and on recorded observations in the clinic and education programs. The fact that the Before and After Surveys were almost identical allows us an additional check on the consistency or reliability of the data. Since we have already shown that the reports of husbands are generally more accurate than those of wives, we can focus our attention in this section on the analysis of discrepancies over time in male responses.

Knowledge and Use of Contraceptives. Taking advantage of the scalar character of our knowledge and use questions, we can combine the responses in such a way that ever admitting use must imply knowledge. Furthermore, if a respondent knew of or had used a method of contraception at the time of the Before Survey, he should have known of at least one method at the time of the After Survey.

Of the 355 couples in which either spouse knew of at least one temporary method at the time of the Before Survey, 21 (6 percent) had no reported knowledge by either spouse in the After Survey. The tendency to disavow prior *use* is greater. Of the 158 couples in which either spouse said in the Before Survey that they had used a method, 28 (18 percent) had no prior use by the reports of either spouse in the After Survey. This figure corresponds very closely with the estimate of underreporting by men derived from clinic records, as described earlier. Two of the 28 couples who disavowed previously reported use even disavowed their knowledge of any methods in the After Survey.

For men and women individually, the inconsistencies are greater. Of the 308 husbands who named at least one temporary contraceptive in the Before Survey, 31 (10 percent) said they knew of none when asked the same question 18 months later. For wives, the corresponding discrepancy in reporting knowledge of any temporary method was 19 percent. In reporting ever using any method in the After Survey, 21 percent of the men and 21 percent of the women disavowed use which they had previously claimed. The fact that 147 of the husbands and only 82 of their wives had previously admitted use, however, makes the 79 percent consistency for women appear to be mainly a matter of consistent underreporting. There is no reason to believe that men were overreporting more in the Before Survey than in the After Survey, but there is no way to measure the extent of overreporting.

Comparing the Before and After responses on specific methods, we found little change in the underreporting rates for the temporary methods emphasized in the program. Among those who mentioned condoms in the Before Survey, 12 percent of the men and 19 percent of the women did not admit their knowledge in the After Survey; 16 percent of the men and 22 percent of the women who had said they had used condoms disavowed ever using them when asked again in the After Survey. Husbands were somewhat more inconsistent in reporting their use of foam tablets, with 30 percent underreporting in the After Survey compared with only 22 percent of the women.

Men were most inconsistent in their reporting of knowledge and use of rhythm and withdrawal as methods of contraception. Seventy percent of those who had mentioned rhythm and 66 percent of those who had named withdrawal as methods they had heard about in the Before Survey failed to mention knowing these methods at the time of the After Survey.

This suggests that one effect of the program was to make certain contraceptive methods more salient at the expense of others. Respondents may have decided that rhythm and withdrawal were not legitimate methods worth mentioning in the After Survey because they had not been promoted during the educational program. On the other hand, these results might indicate the tendency to forget more primitive methods after learning about methods involving material or devices.

Another method not promoted in the program was the diaphragm or cervical cap. We found a similar decline in those mentioning knowledge or use of this method: a total 18 percent of the men and 12 percent of the women in the Before Survey named this method, but in the After Survey only 10 percent of the men and 3 percent of the women named it. Similar declines occurred between the two surveys with other methods not emphasized or discredited in the program, including douche, early abortives, pills, late weaning, rhythm, and withdrawal.

It appears that knowledge and use, as measured in this study, must be operationally defined as contraceptive methods specifically recalled and named by respondents among several which respondents might actually have known or used at some time. In using this measure as a criterion of success in evaluating the programs we must recognize the tendency to forget prior knowledge and use of several methods between the Before and After surveys. There is also the possibility that many respondents in the After Survey decided not to mention recent or current knowledge or use of methods discredited by the program.

Thus, we are inclined to avoid composite measures of reported knowledge and "ever" use in favor of measures of current knowledge and "recent" use of specific methods which were promoted by the program.

Knowledge of Family Planning Sources. We asked respondents in both the Before and After Surveys if they knew of any places in Dacca outside the housing colonies where they could go to obtain information about birth control (Q44). Among the 335 male respondents who said yes in the Before Survey, 11 (3.2 percent) said no in the After Survey. Among wives, however, 38 percent of the 147 who originally said "yes" disavowed knowing of any such place at the time of the After Survey.

Again, the program emphasized the newly established clinics in the housing colonies so that wives, whose mobility was restricted, might have tended to forget sources outside the colonies. As will be shown in Chapter VI, a great many more wives than husbands learned about outside sources during the program, but not as great a percentage of wives among those who did not already know. Thus, we might infer greater overreporting by women in the Before Survey. Some women may have thought they knew of a place where they could get family planning advice but later came to learn that no such place existed or that their presumed source was not in fact in the birth control business.

Whether wives were overreporting in the Before Survey or underreporting in the After Survey, or both, we should be able to interpret our success statistics on this item somewhat more liberally for women than for men.

Consistency in Desire for No More Children. Attitudes toward family size cannot be treated as unreliable responses simply because they are inconsistent, for attitudes are, by definition, changeable. We might assume, however, that a specific declaration in the Before Survey that no more children are desired should not change to a desire for many children by the time of the After Survey 18 months later.

We found that only 26 of the 189 men and only 22 of the 210 women who originally said they wanted no more children (Q26/34) changed their statements in the After Survey. About half in both cases (12 of the men and 10 of the women) changed their response to "no preference." None of the respondents decided they wanted as many as possible (Q29/37) after previously declaring that they wanted none. Five of the men and none of the women who were inconsistent said they wanted the next child "soon" rather than "after some delay" (Q27/35).

We would expect greater inconsistency among men on this item inasmuch as women were much stronger, at the time of the Before Survey, in their attitudes regarding the limitation and spacing of further births. Men tended to be somewhat ambivalent and inconsistent in their attitudes at that time. We are inclined, therefore, to place some confidence in the reliability of responses, within this limited range of this item (Q26/34), as an accurate reflection of desire for no more children.

Attitude Toward Others Using Contraceptives. Again, caution must be exercised in discussing the reliability of an attitude which, by its definition, should be capable of change in any direction. We are willing to assume for the sake of examination only that respondents who clearly state in the Before Survey that they think it is all right for others to use contraceptives should not become clearly opposed by the time of the After Survey (Q42, asked only of those who knew of at least one temporary method). Only 3 of the 122 men and only 6 of the 97 women initially favorable to others using contraceptives made the unexpected conversion to clearly negative responses in the After Survey.

We are inclined, therefore, to accept the proportion of positive responses on this item as a fairly reliable index of the extent of community support for the practice of family planning.

Willingness to Use Contraceptives in the Future. In a related but quite different question, we asked those respondents who had not already used whether they would consider using contraceptives themselves in the future (Q43). Following the same assumption regarding unexpected conversions as in the previous item, we found 10 men who said they would *not* consider future use at the time of the After Survey among the 86 nonusers who said they *would* consider future use in the Before Survey. Among the 94 nonuser wives who said they would consider using at the time of the Before Survey, 18 said they would *not* at the time of the After Survey. The "unreliability" rates of 11.6 percent for men and 19.2 percent for women are not entirely comparable, however, because a larger number of the 86 men (35) than of 94 women (29) admitted having become users at the time of the After Survey. These respondents were not asked the question regarding future use in the After Survey, leaving fewer degrees of freedom for variability in male responses than in female responses.

If we assume that an admission of having used already is tantamount to a willingness to use in the future then we must conclude that men are considerably more reliable in their responses to this item.

As a predictor of subsequent behavior, on the other hand, this attitudinal item leaves much to be desired. The percentages of reported users in the After Survey among declared nonusers giving different responses to Q43 at the time of the Before Survey were as follows:

Before Survey Nonusers Stating Willingness to Become Users	After Survey Percentage Reporting Having Become Users	
	Males	Females
Yes	40.7	30.9
Undecided	27.3	18.5
No	16.6	12.4
All Nonusers	26.6	19.3

Those who said they would consider using in the future were clearly more likely to report having become users by the time of the After Survey 18 months later than those who originally said they were undecided or who said they would not consider using. But the fact that nearly 60 percent of the men and nearly 70 percent of the women who said "yes" did not report even trying a contraceptive method by the end of the program makes stated willingness a rather weak indicator of actual intent.

Part of the discrepancy between stated willingness and subsequent use can be attributed to the underreporting of use in the After Survey rather than to unreliability of declared willingness. In a special analysis of the predictive utility of the willingness item, Miller and Green (1970) employed as the criterion of subsequent use a combination of verbal reports of use in the past year by either spouse in the After Survey and the measure of inferred use from clinic and education records described in the previous section. The resulting differentials in percentages of subsequent users by this criterion were as follows:

Before Survey Nonusers Stating Willingness to Become Users	Percentage Subsequently Using Inferred from Survey and Program Records	
	Males	Females
Yes	42.8	38.5
Undecided	26.4	22.2
No	20.4	26.7
All Nonusers	28.7	28.7

Assuming that these percentages more clearly reflect differentials in correspondence between declared willingness to use and actual subsequent use, it appears that husbands are better predictors than wives of future use by the couple. Couples in which the husband is either willing or undecided are more likely to become users than couples in which the wife is willing or undecided. Conversely, more couples become users despite initial unwillingness expressed by wives than become users over the initial objection of husbands.

Comparing the two sets of percentages, it appears that an expressed objection to future use predisposes to underreporting actual use in the subsequent interview, especially among wives. In the first set, percentages are based on reported use; in the second, inferred actual use is seen to be much higher for wives who initially disavowed their willingness to consider using contraceptives sometime in the future.

Thus, we are inclined to interpret positive responses to Q43 as reasonably reliable indicators of positive attitudes toward future contraception among nonusers, but as poor predictors of actual subsequent use within the 18 month period of the program. We are inclined not to accept negative responses necessarily as negative predispositions to use, but rather as negative perceptions of the social acceptability of birth control practices. "Undecided" responses must be regarded as more akin to negative responses than to positive responses. In fact, undecided wives are more likely to end up nonusers than are "unwilling" wives.

Socioeconomic Background. Husbands were asked in both the Before and After Surveys to state their class of employment (Q8b), their district of origin (Q11a), their level of formal education (Q12a), and the size of the place in which they lived during the first year of marriage (Q13). All of these items were intended to place respondents and couples according to socioeconomic and cultural background. Questions concerning age at marriage were also asked as an internal consistency check against reports on duration of marriage for purposes of standardizing family growth rates. Age at marriage, however, turns out to be as much a socioeconomic indicator as it is a demographic variable. We shall limit our investigation of consistency to male reports inasmuch as we have already established that husbands are more accurate than wives in reporting on these kinds of items.

In reporting their class of employment, husbands were quite consistent between the Before and After Surveys. Only six of the 405 men changed their reports, five moving up from Class IV to Class III and one moving up from Class III to Class II. It is quite possible that all or most of these men did obtain promotions.

District of origin was also very consistently reported by men. Among the four divisions of East Pakistan and India where all of the men were born, only four men gave different places of birth in the two surveys. In the Before Survey all four of these men named a district of East Bengal as their place of birth but in the After Survey they said they were born in a district that is now part of India. One possible explanation for these changes is that some men were afraid to mention their Indian origin because of the enmity between the two countries, but over time they overcame these fears or it became more socially acceptable or possibly even a mark of status to have come from India.

Formal educational level was much less consistently reported by men, 19 percent giving different statements of the highest grade completed when interviewed in the Before and After Surveys. Of the 78 men who gave inconsistent reports, 56 gave higher reports in the After Survey and 22 gave lower reports. It is quite possible that some of the 56 men who upped their education reports could have completed requirements which advanced them to a higher educational level between the two surveys.

Inconsistent reporting was highest at low education levels and the discrepancy rates generally declined with more highly educated respondents. Thus, 52 percent of the men who said in the Before Survey that they had 0 to 3 years of education gave some other amount in their After Survey interviews. Only 9 percent of those reporting college education beyond the twelfth grade were inconsistent in the After Survey. This phenomenon can be attributed primarily to the greater sophistication of the higher educated men in giving consistent replies to the survey questions. But it could be attributed partly to the fact that most discrepancies were in the upward direction between the surveys, so that respondents who started at higher levels had less space in which to move their reported education upward. Most discrepancies, however, were of only one or two grade levels. Only three men increased their reported education by more than two grades.

The socioeconomic item with the greatest inconsistency was Q13 on size of place where respondent lived during the first year of marriage.

This item was intended to separate couples with more urban background from those with more rural or small town backgrounds. Of the 405 men in the panel, 103 (25 percent) were inconsistent in identifying their earlier residence as a place of more or less than 100,000 population. Again, the tendency was more toward raising one's socioeconomic status by claiming the more urban background in the After Survey, which 38 percent of the men did who had earlier said they had lived in a place of less than 100,000 population.

Age at marriage was also reported inconsistently by men in a way which again can be explained by a tendency toward status aggrandizement. Men tended to increase their wives' age at marriage by an average of .52 years between the Before and After Surveys. Of the 405 men, 149 gave consistent reports, 176 gave lower marital ages of wives in the After Survey, and 271 a higher marital ages of wives. The weighted means were -1.47 years for those giving lower marital ages and $+1.99$ for those giving higher marital ages in the After Survey. One-third of all discrepant responses differed from the Before Survey reports by only one year.

We conclude from this series of comparisons that men in this study population became more status conscious and more defensive about their status between the Before and After Survey. This may be a natural process with increasing age in populations of this kind or it may have been the peculiar conditions and events during this particular 18 month interval in Dacca. In either case, we are inclined to place greater credence in the Before Survey responses on socioeconomic items.

Among the different socioeconomic items we found class of employment to be the most reliable indicator of status. Men could hardly deceive the interviewers on this item because the different employment classes were assigned to different types of apartments. This item was also sufficiently correlated with other measures of socioeconomic background to provide an adequate proxy measure in our proposed statistical control in later analyses. (The correlation coefficients between class of employment and education of husband, education of wife, wife's age at marriage, size of community of residence in first year of marriage were respectively .65, .40, .24, and .10). Class of employment was also found to be more consistently correlated with prior fertility and family growth history than the other socioeconomic measures.

Age and Duration of Marriage. Men were rather inconsistent in reporting their ages and years married. Allowing increases of one and two years for the 18 month interval, 167 men (41 percent) gave consistent age reports, 83 (21 percent) reduced their age (or failed to increase it by one or two years), and 155 (38 percent) increased their age too much between the Before and After Surveys. The magnitude of discrepancies average -2.53 for those who made themselves younger, $+2.83$ for those who made themselves older than necessary in the After Survey. The net error for the study population was only .30 (or about 4 months' increase), but the individual discrepancies are disturbing. The distribution of differences between Before and After reports of age in years were as follows:

Actual difference	−8 . . . −4	−3	−2	−1	0	+1	+2	+3	+4	+5	+6	+7 . . . 14
Discrepancy	−9 . . . −5	−4	−3	−2	−1	0	0	+1	+2	+3	+4	+5 . . . 12
Number of men	7	10	14	13	39	79	90	51	40	24	16	24

In reporting duration of present marriage, 60 men (15 percent) failed to increase their reported years enough to account for the 18 months that elapsed between the Before and After Surveys. Another 22 percent increased their marriage duration reports too much. The net error and the distribution of discrepancies were similar to those for reported age, although the average discrepancies were not as great because the range of possible error on duration of marriage is less.

It appears that men tended to lose track of years with the passage of time. There might have been an additional factor pressuring men to increase their age reports, such as the prestige and deference that come with age in this culture, job security, or a desire to exempt themselves from further involvement in the family planning program by claiming themselves too old. Again, we shall use the more credible Before Survey reports on these items in later analyses.

Conclusion

These methodological analyses identified a number of weaknesses in the survey data on which we had to base our evaluation of the experimental programs. By recognizing these problems and noting the direction, magnitude and correlates of specific response biases, we were able to minimize the misuse and misinterpretation of the data and to weight or select the best variables where alternatives were available.

Appendix C

THE NATIONAL SURVEY OF PERSONAL HEALTH PRACTICES AND CONSEQUENCES*

1. First, would you say your health is excellent, good, fair, or poor?

   Excellent Good
   Fair Poor
   Don't Know

2. How often do you eat breakfast?

   Almost every day Sometimes
   Rarely or never

3. On an average day how many of the following do you drink?

   Cups of coffee
   Cups of tea
   Glasses of milk
   Glasses of water
   Cans or bottles of soft drink
   Glasses of fruit or vegetable juice

4. Do you make any conscious effort to limit the amount of red meat in your diet *for health reasons?*

   Yes No

5. How often, if ever, do you take vitamin pills or other vitamin supplements?

   Regularly Occasionally
   Rarely or never

6. On the average how many hours of sleep do you get each day, that is, during a 24-hour period?

   Number of hours

7. On the average, do you now get more sleep, less sleep or about the same amount of sleep as you did 2 years ago?

   More Less
   SKIP TO Q. 9 Same

8. Is this because of a health-related problem or condition that you had?

   Yes No

9. About how tall are you without shoes?

   Feet Inches

*Source: *Toward a Healthy Community: Organizing Events for Community Health Promotion.* DHHS (PHS) Pub. No. 80-50113. Washington, D.C.: Office of Disease Prevention and Health Promotion, 1980. This is an abbreviated version of a questionnaire developed by the Division of Analysis, National Center for Health Statistics, using similar studies conducted in Alameda County, California, and the state of Michigan. The questionnaire was administered in April 1979 during a telephone survey. Persons interested in obtaining the complete questionnaire or learning more about its use should contact the National Center for Health Statistics, Federal Center Building, 3700 East-West Highway, Hyattsville, Maryland 20782.

10. How much do you weigh without clothes on?

Actual weight

11. Do you now weigh more, less, or about the same as you did two years ago?

More	Less
SKIP TO Q. 14	Same

12. Was this change the result of a health-related problem or condition that you had?

Yes	No

13. About how much (MORE/LESS) do you now weigh than you did two years ago?

More	Less

(Number of pounds)

14. Do you *now* consider yourself to be overweight, underweight, or about average?

Overweight	Underweight
Average	Don't Know

15. About how long has it been since you last went to a dentist?

Less than 1 year,
(Less than 12 months)
1–2 years,
(12 months up to 24 months)
2–4 years
(More than 24 months, up to 5 years)
5 or more years
Never
Don't Know
(IF 55 OR OVER.)

16. Have you lost all of your teeth?

Yes	No
SKIP TO Q. 19	CONTINUE

17. How often do you brush your teeth?

More than twice a day
Twice a day
Once a day
Less than once a day

18. And how often, if ever, do you use dental floss or a waterpick?

Every day
3–6 times a week
1–2 times a week
Less than once a week
Never

19. About how long has it been since you last had an eye examination?

Less than 1 year
(Less than 12 months)
1–2 years
(12 months up to 24 months)
2–4 years
(More than 24 months, up to 5 years)
5 or more years
Never
Don't Know

20. Some people get a general physical examination once in a while even though they are feeling well and have not been sick. When was the last time you had a general physical examination when you were not sick?

Less than 1 year
(Less than 12 months)
1–2 years
(12 months up to 24 months)
2–4 years
(More than 24 months, up to 5 years)
5 or more years
Never
Don't Know

21. During the past 12 months, that is, since (*DATE ONE YEAR AGO*), about how many times did you see or speak to a medical doctor about your own health? Please exclude any doctors you may have seen while you were a patient in a hospital.

Number of visits

None	Don't Know

22. About how long has it been since you last saw or talked to a medical doctor about your own health?

    Less than 1 year
    (Less than 12 months)
    1–2 years
    (12 months up to 24 months)
    2–4 years
    (More than 24 months, up to 5 years)
    5 or more years
    Never
    Don't Know

23. How long has it been since you last had your blood pressure checked?

    Less than 1 year
    (Less than 12 months)
    1–2 years
    (12 months up to 24 months)
    2–4 years
    (More than 24 months, up to 5 years)
    5 or more years
    Never
    Don't Know

24. (ASK FEMALES ONLY)
    When was the last time you had a Pap smear test for cancer?

    Less than 1 year
    (Less than 12 months)
    1–2 years
    (12 months up to 24 months)
    2–4 years
    (More than 24 months, up to 5 years)
    5 or more years
    Never
    Don't Know

25. (ASK FEMALES ONLY)
    When was the last time you had a breast examination by a doctor?

    Less than 1 year
    (Less than 12 months)
    1–2 years
    (12 months up to 24 months)
    2–4 years
    (More than 24 months, up to 5 years)
    5 or more years
    Never
    Don't Know

26. Have you smoked at least 100 cigarettes (five packs of cigarettes) in your entire life?

Yes	No
	SKIP TO Q. 36

27. Do you smoke cigarettes now?

Yes	No
SKIP TO Q. 31	CONTINUE

28. Did you ever smoke cigarettes regularly?

Yes	No
SKIP TO Q. 36	

29. During the period when you were smoking most, about how many cigarettes a day did you usually smoke?

    1 Pack = 20 Cigarettes ________
    (# of cigarettes)

30. About how long has it been since you smoked cigarettes fairly regularly?

Years	Months
SKIP TO Q. 36	

31. On the average, how many cigarettes a day do you smoke?

    1 Pack = 20 Cigarettes ________
    (# of cigarettes)

32. Think about the tar or nicotine level of the cigarettes you usually smoke. Would you say they are high, medium, or low tar and nicotine?

    High tar and nicotine
    Medium tar and nicotine
    Low tar and nicotine
    Don't Know

33. Have you changed the *number* of cigarettes you smoke or the *brand* of cigarettes you smoke in the past two years?

Yes No
SKIP TO Q. 35

34. Was this because of a *specific* health related problem or condition that you *had*?

Yes No

35. During the past two years did you make a serious attempt to stop smoking cigarettes?

Yes No

36. Do you ever drink any alcoholic beverages, that is, beer, wine, or liquor?

Yes No
SKIP TO Q. 39

37. Did you drink any alcoholic beverages two years ago?

Yes No
SKIP TO Q. 43

38. Have you changed your drinking pattern during the past two years because of a specific health-related problem or condition that you had?

Yes No
SKIP TO Q. 43

39. On the average, how often do you drink any alcoholic beverages such as beer, wine, or liquor?

40. On the days that you drink, how many drinks do you have per day, on the average?

41. Have you changed your drinking pattern during the past two years because of a specific health-related problem or condition?

Yes No
SKIP TO Q. 43

42. Do you now drink more or less than you did two years ago?

More Less

43. How often do you use seat belts when you ride in a car?

Always or nearly always Seldom
Sometimes Never

The next group of questions asks your personal opinions about health-related matters.

44. How good a job do you feel you are doing in *taking care* of your health?

Excellent Good
Fair Poor
Don't Know

45. How would you compare your level of physical activity with other people your age?

Much more physically active
Somewhat more active
Somewhat less active
Much less active
Don't Know

46. Compared to your level of physical activity two years ago, would you say you are now more physically active, less physically active, or about the same?

More physically active
Less physically active
About the same
SKIP TO Q. 48

47. Is this because of a *specific* health-related problem or condition that you *had*?

Yes No

48. Do you feel that you get as much exercise as you need, or less than you need?

As much as you need
Less than you need
Don't Know

49. In general, how satisfied are you with your overall physical condition?

Very satisfied
Somewhat satisfied
Not too satisfied
Not at all satisfied
Don't Know

50. Compared with two years ago, that is, since 1977, would you say that your health is now better, worse, or about the same?

Better | Worse
Same | Don't Know

51. Over the *past year* has your health caused you a great deal of worry, some worry, hardly any worry, or no worry at all?

A great deal of worry
Some worry
Hardly any worry
No worry at all
Don't Know

52. How much control do you think you have over your future health? Would you say . . .
(READ LIST)

A great deal | Some
Very little | None at all
Don't Know

53. Compared to other people your age, would you say your health is

Excellent | Good
Fair | Poor
Don't Know

54. Compared to other people your age, would you say you have

Much more energy
Somewhat more energy
Somewhat less energy
Much less energy
Don't Know

The following questions pertain to your health status and medical care.

55. Is there a particular clinic, health center, doctor's office, or hospital emergency room that you usually go to if you are sick or need advice about your health?

Yes | No

56. Have you been a patient overnight in a hospital since (*DATE ONE YEAR AGO*)?

Yes | No
SKIP TO Q. 58

57. All together, how many nights were you in the hospital since (*DATE ONE YEAR AGO*)?

Number of nights

58. Do you feel that there are things you can do in your everyday life which will *prevent* you from getting high blood pressure?

Yes | No
Don't Know

59. Have you had high blood pressure or were you treated for it during the last twelve months?

Yes | No
Don't Know

60. How many colds, if any, did you have in the past 12 months?

61. How often, if ever, do you get headaches?

62. Do you ever have any trouble or difficulty with routine physical activities such as walking, using stairs or inclines, standing or sitting for long periods, using your fingers to grasp or handle, or lifting or carrying something heavy?

Yes | No
SKIP TO Q. 64

63. Do your have any trouble or difficulty . . .

	No	Yes: Great deal	Yes: Some
Walking	1	2	3
Using stairs or inclines	1	2	3
Standing or sitting for long periods	1	2	3
Using your fingers to grasp or handle	1	2	3
Lifting or carrying something as heavy as 10 pounds	1	2	3

64. During the past 12 months, that is, since (*DATE ONE YEAR AGO*), about how many days did illness or injury keep you in bed all or most of the day?

____
(Days)

The next few questions will be used to determine trends in longevity patterns within families. Please answer these questions with reference to your *natural* parents and grandparents, if you know about them.

65. Is your father now living?

Yes	CONTINUE
No	SKIP TO Q. 67
Don't Know	SKIP TO Q. 69

66. About how old is he?

____
(Age)
Don't Know
(SKIP TO Q. 69)

67. About how old was he when he died?

____
(Age)
Don't Know

68. Did he die as a result of an accident?

Yes No

69. Is your mother now living?

Yes	CONTINUE
No	SKIP TO Q. 71
Don't Know	SKIP TO Q. 73

70. About how old is she?

____
(Age)
Don't Know
(SKIP TO Q. 73)

71. About how old was she when she died?

____
(Age)
Don't Know

72. Did she die as a result of an accident?

Yes No

73. How many of your grandparents, if any, are now living? ____________

None SKIP TO Q. 75

74. (Is he or she) (Are any of them) 50 years or older?

Yes	SKIP TO Q. 76
No	
Don't Know	

75. Did any of your grandparents live beyond 80 years of age?

Yes No
Don't Know

The following are questions about your present and past employment experiences.

76. Are you now . . .

Working { Full-time / Part-time }
Laid off or on strike
Retired
Unemployed { Looking for work / Not looking for work }

Unable to work (disabled)
Keeping house
Full-time student

77. Have you ever worked?

Yes
No SKIP TO Q. 87

78. Are you self-employed?

Yes SKIP TO Q. 81
No

79. Do you get time off from your job with pay, when you are ill?

Yes No

80. Does your employer give you time off from work with pay for visits to the doctor?

Yes No

81. Does your job involve a variable work shift? That is, do you work the day shift some times and the night shift at other times?

Yes No

82. How much hard physical work is required on your job? I'm referring to things like pushing or carrying heavy objects, handling heavy tools or equipment, or digging.

A great deal Some
Hardly any None at all
Don't Know

83. How would you describe the degree of emotional stress associated with your job? Would you say you are under a great deal of stress, some stress, or hardly any stress?

A great deal Some
Hardly any Don't Know

84. In your current job are you exposed to any special risk of accidents or injuries or to any substances that could endanger your health?

Yes No

85. Did you ever change jobs because you were concerned about occupational hazards or dangers to your health?

Yes No

86. During the past five years, that is, since 1974, how many employers or companies, if any, have you worked for on a full-time basis, including your present job?

No. of employers

87. Would you please tell me whether you have participated in any activities or meetings run by any of the following groups in the last 3 months?

	Yes	No	Don't Know
A labor union, commercial group or professional organization	___	___	___
A church group	___	___	___
A group concerned with children such as PTA, Boy Scouts, Girl Scouts, etc.	___	___	___
Any *other* group that is concerned with community betterment, charity or service	___	___	___
Any *other* group that is mainly social, fraternal or recreational	___	___	___

88. About how often, if ever, do you go to religious services?

____

89. Now I'm going to read you a list of things that people do in their free time. Please tell me how often you participate in these activities.

	Often	Sometimes	Rarely	Never
Go swimming in the summer	___	___	___	___
Take long walks	___	___	___	___
Work on a physically active hobby such as dancing or gardening	___	___	___	___
Go jogging or running	___	___	___	___

90. On the average how many miles a *week* do you usually jog or run?

Less than 5 miles	___	___	___	___
5 to 15 miles	___	___	___	___
More than 15 miles	___	___	___	___

91. And how often do you . . .

	Often	Sometimes	Rarely	Never
Ride a bicycle	___	___	___	___
Do calisthenics or physical exercise	___	___	___	___
Participate in any other active sports I haven't already mentioned	___	___	___	___

92. How much enjoyment do you get out of your free time?

A great deal — Some
A little — Don't Know

93. And how often do you find that you have time on your hands that you don't know what to do with?

Very often — Sometimes
Rarely — Never
Don't Know

94. All in all how happy are you these days?

Very happy — Pretty happy
Not too happy — Don't Know

95. How many *close* relatives do you have? These are people that you feel at ease with, can talk to about private matters, and can call on for help.

No. of close relatives ____________

96. And how many friends do you have that you feel *really close* to? These are friends that you feel at ease with, can talk to about private matters, and can call on for help.

Number of close friends __________

97. How many of these *close* friends or relatives do you see at least once a month?

98. About how often do you visit with any close relatives or friends?

99. Do you feel that you have enough close friends or relatives?

Yes — No
Don't Know

100. Are you now . . .

Married — Widowed
Divorced — Separated
Never married

101. All in all, how happy has your marriage been for you?

Very happy   Pretty happy
Not too happy   Don't Know

102. How often in the *past month* have you felt . . .

	Very Often	Sometimes	Rarely	Never	Don't Know
Cheerful and lighthearted	___	___	___	___	___
Loved and wanted	___	___	___	___	___
Downhearted and blue	___	___	___	___	___
Lonely	___	___	___	___	___

103. Does it *ever* happen that you do not have enough money to afford the kind of *medical care* you or your family should have?

Yes   No

104. Would you say this happens . . .

Very often   Sometimes
Rarely

105. I'm now going to read you a list of things that can happen to people. Please tell me which of these events, if any, happened in your life during the *past five years.* (READ ENTIRE LIST)

Death of your (husband/wife) or one of your children

Problems or difficulties with a steady date or fiance

Serious financial difficulties or problems

. . . And in the past five years did any of these events happen in your life?

Your own serious illness, injury, or operation

Serious illness, injury, or operation of your children

Serious illness, injury, or operation of your (husband/wife)

Being unable to get medical treatment when it was seriously needed for yourself or your (husband/wife) or your children

Your own marital separation or divorce

Other problems or difficulties related to your marriage

106. Did you have any *severe* personal, emotional, behavioral or mental problems that concerned you in the past year?

Yes   No
SKIP TO Q. 108   Don't Know

107. Would you say you had no problems of this kind at all, or no *severe* problems?

No problems at all   SKIP TO Q. 110
No *severe* problems

108. Did you consider any of these to be severe enough that you felt you needed professional help?

Yes   No
Don't Know   SKIP TO Q. 110

109. Did you seek professional help?

Yes   No

110. Have you ever had a nervous breakdown?

Yes   No
SKIP TO Q. 112   Don't Know

111. Did you ever feel that you were going to have, or were close to having a nervous breakdown?

Yes   No
Don't know   SKIP TO Q. 114

112. Was that during the past year?

Yes   No
Don't Know

113. Are you still bothered by that condition or are you completely over it?

Still bothered by it
Completely over it
Don't Know

114. In the past five years, since (*MONTH, YEAR*), how many addresses have you lived at, including your present address?

____
(# of addresses)

115. What was the last grade or year of school you completed?

116. And what is your date of birth?

Day Month
Year

(See type of residence on screener. If "private residence," ask Q. 117. If "group quarters," skip to Q. 120.)

117. And now I'd like to know the age and sex of members of your household who are younger than 20 or older than 64.

____

____

____

118. Are there any telephone numbers other than the one I've dialed at which household members can be reached *at this residence?*

Yes
No
SKIP TO Q. 124

I would just like to make sure you are referring to a phone number other than the one you are using right now.

Yes
No
SKIP TO Q. 124

119. In total, at how many *other* phone numbers in this residence can household members be reached?

None
(SKIP TO Q. 124)
____
(No.)

120. How many people between the ages of 20 and 64 live here?

Number of people
Don't Know

121. How many of these people have regular access to this phone number?

Number of people
Don't Know

122. Are there any telephone numbers in this residence other than the one I've dialed, at which these (*# IN Q. 121*) people can be reached?

Yes
No
SKIP TO Q. 124

123. In total, at how many *other* phone numbers in this residence can these (*# IN Q. 121*) people be reached?

Number
Don't Know

124. Please tell me which *one* of the following racial groups *best* describes your racial background. Are you . . .

White SKIP TO Q. 126
Black
American Indian
Asian
Pacific Islander
Some other group

125. To which racial group do you belong?

Puerto Rican
Cuban
Mexican, Mexicano, Mexican American, or Chicano
Some other Latin American or Spanish group

Other (SPECIFY) SKIP TO Q. 127

126. Now I'm going to read you a list of groups which describes some people's national origin or ancestry.

Please tell me if any of these groups is your national origin or ancestry.

Puerto Rican

Cuban

Mexican, Mexicano, Mexican American, or Chicano

Some other Latin American or Spanish group

None of these groups

Don't Know

127. And finally, so that we can group our answers, please tell me into which of the following groups your family's combined income fell in 1978, before taxes. Would that be . . . (READ LIST)

Less than $5,000

$5,000 to $10,000

$10,000 to $15,000

$15,000 to $25,000

$25,000 or more

Don't Know

Appendix D

A SAMPLE OF EVALUATIONS IN HEALTH EDUCATION AND HEALTH PROMOTION

To provide the student with a variety of examples for purposes of illustrating problems and approaches in measurement and evaluation, we have compiled an unsystematic sample of published reports on evaluation of programs in patient education, community health education, worksite health promotion, school health education, and continuing education for health professionals. They are listed alphabetically in the numbered reference list at the end of this appendix. The following classified index is designed to simplify your search for the kind of example you wish to review.

SETTING

Studies in hospital settings: 4, 5, 7, 10, 17, 26, 35, 36, 37, 38, 43, 44, 46, 49, 50, 53, 63, 64, 67, 72, 73, 74, 75, 77, 80, 86, 97, 100, 102, 103, 109, 110, 111, 117, 121, 124, 125, 126, 130, 131, 134, 139, 140, 156, 167, 175, 176, 178, 185, 189, 204, 205, 209, 217, 219, 223, 224, 225, 226, 228, 233, 237, 238, 240, 241, 244

Studies in outpatient clinical or primary care settings: 3, 8, 13, 14, 18, 20, 21, 22, 29, 32, 39, 40, 47, 48, 65, 68, 69, 83, 91, 94, 95, 96, 98, 101, 106, 108, 114, 115, 118, 127, 128, 135, 141, 142, 144, 154, 160, 161, 164, 170, 188, 190, 196, 198, 207, 211, 218, 231, 239, 242, 245

Studies on continuing education: 1, 2, 9, 11, 15, 16, 19, 24, 25, 27, 28, 30, 33, 41, 45, 51, 52, 53, 54, 55, 56, 57, 58, 59, 62, 66, 70, 79, 81, 84, 85, 87, 88, 89, 92, 93, 99, 104, 105, 112, 113, 116, 120, 122, 123, 129, 132, 136, 137, 143, 145, 147, 148, 149, 150, 151, 152, 153,

TARGET POPULATIONS

DESIGN

With two groups: 42, 60, 68, 85, 171, 195, 220, 236

With three or more groups: 9, 33, 58, 71, 76, 105, 138, 161, 173, 213, 235, 239

Studies using single subject designs: 20, 94, 115, 144

Time series designs: 12, 19, 61, 113, 168, 169, 179, 180, 182, 221, 230

Posttest-only designs: 15, 16, 24, 27, 28, 30, 41, 45, 54, 55, 57, 79, 81, 84, 93, 116, 119, 120, 122, 123, 129, 143, 148, 155, 157, 158, 159, 165, 172, 175, 181, 183, 193, 200, 206

OUTCOME OR IMPACT MEASURES

Studies measuring impact on knowledge (cognitive effects): 1, 2, 6, 9, 22, 23, 27, 31, 33, 38, 47, 51, 52, 56, 57, 58, 59, 60, 62, 66, 70, 71, 83, 85, 87, 88, 89, 99, 105, 106, 112, 119, 121, 133, 136, 137, 138, 145, 147, 149, 150, 153, 154, 157, 158, 162, 163, 165, 171, 173, 175, 176, 177, 185, 186, 191, 192, 195, 196, 203, 204, 205, 207, 210, 211, 213, 214, 222, 229, 235, 241, 243

Studies measuring impact on attitudes: 1, 10, 15, 16, 21, 23, 24, 25, 27, 28, 34, 35, 36, 41, 45, 51, 54, 55, 56, 59, 60, 66, 70, 71, 72, 74, 75, 76, 78, 80, 82, 84, 85, 89, 90, 93, 107, 116, 122, 124, 130, 136, 138, 140, 143, 146, 147, 149, 150, 151, 152, 153, 157, 158, 159, 162, 163, 165, 166, 168, 169, 171, 172, 173, 175, 179, 180, 182, 193, 195, 200, 201, 202, 212, 213, 217, 224, 225, 226, 229, 232, 234, 240

Studies measuring impact on satisfaction: 2, 9, 21, 33, 57, 79, 88, 92, 96, 105, 107, 108, 123, 148, 153, 191, 197, 206, 229

Studies measuring impact on behavior: 1, 2, 3, 5, 8, 11, 12, 13, 14, 18, 19, 20, 21, 27, 30, 32, 34, 38, 40, 41, 42, 44, 48, 49, 51, 52, 57, 68, 69, 71, 74, 76, 80, 83, 86, 88, 94, 95, 96, 98, 99, 101, 104, 106, 108, 113, 114, 115, 116, 118, 120, 124, 129, 132, 135, 136, 138, 139, 142, 144, 153, 154, 155, 160, 161, 162, 163, 168, 169, 170, 173, 179, 180, 181, 182, 183, 184, 187, 188, 189, 190, 193, 194, 195, 197, 198, 199, 205, 206, 207, 208, 213, 215, 216, 219, 220, 221, 224, 227, 228, 229, 230, 232, 234, 236, 239, 243

Studies measuring physiological or health outcomes: 3, 4, 7, 8, 10, 22, 29, 32, 34, 35, 36, 39, 48, 61, 63, 65, 67, 71, 72, 73, 74, 75, 80, 82, 86, 91, 96, 98, 100, 106, 108, 111, 115, 121, 124, 125, 126, 127, 128, 129, 130, 131, 132, 138, 140, 141, 144, 154, 156, 164, 167, 168, 169, 173, 179, 180, 185, 187, 196, 199, 212, 213, 215, 217, 231, 232, 233, 236, 240, 242, 244, 245

Studies measuring mortality outcomes: 10, 80, 185, 217, 230

HEALTH PROBLEMS

REFERENCES TO APPENDIX D

1. Abrahamson, S., et al. The use of self-instructional material in continuing education. *Complete Papers, Ninth Annual Conference on Research in Medical Education.* Washington, D.C.: Association of American Medical Colleges, pp. 143–148, 1970.
2. Adler, L. M., & Enelow, A. J. Attempts to evaluate postgraduate teaching of psychiatry to nonpsychiatrist physicians. *Proceedings, Second Colloquium of Postgraduate Teaching of Psychiatry.* Washington, D.C.: American Psychiatric Association, pp. 62–78, 1963.
3. Agras, S., & Weme, J. Behavior modification in anorexia nervosa: Research foundations. In R. A. Vigersky (Ed.), *Anorexia Nervosa.* New York: Raven Press, 1977.
4. Aiken, L. H., & Henrichs, T. F. Systematic relaxation as a nursing intervention technique with open heart surgery patients. *Nursing Research* 20:212–217, 1971.
5. Allan, D. B., & Bergman, A. B. Social learning approaches to health education: Utilization of infant auto restraint devices. *Pediatrics* 58:323–328, 1976.
6. American Lung Association of Southeastern Michigan. *School Health Curriculum Project Summary Evaluation Report.* Detroit: The Association, 1977.
7. Andrew, J. M. Recovery from surgery with and without preparatory instruction, for three coping styles. *Journal of Personal Social Psychology* 15:223–226, 1970.
8. Aragona, J., Cassady, J., & Drabman, R. S. Treating overweight children through parental training and contingency contracting. *Journal of Applied Behavioral Analysis* 8:269–278, 1975.
9. Arney, W. R. Evaluation of a continuing nursing education program and its implications. *Journal of Continuing Education in Nursing* 9:45–51, 1978.

10. Auerbach, S. M., Kendall, P. C., Cuttler, H. F., et al. Anxiety, locus of control, type of preparatory information, and adjustment to dental surgery. *Journal of Consulting and Clinical Psychology* 44:809–818, 1976.
11. Avorn, J., & Soumerai, S. B. Improving drug-therapy decision through educational outreach: A randomized controlled trial of academically based "detailing." *New England Journal of Medicine* 308:1457–1463, 1983.
12. Bailey, J. An evaluative look at a family planning radio campaign in Latin America. *Studies in Family Planning* 4:275–278, 1973.
13. Bass, L. W., & Wilson, T. R. The pediatricians' influence in private practice measured by a controlled seat belt study. *Pediatrics* 34:700–704, 1964.
14. Beck, D. E., Fennell, R. S., Yost, R. L., Robinson, J. D., Geary, M. B., & Richards, G. A. Evaluation of an educational program on compliance with medication regimens in pediatric patients with renal transplants. *Pediatrics* 96:1094–1097, 1980.
15. Bell, A. E., & Shaw, G. Scottish television medical programmes: A preliminary assessment. *Scottish Medical Journal* 11:250–257, 1966.
16. Bergen, S. S. Use of two-way radio by a voluntary health organization for continuing medical education. *New York State Journal of Medicine* 66:2694–2697, 1966.
17. Best, J. K. Reducing length of hospital stay and facilitating the recovery process of orthopedic surgical patients through crisis intervention and pastoral care. (Doctoral dissertation, Northwestern University). *Dissertation Abstracts International* 42:3631B, 1981.
18. Bigelow, G., Strickler, D., Liebson, I., & Griffiths, R. Maintaining disulfiram ingestion among outpatient alcoholics: A security-deposit contingency contracting procedure. *Behavioral Research Therapy* 14:378–381, 1976.
19. Bille, D. A. A study of patients' knowledge in relation to teaching format and compliance. *Supervising Nurses* 8:55–62, 1977.
20. Boudin, H. M. Contingency contracting as a therapeutic tool in the deceleration of amphetamine use. *Behavioral Therapy* 3:604–608, 1972.
21. Boudin, H. M., Valentine, V. E., Inghram, R. D., Brandley, J. M., Buis, M. R., Smith, G. G., Catlin, R. P., III, & Regan, E. J., Jr. Contingency contracting with drug abusers in the natural environment. *Internatinal Journal of Addictions* 12:1–16, 1977.
22. Bowen, R. G., Rich, R., & Schlotfeldt, R. M. Effects of organized instruction for patients with the diagnosis of diabetes mellitus. *Nursing Research* 10:151–159, 1961.
23. Bowers, P. A. The effects of a stress management program on the knowledge, attitudes, symptomatology, and behavior of workers employed by an urban electronics industrial plant: A demonstration project. *Occupational Health Nursing* 131:13–16, 1983.
24. Brandt, E. N., Jr. An experiment in continuing education developed for the annual meeting of a professional society. *Journal of Medical Education* 49:1189–1191, 1974.
25. Brennan, J. G., Dixon, W. T., & Snider, S. Continuing education in alcoholism: Attitude change as a measure of seminar effectiveness. *Maryland State Medical Journal* 23:63–67, 1974.
26. Budd, S., & Brown, W. Effect of a reorientation technique on postcardiotomy delirium. *Nursing Research* 23:341–348, 1974.
27. Byrne, P. S. Evaluation of courses for general practitioners. *Journal of Royal College of General Practitioners* 21:719–725, 1971.

28. California Medical Association. A survey of continuing medical education for physicians. *California Medicine* 109:245–251, 1968.
29. Caplan, R. D., Robinson, E. A. R., French, J. R. P., Jr., Caldwell, J. R., & Shinn, M. *Adhering to Medical Regimens: Pilot Experiments in Patient Education and Social Support.* Ann Arbor: Institute for Social Research, University of Michigan, 1976.
30. Caplan, R. M. Measuring the effectiveness of continuing medical education. *Journal of Medical Education* 48:1150–1152, 1973.
31. Caramanica, V., Feiler, E. G., & Olsen, L. K. Evaluation of the effects of performance-based teacher education on the health knowledge and attitudes of fifth-grade students. *Journal of School Health* 44:449–454, 1974.
32. Carnahan, J. E., & Nugent, C. A. The effects of self-monitoring by patients on the control of hypertension. *American Journal of Medical Science* 269:69–73, 1975.
33. Carpenter, K. F., & Kroth, J. Effects of videotaped role playing on nurses' therapeutic communication skills. *Journal of Continuing Education in Nursing* 7:47–53, 1976.
34. Carrington, P., Collings, G., Benson, H., Robinson, H., Wood, L., Lebrer, P., Woolfolk, R., & Cole, J. The use of meditation-relaxation techniques for the management of stress in a working population. *Journal of Occupational Medicine* 22:221–231, 1980.
35. Cassell, S. Effect of brief puppet therapy upon the emotional responses of children undergoing cardiac catheterization. *Journal of Consulting Clinical Psychology* 29:1–8, 1965.
36. Cassell, S., & Paul, M. H. The role of puppet therapy on the emotional responses of children hospitalized for cardiac catheterization. *Journal of Pediatrics* 71:233–239, 1967.
37. Chapman, J. S. Effects of different nursing approaches on psychological and physiological responses. *Nursing Research Report* 5:5–7, 1970.
38. Choi-Lao, A. T. H. A preliminary study designed to explore the difference in effectiveness of group and individual teaching in self-medication. *Nursing Patients* 8:22–29, 1976.
39. Clark, N. M., Feldman, C. H., Evans, D., Millman, E. J., Wasilewski, Y., & Valle, I. The effectiveness of education for family management of asthma in children: A preliminary report. *Health Education Quarterly* 8:166–174, 1981.
40. Clinite, J., & Kabat, H. Improving patient compliance. *Journal of American Pharmacology Association* 16:74–76, 1976.
41. Clute, K. F. *The General Practitioner.* Toronto: University of Toronto Press, 1963.
42. Cohen, F. Psychological preparation, coping, and recovery from surgery. (Doctoral dissertation, University of California, Berkeley). *Dissertation Abstracts International* 37:454B, 1976.
43. Cohen, M. N., & Abelson, H. I. *Impacts, Benefit and Consequences of "Feeling Good."* Princeton, N.J.: Response Analysis Corporation, 1976.
44. Cole, P., & Emmanuel, S. Drug consultation: Its significance to the discharged patient and its relevance as a role for the pharmacist. *American Journal of Hospital Pharmacists* 28:954, 1971.
45. Conklin, J. L., et al. Slide-tape programs in independent study in continuing medical education. *Proceedings, Tenth Annual Conference on Research in*

Medical Education, Washington, D.C.: Association of American Medical Colleges, pp. 100–103, 1971.
46. Crabtree, M. S. Application of cost-benefit analysis to clinical nursing practice: A comparison of individual and group preoperative teaching. *Journal of Nursing Administration* 8:11–16, 1978.
47. Crichton, E. F., Smith, D. L., & Demanuele, F. Patient recall of medication information. *Drug Intelligence and Clinical Pharmacology* 12:591–599, 1978.
48. Cummings, K. M., Becker, M. H., Kirscht, J. P., & Levin, N. W. Intervention strategies to improve compliance with medical regimens by ambulatory hemodialysis patients. *Journal of Behavioral Medicine* 4:111–127, 1981.
49. D'Altroy, L. H., Blissenbach, H. F., & Lutz, D. Patient drug self-administration improves regimen compliance. *Hospital: Journal of the American Hospital Association* 52:131–136, 1978.
50. Davis, H. S. The role of a crisis intervention treatment in the patient's recovery from elective surgery. (Doctoral dissertation, Northwestern University). *Dissertation Abstracts International* 36:3490B, 1973.
51. Deets, C., & Blume, D. Evaluating the effectiveness of selected continuing education offerings. *Journal of Continuing Education in Nursing* 8:63–71, 1977.
52. del Bueno, D. Verifying the nurses' knowledge of pharmacology. *Nursing Outlook* 20:462–463, 1972.
53. DeLong, R. D. Individual differences in patterns of anxiety arousal, stress-relevant information and recovery from surgery. (Dissertation, University of California, Los Angeles). *Dissertation Abstracts International* 32:554B–555B, 1971.
54. Denne, K. T., & Ulicny, S., & Schorow, M. Open-circuit television: A dying medium for continuing medical education. *Proceedings, Tenth Annual Conference on Research in Medical Education.* Washington, D.C.: Association of American Medical Colleges, pp. 88–91, 1971.
55. Denne, K. T., Ulicny, S., & Schorow, M. Two-way radio: An evaluation of its effectiveness in continuing medical education. *Proceedings, Tenth Annual Conference on Research in Medical Education.* Washington, D.C.: Association of American Medical Colleges. pp. 92–95, 1971.
56. Distefano, M. K., & Pryer, M. Effect of brief training on mental health knowledge and attitudes of nurses and nurse's aides in a general hospital. *Nursing Research* 24:40–42, 1975.
57. Dollinger, M. R., Korenman, S. G., Soloman, D. H., & Brayton, D. F. A novel program of continuing medical education. *Journal of the American Medical Association* 220:714–716, 1972.
58. Donegan, J. H., Reid, J. C., & Eggers, G. W., Jr. The use of test results from ASA workshops to evaluate workshop effectiveness. *Journal of Medical Education* 51:500–505, 1976.
59. Donnelly, F. A., Ware, J. E., Wolkon, G. H., & Naftulin, D. H. Evaluation of weekend seminars for physicians. *Journal of Medical Education* 47:184–187, 1972.
60. Douglas, D., Wertley, B., & Chaffee, S. An information campaign that changed community attitudes. *Journalism Quarterly* 47:220–227, 1970.
61. Drazen, M., Nevid, J. S., Pace, N., & O'Brien, R. M. Worksite-based behavioral

treatment of mild hypertension. *Journal of Occupational Medicine* 24:511–514, 1982.
62. Driver, S. C., Shepherd, D. V., & Walpole, G. R. A comparison of three methods of using television for the continuing medical education of general practitioners. *British Journal of Medical Education* 6:246–252, 1972.
63. Dumas, R. G., & Leonard, R. C. The effect of nursing on the incidence of postoperative vomiting. *Nursing Research* 12:12–15, 1963.
64. Dziurbejko, M. M., & Larkin, J. C. Including the family in preoperative teaching. *American Journal of Nursing* 78:1892–1894, 1978.
65. Earp, J. L., Ory, M. G., & Strogatz, D. S. The effects of family involvement and practitioner home visits on the control of hypertension. *American Journal of Public Health* 72:1146–1154, 1982.
66. Edson, J. N., DiGregorio, N. J., & Hukin, J. An evaluation of a clerkship in cardiology for general practitioners. *Journal of Medical Education* 45:1150–1155, 1969.
67. Egbert, L. D., Battit, G. E., Welch, C. E., & Bartlett, M. K. Reduction of postoperative pain by encouragement and instruction of patients. *New England Journal of Medicine* 270:825–827, 1964.
68. Elliott, R., & Tighe, T. Breaking the cigarette habit: Effects of a technique involving threatened loss of money. *Psychology Record* 18:503–513, 1968.
69. Eney, R. D., & Goldstein, E. O. Compliance of chronic asthmatics with oral administration of theophylline as measured by serum and salivary levels. *Pediatrics* 57:513–517, 1976.
70. Fahs, I. J., & Miller, W. R. Continuing medical education and educational television: An evaluation of a series for physicians in Minnesota. *Journal of Medical Education* 45:578–587, 1970.
71. Farquhar, J. W., Maccoby, N., Wood, P. D., Alexander, J. K., Breitrose, H., Brown, B. W., Jr., Haskell, W. L., McAlister, A. L., Meyer, A. J., Nash, J. D., & Stern, M. P. Community education for cardiovascular health. *Lancet* 1:1192–1198, 1977.
72. Felton, G., Huss, K., Payne, E. A., & Srisic, K. Preoperative nursing intervention with the patient for surgery: Outcomes of three alternative approaches. *International Journal of Nursing Studies* 13:83–96, 1976.
73. Field, P. B. Effects of tape-recorded hypnotic preparation for surgery. *International Journal of Experimental Hypnosis* 22:54–61, 1974.
74. Finesilver, C. Preparation of adult patients for cardiac catheterization and coronary cineangiography. *International Journal of Nursing Studies* 15:211–221, 1978.
75. Flaherty, G. G., & Fitzpatrick, J. J. Relaxation technique to increase comfort level of postoperative patients: A preliminary study. *Nursing Research* 27:352–355, 1978.
76. Fleisher, G. A. A study of a radio/TV campaign on safety belt use. *Journal of Safety Research* 5:3–11, 1973.
77. Florell, J. L. Crisis intervention in orthopedic surgery. (Doctoral dissertation, Northwestern University). *Dissertation Abstracts International* 32:3633B, 1971.
78. Forman, S. G. Stress-management training: Evaluation of effects of school psychological services. *Journal of School Psychology* 19:233–241, 1981.
79. Forni, P., & Overman, R. Does continuing education have an effect on the

practice of nursing? A survey. *Journal of Continuing Education in Nursing* 5:44–51, 1974.
80. Fortin, F., & Kirouac, S. A randomized controlled trial of preoperative patient education. *International Journal of Nursing Studies* 13:11–24, 1976.
81. Fox. H. M. Psychiatric consultation in general medical clinics: An experiment in postgraduate education. *Journal of the American Medical Association* 185:999–1003, 1963.
82. Ganster, D. C., Mayes, B. T., Sime, W. E., & Tharp, G. D. Managing organizational stress: A field experiment. *Journal of Applied Psychology* 67:533–542, 1982.
83. Garnett, W. R., Davis, L. J., McKenney, J. M., & Steiner, K. C. Effect of telephone follow-up on medication compliance. *American Journal of Hospital Pharmacists* 38:676–679, 1981.
84. Gauvain, S., & Bowie, D. C. Continuing medical education: Assessment of courses. *Journal of the Royal College of General Practitioners* 19:223–227, 1970.
85. Gauvain, S., Wood, C. H., Walford, J., & Schilling, R. S. F. An experiment in postgraduate education to evaluate teaching and examination techniques. *Journal of Medical Education* 40:516–523, 1965.
86. German, P. S., Klein, L. E., McPhee, S. J., & Smith, C. R. Knowledge of and compliance with drug regimens in the elderly. *Journal of the American Geriatric Society* 30:568–571, 1982.
87. Gilliland, I. C., & Gibbons, J. L. The assessment of advanced courses of medical education. *British Journal of Medical Education* 5:305–306, 1971.
88. Grannan, M. A., McFarland, M., & Palmer, J. A nontraditional course of intensive care nursing... University of Hawaii, School of Nursing, Honolulu, Hawaii. *Journal of Continuing Education in Nursing* 6:32–36, 1975.
89. Gravenstein, J. S., & Rhoton, M. F. A brief note on a technique for postgraduate education: An educational experiment involving 465 physicians. *Anaesthetist* 22:249–250, 1973.
90. Gray-Toft, P. Effectiveness of a counseling support program for hospice nurses. *Journal of Counseling Psychology* 27:346–354, 1980.
91. Green, L. W., Werlin, S. H., Schauffler, H. H., & Avery, C. H. Research and demonstration issues in self-care: Measuring the decline of medicocentrism. *Health Education Monographs* 5:176–183, 1977.
92. Greenburg, A. G., McClure, D. K., Kink, R., Stubbs, J. A., & Peskin, G. W. Computerization of the surgical intensive care unit: Improvement of patient care via education. *Surgery* 77:799–806, 1975.
93. Groom, D. The South Carolina experiment in medical television. *Journal of Medical Education* 38:202–206, 1963.
94. Hall, S. M., Cooper, J. L., Burmaster, S., & Polk, A. Contingency contracting as a therapeutic tool with methadone maintenance clients: Six single-subject studies. *Behavioral Research Therapy* 15:438–441, 1977.
95. Hall, W. L., & Council, F. M. *Effects of Pediatric Education on the Use of Child Restraint Devices in North Carolina.* Charlotte: University of North Carolina, Highway Safety Research Center, 1979.
96. Harris, M. B., & Bruner, C. G. A comparison of a self-control and a contract procedure for weight control. *Behavioral Research Therapy* 9:347–354, 1971.
97. Hart, R. R. The influence of a taped hypnotic induction treatment procedure

on the recovery of surgical patients. *International Journal of Clinical and Experimental Hypnosis* 28:324–332, 1980.
98. Haynes, R. B., Sackett, D. L., Gibson, E. S., Taylor, D. W., Hackett, B. C., Roberts, R. S., & Johnson, A. L. Improvement of medication compliance in uncontrolled hypertension. *Lancet* 1:1265–1268, 1976.
99. Hazlett, C. B., Bachynski, J. E., & Embleton, J. Evaluation of on-campus continuing medical education programs in Alberta. *Canadian Medical Association Journal* 108:1282–1287, 1973.
100. Healy, K. M. Does preoperative instruction make a difference? *American Journal of Nursing* 68:62–67, 1968.
101. Hecht, A. B. Improving medication compliance by teaching outpatients. *Nursing Forum* 13:112–129, 1974.
102. Hegyvary, S. T., & Chamings, P. A. The hospital setting and patient care outcomes. *Journal of Nursing Administration* 5(3):29–32, 36–42, 1975.
103. Hill, B. J. Sensory information, behavioral instructions, and coping with sensory alteration surgery. *Nursing Research* 31:17–21, 1982.
104. Hirsch, E. O. Utilization review as a means of continuing education. *Medical Care* 12:358–362, 1974.
105. Huckabey, L., Cooper, P., & Neal, M. Effect of specific teaching techniques. *Nursing Research* 26:380–385, 1977.
106. Inui, T. S., Yourtee, E. L., & Williamson, J. W. Improved outcomes in hypertension after physician tutorials. *Annals of Internal Medicine* 84:646–651, 1976.
107. Jackson, S. E. Participation in decision making as a strategy for reducing job-related strain. *Journal of Applied Psychology* 68:3–19, 1983.
108. Jeffery, R. W., Thompson, P. D., & Wing, R. R. Effects on weight reduction of strong monetary contracts for calorie restriction or weight loss. *Behavioral Research Therapy* 16:363–369, 1978.
109. Johnson, J. E., Fuller, S. S., Endress, M. P., & Rice, V. H. Altering patients' responses to surgery: An extension and replication. *Research in Nursing and Health* 1:111–121, 1978.
110. Johnson, J. E., Rice, V. H., Fuller, S. S., & Endress, M. P. Sensory information, instruction in a coping strategy, and recovery from surgery. *Research in Nursing and Health* 1:4–17, 1978.
111. Johnson, P. A., & Stockdale, D. F. Effects of puppet therapy on palmar sweating of hospitalized children. *Johns Hopkins Medical Journal* 137:1–5, 1975.
112. Jones, R., & Taxay, E. P. Methodology and effectiveness of a program of postgraduate education for Cuban physicians. *Journal of Medical Education* 38:949–960, 1963.
113. Kane, R., & Bailey, R. Q. Evaluation of a postgraduate educational programme in early cancer detection. *British Journal of Medical Education* 5:134–137, 1971.
114. Kanthor, H. A. Car safety for infants: Effectiveness of prenatal counseling. *Pediatrics* 58:320–322, 1976.
115. Keane, T. M., Prue, D. M., & Collins, F. L., Jr. Behavioral contracting to improve dietary compliance in chronic renal dialysis patients. *Journal of Behavioral Therapy and Experimental Psychiatry* 12:63–67, 1981.
116. Kern, H. M., Jr., Jacobson, J. E., & Hess, J. B. Continuing education in psychiatry: A report of a program based upon the inductive method. *Johns Hopkins Medical Journal* 123:78–84, 1968.
117. King, I., & Tarsitano, B. The effect of structured and unstructured pre-operative teaching: A replication. *Nursing Research* 31:324–329, 1982.

118. Kirscht, J. P., Kirscht, J. L., & Rosenstock, I. M. A test of interventions to increase adherence to hypertensive medical regimens. *Health Education Quarterly* 8:261–272, 1981.
119. Kline, F. G., Miller, P., & Morrison, A. Adolescents and family planning information: An exploration of audience needs and media effects. In J. Blumler & E. Katz (Eds.), *The Uses of Mass Communications: Current Perspectives on Gratifications Research.* Beverly Hills, Calif.: Sage, 1974.
120. Konefal, M. M. Continuing education pays off in the care of high risk infants. *Journal of Continuing Education in Nursing* 8:22–25, 1977.
121. Korhonen, T., Huttunen, J. K., Aro, A., Hentinen, M., Ihalainen, O., Majander, H., Siitonen, O., Uusitupa, M., & Pyorala, K. A controlled trial of the effects of patient education in the treatment of insulin-dependent diabetes. *Diabetes Care* 6:256–261, 1983.
122. Kotre, J. N., et al. The Michigan physician: His use and evaluation of the professional meeting and postgraduate course. *Michigan Medicine* 70:111–117, 1971.
123. Lancour, J., & Reinders, A. A pilot project in continuing education for critical care nursing... Marquette University, Milwaukee, Wisconsin. *Journal of Nursing Administration* 5:38–41, 1975.
124. Langer, E. J., Janis, I. L., & Wolfer, J. A. Reduction of psychological stress in surgical patients. *Journal of Experimental Social Psychology* 11(2):155–165, 1975.
125. Layne, O. L., & Yudofsky, S. C. Postoperative psychosis in cardiotomy patients. *New England Journal of Medicine* 284:518–520, 1971.
126. Lazarus, H. R., & Hagens, J. H. Prevention of psychosis following open-heart surgery. *American Journal of Psychiatry* 124:1190–1195, 1968.
127. Levine, D. M., Green, L. W., Deeds, S. G., Chwalow, J., Russell, R. P., & Finlay, J. Health education for hypertensive patients. *Journal of the American Medical Association* 241:1700–1703, 1979.
128. Levine, P. H., & Britten, A. F. H. Supervised patient-management of hemophilia. *Annals of Internal Medicine* 78:195–201, 1973.
129. Lewis, C. E., & Hassanein, R. S. Continuing medical education: An epidemiologic evaluation. *New England Journal of Medicine* 282:254–259, 1970.
130. Lindeman, C. A., & Stetzer, S. L. Effects of preoperative visits by operating room nurses. *Nursing Research* 22:4–16, 1973.
131. Lindeman, C. A., & Van Aernam, B. Nursing intervention with the presurgical patient: The effects of structured and unstructured preoperative teaching. *Nursing Research* 20:319–332, 1971.
132. Linn, B. S. Continuing medical education: Impact on emergency room burn care. *Journal of the American Medical Association* 244:565–570, 1980.
133. Lorton, P. Evaluation of the effect of health education units on the smoking attitudes and behavior of fifth-, sixth-, and seventh-grade students. Report for the Institute for Math Studies in the Social Sciences, 1970.
134. Lucas, R. H. The affective and medical effects of different preoperative interventions with heart surgery patients. (Doctoral dissertation, University of Houston). *Dissertation Abstracts International* 36:5763B, 1976.
135. Ludy, J. A., Gagnon, J. P., & Caiola, S. M. The patient-pharmacist interaction in two ambulatory settings: Its relationship to patient satisfaction and drug misuse. *Drug Intelligence and Clinical Pharmacology* 11:81–89, 1977.
136. Lynch, L. Toward appropriate change in behavior measuring knowledge, attitude, and skills in continuing education. *Journal of Continuing Education in Nursing* 3:6–10, 1972.

137. Lytton, B., Weiss, R. M., Schiff, M. J., McGuire, E. J., Scott, R., Jr., & Glenn, J. F. Results of objective evaluation of postgraduate urologic seminar. *Journal of Urology* 110:582–584, 1973.
138. Maccoby, N., Farquhar, J. W., Wood, P. D., & Alexander, J. Reducing the risk of cardiovascular disease. *Journal of Community Health* 3:100–114, 1977.
139. MacDonald, E. T., MacDonald, J. B., & Phoenix, M. Improving drug compliance after hospital discharge. *British Medical Journal* 2:618–621, 1977.
140. Mahaffy, P. R. The effects of hospitalization on children admitted for tonsillectomy and adenoidectomy. *Nursing Research* 14:12–19, 1965.
141. Maiman, L. A., Green, L. W., Gibson, G., & MacKenzie, E. J. Education for self-treatment by adult asthmatics. *Journal of the American Medical Association* 241:1919–1922, 1979.
142. Malahy, B. The effect of instruction and labeling on the number of medication errors made by patients at home. *American Journal of Hospital Pharmacists* 23:283–292, 1966.
143. Mann, F. C., Kotre, J., Rielly, A., Vanselow, N. A., & Arbor, A. The Michigan physician and his continuing education: MARMP study purpose, design, and first findings. *Michigan Medicine* 69:981–990, 1970.
144. Mann, R. A. The behavior-therapeutic use of contingency contracting to control an adult behavior problem: Weight control. In R. C. Katz & S. Zlutnick (Eds.), *Behavior Therapy and Health Care: Principles and Applications.* New York: Pergamon Press, 1975.
145. Manning, P. R., Abrahamson, S., & Dennis, D. Comparison of four teaching techniques: Programmed text, textbook, lecture-demonstration, and lecture-workshop. *Journal of Medical Education* 43:356–359, 1968.
146. Manuso, J. S. J. The Equitable Life Assurance Society program. *Preventive Medicine* 12:658–662, 1983.
147. Margolis, C. Z., Sheehan, T. J., & Meyers, A. Using a workshop to determine the effectiveness of a text on the problem-oriented medical record. *Journal of Medical Education* 51:767–768, 1976.
148. Mathie, J. Intensive care course planning, progress, and evaluation. *Nursing Times* 70:135–209, 1974.
149. McGuinness, A. C., Menzel, H., Rogers, C., & Bodden, U. R. Continuation medical education by open-circuit television: A preliminary report. *Journal of Medical Education* 39:735–745, 1964.
150. McGuinness, A. C. The New York Academy of Medicine TV-PG efforts in a metropolis. *Journal of Medical Education* 40:878–881, 1965.
151. McGuinness, A. C. Physician interest in the New York Academy of Medicine television program after four years. *Journal of Medical Education* 43:852–855, 1968.
152. McGuinness, A. C. The medical television audience of the New York Academy of Medicine after four years. *Bulletin of the New York Academy of Medicine* 44:332–345, 1968.
153. McGuire, C., Hurley, R. E., Babbott, D., & Butterworth, J. S. Auscultatory skill: Gain and retention after intensive instruction. *Journal of Medical Education* 39:120–131, 1964.
154. McKenney, J. M., Slining, J. M., Henderson, H. R., Devins, D., & Barr, M. The effect of clinical pharmacy services on patients with essential hypertension. *Circulation* 48:1104–1111, 1973.
155. McMahon, J., & Neuman, M. Tool for evaluating the impact of an inservice program on nursing care. *Journal of Continuing Education in Nursing* 3: 5–7, 1972.

156. Melamed, B. G., & Siegel, L. J. Reduction of anxiety in children facing hospitalization and surgery by use of filmed modeling. *Journal of Consulting Clinical Psychology* 43:511–521, 1975.
157. Menzel, H., Maurice, R., & McGuinness, A. C. Evaluation of the New York Academy of Medicine's television programs. *Journal of Medical Education* 41:826–843, 1966.
158. Menzel, H., Maurice, R., & McGuinness, A. C. The effectiveness of the televised clinical science seminars of the New York Academy of Medicine. *Bulletin of the New York Academy of Medicine* 42:679–714, 1966.
159. Meyer, T. C., Hansen, R. H., & Keliher, J. J. Report of an experiment in the use of telelectures for the continuing education of physicians and allied health personnel. *Journal of Medical Education* 43:73–77, 1968.
160. Miller, J. R., & Pless, I. B. Child automobile restraints: Evaluation of health education. *Pediatrics* 59:907–911, 1977.
161. Miller, P. M., Hersen, M., & Eisler, R. M. Relative effectiveness of instructions, agreements, and reinforcement in behavioral contracts with alcoholics. *Journal of Abnormal Psychology* 83:548–553, 1974.
162. Minor, M. J., & Bradburn, N. M. *The Effects of Viewing "Feeling Good": Results from a Field Experiment in a Low-Income Community.* Chicago: National Opinion Research Center, 1976.
163. Mock, R. L., McCoard, B. F., & Prestwood, R. Northern California postgraduate medical television: An evaluation. *Journal of Medical Education* 45:40–46, 1970.
164. Morisky, D. E., Levine, D. M., Green, L. W., Shapiro, S., Russell, R. P., & Smith, C. R. Five-year blood pressure control and mortality following health education for hypertensive patients. *American Journal of Public Health* 73:153–162, 1983.
165. Morrison, A. F., Kline, F. G., & Miller, P. Aspects of adolescent information acquisition about drugs and alcohol topics. In R. Ortman (Ed.), *Communication Research and Drug Education.* Beverly Hills, Calif.: Sage, 1976.
166. Moses, C., & Wolfe, R. Grand rounds via television: An experiment in continuing education. *Pennsylvania Medical Journal* 67:23–28, 1964.
167. Muhlhauser, I., Jorgens, V., Berger, M., Graninger, W., Gurtler, W., Hornke, L., Kunz, A., Schernthaner, G., Scholz, V., & Voss, H. E. Bicentric evaluation of a teaching and treatment programme for Type 1 (insulin-dependent) diabetic patients: Improvement of metabolic control and other measures of diabetes care for up to 22 months. *Diabetologia* 25:470–476, 1983.
168. Murphy, L. R. A comparison of relaxation methods for reducing stress in nursing personnel. *Human Factors* 25:431–440, 1983.
169. Murphy, L. R. Stress management in highway maintenance workers. *Journal of Occupational Medicine* 26:436–442, 1984.
170. Myers, E. D., & Calvert, E. J. The effect of forewarning on the occurrence of side effects and discontinuance of medication in patients on dothiepin. *Journal of Internal Medicine Research* 4:237–240, 1976.
171. Naftulin, D. H., Donnelly, F. A., & Wolkon, G. H. Psychiatry education programs for nonpsychiatrist physicians: A 10-year perspective. *Comprehensive Psychiatry* 15:133–139, 1974.
172. Naftulin, D. H., & Ware, J. E., Jr. Continuing education, clinical competence, and specialty certification. *Journal of Medical Education* 46:901–903, 1971.
173. Nash, J. D., & Farquhar, J. W. Community approaches to dietary modification and obesity. In A. J. Stunkard (Ed.), *Psychiatric Clinics of North America: Obesity.* Philadelphia: Saunders, 1978.

174. Neu, H. C., & Howrey, S. P. Testing the physician's knowledge of antibiotic use. *New England Journal of Medicine* 293:1291–1295, 1975.
175. Newble, D. I., Grant, K. A., Sage, R. E., & Burston, R. A. An experiment in continuing education for physicians. *Australian and New Zealand Journal of Medicine* 3:512–515, 1973.
176. Newcomer, D. R., & Anderson, R. W. Effectiveness of a combined drug self-administration and patient teaching program. *Drug Intelligence and Clinical Pharmacology* 8:374–381, 1974.
177. Olsen, L. K., Stone, D. B., & Saunders, J. A. In-service training for elementary school health education. *Health Education* 7:27–29, 1976.
178. Ortmeyer, J. A. Anxiety and repression coping styles, and treatment approaches in the integration of elective orthopedic surgical stress. (Doctoral dissertation, Northwestern University). *Dissertation Abstracts International* 38:5536A, 1978.
179. Peters, R. K., Benson, H., & Peters, J. M. Daily relaxation in a working population: II. Effects on blood pressure. *American Journal of Public Health* 67:954–959, 1977.
180. Peters, R. K., Benson, H., & Porter, D. Daily relaxation response breaks in a working population: I. Effects on self-reported measures of health, performance, and well-being. *American Journal of Public Health* 67:946–953, 1977.
181. Peterson, O. L., Andrews, L. P., Spain, R. S., & Greenberg, R. G. An analytical study of North Carolina general practice. *Journal of Medical Education* 31 (pt. II):1–165, 1956.
182. Popiel, E. Long-range evaluation of a continuing education course. *Journal of Continuing Education in Nursing* 4:15–17, 1973.
183. Puetz, B. E., & Rytting, M. Evaluation of the effect of continuing education on health care. *Journal of Continuing Education in Nursing* 10:22–25, 1979.
184. Putnum, W., & Curry, L. Patient care appraisal in the ambulatory setting: Effectiveness as a continuing medical education tool. *Annual Conference on Research in Medical Education.* Washington, D.C.: Association of American Medical Colleges, pp. 207–212, 1980.
185. Rahe, R. H., O'Neil, T., Hagan, A., & Arthur, R. J. Brief group therapy following myocardial infarction: Eighteen-month follow-up of a controlled trial. *International Journal of Psychiatric Medicine* 6:349–358, 1975.
186. Redican, K. J., Olsen, L. K., & Stone, D. B. Effects of a prototype health education curriculum on health knowledge of lower socioeconomic sixth-grade students. *Health Values* 2:84–91, 1978.
187. Reed, D. E., Lapenas, C., & Rogers, K. Continuing education based on record audit in a community hospital. *Journal of Medical Education* 48:1152–1155, 1973.
188. Rehder, T. L., McCoy, L. K., Blackwell, B., Whitehead, W., & Robinson, A. Improving medication compliance by counseling and special prescription container. *American Journal of Hospital Pharmacists* 37:379–384, 1980.
189. Reisinger, K. S., & Williams, A. F. Evaluation of programs designed to increase the protection of infants in cars. *Pediatrics* 62:280–287, 1978.
190. Reisinger, K. S., Williams, A. F., Wells, J. K., John, C. E., Roberts, T. R., & Podgainy, M. J. The effect of pediatricians' counseling on infant restraint use. *Pediatrics* 67:201–206, 1981.

191. Repicky, P., & Hotvedt, M. The role of formative evaluation in a continuing education program: Basic rehabilitation nursing techniques. *Journal of Continuing Education in Nursing* 8:29–34, 1977.
192. Richardson, F. M. Examinations as devices for evaluation. *Journal of Medical Education* 40:972–977, 1965.
193. Rittelmeyer, L. F., Jr. Continuing education in psychiatry for physicians. *Journal of the American Medical Association* 220:710–713, 1972.
194. Robertson, L., Kelley, A. B., O'Neill, B., Wixon, C. W., Eisworth, R. S., & Haddon, W. J. A controlled study of the effect of television messages on safety belt use. *American Journal of Public Health* 64:1071–1080, 1974.
195. Roney, J. G., & Roark, G. M. *Continuing Education of Physicians in Kansas: An Exploratory End-Result Study.* Menlo Park, Calif.: Stanford Research Institute, 1967.
196. Rosenberg, S. G. Patient education leads to better care for heart patients. *HSMHA Health Report* 86:793–802, 1971.
197. Rubenstein, E. Continuing medical education at Stanford: The back-to-medical school program. *Journal of Medical Education* 48:911–918, 1973.
198. Sackett, D. L., Haynes, R. B., Gibson, E. S., Hackett, B. C., Taylor, D. W., Roberts, R. S., & Johnson, A. L. Randomized clinical trial of strategies for improving medication compliance in primary hypertension. *Lancet* 1:205–207, 1975.
199. Sanazaro, P. J., & Worth, R. M. Concurrent quality assurance in hospital care: Report of a study by private initiative in PSRO. *New England Journal of Medicine* 298:1171–1177, 1978.
200. Schlesinger, L. E. Evaluation of a symposium on epilepsy as a method of training. *Public Health Reports* 81:929–937, 1966.
201. Seamonds, B. C. Stress factors and their effect on absenteeism in a corporate employee group. *Journal of Occupational Medicine* 24:393–397, 1982.
202. Seamonds, B. C. Extension of research into stress factors and their effect on illness absenteeism. *Journal of Occupational Medicine* 25:821–822, 1983.
203. Secarea, R. V., & Olsen, L. K. An evaluation instrument for appraising the health knowledge of seventh-grade students participating in a special School Health Education Project. Presented at the Annual Convention of the American School Health Association, October 1974.
204. Sechrist, K. R. The effect of repetitive teaching on patient's knowledge about drugs to be taken at home. *International Journal of Nursing Studies* 16:51–58, 1979.
205. Seltzer, A., Roncari, I., & Garfinkel, P. Effect of patient education on medication compliance. *Canadian Journal of Psychiatry* 25:638–645, 1980.
206. Shepherd, R. M. Evaluation of continuing education. *Proceedings of the Royal Society of Medicine* 64:149–150, 1971.
207. Shope, J. T. Intervention to improve compliance with pediatric anticonvulsant therapy. *Patient Counseling and Health Education* 2:135–141, 1980.
208. Sibley, J. C., Sackett, D. L., Neufeld, V. R., Gerrard, B., Rudnick, K., & Fraser, W. A randomized trial of continuing medical education. *New England Journal of Medicine* 306:511–515, 1982.
209. Solomon, A. J. The effect of a psychotherapeutic interview on the physical results of thoracic surgery. (Doctoral dissertation, California School of Professional Psychology, San Francisco). *Dissertation Abstracts International* 34:2319B, 1973.

210. Stafford, J., Helm, A., & Beaver, D. The value of short courses: An attempt to evaluate a four-day teaching programme in Christchurch for diabetes educators. *New Zealand Nursing Journal* 72:24, 1979.
211. Steckel, S. B., & Swain, M. A. Contracting with patients to improve compliance. *Hospitals: Journal of the American Hospital Association* 51:81–84, 1977.
212. Steinmetz, J., Kaplan, R. M., & Miller, G. L. Stress management: An assessment questionnaire for evaluating interventions and comparing groups. *Journal of Occupational Medicine* 24:923–931, 1982.
213. Stern, M. P., Farquhar, J. W., McCuby, N., & Russell, S. H. Results of a two-year health education campaign of dietary behavior. *Circulation* 54:826–833, 1976.
214. Stone, E. J. The effects of a prototype health education curriculum model on locus of control, perceived vulnerability, and health attitudes of fifth-graders. *Journal of School Health* 48:667–671, 1978.
215. Stross, J. K., & Bole, G. G. Evaluation of a continuing education program on rheumatoid arthritis. *Arthritis and Rheumatism* 23:846–849, 1980.
216. Stross, J. K., Hiss, R. G., Watts, C. M., Davis, W. K., & MacDonald, R. Continuing education in pulmonary disease for primary care physicians. *American Review of Respiratory Diseases* 127:739–746, 1983.
217. Surman, O. S., Hackett, T. P., Silverberg, E. L., & Behrendt, D. M. Usefulness of psychiatric intervention in patients undergoing cardiac surgery. *Archives of General Psychiatry* 30:830–835, 1974.
218. Swain, M. A., & Steckel, S. B. Influencing adherence among hypertensives. *Research in Nursing Health* 4:213–222, 1981.
219. Tagliacozzo, D. M., Luskin, D. B., Lashof, J. C., & Ima, K. Nurse intervention and patient behavior. *American Journal of Public Health* 64:596–603, 1974.
220. Trinca, J. C., & Rowe, I. L. Evaluation of a medical education programme. Diabetes Mellitus Telecast, 1968. *Medical Journal of Australia* 2:140–145, 1970.
221. Udry, J. R., Clark, L. T., Chare, C. L., & Levy, L. Can mass media advertising increase contraceptive use? *Family Planning Perspectives* 4:37–44, 1972.
222. Valish, A. V., & Boyd, N. The role of computer-assisted instruction in continuing education of registered nurses: An experimental study. *Journal of Continuing Education in Nursing* 6:13–32, 1975.
223. Van Steenhouse, A. L. A comparison of three types of presurgical psychological intervention with male open heart surgery patients. (Doctoral dissertation, Michigan State University, East Lansing). *Dissertation Abstracts International* 39:1449A, 1978.
224. Vaughan, C. F. Children in hospital. *Lancet* 12:1117–1120, 1957.
225. Vernon, D. T. A., & Bailey, W. C. The use of motion pictures in the psychological preparation of children for induction of anesthesia. *Anesthesiology* 40:68–72, 1974.
226. Vernon, D. T. A., & Bigelow, D. A. Effect of information about a potentially stressful situation on responses to stress impact. *Journal of Personal Social Psychology* 29:50–59, 1974.
227. Wallston, K., Cohen, B. D., Wallston, B. S., Smith, R. A., & DeVellis, B. M. Increasing nurses' person-centeredness. *Nursing Research* 27:56–59, 1978.
228. Wandless, I., & Whitmore, J. The effect of counseling by a pharmacist on drug compliance in elderly patients. *Journal of Clinical Hospital Pharmacology* 6:51–56, 1981.

229. Ware, J. E., Jr., & Naftulin, D. H. Continuing education and clinical skills: A second look. *Proceedings, Tenth Annual Conference on Research in Medical Education.* Washington, D.C.: Association of American Medical Colleges, pp. 96–99, 1971.
230. Warner, K. E. The effects of the anti-smoking campaign on cigarette consumption. *American Journal of Public Health* 67:645–650, 1977.
231. Webb, P. A. Effectiveness of patient education and psychosocial counseling in promoting compliance and control among hypertensive patients. *Journal of Family Practice* 10:1047–1055, 1980.
232. West, D. J., Horan, J. J., & Games, P. A. Component analysis of occupational stress inoculation applied to registered nurses in an acute care hospital setting. *Journal of Counseling Psychology* 31:209–218, 1984.
233. Whitehouse, F. W., Whitehouse, I. J., Smith, J., & Hohl, R. D. Teaching the person with diabetes: Experience with a follow-up session. *Diabetes Care* 2:35–38, 1979.
234. Williamson, J. W., Alexander, N., & Miller, G. Continuing education and patient care research. *Journal of the American Medical Association* 201: 118–122, 1967.
235. Williamson, J. W., Aronovitch, S., Simonson, L., Ramirez, C., & Kelley, D. Health accounting: An outcome-based system of quality assurance—illustrative application to hypertension. *Bulletin of the New York Academy of Medicine* 51:727–738, 1975.
236. Williamson, J. W., & McGuire, C. Consecutive case conference: An educational evaluation. *Journal of Medical Education* 43:1068–1074, 1968.
237. Wilson, J. F. Determinants of recovery from surgery: Preoperative instruction, relaxation training, and defensive structure. (Doctoral dissertation, University of Michigan). *Dissertation Abstracts International* 38:1476B, 1977.
238. Wilson, J. F. Behavioral preparation for surgery—benefit or harm? *Journal of Behavioral Medicine* 4:79–101, 1981.
239. Winett, R. A. Parameters of deposit contracts in the modification of smoking. *Psychological Record* 23:49–60, 1973.
240. Wolfer, J. A., & Visintainer, M. A. Pediatric surgical patients' and parents' stress responses and adjustment as a function of psychologic preparation and stress-point nursing care. *Nursing Research* 24:244–255, 1975.
241. Woroniecki, C. L., McKercher, P. L., Flagler, D. G., Berchou, R., & Cook, J. A. Effect of pharmacists' counseling on drug information recall. *American Journal of Hospital Pharmacists* 39:1907–1910, 1982.
242. Worth, R., Home, P. D., Johnston, D. G., Anderson, J., Ashworth, L., Burrin, J. M., Appleton, D., Binder, C., & Alberti, K. G. M. M. Intensive attention improves glycemic control in insulin-dependent diabetes without further advantage from home blood glucose monitoring: Results of a controlled trial. *British Medical Journal* 285:1233–1240, 1982.
243. Youmans, J. B. Experience with a postgraduate course for practitioners: Evaluation of results. *Journal of Association of American Medical Colleges* 10:154–172, 1935.
244. Zaremba, M. *Maine Diabetes Control Project.* Augusta: Maine Department of Human Services, 1984.
245. Zismer, D. K., Gillum, R. F., Johnson, C. A., Becerra, J., & Johnson, T. H. Improving hypertension control in a private medical practice. *Archives of Internal Medicine* 142:297–299, 1982.

Glossary

Assessment: The estimation of the relative magnitude, importance, or value of objects observed.

Behavioral diagnosis: The assessment of the causes of a problem or goal that can be changed by an adaptation of human actions.

Behavioral evaluation: The comparison of an action or set of actions against an objective or standard (e.g., a criterion or a norm).

Blinding: Methods of preventing subjects, educators, or data gatherers from knowing which experimental or control group the subject is in.

Case control study: An inquiry in which groups of individuals are selected according to whether they do or do not have the disease, behavior, or other characteristic of which the cause is to be studied. The groups are compared with respect to existing or past characteristics judged to be of possible relevance to the cause of the disease, behavior, or other characteristic. (Also called *case comparison, case compeer, case referent, retrospective study.*)

Cluster sampling: A method for approximating a random sample by aggregating individuals in larger units of observation that occur naturally (e.g., classrooms, census tracts, institutions), taking a random sample of the larger units (clusters), and then observing all or a sample of the individuals within the sampled clusters.

Cohort study: The observation over time of one or more groups of people that have some common characteristic (usually year of birth) or exposure (usually date of enrollment in program). Sometimes called a *panel study.*

Colinear: Two or more variables all having a similar linear relationship with each other or with a common referent variable.

Concept: An idea of the attributes or relationships common to a class of objects; an abstraction of particulars to a more global idea.

Confidence limits: The band of values above and below a statistical estimate to show the range of true values the estimate might have with a given probability (e.g., 95 percent confidence limits for a mean of 2.0 might be −0.15 to 4.15).

Construct: The specific representation of a concept within a causal explanation or theoretical framework.

Continuous variable: A variable that can take on any value in a specified interval. See also *Discrete variable.*

Cost-benefit: A measure of the cost of an intervention relative to the benefits it yields, usually expressed as a ratio of dollars saved or gained for every dollar spent on the program. See also *Cost-effectiveness.*

Cost-effectiveness: A measure of the cost of an intervention relative to its impact, usually expressed in dollars per unit of effect. See also *Cost-benefit.*

Coverage: The percentage of an eligible or target population reached by a program.

Cronbach's alpha: A coefficient calculated from the intercorrelations of all items in a questionnaire or other measurement instrument to estimate the internal consistency reliability of the items of a measurement scale.

Cross-sectional study: A study that tries to infer cause and effect from observations made at the same time.

Data: Two or more measures resulting from observations. *Data* is the plural form of *datum.*

Datum: A single observation recorded as a point of measurement.

Diagnosis: The identification of a problem and the determination of its causes.

Dichotomous characteristic: A characteristic that is classified into one of two classes.

Discrete variable: A variable that can take on only certain prescribed values in an interval (e.g., 0, 1, and 2; not 0.5 and 1.456).

Dose-response study: A study that seeks to determine how the risk of a specified event increases with the amount of exposure to a causative agent.

Educational diagnosis: The assessment of causes of a behavior that can be changed by learning.

Educational evaluation: The comparison of some combination of predisposing, enabling, and reinforcing factors regarded as causes of a behavior of interest against a standard or objectives for these factors (e.g., criteria or norms).

Effectiveness: The ability of an intervention to achieve its intended effect in reducing a need or problem in a population.

Efficacy: The ability of an intervention to achieve its intended effect in those individuals exposed to it.

Efficiency: A measure of resources consumed (time, labor, material) in relation to the number of people served or units of effect produced.

Epidemiology: The study of the distribution and determinants of disease frequency in populations.

Evaluation: The comparison of an object of interest against a standard of acceptability.

Experiment: A set of procedures applied to an object of interest in order to answer a specific question about it according to scientific rules of evidence.

Experimental design: A set of procedures distinguished from other designs for evaluation by the presence of a truly equivalent control group, which is best assured by random assignment of large numbers of subjects to each group.

External validity: Assurance that the results of an evaluation can be generalized to other settings.

Extraneous event: Something other than the program or method being evaluated that could account for the changes observed during the history of the program.

Focus group: A method used in testing the perception and receptivity of a target population to an idea or method by recording the reactions of a sample of eight to ten people discussing it with each other.

Formative evaluation: Any combination of measurements obtained and judgments made before or during the implementation of materials, methods, activities or programs to control, assure or improve the quality of performance or delivery. (Measurements *during* the program are sometimes called *process evaluation.*)

Frequency distribution: A table showing the numbers or proportions of individuals falling in each subgroup.

Hawthorne effect: A specific reactive effect when subjects are responding favorably to the attention being paid to them.

Health evaluation: The comparison of a health condition against a standard of acceptable health (e.g., an objective or a norm).

Historical prospective study: See *Retrospective-prospective study.*

History: A threat to internal validity caused by secular trends or extraneous events that could account for the results of an evaluation.

Impact: The immediate observable effects of a program, leading to the intended outcomes of the program; intermediate outcomes.

Incidence: The number of new cases of a condition that come into being or are discovered during a specified period of time.

Indicator: One observable and measurable representation of a property or its construct.

Internal consistency: One operational form of reliability based on how well the results on items in a measurement instrument are correlated with each other.

Internal validity: Assurance that the results of an evaluation can be attributed to the object (program or method) evaluated.

KR-20 coefficient: An internal consistency reliability estimate based on the Kuder-Richardson formula for a measurement scale made up of dichotomous items such as true-false questions.

Linear: A relationship in which each unit of change in one variable is associated with a proportionate change in the other variable, and in which the direction of the relationship does not change.

Longitudinal: Data analyzed to connect events or characteristics at two or more points in time for the same individuals, either prospectively or retrospectively.

Maturation: A threat to internal validity caused by the growth, development, or maturation of participants, which could account for the results of an evaluation.

Measure: Assignment of a number or numbers to objects observed.

Measurement: Methods and procedures for systematic observation, assessment, and assignment of numbers.

Mediating variable: A factor responsible for altering or enabling the relationship between a cause and an effect. For example, age and attitudes are mediating variables in the relationship between drug information and drug use behavior.

Natural history study: A study of the factors that are involved in determining the course of a disease, the development of a behavior, or the typical pattern of social processes over time without controlled interventions.

Need: An estimation of the interventions required based on a diagnosis of the problem and, in populations, the number of people eligible to benefit from the intervention(s).

Observation: Notice taken of an indicator.

Operating cost-effectiveness: A ratio of the operating costs of a program to a specific effect or impact of the program.

Operating costs: Total costs of a program minus start-up costs.

Outcome: An ultimate goal or product of a program or treatment, generally measured in the health field in terms of morbidity or mortality statistics in a population, vital measures, symptoms, signs, or physiological indicators on individuals.

Period prevalence: The number of cases of a condition known to have existed during a specified period of time, regardless whether they began during that period or an earlier period.

Placebo effect: A specific reactive effect when the subject's change is a result of believing so strongly in the treatment that he or she responds to his or her belief rather than to the education.

Point prevalence: The frequency of a condition at a designated point in time.

Policy analysis: An application of measurement and evaluation procedures in which the broadest questions of need, scope, and allocation of resources and goals are critically assessed.

Power of a statistical test: The probability that the sample size is large enough to reject a false alternative hypothesis.

Process evaluation: Any combination of measurements obtained during the implementation of program activities to control, assure, or improve the quality of performance or delivery. Together with preprogram studies, makes up formative evaluation.

Property: One dimension or element of a construct.

Prospective: Collection or analysis of additional data at one or more points in time after subjects are first seen, usually from the present to the future. See also *Retrospective-prospective.*

Prospective study: A study in which exposed and nonexposed cohorts are observed over time for the occurrence of a specified event. (Also called *cohort study.*)

Quality: The appropriateness of a specific set of professional activities as performed in relation to the educational objectives they are intended to serve.

Quality assurance: Long-range accountability for professional activities whereby consumers and other relevant publics can know that they are appropriately performed.

Quality control: The monitoring and surveillance mechanisms or procedures for producing evidence of quality.

Quasi-experimental design: A design that is experimental in all respects except assurance of equivalence between experimental and control groups prior to treatment.

Quota sampling: A method for approximating a random sample by selecting individuals or other units of observations as they appear until certain characteristics (e.g., age, sex, race, blood pressure, weight) are represented in the sample according to their known proportion of the population.

Random assignment: Procedures by which each individual or other unit of observation has an equal opportunity to appear in experimental or control groups, thereby assuring equivalent compositions of the groups. Also called *random allocation.*

Random error: An unbiased and unpredictable form of error whose mean, in repeated measurements, usually tends toward zero (see also *Systematic error*).

Random sampling: Procedures by which each individual or other unit of observation (e.g., family, neighborhood, classroom, clinic, or worksite) has an equal or known probability of being included in a study, thereby assuring that the sample studied is representative of the population to which results are to be generalized.

Reach: The number of people attending or exposed to an intervention or program.

Reactive effects: Threats to the external validity of evaluation that result when the subjects are responding to the experimental conditions as well as to the health education program being tested.

Regression to the mean: A threat to internal validity when the pretest scores are sufficiently deviant from population averages that they will predictably be closer to the population averages at the time of the posttest, regardless of the independent variable.

Relative risk: The ratio of the rate of disease or injury among those exposed to the rate among those not exposed.

Repeated measurement study: A cohort study in which the same characteristics are measured over a period of time.

Result: A value or quantity arrived at by calculation, representing the impact or outcome of an intervention.

Retrospective: Collection or analysis of data pertaining to a time before the subjects are first seen or recorded in a study.

Retrospective-prospective study: A study of a cohort in which data collection was begun in the past. (Also called *historical-prospective, historical-cohort,* or *nonconcurrent prospective study.*)

Retrospective study: A study in which the previous histories of people are examined for exposure to a potentially causative agent. (Also called *case-control study.*)

Sampling frame: A list that identifies all individuals or households or other units in a given population at a point in time.

Secular trend: The continuation of a slope that was occurring in the population at large as a part of history.

Selection: A threat to internal validity arising from differences between experimental and comparison groups in their characteristics that might account for their posttest differences on outcomes.

Sensitivity: The extent to which a method gives results free from false negative measurements. See also *specificity.*

Sleeper effect: A delay in the impact of an intervention, usually associated with the time required for knowledge or attitudes to be converted into action.

Social desirability effect: A specific reactive effect or source of bias in measurements when the subject is trying to satisfy the evaluator.

Specificity: The extent to which a method gives results free from false positive measures. See also *sensitivity.*

Split-half reliability: An estimate of internal consistency reliability based on the magnitude of the correlation of scores between two halves of a measurement instrument.

Stability reliability: A form of reliability estimation based on the correlation of scores on the same measurement instrument taken on the same people at two or more points in time.

Standards: The minimum acceptable levels of performance (in formative evaluation), effectiveness (in impact evaluation), or benefits (in outcome evaluation) used to judge the value.

Start-up costs: The nonrecurring costs of initiating a program, including planning and capital outlays.

Stratified sample: Random sample from a subgroup (stratum) of a population divided according to known characteristics such as age or income.

Summative evaluation: Any combination of measurements and judgments that permit conclusions to be drawn about the impact, outcomes, or benefits of a program or method.

Synthetic estimate: A statistic produced from a synthesis of local population data and proportions or means from another population, usually designed to give an estimate of need.

Systematic error: A biased form of measurement error—for example, where the overestimates are not balanced by the underestimates.

Testing: A threat to internal validity when the pretest on the dependent variable prepares subjects to perform better on the posttest, independent of the intervention or of real change.

Test-retest reliability: An operational method of estimating stability reliability.

Trigger effect: A temporary increase in behavior, usually associated with mass media "triggering" an already motivated behavior, or a change in rules or resources that enable a behavior that would have occurred eventually to occur sooner. Also referred to in evaluation as "borrowing from the future."

Validity: Assurance that results obtained from measurement or evaluation are an accurate reflection of reality.

Variable: An observable indicator or property that takes on different values among objects assessed. Measurement may be either qualitative (assigning individuals to classes) or quantitative (assigning numerical scores to individuals).

Weighted sample: A stratified sample in which the sampling fraction is disproportionately higher in a particular stratum so that more cases of the object of interest will be available for study in that stratum. (Also called *enriched sample.*)

References

Aday, L. A., & Eichhorn, R. *The Utilization of Health Services: Indices and Correlates.* DHEW Pub. No. (HSM) 73-3003. Washington, D.C.: National Center for Health Services Research, 1973.

Aday, L. A., Sellers, C., & Andersen, R. M. Potentials of local health surveys: A state-of-the-art summary. *American Journal of Public Health* 71:835–840, August 1981.

Alkhateeb, W., Lukeroth, C. T., & Riggs, M. A. Comparison of three educational techniques used in a venereal disease clinic. *Public Health Reports* 90:159–164, 1975.

Alkin, M. C., & Solmon, L. C. *The Costs of Evaluation.* Beverly Hills, Calif.: Sage, 1983.

Alwin, D. F. (Ed.). *Survey Design and Analysis: Current Issues.* Beverly Hills, Calif.: Sage, 1978.

American Hospital Association. *Implementing Patient Education in the Hospital.* Chicago: American Hospital Association, 1979.

American Psychological Association. *Standards for Educational and Psychological Tests.* Washington, D.C.: American Psychological Association, 1974.

Anastasi, A. *Psychological Assessment* (4th ed.). Boston: Houghton Mifflin, 1978.

Anderson, C. L., & Creswell, W. H. *School Health Practice* (8th ed.). St. Louis: Mosby, 1985.

Anderson, L. W. *Assessing Affective Characteristics in the Schools.* Newton, Mass.: Allyn & Bacon, 1981.

Anderson, S. B., & Ball, S. *The Profession and Practice of Program Evaluation.* San Francisco: Jossey-Bass, 1980.

Andrews, F. M., & Withey, S. B. *Social Indicators of Well-Being: America's Perception of Life Quality.* New York: Plenum Press, 1976.

Armor, D. J. Theta reliability and factor scaling. In H. Costner (Ed.), *Sociological Methodology,* pp. 17–50. San Francisco: Jossey-Bass, 1974.

Association for the Advancement of Health Education. *Evaluation Instruments in Health Education.* Reston, Va.: Alliance for Health, Physical Education, Recreation and Dance, 1979.

Atwater, J. B. Adapting the venereal disease clinic to today's problem. *American Journal of Public Health* 64(5):433–437, May 1974.

Atwood, J., & Hinshaw, A. S. Multiple indicators of nurse and patient outcomes as a method for evaluating a change in staffing patterns. *Communicating Nursing Research* 10:235–256, September 1977.

Aujoulet, L. P. L'education pour la santé. Peut-on en evaluer la rentabilité. *International Journal of Health Education* 16(1):21–27, 1973.

Bachman, J. G., O'Malley, P. M., & Johnston, J. *Change and Stability in the Lives of Young Men: Adolescence to Adulthood* (Vol. 6). Ann Arbor, Mich.: Institute for Social Research, 1978.

Back, K. W., & Stycos J. M. *The Survey Under Unusual Conditions: Methodological Facets of the Jamaica Human Fertility Investigation,* Monograph No. 1. Ithaca, N.Y.: Society for Applied Anthropology, 1959.

Baggaley, A. R. Multivariate analysis, an introduction for consumers of behavioral research. *Evaluation Review* 5:123–131, February 1981.

Baker, E. L., & Quellmalz, E. S. *Educational Testing and Evaluation.* Beverly Hills, Calif.: Sage, 1980.

Baker, S. P., & Dietz, P. E. Injury prevention. In U.S. Department of Health, Education, and Welfare, *Healthy People: The Surgeon General's Report on Health Promotion and Disease Prevention, Background Papers.* DHEW (PHS) Pub. No. 79-55071A. Washington, D.C.: Office of the Assistant Secretary for Health, 1979.

Balinsky, W., & Berger, R. A review of the research on general health status indexes. *Medical Care* 13:283–293, 1975.

Banta, H. D., & Luce, B. R. Assessing the cost-effectiveness of prevention. *Journal of Community Health* 9:145–165, Winter 1983.

Baskerville, J. C. A systematic study of the consulting literature as an integral part of applied training in statistics. *American Statistician* 35:121–123, 1981.

Batey, M. V., & Lewis, F. M. Clarifying autonomy and accountability in nursing service: Part 1. *Journal of Nursing Administration* 12(9):13–18, September 1982.

Bauer, K. *Improving the Chances for Health.* Report to the Robert Wood Johnson Foundation. San Francisco: National Center for Health Education, 1978.

Beery, W. A shopper's guide to appraisal instruments. *Promoting Health* (American Hospital Association), pp. 6–9, July–August 1981.

Berelson, B. KAP studies on fertility. In B. Berelson, R. K. Anderson, O. Harkavy, J. Maier, W. P. Mauldin, & S. J. Segal (Eds.), *Family Planning and Population Policies: A Review of World Developments.* Chicago: University of Chicago Press, 1966.

Berg, H. V. Nursing audit and outcome criteria. *Nursing Clinics of North America* 9:331–335, 1974.

Berger, P. L., & Luckmann, T. *The Social Construction of Reality.* New York: Doubleday, 1967.

Bergner, M., Bobbitt, R. A., Pollard, W. E., Martin, D. P., & Gibson, B. S. The sickness impact profile: Validation of a health status measure. *Medical Care* 14(1):57–67, January 1976.

Berk, R. A. (Ed.). *Criterion-Referenced Measurement: The State of the Art.* Baltimore: Johns Hopkins University Press, 1980.

Berk, R. A. (Ed.). *Handbook of Methods for Detecting Test Bias.* Baltimore: Johns Hopkins University Press, 1982.

Bernstein, I. N. (Ed.). *Validity Issues in Evaluation Research.* Beverly Hills, Calif.: Sage, 1976.

Bernstein, I. N., & Freeman, H. E. *Academic and Entrepreneurial Research: The Consequences of Diversity in Federal Evaluation Studies.* New York: Russell Sage Foundation, 1975.

Bertera, R., & Green, L. W. Cost-effectiveness evaluation of a home visiting triage program for family planning in Turkey. *American Journal of Public Health* 69:950–953, September 1979.

Bertram, D. A., & Brooks-Bertram, P. A. The evaluation of continuing medical education: A literature review. *Health Education Monographs* 5:330–362, Winter 1977.

Blackburn, H. Research and demonstration projects in community cardiovascular disease prevention. *Journal of Public Health Policy* 4:398–421, 1983.

Blackburn, H. W., Luepker, R. V., Kline, F. G., Bracht, N., Carlaw, R., Jacobs, D., Mittlemark, M., Stauffer, L., & Taylor, H. L. The Minnesota Heart Health Program: A research and demonstration project in cardiovascular disease prevention. In J. D. Matarazzo, S. M. Weiss, J. A. Herd, N. E. Miller, & S. M. Weiss (Eds.), *Behavioral Health: A Handbook of Health Enhancement and Disease Prevention.* New York: Wiley, 1984.

Blackwell, B. Treatment adherence in hypertension. *American Journal of Pharmacy* 148:75–85, 1976.

Blalock, H. M., Jr. *Causal Inferences in Non-experimental Research.* New York: Norton, 1964.

Blalock, H. M., Jr. *Theory Construction.* Englewood Cliffs, N.J.: Prentice-Hall, 1969.

Blalock, H. M., Jr. (Ed.). *Causal Models in the Social Sciences.* New York: Aldine-Atherton, 1971.

Blalock, H. M., Jr. *Social Statistics* (2nd ed.). New York: McGraw-Hill, 1972.

Blalock, H. M., Jr. *Conceptualization and Measurement in the Social Sciences.* Beverly Hills, Calif.: Sage, 1982.

Blalock, H. M., Jr., & Blalock, A. B. *Methodology in Social Research.* New York: McGraw-Hill, 1968.

Bloch, D. Evaluation of nursing care in terms of process and outcome. Issues in research and quality assurance. *Nursing Research* 24:256–263, 1975.

Bloom, J. R. Psychosocial measurement and specific hypotheses: A research note. *Journal of Consulting and Clinical Psychology* 47(3):637–639, 1979.

Boatman, R. H., Levin, L. S., Roberts, B. J., & Rugen, M. E. Professional preparation in health education in schools of public health (United States and Canada): A report prepared for the 1965 annual meeting of the Association of Schools of Public Health. *Health Education Monographs* 1(21):1–35, 1966.

Bogue, D. J., Burs, R., & Mayo, J. *Communicating to Combat VD: The Los Angeles Experiment.* Chicago: Center for Community and Family Studies, University of Chicago, 1979.

Bohrnstedt, G. W. Observations on the measurement of change. In E. R. Borgatta (Ed.), *Sociological Methodology*, pp. 113–133. San Francisco: Jossey-Bass, 1969.

Bohrnstedt, G. W. Reliability and validity assessment in attitude measurement. In G. H. Summers (Ed.), *Attitude Measurement*, pp. 80–99. Chicago: Rand McNally, 1970.

Bohrnstedt, G. W., & Borgatta, E. F. *Social Measurement: Current Issues.* Beverly Hills, Calif.: Sage, 1981.

Bond, B. W. *Group Discussion-Decision: An Appraisal of Its Use in Health Education.* Minneapolis: Minnesota Department of Health, 1956.

Boruch, R. F., & Rindskopf, D. On randomized experiments, approximation to experiments, and data analysis. In L. Rutman (Ed.), *Evaluation Research Methods: A Basic Guide*, pp. 143–176. Beverly Hills, Calif.: Sage, 1977.

Bowler, M. H., & Morisky, D. E. A small group strategy for improving compliance behavior and blood pressure control. *Health Education Quarterly* 10:56–69, Spring 1983.

Bracht, G. H., & Glass, G. V. The external validity of experiments. *American Educational Research Journal* 5:437–474, 1968.

Breckon, D. J. *Hospital Health Education.* Rockville, Md.: Aspen Systems Corporation, 1982.

Breslow, L., & Enstrom, J. E. Persistence of habits and their relationship to mortality. *Preventive Medicine* 9(4):469–483, 1980.

Broadhead, R. S. Qualitative analysis in evaluation research: Problems and promises of an interactionist approach. *Symbolic Interaction* 3:23–40, 1980.

Brown, C. R., & Uhl, H. S. Mandatory continuing education: Sense or nonsense? *Journal of the American Medical Association* 213:1660–1668, September 7, 1970.

Brown, S. *What Do They Know? A Review of Criterion-Referenced Assessment.* Edinburgh, Scotland: Scottish Education Department, 1980.

Bruess, C. E., & Gay, J. E. *Implementing Comprehensive School Health.* New York: Macmillan, 1978.

Bryant, N. H., Stender, W., Frist, W., & Somers, A. R. VD hotline: An evaluation. *Public Health Reports* 91:231–235, 1976.

Buros, O. K. (Ed.). *Tests in Print.* Highland Park, N.J.: Gryphon Press, 1974.

Buros, O. K. (Ed.). *Personality Tests and Reviews. II.* Highland Park, N.J.: Gryphon Press, 1975.

Butman, R. C. CAI—there is a way to make it pay (but not in conventional schooling). *Educational Technology* 13:5–9, 1973.

Byler, R. *Teach Us What We Want to Know.* Hartford, Conn.: State Board of Education, Mental Health Materials Center, 1969.

Campbell, D. T. Reforms as experiments. *American Psychologist* 24(4): 409–429, 1969.

Campbell, D. T. Assessing the impact of planned social change. *Evaluation and Program Planning* 2(1):67–90, 1979a.

Campbell, D. T. Degrees of freedom and the case study. In T. D. Cook & C. S. Reichardt (Eds.), *Qualitative and Quantitative Methods in Evaluation Research.* Beverly Hills, Calif.: Sage, 1979b.

Campbell, D. T., & Fiske, D. W. Convergent and discriminant validation by the multitrait-multimethod matrix. *Psychological Bulletin* 56:81–105, 1959.

Campbell, D. T., & Stanley, J. C. *Experimental and Quasi-Experimental Designs for Research.* Chicago: Rand McNally, 1963.

Campeau, P. L. Selective review of the results of research on the use of audiovisual media to teach adults. *AV Communications Review* 22:5–40, 1974.

Carmines, E. G., & Zeller, R. A. *Reliability and Validity Assessment.* Beverly Hills, Calif.: Sage, 1979.

Cartwright, A., Martin, F. M., & Thomson, J. G. Efficacy of an anti-smoking campaign. *Lancet* 1:327–329, February 1960.

Center for Health Promotion and Education. *Behavioral Risk Factor Surveillance System Data Collection Instrument.* Atlanta: Centers for Disease Control, 1983a.

Center for Health Promotion and Education. *Health Risk Appraisal Users Confer-*

ence, Summary of Proceedings. Atlanta, Ga.: Centers for Disease Control, 1983b.

Cernada, G. P. *Knowledge into Action: A Guide to Research Utilization.* Farmingdale, N.Y.: Baywood, 1982.

Chein, I. An introduction to sampling. (Appendix A). In C. Selltiz, L. W. Wrightsman, & S. W. Cook (Eds.), *Research Methods in Social Relations* (3rd ed.), pp. 511–540. New York: Holt, Rinehart & Winston, 1976.

Choldin, H. M., Khan, A. M., & Ara, B. H. Cultural complications in fertility interviewing. *Demography* 4:244–252, 1967.

Chun, K. T., Cobb, S., & French, J. R. P., Jr. *Measures for Psychological Assessment: A Guide to 3,000 Original Sources and Their Applications.* Ann Arbor: University of Michigan Survey Research Center, Institute for Social Research, 1975.

Chwalow, A. J., Green, L. W., Levine, D. M., & Deeds, S. G. Effects of the multiplicity of interventions on the compliance of hypertensive patients with medical regimens in an inner city population. *Preventive Medicine* 7(1):51, 1978.

Clark, C. M., & Walck, E. A. Evaluation of the use of programmed instruction for patients maintained on Warfarin therapy. *American Journal of Public Health* 62:1135–1139, August 1972.

Clark, N. M., Feldman, C. H., Freudenberg, N., Millman, E. J., Wasilewski, Y., & Valle, I. Developing education for children with asthma through study of self-management behavior. *Health Education Quarterly* 7(4):278–297, 1980.

Clearinghouse of Health Indexes. Published by the Division of Analysis, National Center for Health Statistics, U.S. Department of Health and Human Services. Center Building, Room 2-27, 3700 East-West Highway, Hyattsville, MD 20782.

Cleary, H. P., Kornacki, M. J., & Grancio, S. Planning the educational component of a hypertension control program: A case study. *Health Education Quarterly* 7(4):263–277, 1980.

Coates, T. J., Petersen, A. C., & Perry C. (Eds.). *Promoting Adolescent Health: A Dialog on Research and Practice.* New York: Academic Press, 1982.

Cochran, W. G. *Sampling Techniques* (2nd ed.). New York: Wiley, 1963.

Cohen, C. I., & Cohen, E. J. Health education: Panacea or pernicious? *New England Journal of Medicine* 299:718–720, 1978.

Cohen, J. *Statistical Power Analysis for the Behavioral Sciences.* New York: Academic Press, 1969.

Comrey, A. L., Backer, T. E., & Glaser, E. M. *A Sourcebook for Mental Health Measures.* Los Angeles: University of California, Los Angeles, Human Interaction Research Institute, 1973.

Cook, T. D., & Campbell, D. T. (Eds.). *Quasi-Experimentation, Design and Analysis Issues for Field Settings.* Chicago: Rand McNally, 1979.

Cook, T. D., Cook, F. L., & Mark, M. M. Randomized and quasi-experimental designs in evaluation research: An introduction. In L. Rutman (Ed.), *Evaluation Research Methods: A Basic Guide,* pp. 103–135. Beverly Hills, Calif.: Sage, 1977.

Cook, T. D., & Reichardt, C. S. (Eds.). *Qualitative and Quantitative Methods in Evaluation Research.* Beverly Hills, Calif.: Sage, 1979.

Cornacchia, H. F., & Staton, W. M. *Health in Elementary Schools.* St. Louis: Mosby, 1979.

Cornell, R. G., Landis, J. R., Zemach, R., Manela, R., Wainstock, E. J., & Gardner, H. H. The Michigan Ambulatory Medical Care Survey: Results and utility relative to the national survey. *Public Health Reports* 95:369–376, July–August 1980.

Corsa, L., Jr. The sample survey in a national population program. *Public Opinion Quarterly,* 28:383–388, Fall 1964.

Cronbach, L. J. Coefficient alpha and the internal structure of tests. *Psychometrika* 16:297–334, 1951.

Cronbach, L. J. *Essentials of Psychological Testing* (3rd ed.). New York: Harper & Row, 1970.

Cronbach, L. J. Test validation. In R. L. Thorndike (Ed.), *Educational Measurement,* pp. 443–507. Washington, D.C.: American Council on Education, 1971.

Cronbach, L. J. Beyond the two disciplines of scientific psychology. *American Psychologist* 30:116–127, 1975.

Cronbach, L. J. *Designing Evaluations of Educational and Social Programs.* San Francisco: Jossey-Bass, 1983.

Cronbach, L. J., Ambron, S. R., Dornbusch, S. M., Hess, R. D., Hornik, R. C., Phillips, D. C., Walker, D. F., & Weiner, S. S. *Toward Reform of Program Evaluation: Aims, Methods and Institutional Arrangements.* San Francisco: Jossey-Bass, 1980.

Cronbach, L. J., & Furby, L. How should we measure "change"—or should we? *Psychological Bulletin* 74:68–80, 1970.

Cummings, K. M., Jette, A. M., & Rosenstock, I. M. Construct validation of the Health Belief Model. *Health Education Monographs* 6(4):394–405, Winter 1978.

Cuskey, W. R., & Premkumar, T. A differential counselor role model for the treatment of drug addicts. *Health Services Reports* 88:663–668, 1973.

D'Altroy, L. H., Blissenbach, H., Lutz, D., Beardsley, R., Cain, H., Mardt, R., & Quarn, J. Patient drug self-administration improved regimen compliance. *Hospitals* 52:31–36, 1978.

Deeds, S. G. Promises! Promises! Educational technology for health education audiences. Presented at the annual meeting of the American Public Health Association, San Francisco, 1973.

Deniston, O. L., & Rosenstock, I. M. The validity of nonexperimental designs for evaluating health services. *Health Services Reports* 88:153–164, 1973.

Dennison, D. *The DINE System: The Nutritional Plan for Better Health.* St. Louis: Mosby, 1982.

Dennison, D. The DINE System: *Pulse* 6(1):25–26, January–February–March 1983.

Dennison, D., Frauenheim, K., & Izu, L. The DINE Microcomputer Program: An innovative curricular approach. *Health Education* 44–47, March–April 1983.

Dershewitz, R. A., & Williamson, J. W. Prevention of childhood household injuries: A controlled clinical trial. *American Journal of Public Health* 67(12):1148–1153, December 1977.

Deutcher, I. Toward avoiding the goal trap in evaluation research. In F. G. Caro (Ed.), *Readings in Evaluation Research* (2nd ed.). New York: Russell Sage Foundation, 1977.

Deutcher, I., & Gold, M. Traditions and rules as obstructions to useful program evaluation. In N. Denzin (Ed.), *Studies in Symbolic Interaction* (Vol. 2). Greenwich, Conn.: JAI Press, 1978.

Devine, E. C., & Cook, T. D. A meta-analytic analysis of effects of psychoeducational interventions on length of postsurgical hospital stay. *Nursing Research* 32:267–274, 1983.

Dielman, T. E., Leech, S. L., Becker, M. H., Rosenstock, I. M., Horvath, W. J., & Radius, S. M. Dimensions of children's health beliefs. *Health Education Quarterly* 7(3):219–238, Fall 1980.

Dillman, D. A. *Mail and Telephone Surveys: The Total Design Method.* New York: Wiley, 1978.

Dishman, R. K., & Ickes, W. Self-motivation and adherence to therapeutic exercise. *Journal of Behavioral Medicine* 4(4):421–438, December 1981.

D'Onofrio, C. N. Evaluating patient education: Purposes, politics, and a proposal for practitioners. In W. D. Squyres (Ed.), *Patient Education: An Inquiry into the State of the Art.* New York: Springer, 1980.

Dornbusch, S. M., & Scott, W. R. *Evaluation and the Exercise of Authority: A Theory of Control Applied to Diverse Organizations.* San Francisco: Jossey-Bass, 1975.

Dumbauld, S. *National Health Status Objectives for 1990: An Assessment of California.* Sacramento, Calif.: Department of Health Services, Center for Health Statistics, 1981.

Duncan, B., Boyce, W. T., Itami, R., & Puffenbarger, N. A controlled trial of a physical fitness program for fifth grade students. *Journal of School Health* 53:467–471, October 1983.

Duncan, O. T. *Introduction to Structural Equation Models.* New York: Academic Press, 1975.

Durant, W. *The Story of Philosophy.* New York: Washington Square Press, 1926.

Eastaugh, S. R., & Hatcher, M. E. Improving compliance among hypertensives: A triage criterion with cost-benefit implications. *Medical Care* 20:1001–1017, October 1982.

Edwards, A. L. *The Social Desirability Variable in Personality Assessment and Research.* New York: Dryden Press, 1957.

Eisen, M., Donald, C. A., Ware, J. E., & Brook, R. H. *Conceptualization and Measurement of Health for Children in the Health Insurance Study.* R-2312-HEW. Santa Monica, Calif.: Rand Corporation, 1980.

Elashoff, J. D. Analysis of covariance: A delicate instrument. *American Educational Research Journal* 6(3):383–401, May 1969.

Elinson, J., & Siegmann, A. E. *Socio-Medical Health Indicators.* Farmingdale, N.Y.: Baywood, 1983.

Eriksen, M. P., & Gielen, A. C. The application of health education principles to automobile child restraint programs. *Health Education Quarterly* 10:30–55, Spring 1983.

Espenshade, J. E. *Staff Manual for Teaching Patients About Diabetes Mellitus.* Chicago: American Hospital Association, 1979.

Etzioni, A., & Lehman, E. W. Some dangers in "valid" social measurement. *American Academy of Political and Social Science* 2:1–15, 1967.

Evans, R. I., Hill, P. C., Raines, B. E., & Henderson, A. H. Current behavioral, social and educational programs in control of smoking: A selective, critical review. In S. Weiss, A. Herd, & B. Fox (Eds.), *Perspectives on Behavioral Medicine.* New York: Academic Press, 1981.

Evans, R. I., & Raines, B. E. Control and prevention of smoking in adolescents: A psychosocial perspective. In T. J. Coates, A. C. Petersen, & C. Perry (Eds.), *Promoting Adolescent Health: A Dialog on Research and Practice.* New York: Academic Press, 1982.

Faber, M. (Ed.). Risk reduction for health promotion and maintenance. *Family and Community Health* 3:1–113, May 1980.

Faber, M. M., & Reinhardt, A. M. (Eds.). *Promoting Health Through Risk Reduction.* New York: Macmillan, 1982.

Faden, R. Disclosure and informed consent: Does it matter how we tell it? *Health Education Monographs* 5(3):198–214, Fall 1977.

Fanamanu, J. Working through the community leaders: An experiment in Tonga. *International Journal of Health Education* 9:130–137, July–September 1966.

Farquhar, J. W. *The American Way of Life Need Not Be Hazardous to Your Health.* New York: Norton, 1978.

Farquhar, J., Maccoby, N., & Solomon, D. S. Community applications of behavioral medicine. In W. D. Gentry (Ed.), *Handbook of Behavioral Medicine.* New York: Gilford Press, 1984.

Farquhar, J., Maccoby, N., Wood, P. D., Breitrose, H., Haskell, W. L., Meyer, A. J., Alexander, J. K., Brown, B. W., Jr., McAlister, A. L., Nash, J. D., & Stern, M. P. Community education for cardiovascular health. *Lancet* 1(8023):1192–1195, 1977.

Fass, M. F., Green, L. W., & Deeds, S. G. The effect of family education on patient adherence to antihypertensive regimens. *Proceedings of the National High Blood Pressure Conference.* Washington, D.C.: National Heart, Lung and Blood Institute, 1977.

Ferlic, M., Goldman, A., & Kennedy, B. J. Group counseling in adult patients with advanced cancer. *Cancer* 43:760–766, 1979.

Filstead, W. J. Qualitative methods: A needed perspective in evaluation research. In T. D. Cook & C. S. Reichardt (Eds.), *Qualitative and Quantitative Methods in Evaluation Research.* Beverly Hills, Calif.: Sage, 1979.

Finney, D. J. The questioning statistician. *Statistics in Medicine* 1:5–14, 1982.

Fisher, A. A. The characteristics of family planning opinion leaders and their influence on the contraceptive behavior of others. Unpublished doctoral dissertation. Johns Hopkins University, School of Hygiene and Public Health, 1974.

Fisher, A. A., & Carlaw, R. W. Family planning field research projects: Balancing internal against external validity. *Studies in Family Planning* 14(1):3–8, 1983.

Fisher, A. A., Laing, J., & Stoeckel, J. *Handbook for Family Planning Operations Research Design.* New York: Population Council, 1983.

Flay, B. R., & Best, J. A. Overcoming design problems in evaluating health behavior programs. *Evaluation and the Health Professions* 5:43–69, March 1982.

Flay, B. R., & Cook, T. D. Evaluation of mass media prevention campaigns. In R. E. Rice & W. J. Paisley (Eds.), *Public Communication Campaigns.* London: Sage, 1981.

Fletcher, S. R. A study of effectiveness of a follow-up clerk in an emergency room. Unpublished master's thesis. Johns Hopkins University, School of Hygiene and Public Health, 1973.

Franz, J. C., & Weisser, R. J., Jr. Venereal disease education in West Virginia, USA. *British Journal of Venereal Disease* 54(2):269–273, 1978.

Freeman, H. E. Evaluation research and public policy. Presented at the Dartmouth/OECD Seminar on Social Research and Public Policy, Dartmouth, New Hampshire, September 13–15, 1974.

Freudenberg, N. Citizen action for environmental health: Report on a survey of community organizations. *American Journal of Public Health* 74:444–448, May 1984.

Frieman, J. A., Smith, H., & Chalmers, T. C. Validity of negative randomized clinical trials. *Clinical Research* 25:512A, 1977.

Fuchs, V. *Who Shall Live? Health, Economics and Social Choice.* New York: Basic Books, 1974.
Galtung, J. *Theory and Methods of Social Research.* New York: Columbia University Press, 1967.
Gebhardt, M. E. Health education evaluation: An alternate research paradigm. *Evaluation and the Health Professions* 3(2):205–210, 1980.
Gillum, R. F., Williams, P. T., & Sondik, E. Some considerations for the planning of total-community prevention trials: When is sample size adequate? *Journal of Community Health* 5:270–278, Summer 1980.
Glaser, B. G. *Theoretical Sensitivity: Advances in the Methodology of Grounded Theory.* Mill Valley, Calif.: Sociology Press, 1978.
Glaser, B. G., & Strauss, A. L. *The Discovery of Grounded Theory: Strategies for Qualitative Research.* Chicago: Aldine-Atherton, 1967.
Glaser, R. Instructional technology and the measurement of learning outcomes: Some questions. *American Psychologist* 18(7):519–521, August 1963.
Glaser, W. A., & McVey, F. A. Effects of public health field practice upon career preferences and career plans. *Nursing Research* 14:61–65, Winter 1965.
Glass, G. V. Primary, secondary, and meta-analysis of research. *Educational Researcher* 5(5):3–8, November 1976.
Glass, G. V. Integrating findings: The meta-analysis of research. *Review of Research in Education* 5:351–379, 1977.
Goetz, A., Duff, J., & Bernstein, J. Health risk appraisal: The estimation of risk. *Public Health Reports* 95:119–126, March–April 1980.
Gold, R. S., & Basch, C. E. Multi-matrix sampling: An approach to evaluation of health education programs. *Health Education Quarterly* 10:135–148, 1983.
Goldstein, G., & Hersen, M. *Handbook of Psychological Assessment.* New York: Pergamon Press, 1984.
Goldstein, R. A., Green, L. W., & Parker, S. R. Self-management of childhood asthma. *Journal of Allergy and Clinical Immunology* 72(5, Suppl.):522–525, 1983.
Goodwin, L. D., & Prescott, P. A. Issues and approaches to estimating interrater reliability in nursing research. *Research in Nursing and Health* 4:323–337, 1981.
Gottlieb, N. H., & Green, L. W. Life events, social network, lifestyle and health: An analysis of the National Survey of Personal Health Practices and Consequences. *Health Education Quarterly* 11(1):91–105, 1984.
Gouldner, A. W. Anti-minotaur: The myth of a value-free sociology. In I. L. Horowitz (Ed.), *The New Sociology,* pp. 196–217. New York: Oxford University Press, 1964.
Green, B. F., & Hall, J. A. Quantitative methods for literature reviews. *Annual Review of Psychology* 35:37–53, 1984.
Green, L. W. East Pakistan: Knowledge and use of contraceptives. *Studies in Family Planning* 1:9–14, March 1969.
Green, L. W. A manual for scoring socioeconomic status for research on health behavior. *Public Health Reports* 85(9):815–827, September 1970.
Green, L. W. Toward cost-benefit evaluations of health education: Some concepts, methods, and examples. *Health Education Monographs* 2(Suppl. No. 1):34–65, 1974.
Green, L. W. Diffusion and adoption of innovations related to cardiovascular risk behavior in the public. In A. J. Enelow & J. B. Henderson (Eds.), *Applying Behavioral Science to Cardiovascular Risk.* New York: American Heart Association, 1975.

Green, L. W. Methods available to evaluate the health education components of preventive health programs. In *Preventive Medicine USA: Health Promotion and Consumer Health Education.* New York: Prodist, 1976a.

Green, L. W. The potential of health education includes cost-effectiveness. *Hospitals* 50:57–61, 1976b.

Green, L. W. Suggested procedures for moving from programmatic accreditation to peer review under broader institutional accreditation. *Health Education Monographs* 4(3):278–284, Fall 1976c.

Green, L. W. Evaluation and measurement: Some dilemmas for health education. *American Journal of Public Health* 67(2):155–161, February 1977.

Green, L. W. Determining the impact and effectiveness of health education as it relates to federal policy. *Health Education Monographs* 6:28–66, Spring 1978.

Green, L. W. Health promotion policy and the placement of responsibility for personal health care. *Family and Community Health* 2:51–64, 1979a.

Green, L. W. Research methods translatable to the practice setting: From rigor to reality and back. In S. J. Cohen (Ed.), *New Directions in Patient Compliance.* Lexington, Mass.: Lexington Books, 1979b.

Green, L. W. Healthy people: The Surgeon General's report and the prospects. In W. J. McNerny (Ed.), *Working for a Healthier America.* Cambridge, Mass.: Ballinger, 1980a.

Green, L. W. To educate or not to educate. Is that the question? *American Journal of Public Health* 70(6):625–626, 1980b.

Green, L. W. What is quality in patient education and how do we assess it? In W. D. Squyres (Ed.), *Patient Education: An Inquiry into the State of the Art.* New York: Springer, 1980c.

Green, L. W. National policy in the promotion of health. In M. D. Hiller (Ed.), *Medical Ethics and the Law: Implications for Public Policy.* Cambridge, Mass.: Ballinger, 1981.

Green, L. W. A triage and stepped approach to self-care education. *Medical Times* 111(3):75–82, May 1983.

Green, L. W. Modifying and developing health behavior. *Annual Review of Public Health,* 5:215–236, 1984.

Green, L. W., & Brooks-Bertram, P. Peer review and quality control in health education. *Health Values* 2(4):191–197, 1978.

Green, L. W., & Figa-Talamanca, I. Suggested designs for evaluation of patient education programs. *Health Education Monographs* 2(1):54–71, Spring 1974.

Green, L. W., & Gordon, N. Productive research designs for health education. *Health Education* 13(3):4–10, 1982.

Green, L. W., Gustafson, H. C., Griffiths, W., & Yaukey, D. *The Dacca Family Planning Experiment: A Comparative Evaluation of Programs Directed at Males and Females.* Pacific Health Education Reports, No. 3. Berkeley: University of California School of Public Health, 1972.

Green, L. W., Heit, P., Iverson, D. C., Kolbe, L. J., & Kreuter, M. W. The School Health Curriculum Project: Its theory, practice, and measurement experience. *Health Education Quarterly* 7(1):14–34, Spring 1980.

Green, L. W., & Iverson, D. C. School health education. *Annual Review of Public Health* 3:321–338, 1982.

Green, L. W., & Jan, Y. A. Family-planning knowledge and attitude surveys in Pakistan. *Pakistan Development Review* 4(3):332–355, Summer 1964.

Green, L. W., & Johnson, K. W. Health education and health promotion, In D. Mechanic (Ed.), *Handbook of Health, Health Care and the Health Professions.* New York: Wiley, 1983.

Green, L. W., & Kansler, C. C. *The Professional and Scientific Literature on Patient Education.* Detroit: Gale Research Company, 1980.

Green, L. W., Kreuter, M. W., Deeds, S. G., & Partridge, K. B. *Health Education Planning: A Diagnostic Approach.* Palo Alto, Calif.: Mayfield, 1980.

Green, L. W., & Krotki, K. J. Proximity and other geographical factors in family planning clinic utilization in Pakistan. *Pakistan Development Review* 6(2): 80–104, Spring 1966.

Green, L. W., & Krotki, K. J. Class and parity biases in family planning programs: The case of Karachi. *Eugenics Quarterly (Social Biology)* 15:235–251, 1968.

Green, L. W., Levine, D. M., & Deeds, S. G. Clinical trials of health education for hypertensive outpatients: Design and baseline data. *Preventive Medicine* 4(4):417–425, 1975.

Green, L. W., Levine, D. M., Wolle, J., & Deeds, S. G. Development of randomized patient education experiments with urban poor hypertensives. *Patient Counselling and Health Education* 1(1):106–111, 1979.

Green, L. W., & Lewis, F. M. Issues in relating evaluation to theory, policy and practice in continuing education and health education. *Mobius* 1(2):46–58, April 1981.

Green, L. W., Lewis, F. M., & Levine, D. M. Balancing statistical data and clinician judgments in the diagnosis of patient educational needs. *Journal of Community Health* 6(2):79–91, Winter 1980.

Green, L. W., & McAlister, A. L. Macro-interventions to support health behavior: Some theoretical perspectives and practical reflections. *Health Education Quarterly* 11(3):323–339, Fall 1984.

Green, L. W., Rimer, B., & Bertera, R. How cost-effective are smoking cessation strategies? *World Smoking and Health* 3:33–40, 1978.

Green, L. W., Squyres, W. D., D'Altroy, L. H., & Herbert, B. What do recent evaluations of patient education tell us? In W. D. Squyres (Ed.), *Patient Education: An Inquiry into the State of the Art.* New York: Springer, 1980.

Green, L. W., Werlin, S. H., Schauffler, H. H., & Avery, C. H. Research and demonstration issues in self-care: Measuring the decline of medicocentrism. *Health Education Monographs* 5(2):161–189, Summer 1977.

Green, L. W., Wilson, R. W., & Bauer, K. G. Objectives for the nation in health promotion and disease prevention and requirements to measure our progress. *Proceedings of the 18th National Meeting of the Public Health Records.* DHHS Pub. No. (PHS) 81-1214. Washington, D.C.: Office of Health Research, Statistics and Technology, National Center for Health Statistics, 1980.

Green, L. W., Wilson, R. W., & Bauer, K. G. Data required to measure progress on the Objectives for the Nation in health promotion and disease prevention. *American Journal of Public Health* 73(1):18–24, January 1983.

Greenwald, H. J., & Satow, Y. A short social desirability scale. *Psychological Reports* 27:131–135, 1970.

Guba, E. G. *Toward A Methodology of Naturalistic Inquiry in Educational Evaluation.* Los Angeles: University of California, Center for the Study of Evaluation, 1978.

Guba, E. G., & Lincoln, Y. S. *Effective Evaluation.* San Francisco: Jossey-Bass, 1981.

Guilford, J. P. *Psychometric Methods.* New York: McGraw-Hill, 1954.

Guilford, J. P., & Fruchter, D. *Fundamental Statistics in Psychology and Education* (5th ed.). New York: McGraw-Hill, 1973.

Habermas, J. *Knowledge and Human Interests.* Boston: Beacon Press, 1971.

Haddon, W., Jr. Strategy in preventive medicine: Passive versus active approaches to reducing human wastage. *Journal of Trauma* 14:353, 1978.

Haddon, W., Jr., & Baker, S. P. Injury control. In D. Clark & B. MacMahon (Eds.), *Preventive Medicine* (2nd ed.). Boston: Little, Brown, 1974.

Hall, J. Which health-screening techniques are cost-effective? *Diagnosis* 2:60–82, February 1980.

Hall, J. H., & Zwemer, J. D. *Prospective Medicine.* Indianapolis: Methodist Hospital of Indiana, 1979.

Hambleton, R. K., & Eignor, D. R. Guidelines for evaluating criterion-referenced tests and manuals. *Journal of Educational Measurement* 15:321–327, 1978.

Hambleton, R. K., Swaminathan, H., Algina, J., & Coulson, D. B. Criterion-referenced testing and measurement: A review of technical issues and development. *Review of Educational Research* 48(1):1–48, Winter 1978.

Havelock, R. G. (Ed.). *Planning for Innovation Through Dissemination and Utilization of Knowledge.* Ann Arbor, Mich.: Center for Research on Utilization of Knowledge, Institute for Social Research, 1979.

Hawkins, J. D., & Sloma, D. Recognizing the organizational context: A strategy for evaluation research. *Administration in Social Work* 2(3):283–294, Fall 1978.

Hayes-Bautista, D. E. Coaches, arbitrators, and access to medical care. *Journal of Health and Social Behavior* 20:52–60, March 1979.

Hays, W. L., & Winkler, R. L. *Statistics, Probability, Inference and Decision* (Vol. 2). New York: Holt, Rinehart & Winston, 1970.

Health Manpower Coordinating Committee. *A Proposal for Credentialing Health Manpower.* Rockville, Md.: Health Resources Administration, U.S. Department of Health, Education, and Welfare, June 1976.

Heath, L., Kendzerski, D., & Borgida, E. Evaluation of social programs: A multimethodological approach combining a delayed treatment true experiment and multiple time series. *Evaluation Review* 6:233–246, April 1982.

Hedges, L. V. Advances in statistical methods for meta-analysis. In W. H. Yeaton & P. M. Wortman (Eds.), *Issues in Data Synthesis.* San Francisco: Jossey-Bass, 1984.

Heise, D. R. Separating reliability and stability in test-retest correlations. *American Sociological Review* 34(1):93–101, 1969.

Heshmat, M. Y. Evaluating various forms of publicity. *International Journal of Health Education* 8:86–94, April–June 1965.

Highlights of the Eighth International Conference on Health Education. *International Journal of Health Education* 16 (Suppl. 3), 1973.

Hirschhorn, N., Goldy, A. S., Plager, B., Bell, P., Brier, J., Parenteau, T., McIntosh, E. N., & Robbins, J. A focused approach to quality of care assessment in family planning. *American Journal of Public Health* 74:825–833, August 1984.

Hochbaum, G. M. Research relating to health education. *Health Education Monographs* 1(8):10–20, 1960.

Hochbaum, G. M. Research to improve health. *International Journal of Health Education* 8(3):141–148, 1965.

Hoepfner, R. (Ed.). *CSE-RBS Test Evaluations: Tests of Higher and Cognitive, Affective and Interpersonal Skills.* Los Angeles: University of California, Center for the Study of Evaluation, 1972.

Holmes, A. C. Evaluation in health education. *Journal of Tropical Medicine and Hygiene* 66:23–24, 1963.

Hongladarom, G. C. A mobile cancer nursing outreach program: Assumptions and realities. *Cancer Nursing* 6(1):49–54, 1983.

Horn, D. Modifying smoking habits in high school students. *Children* 7:63, 1960.

House, E. R. *Evaluating with Validity.* Beverly Hills, Calif.: Sage, 1980.

Houston, T. R., Jr. The behavioral sciences impact-effectiveness model. In P. H. Rossi & W. Williams (Eds.), *Evaluating Social Programs,* pp. 59–65. New York: Seminar Press, 1972.

Hovland, C. I., Lumsdaine, A., & Sheffield, F. D. *Experiments on Mass Communication.* New York: Wiley, 1949.

Howard, D. M. Health education needs assessment in an HMO: A case study. *Health Education Quarterly* 9:23–41, Spring 1982.

Hultsch, D. F., & Hickey, T. External validity in the study of human development: Theoretical and methodological issues. *Human Development* 21:76–91, 1978.

Hunt, W. A., & Bespalec, D. A. An evaluation of current methods of modifying smoking behavior. *Journal of Clinical Psychology* 30:431–438, 1974.

Iammarino, N., Weinberg, A., & Holcomb, J. The state of school heart health education: A review of the literature. *Health Education Quarterly* 7(4):298–320, Winter 1980.

International Classification of Diseases, 9th Revision, Clinical Modification. DHHS Pub. No. (PHS) 80-1260. Public Health Service and Health Care Financing Administration. Washington, D.C.: U.S. Government Printing Office, 1980.

Inui, T. Effects of post-graduate physician education on the management and outcomes of patients with hypertension. Unpublished master's thesis, Johns Hopkins University, School of Hygiene and Public Health, 1973.

Inui, T. S., Yourtee, E. I., & Williamson, J. W. Improved outcomes in hypertension after physician tutorial. *Annals of Internal Medicine* 84:646–651, 1976.

IOX Assessment Associates. *An Evaluation Handbook for Health Education Programs in* ... [7 handbooks:] *Alcohol and Substance Abuse./ Diabetes./ Exercise./ Immunization./ Nutrition./ Smoking./ Stress Management.* Atlanta: Centers for Disease Control, Center for Health Promotion and Education, 1983.

Isley, R. B. Planning for community participation in water supply and sanitation. *Hygie* 1(1):39–42, 1982.

Iverson, D. C. Issues related to designing and conducting school health education research. *Journal of School Health* 54(6):50–56, 1984.

Jaeger, R. *Statistics: A Spectator Sport.* Beverly Hills, Calif.: Sage, 1983.

James, G. Evaluation in public health practice. *American Journal of Public Health* 50(7):1145–1154, July 1962.

Jenne, F. H., & Greene, W. H. *Turner's School Health and Health Education.* St. Louis: Mosby, 1976.

Jöreskog, K. G. Structural analysis of covariance and correlation matrices. *Psychometrika* 43:443–477, 1978.

Jöreskog, K. G., & Sörbom, D. *Advances in Factor Analysis and Structural Equation Models.* Cambridge, Mass.: Abt Books, 1979.

Kar, S. B. Community interventions in health and family planning programs: A conceptual framework. *International Journal of Health Education* 20(Suppl.):1–15, January–March 1977.

Kerlinger, F. N. *Foundations of Behavioral Research* (2nd ed.). New York: Holt, Rinehart & Winston, 1973.

Kerlinger, F. N., & Pedhazur, E. J. *Multiple Regression in Behavioral Research.* New York: Holt, Rinehart & Winston, 1973.

Kirscht, J. P., Kirscht, J. L., & Rosenstock, I. M. A test of interventions to increase adherence to hypertensive medical regimens. *Health Education Quarterly* 8:261–272, Fall 1981.

Kish, L. *Survey Sampling.* New York: Wiley, 1965.

Klein, R. Evaluation and social policy. *Evaluation and Program Planning* 5(2):133–140, 1982.

Kolbe, L. J. Evaluating effectiveness: The problems of behavioral criteria. *Health Education* 10:12–16, 1979.

Kolbe, L. J. What can we expect from school health education? *Journal of School Health* 52:145–150, 1982.

Kolbe, L. J., Green, L. W., Foreyt, J., Goodrick, K., Williams, H., Ward, D., Korton, A., Karacan, I., Widmeyer, R., & Stainbrook, G. Appropriate functions of health education in schools. In N. Krasnegor, J. Arasteh, & M. Cataldo (Eds.), *Proceedings of the Conference on Child Health Behavior: Behavioral Pediatrics.* New York: Wiley, in press.

Kosecoff, J., Fink, A., Cullen, J., Kean, T., Arnold, M., & Greenwald, P. Guidelines for evaluating cancer control programs. *Preventive Medicine* 11:187–198, 1982.

Kreuter, M. W., & Christianson, G. M. School health education: Does it cause an effect? *Health Education Quarterly* 8(1):43–56, Spring 1981.

Kreuter, M. W., & Green, L. W. Evaluation of school health education: Identifying purpose, keeping perspective. *Journal of School Health* 48(4):228–235, 1978.

Krippendorf, K. *Content Analysis: An Introduction to Its Methodology.* Beverly Hills, Calif.: Sage, 1980.

Kroger, F. Compliance strategies in a clinic for treatment of sexually transmitted diseases. *Sexually Transmitted Diseases* 7:178–182, 1980.

Kroger, F., & Yarber, W. L. STD content in school health textbooks: An evaluation using the worth assessment procedure. *Journal of School Health* 54(1): 41–44, 1984.

Kruglanski, A. W., & Kroy, M. Outcome validity in experimental research: A reconceptualization. *Journal of Representative Research in Social Psychology* 7:168–178, 1975.

Kurz, D. E. The use of participant observation in evaluation research. *Evaluation and Program Planning* 6(1):93–102, 1983.

Lake, D. G., Miles, M. B., & Earle, R. B. *Measuring Human Behavior.* New York: Teachers College Press, Columbia University, 1973.

Lana, R. E. Pretest sensitization. In R. Rosenthal & R. Rosnow (Eds.), *Artifact in Behavioral Research.* New York: Academic Press, 1969.

Lasater, T., Abrahams, D., Artz, L., Beaudein, P., Caprera, L., Elder, J., Ferreira, A., Knisley, P., Peterson, G., Rodrigues, A., Rosenberg, T., Snow, R., & Carleton, R. Lay volunteer delivery of a community-based risk factor change program: The Pawtucket Experiment. In J. D. Matarazzo, S. M. Weiss, J. A. Herd, N. E. Miller, & S. M. Weiss (Eds.), *Behavioral Health: A Handbook of Health Enhancement and Disease Prevention.* New York: Wiley, 1984.

Lau, R., Kane, R., Berry, S., Ware, J., & Roy, D. Channeling health: A review of the evaluation of televised health campaigns. *Health Education Quarterly* 71(1):56–89, Spring 1980.

Lazerwitz, B. Sampling theory and procedures. In H. M. Blalock, Jr., & A. B. Blalock (Eds.), *Methodology in Social Research.* New York: McGraw-Hill, 1968.

Lefcourt, H. M. Internal versus external control of reinforcement: A review. *Psychological Bulletin* 65:206–220, April 1966.

Levine, D. M., Green, L. W., Deeds, S. G., Chwalow, A. J., Russell, R. P., & Finlay, J. Clinical and behavioral effects of randomized health education trials with

hypertensive patients. *Journal of the American Medical Association* 241(16):1700–1703, April 20, 1979.
Leviton, L. C., & Hughes, E. F. X. A review and synthesis of research on utilization of evaluations. *Evaluation Review* 5:525–545, 1981
Levy, S. R., Iverson, B. K., & Wahlberg, H. J. Nutrition-education research: An interdisciplinary evaluation and review. *Health Education Quarterly* 7(2): 107–126, 1980.
Lewin, K. Group decision and social change. In E. Maccoby, T. Newcomb, & E. L. Hartley (Eds.), *Readings in Social Psychology.* New York: Holt, 1947.
Lewis, F. M. Organizational control and discretionary activity. Unpublished doctoral dissertation, Stanford University, 1977a.
Lewis, F. M. A time to live and a time to die: An instructional drama. *Nursing Outlook* 25:762–765, December 1977b.
Lewis, F. M. Rigor in health education evaluation: Myth or mandate. Second Annual Arizona Patient Education Conference. Sponsored by Arizona State Health Department, Scottsdale, Arizona, May 4, 1979.
Lewis, F. M. Experienced personal control and quality of life in late-stage cancer patients. *Nursing Research* 31:113–119, March–April 1982a.
Lewis, F. M. Health locus of control. *Oncology Nursing Forum* 9:108–109, Summer 1982b.
Lewis, F. M. The client's sense of personal control. Do we know what we mean when we say it? Poster session presented at Annual Meeting, American Public Health Association, Dallas, Texas, November 1983a.
Lewis, F. M. The concept of personal control: Specification and measurement. Paper presented at Sixteenth Annual Communicative Nursing Research Conference, Western Interstate Commission for Higher Education (WICHE), Portland, Oregon, May 4–6, 1983b.
Lewis, F. M., & Batey, M. V. Clarifying autonomy and accountability in nursing service: Part 2. *Journal of Nursing Administration* 12:10–15, October 1982.
Lewis, F. M., Firsich, S. C., & Parsell, S. Clinical tool development for adult chemotherapy patients: Process and content. *Cancer Nursing* 2(2):99–108, April 1979.
Lewis, F. M., Morisky, D. M. & Flynn, B. S. A test of the construct validity of health locus of control: Effects on self-reported compliance for hypertension patients. *Health Education Monographs* 6(2):138–148, Spring 1978.
Ley, P. Primacy, rated importance, and the recall of medical statements. *Journal of Health and Social Behavior* 13:311–317, September 1972.
Ley, P. Memory for medical information. Presented at Conference on Practical Aspects of Memory, Swansca, Wales, 1978.
Light, R. S. & Pillemer, D. B. *Summing Up.* Cambridge, Mass.: Harvard University Press, 1984.
Lindeman, C. A. Measuring quality of nursing care, Part I. *Journal of Nursing Administration* 6(5):7–9, June 1976a.
Lindeman, C. A. Measuring quality of nursing care, Part II. *Journal of Nursing Administration* 6(8):16–19, September 1976b.
Lindeman, C. A., & Van Aernam, B. Nursing intervention with the presurgical patient. *Nursing Research* 20:319–331, July–August 1971.
Linn, B. S., & Linn, M. W. Late-stage cancer patients: Age differences in their psychophysical status and response to counseling. *Journal of Gerontology* 36:689–692, 1981.
Lord, F. M., & Novick, M. R. *Statistical Theories of Mental Test Scores.* Reading, Mass.: Addison-Wesley, 1968.

Maccoby, N., Farquhar, J. W., Wood, P. D., & Alexander, J. Reducing the risk of cardiovascular disease: Effects of a community-based campaign on knowledge and behavior. *Journal of Community Health* 3:100–114, Winter 1977.

Madaus, G. F., Scriven, M. S., & Stufflebeam, D. L. *Evaluation Models, Viewpoints on Educational and Human Services Evaluation.* Boston: Kluwer-Nijhoff, 1983.

Madnick, M. E. *Consumer Health Education: A Guide to Hospital-Based Programs.* Wakefield, Mass.: Nursing Resources, 1980.

Maiman, L. A., Becker, M. H., Kirscht, J. P., Haefner, D. P., & Drachman, R. H. Scales for measuring Health Belief Model dimensions: A test of predictive value, internal consistency, and relationship among beliefs. *Health Education Monographs* 5(3):215–230, Fall 1977.

Maiman, L. A., Green, L. W., Gibson, G., & MacKenzie, E. J. Education for self-treatment by adult asthmatics. *Journal of the American Medical Association* 241(18):1919–1922, May 4, 1979.

Mannheim, K. Ideology and the sociology of knowledge. In M. Brodbeck (Ed.), *Readings in the Philosophy of the Social Sciences.* London: Macmillan, 1968. Originally published 1936.

Mazelis, S. Evaluation, a planned approach to an educational program. *Health Educators at Work* 13:61–66, June 1962.

Mazzuca, S. A. Does patient education in chronic disease have therapeutic value? *Journal of Chronic Diseases* 35:521–529, 1982.

McAlister, A. Tobacco, alcohol, and drug abuse: Onset and prevention. In *Healthy People: The Surgeon General's Report on Health Promotion and Disease Prevention.* Background Papers. Rockville, Md.: U.S. Department of Health, Education, and Welfare, Public Health Service, Office of the Assistant Secretary for Health, and Surgeon General, 1979.

McAlister, A. The development and prevention of substance abuse: An introduction to research and policy. In T. J. Coates, A. C. Petersen, & C. Perry (Eds.), *Promoting Adolescent Health: A Dialog on Research and Practice.* New York: Academic Press, 1982.

McAlister, A. Community studies of smoking cessation and prevention. In *The Health Consequences of Smoking: A Report of the Surgeon General.* Rockville, Md.: U.S. Department of Health and Human Services, Public Health Service, Office of the Assistant Secretary for Health, Office on Smoking and Health, 1984.

McCormick, R. D., & Gilson-Parkevich, T. *Patient and Family Education: Tools, Techniques, and Theory.* New York: Wiley, 1979.

McCusker, J., & Morrow, G. The relationship of health locus of control to preventive health behaviors and health beliefs. *Patient Counseling and Health Education* 1(4):146–156, 1979.

McGaw, B., & Glass, G. V. Choice of metric for effect size in meta-analysis. *American Educational Research Journal* 17:325–337, 1980.

McGinnis, J. M. Targetting progress in health. *Public Health Reports* 97(4):295–307, April 1982.

McLeroy, K. R., Green, L. W., Mullen, K. D., & Foshee, V. Assessing the effects of health promotion in worksites: A review of the stress program evaluations. *Health Education Quarterly* 11:379–401, 1984.

Mechanic, D. The stability of health and illness behavior: Results from a 16-year follow-up. *American Journal of Public Health* 69(11):1142–1145, 1979.

Mendenhall, W., Ott, L., & Scheaffer, R. L. *Elementary Survey Sampling.* Belmont, Calif.: Wadsworth, 1971.

Messick, S. Evidence and ethics in the evaluation of tests. *Educational Researcher* 10(9):9–20, 1981.

Metsch, J. M., Berson, A., & Weitzner, M. The impact of training on consumer participation in the delivery of health services. *Health Education Monographs* 3:251–261, Fall 1975.

Meyers, R., Donham, G. W., & Lundenia, K. The psychometric properties of the health locus of control scale with medical and surgical patients. *Journal of Clinical Psychology* 38(4):783–787, October 1982.

Mezirow, J., Darkenwald, G. G., & Knox, A. B. *Last Gamble on Education Dynamics of Adult Basic Education.* Washington, D.C.: Adult Education Association of the USA, 1975.

Mico, P. R., & Ross, H. S. *Health Education and Behavioral Science.* Oakland, Calif.: Third Party Associates, 1975.

Miller, D. C. *Handbook of Research Design and Social Measurement.* New York: McKay, 1974.

Miller, G. H., & Willmer, B. Information systems for evaluation and feedback in mental health organizations. In L. Rutman (Ed.), *Evaluation Research Methods: A Basic Guide,* pp. 199–215. Beverly Hills, Calif.: Sage, 1977.

Miller, J. R., & Lewis, F. M. Closing the gap in quality assurance: A tool for evaluating group leaders. *Health Education Quarterly* 9(1):55–66, Spring 1982.

Miller, R. A., & Green, L. W. The validity of personal predictions of future use of contraceptives. Unpublished paper, University of California Public Health Education Research Project, Berkeley, April 1970.

Millman, J. In W. J. Popham (Ed.), *Evaluation in Education: Current Applications.* Berkeley, Calif.: McCutchan, 1974.

Millman, J. *Handbook of Teacher Evaluation.* Beverly Hills, Calif.: Sage, 1981.

Minkler, M. Citizen participation in health in the Republic of Cuba. *International Quarterly of Community Health Education* 1:65–78, 1980–1981.

Monk, M., Tayback, M., & Gordon, J. Evaluation of an anti-smoking program among high school students. *American Journal of Public Health* 55:994–1004, July 1965.

Moos, R. H., Insel, P. M., & Humphrey, B. *Combined Preliminary Manual, Family Work and Group Environment Scales.* Palo Alto, Calif.: Consulting Psychologists Press, 1974.

Moos, R. H., & Moos, B. S. A typology of family social environments. *Family Process* 15(4):357–371, 1976.

Morisky, D. E., Levine, D. M., Green, L. W., Russell, R. P., & Smith, C. R. The relative impact of health education for low- and high-risk patients with hypertension. *Preventive Medicine* 9(4):550–558, 1980.

Morisky, D. E., Levine, D. M., Green, L. W., Shapiro, S., Russell, R. P., & Smith, C. R. Five-year blood pressure control and mortality following health education for hypertensive patients. *American Journal of Public Health* 73(2):153–162, 1983.

Morisky, D. E., Levine, D. M., Green, L. W., & Smith, C. R. Health education program effects on the management of hypertension in the elderly. *Archives of Internal Medicine* 142:1835–1838, 1982.

Morris, M. D. *Measuring the Condition of the World's Poor: The Physical Quality of Life Index.* Washington, D.C.: Pergamon Press, for Overseas Development Council, 1979.

Morton, R. F., & Hebel, J. R. *A Study Guide to Epidemiology and Biostatistics* (2nd ed.). Baltimore: University Park Press, 1984.

Moses, L., & Louis, T. A. Statistical consulting in clinical research: The two-way street. *Statistics in Medicine* 3:1–5, 1984.

Mosher, L. R., & Menn, A. Z. Community residential treatment for schizophrenia: Two-year followup. *Hospital and Community Psychiatry* 29(22):715–723, 1978.

Moss, N. An organization-environment framework for assessing program implementation. *Evaluation and Program Planning* 6:153–164, 1983.

Moynihan, D. P. *Maximum Feasible Misunderstanding: Community Action in the War on Poverty.* New York: Free Press, 1969.

Mullen, P. D. Generating theory in multi-site evaluations. Presented to the American Public Health Association Annual Meeting, Los Angeles, California, November 1981.

Mullen, P. D., & Culjat, D. Improving attendance in weight-control programs. *Health Education Quarterly* 7:4–13, Spring 1980.

Mullen, P. D., & Green, L. W. *Measuring Patient Drug Information Transfer: An Assessment of the Literature.* Washington, D.C.: Pharmaceutical Manufacturers Association, 1984.

Mullen, P. D., Green, L. W., & Persinger, G. Clinical trials of patient education for chronic conditions: A comparative meta-analysis. *Preventive Medicine* 15:in press, 1986.

Mullen, P. D., & Iverson, D. C. Qualitative methods for evaluative research in health education programs. *Journal of Health Education* 13(3):11–18, May–June 1982.

Mullen, P. D., Ottoson, J., & Williams, T. R. *Guidelines for Health Promotion and Disease Prevention Services in Reproductive Health Care Settings.* Rockville, Md.: U.S. Department of Health and Human Services, Public Health Service, Bureau of Community Health Services, Office of Health Information, Health Promotion and Physical Fitness and Sports Medicine, 1981.

Mullen, P. D., & Reynolds, R. The potential of grounded theory for health education research. *Health Education Monographs* 6:280–294, Fall 1978.

Mullen, P. D., & Zapka, J. G. Health education and promotion in HMOs: The recent evidence. *Health Education Quarterly* 8(4):292–315, Winter 1981.

Mullen P. D., & Zapka, J. G. *Guidelines for Health Promotion and Education Services in HMOs.* Washington, D.C.: U.S. Goverment Printing Office, Department of Health and Human Services, 1982.

Mumford, E., Schlesinger, H. J., & Glass, G. V. The effects of psychological intervention on recovery from surgery and heart attacks: An analysis of the literature. *American Journal of Public Health* 72(2):141–151, 1982.

Murphy, R. F. An attitude scale for dental health. *Journal of School Health* 40(5):268–270, May 1970.

Mustard, H. S. *Government in Public Health.* New York: Commonwealth Fund, 1945.

National Center for Health Services Research. *Experiments in Interviewing Techniques: Field Experiments in Health Reporting, 1971–1977.* DHEW Pub. No. (HRA) 78-3204. Washington, D.C.: Public Health Service, 1977.

National Center for Health Statistics. *Basic Data from Wave I of the National Survey of Personal Health Practices and Consequences: United States, 1979.* Series 15, No. 2, DHHS Pub. No. 81-1163. Washington, D.C.: U.S. Government Printing Office, 1981a.

National Center for Health Statistics. *User's Manual: The National Death Index.*

DHHS Pub. No. (PHS) 81-1148. Washington, D.C.: U.S. Government Printing Office, 1981b.

National Commission on Excellence in Education. *A Nation at Risk: The Imperative for Educational Reform.* Washington, D.C.: U.S. Government Printing Office, 1983.

National Heart, Lung and Blood Institute and Dynamic Corporation. *Evaluation of Health Hazard Appraisal Strategies in Industrial Cardiovascular Risk Factor Reduction Programs.* Springfield, Va.: National Technical Information Service, 1982.

Nehemkis, A., Macari, M. A., & Lettieri, D. L. (Eds.). *Drug-Abuse Instrument Handbook.* Washington, D.C.: U.S. Government Printing Office, 1976.

Neill, J. S., & Bond, J. O. *Hillsborough County Oral Polio Vaccine Program.* Florida State Board of Health Monograph No. 6. Jacksonville: Florida State Board of Health, 1964.

Neufeld, V. R. Patient education: A critique. In D. L. Sackett & R. B. Haynes (Eds.), *Compliance with Therapeutic Regimens.* Baltimore: Johns Hopkins University Press, 1976.

New, P. K., & Hessler, R. M. Community researchers meet community residents: Interpretation of findings. *Human Organization* 32(3):243–255, Fall 1973.

Nie, N. H., Hull, C. H., Jenkins, J. G., Steinbrenner, K., & Bent, D. H. *Statistical Package for the Social Sciences* (2nd ed.). New York: McGraw-Hill, 1975.

Nunnally, J. C. *Psychometric Theory.* New York: McGraw-Hill, 1967.

Nursing Development Conference Group. *Concept Formalization in Nursing: Process and Product.* Boston: Little, Brown, 1973.

Oettenger, A. G. *Run, Computer, Run: The Mythology of Education Innovation.* Cambridge, Mass.: Harvard University Press, 1969.

Oettenger, A. G., & Zapol, N. Will information technologies help learning? *Teachers College Record* 74:5–54, September 1972.

Office of the Assistant Secretary for Health. *Forward Plan for Health, 1978–1982.* Washington, D.C.: U.S. Government Printing Office, 1976.

Olsen, L. K. An evaluation instrument for appraising health-related attitudes of college students. *Journal of School Health* 42:408–411, September 1972.

Olsen, L., Redican, K., & Kruz, P. The School Health Curriculum Project: A review of research studies. *Health Education* 116:16–21, 1980.

Oman, R. C., & Chitwood, S. R. Factors affecting the acceptance of recommendations. *Evaluation Review* 8:283–305, 1984.

Oppenheim, A. N. *Questionnaire Design and Attitude Measurement.* New York: Basic Books, 1966.

Orem, D. E. *Nursing Concepts of Practice.* New York: McGraw-Hill, 1971.

Osgood, C. E., Suci, G. J., & Tannenbaum, P. H. *The Measurement of Meaning.* Urbana: University of Illinois Press, 1967.

Ottoson, J. M. Evaluation of continuing education for nurses: A literature review. Unpublished paper, Harvard Graduate School of Education, May 1981.

Padilla, G. P., Baker, R. E., & Dolan, V. A. *Interacting with Dying Patients: An Inter-hospital Nursing Research and Nursing Education Project.* Duarte, Calif.: City of Hope Medical Center, 1975.

Parcel, G., & Nader, P. Evaluation of a pilot school health education program for asthmatic children. *Journal of School Health* 47(8):453–456, 1977.

Parkinson, R. S., Green, L. W., McGill, A. M., Eriksen, M., Pearson, C. E., Merwin, D., Ware, B. G., Collings, G. H., & Beck, R. N. *Managing Health Promotion in the Workplace: Guidelines for Implementation and Evaluation.* Palo Alto, Calif.: Mayfield, 1982.

Parlett, M., & Hamilton, D. Evaluation as illumination: A new approach to the study of innovative program. In G. V. Glass (Ed.), *Evaluation Studies: Review Annual* (Vol. 1). Beverly Hills, Calif.: Sage, 1976.

Patton, M. Q. *Utilization-Focused Evaluation.* Beverly Hills, Calif.: Sage, 1978.

Patton, M. Q. *Qualitative Evaluation Methods.* Beverly Hills, Calif.: Sage, 1980.

Payne, S. *The Art of Asking Questions.* Princeton, N.J.: Princeton University Press, 1951.

Perry, S. Special report: The brief life of the National Center for Health Care Technology. *New England Journal of Medicine* 307:1095–1100, 1982.

Pfeiffer, J. W., Heslin, R., & Jones, J. E. (Eds.). *Instrumentation in Human Relations Training: A Guide to 92 Instruments with Wide Application to the Behavioral Sciences* (2nd ed.). La Jolla, Calif.: University Associates, 1976.

Phillips, D. L. *Knowledge from What?* Chicago: Rand McNally, 1971.

Phillips, J. F., Silayan-Go, A., & Pal-Montano, A. An experiment with payment, quota, and clinic affiliation schemes for lay motivators in the Philippines. *Studies in Family Planning* 6(9):326–334, September 1975.

Pigg, R. M., Jr. Recent developments in the evaluation of school health education. *Health Education* 14(4):29–35, 1983.

Pinckeny, C., & Pinckeny, E. R. *The Encyclopedia of Medical Tests.* New York: Facts on File Publications, 1982.

Podell, R. N. *Physicians' Guide to Compliance in Hypertension.* Rahway, N.J.: Merck, 1975.

Polit, D. F., & Hungler, B. P. *Nursing Research Methods: Principles and Methods.* Philadelphia: Lippincott, 1978.

Popham, W. J. *Educational Evaluation.* Englewood Cliffs, N.J.: Prentice-Hall, 1975.

Popham, W. J. (Ed.). *Criterion-Referenced Measurement.* Englewood Cliffs, N.J.: Prentice-Hall, 1978.

Popham, W. J. *Modern Educational Measurement.* Englewood Cliffs, N.J.: Prentice-Hall, 1981.

Popham, W. J. Appropriate measuring instruments for health education investigations. *Health Education* 13(3):23–26, May–June 1982.

Population Council. *Selected Questionnaires on Knowledge, Attitudes and Practices of Family Planning.* New York: Population Council, 1967.

Posavac, E. J. Evaluations of patient education programs: A metaanalysis. *Evaluation and the Health Professions* 3:47–62, 1980.

Postgraduate Preparation of Health Workers in Health Education. Technical Report Series No. 278. Geneva, Switzerland: World Health Organization, 1964.

Poti, S. J., Chakraborti, B., & Malaker, C. R. Reliability of data relating to contraceptive practices. In C. V. Kiser (Ed.), *Research in Family Planning.* Princeton, N.J.: Princeton University Press, 1962.

Potterat, J. J., & Rothenberg, R. The case-finding effectiveness of a self-referral system for gonorrhea: A preliminary report. *American Journal of Public Health* 67(2):174–179, February 1977.

Preventive Medicine U.S.A.—Health Promotion and Consumer Health Education. New York: Prodist, 1976.

Pritchard, M. J. Temporal reliability of a questionnaire measuring psychological response to illness. *Psychosomatic Research* 25:63–66, 1981.

Pritchett, S. *Patient, Family and Community Health Education: Design and*

Management of Hospital-Based Programs. Atlanta: Pritchett and Hull Associates, 1977.

Provus, M. Evaluation on ongoing programs in the public school system. In R. B. Worthen & J. R. Sanders (Eds.), *Educational Evaluation: Theory and Practice.* Belmont, Calif.: Wadsworth, 1973.

Psathas, G. *Phenomenological Sociology.* New York: Wiley, 1973.

Ratcliffe, J. W. Notions of validity in qualitative research methodology. Presented to the American Public Health Association Annual Meeting, Detroit, October 1980.

Ratcliffe, L. *Health Hazard Appraisal: Clues for a Healthier Lifestyle.* New York: Public Affairs Committee, 1978.

Redman, B. K. *The Process of Patient Teaching in Nursing* (3rd ed.). St. Louis: Mosby, 1976.

Reeder, L. G., Ramacher, L., & Gorelnik, S. *Handbook of Scales and Indices of Health Behavior.* Pacific Palisades, Calif.: Goodyear, 1976.

Reichardt, C. S., & Cook, T. D. Beyond qualitative *versus* quantitative methods. In T. D. Cook & C. S. Reichardt (Eds.), *Qualitative and Quantitative Methods in Evaluation Research.* Beverly Hills, Calif.: Sage, 1979.

Reiner, J. S., Reimer, E., & Reiner, T. A. Client analysis and the planning of public programs. *Journal of the American Institute of Planners* 29(4):270–282, 1963.

Research in Health Education: Report of a WHO Scientific Group. Technical Report Series No. 432. Geneva: World Health Organization, 1969.

Rezmovic, E. L., Cook, T. J., & Dobson, L. D. Beyond random assignment, factors affecting evaluation integrity. *Evaluation Review* 5:51–67, 1981.

Rhodes, R. L., Hafen, B. Q., Karren, K. J., & Rollins, L. M. *Elementary School Health: Education and Service.* Boston: Allyn & Bacon, 1981.

Richardson, G. F., & Kuder, M. The theory of the estimation of test reliability. *Psychometrika* 2:135–138, 1937.

Risser, N. L. Development of an instrument to measure patient satisfaction with nurses and nursing care in primary care settings. *Nursing Research* 24(1):45–52, January–February 1975.

Rist, R. D. On the relations among educational research paradigms: From disdain to detente. *Anthropology and Education Quarterly* 8:42–49, 1977.

Robbins, L. C., & Blankenbaker, R. Prospective medicine and the health hazard appraisal. In R. B. Taylor, J. R. Ureda, & J. W. Denham (Eds.), *Health Promotion: Principles and Clinical Applications.* Norwalk, Conn.: Appleton-Century-Crofts, 1982.

Roberts, B. J. Concepts and methods of evaluation in health education. *International Journal of Health Education* 5:1–11, 1962.

Roberts, B. J., & Green, L. W. *International Survey of Research and Studies in Health Education by Ministries of Health and Universities.* Background Paper for World Health Organization Study Group, Berkeley, Calif.: University of California School of Public Health, 1968.

Roberts, B. J., Mico, P. R., & Clark, E. W. An experimental study of two approaches to communication. *American Journal of Public Health* 53(9):1361–1381, September 1963.

Robertson, L. S. Crash involvement of teenaged drivers when driver education is eliminated from high school. *American Journal of Public Health* 70(6): 599–603, June 1980.

Robertson, L. S., Kelley, A. B., O'Neill, B., Wixom, C. W., Eiswirth, R. S., & Haddon, W., Jr. A controlled study of the effect of television messages on safety belt use. *American Journal of Public Health* 64:1071–1080, November 1974.

Robertson, L. S., & Zador, P. L. Driver education and fatal crash involvement of teenaged drivers. *American Journal of Public Health* 68(10):959–965, 1978.

Robinson, E. A comparative evaluation of the scrub and bass methods of tooth-brushing with flossing as an adjunct (in fifth and sixth graders). *American Journal of Public Health* 66(11):1078–1081, November 1976.

Robinson, J. P., Athanasiou, R., & Head, K. B. *Measures of Occupational Attitudes and Occupational Characteristics.* Ann Arbor: University of Michigan Survey Research Center, Institute for Social Research, 1969.

Robinson, J. P., & Shaver, P. R. *Measures of Social Psychological Attitudes* (rev. ed.). Ann Arbor: University of Michigan Survey Research Center, Institute for Social Research, 1973.

Romano, R. M. *Making PSAs Work: A Handbook for Health Communication Professionals.* National Institute of Health, Pub. No. 83-2485. Bethesda, Md.: National Cancer Institute, 1983.

Romney, A. K., Shepard, R. N., & Nerlove, S. B. *Multidimensional Scaling.* New York: Seminar Press, 1972.

Roos, N. P. Evaluating health programs: Where do we find the data? *Journal of Community Health* 1(1):39–51, Fall 1975.

Rose, G. A., Blackburn, H., Gillum, R. F., & Prineas, R. J. *Cardiovascular Survey Methods* (2nd ed.). Geneva: World Health Organization, 1982.

Rosenberg, S. G. Patient education leads to better care for heart patients. *HSMHA Reports* 86:793–802, September 1971.

Rosenblatt, D., & Kabasakalian, L. Evaluation of a venereal disease information campaign for adolescents. *American Journal of Public Health* 56:1104–1114, July 1966.

Rosenstock, I. M. Gaps and potentials in health education research. *Health Education Monographs* 1(8):21–27, 1960.

Rosnow, R. L., & Suls, J. M. Reactive effects of pretesting in attitude research. *Journal of Personality and Social Psychology* 15:338–343, 1970.

Ross, H. S. Redefining the future of health education. *Health Education* 7(4):5–6, 1976.

Ross, H. S., & Mico, P. R. *Theory and Practice in Health Education.* Palo Alto, Calif.: Mayfield, 1980.

Rossi, P. H., & Berk, R. A. An overview of evaluation strategies and procedures. *Human Organization* 40:287–299, 1981.

Rossi, P. H., & Freeman, H. E. (Eds.). *Evaluation: A Systematic Approach.* Beverly Hills, Calif.: Sage, 1982.

Roter, D. L. Patient participation in the patient-provider interaction: The effects of patient question asking on the quality of interaction, satisfaction and compliance. *Health Education Monographs* 5:281–315, Winter 1977.

Rotter, J. B. *Social Learning and Clinical Psychology.* Englewood Cliffs, N.J.: Prentice-Hall, 1954.

Rotter, J. B. Generalized expectancies for internal versus external control of reinforcement. *Psychological Monographs* 80 (Whole No. 609):1–28, 1966.

Rotter, J. B. Some problems and misconceptions related to the construct of internal versus external control of reinforcement. *Journal of Consulting and Clinical Psychology* 43(1):56–67, 1975.

Rubin, D. B. Estimating causal effects of treatments in randomized and nonrandomized studies. *Journal of Educational Psychology* 66(5):668–701, 1974.
Rutman, L. (Ed.). *Evaluation Research Methods: A Basic Guide.* Beverly Hills, Calif.: Sage, 1977a.
Rutman, L. Planning an evaluation study. In L. Rutman (Ed.), *Evaluation Research Methods: A Basic Guide.* Beverly Hills, Calif.: Sage, 1977b.
Safter, M. A. An evaluation of the health hazard appraisal based on survey data from a randomly selected population. *Public Health Reports* 97:31–37, January–February 1982.
Schaps, E., DiBartolo, R., Moskowitz, J., Polly, C., & Churgin, S. A review of 127 drug abuse prevention program evaluations. *Journal of Drug Issues* 11(1): 17–43, 1981.
Schatzman, L., & Strauss, A. L. *Field Research: Strategies for a Natural Sociology.* Englewood Cliffs, N.J.: Prentice-Hall, 1973.
Schecter, C., Stunkard, A. J., & Stolley, P. The Pennsylvania County Health Improvement Program. *Pennsylvania Medicine* 85:18–20, 1982.
Schlesinger, E. R. A controlled study of health education in accident prevention. *American Journal of Diseased Children* 111:490–496, May 1966.
Schulberg, H. C., & Baker, F. Program evaluation models and the implementation of research findings. *American Journal of Public Health* 58(7):1248–1255, July 1968.
Schutz, A. *Collected Papers, I: The Problem of Social Reality.* The Hague: Martinus-Nijhoff, 1973.
Schuurman, J., & de Haes, W. Sexually transmitted diseases: Health education by telephone. *International Journal of Health Education* 23:94–106, 1980.
Scriven, M. *Pros and Cons About Goal-Free Evaluation: Evaluation Comment.* Los Angeles: University of California, Los Angeles, Center for the Study of Evaluation, 3(4):1–5, 1972.
Seeman, M., & Seeman, T. E. Health behavior and personal autonomy: A longitudinal study of the sense of control in illness. *Journal of Health and Social Behavior* 24:144–160, 1983.
Seffrin, J. R., & Veenker, C. H. A standardized achievement test of health education objectives in the cognitive domain. *Journal of School Health* 42(1): 43–47, January 1972.
Selltiz, C., Wrightsman, L. S., & Cook, S. W. *Research Methods in Social Relations* (3rd ed.). New York: Holt, Rinehart & Winston, 1976.
Shapiro, A. K., & Shapiro, E. Patient-provider relationships and the placebo effect. In J. D. Matarazzo, S. M. Weiss, J. A. Herd, N. E. Miller, & S. M. Weiss (Eds.), *Behavioral Health: A Handbook of Health Enhancement and Disease Prevention.* New York: Wiley, 1984.
Shortell, S. M., & Richardson, W. C. *Health Program Evaluation.* St. Louis: Mosby, 1978.
Siegel, S. *Non-Parametric Statistics for the Behavioral Sciences.* New York: McGraw-Hill, 1956.
Sills, J. F. Preparing the entry level community health educator. *Health Education* 7(4):7–9, 1976.
Simmons, J. J. Lessons for health educators. (Editorial). *American Journal of Public Health* 67:1137–1138, December 1977.
Simon, A., & Boyer, E. G. (Eds.). *Mirrors for Behavior III: An Anthology of Observation Instruments.* Wyncote, Pa.: Communication Materials Center, 1974.
Skipper, J. K., & Leonard, R. Children, stress and hospitalization: A field experi-

ment. *Journal of Health and Social Behavior* 9:275–287, December 1968.

Smith, H. W. Sampling: The search for typicality. In *Strategies of Social Research.* Englewood Cliffs, N.J.: Prentice-Hall, 1975.

Smith, M. B. Motivation, communications research and family planning. In M. C. Sheps & J. C. Ridley (Eds.), *Public Health and Population Change: Current Research Issues.* Pittsburgh: University of Pittsburgh Press, 1965.

Snow, M., & Thurber, S. Factorial validity of the health locus of control (HLC) scale. *Educational and Psychological Measurement* 43(3):893–895, 1983.

Society for Prospective Medicine. *Guidelines for Health Risk Appraisal/Risk Reduction Systems.* Bethesda, Md.: Society of Prospective Medicine, 1981.

Society for Public Health Education, Ad Hoc Task Force. Guidelines for the preparation and practice of professional health educators. *Health Education Monographs* 5:75–89, Spring 1977.

Society for Public Health Education, Committee on Professional Preparation and Practice. Criteria and guidelines for baccalaureate programs in community health education. *Health Education Monographs* 5:90–98, Spring 1977.

Solleder, M. K. *Evaluation Instruments in Health Education* (4th ed.). Washington, D.C.: American Alliance for Health, Physical Education, Recreation and Dance, 1979.

Solomon, R. L. An extension of control group design. *Psychological Bulletin* 46:137–150, 1949.

Sorochan, W. D. *Personal Health Appraisal.* New York: Wiley, 1976.

Specter, G. An evaluation of the effect of health education methods on prenatal clinic attendance. *International Journal of Health Education* 9(4):183–187, October–December 1966.

Spirduso, W. Exercise and the aging brain. *Research Quarterly for Exercise and Sport* 54:208–218, 1983.

Spolsky, V. W., Kamberg, C. J., Lohr, K. N., & Feldman, B. G. *Measurement of Dental Health Status.* R-2902-HHS. Santa Monica, Calif.: Rand Corporation, 1983.

Spradley, J. P. *Participant Observation.* New York: Holt, Rinehart & Winston, 1980.

Squyres, W. The professional health educator in HMOs: Implications for training and our future in medical care. *Health Education Quarterly* 9(1):67–80, 1982.

Stahl, S. M., Lawrie, T., Neill, P., & Kelley, C. Motivational interventions in community hypertension screening. *American Journal of Public Health* 67:345–352, April 1977.

Stake, R. E. The countenance of educational evaluation. In B. R. Worthen & J. R. Sanders (Eds.), *Educational Evaluation: Theory and Practice.* Belmont, Calif.: Jones, 1973.

Stallones, R. A. To advance epidemiology. *Annual Review of Public Health* 1:69–82, 1980.

Steckler, A., Dawson, L., Dellinger, N., & Williams, A. Consumer participation and influence in a health systems agency. *Journal of Community Health* 6:181–193, Spring 1981.

Steckler, A., Dawson, L., & Herndon, S. Analysis of health education sections of health system plans. *Health Education Quarterly* 7(3):186–202, Fall 1980.

Steinberg, S., & Fitzpatrick, D. The Paducah Health Education Survey, 1958. *American Journal of Public Health* 51:732–745, 1961.

Steuart, G. W. Scientist and professional: The relations between research and action. *Health Education Monographs* 1(29):1–10, 1969.

Stine, O. C., Pacanowski, J. P., Roffman, R.V., & Heald, F. P. Two health questionnaires for adolescents. *Journal of School Health* 44:136–139, March 1974.

Stone, E. (Ed.). Proceedings of the National Conference on School Health Education Research in the Heart, Lung, and Blood Areas. Bethesda, Md.: National Institutes of Health, 1983.

Stufflebeam, D. L. An introduction to the PDK book: Educational evaluation and decision-making. In B. R. Worthen & J. R. Sanders (Eds.), *Educational Evaluation: Theory and Practice.* Belmont, Calif.: Jones, 1973.

Suchman, E. A. *Evaluation Research: Principles and Practice in Public Service and Social Action Programs.* New York: Russell Sage Foundation, 1967.

Sudman, S. *Applied Sampling.* New York: Academic Press, 1976.

Summers, G. F. (Ed). *Attitude Measurement.* Chicago: Rand McNally, 1979.

Texas Department of Health. *Proceedings of the Texas Conference on Disease Prevention and Health Promotion: 1990 Objectives.* Austin: Texas Department of Health, 1984.

Thomas, P. D., & Hooper, E. M. Healthy elderly: Social bonds and locus of control. *Research in Nursing and Health* 6(1):11–16, March 1983.

Thompson, E. L. Smoking education programs, 1960–1976. *American Journal of Public Health* 68:250–257, March 1978.

Thompson, J. D. On reasonable costs of hospital services. In J. B. McKinlay (Ed.), *Economic Aspects of Medical Care.* New York: Prodist, 1973.

Tonon, M. A. Concepts of community participation: A case of sanitary change in a Guatemalan village. *International Journal of Health Education* 23(Suppl. 4): 1–15, October–December 1980.

United Nations. *Foetal, Infant, and Early Childhood Mortality.* Population Studies No. 13. New York: Department of Social Affairs, Population Division, 1954.

U.S. Department of Health, Education, and Welfare. Office of the Assistant Secretary for Health. *Disease Prevention and Health Promotion: Federal Programs and Prospects.* DHEW (PHS) Pub. No. 79-55071B. Stock Number 017-001-00418-9. Washington, D.C.: U.S. Government Printing Office, 1978.

U.S. Department of Health, Education, and Welfare. Office of the Assistant Secretary for Health. *Healthy People: The Surgeon General's Report on Health Promotion and Disease Prevention.* Stock Number 017-001-00416-2. Washington, D.C.: U.S. Government Printing Office, July 1979.

U.S. Department of Health and Human Services. Office of the Assistant Secretary for Health. *Promoting Health, Preventing Disease: Objectives for the Nation.* Stock Number 017-001-00435-9. Washington, D.C.: U.S. Government Printing Office, Fall 1980.

U.S. Department of Health and Human Services. *Basic Data from Wave I of the National Survey of Personal Health Practices and Consequences: United States, 1979.* DHHS (PHS) Pub. No. 81-1163. Washington, D.C.: National Center for Health Statistics, 1981a.

U.S. Department of Health and Human Services. Office of the Assistant Secretary for Health. *Strategies for Promoting Health for Specific Populations.* DHHS (PHS) Pub. No. 81-50169. Washington, D.C.: U.S. Government Printing Office, 1981b.

U.S. Department of Health and Human Services. *Health Risk Appraisals: An Inventory.* Washington, D.C.: Office of Disease Prevention and Health Promotion, 1981c.

Ureda, J. R. Effect of contract witnessing on motivation and weight loss in a weight control program. *Health Education Quarterly* 7(3):163–185, Fall 1980.

Vickery, D. M. *Life Plan for Your Health.* Reading, Mass.: Addison-Wesley, 1979.

Wagner, E. H. An assessment of health hazard/health risk appraisal. *American Journal of Public Health* 72:347–352, April 1982.

Wallack, L. M. Mass media campaigns: The odds against finding behavior change. *Health Education Quarterly* 8:209–260, Fall 1981.
Wallston, B. S., & Wallston, K. A. Locus of control and health: A review of the literature. *Health Education Monographs* 6(2):107–117, Spring 1978.
Wallston, K. A., Wallston, B. S., & DeVellis, R. Development of the multi-dimensional health locus of control (MHLC) scales. *Health Education Monographs* 6(2):160–170, Spring 1978.
Wallston, B. S., Wallston, K. A., Kaplan, G. D., & Maides, S. A. Development and validation of the health locus of control (HLC) scale. *Journal of Consulting and Clinical Psychology* 44:580–585, August 1976.
Waltz, C., & Bausell, R. B. *Nursing Research: Design, Statistics and Computer Analysis.* Philadelphia: Davis, 1981.
Wang, V. L., Ephross, P., & Green, L. W. The point of diminishing returns in nutrition education through home visits by aides: An evaluation of EFNEP. *Health Education Monographs* 3(1):70–88, 1975.
Wang, V. L., Terry, P., Flynn, B. S., Williamson, J., Green, L., & Faden, R. Multiple indicators of continuing medical education priorities for chronic lung diseases in Appalachia. *Journal of Medical Education,* 54:803–811, October 1979.
Ward, G. H. Changing trends in control of hypertension. *Public Health Reports* 93(1):31–34, 1978.
Ware, J. E., Brook, R. H., Davies-Avery, A., Williams, K. N., & Stewart, A. L. *Conceptualization and Measurement of Health for Adults in the Health Insurance Study.* Vol. 1: *Model of Health.* R-1987/1-HEW. Santa Monica, Calif.: Rand Corporation, 1980.
Ware, J. E., Davies-Avery, A., & Donald, C. A. *Conceptualization and Measurement of Health for Adults in the Health Insurance Study.* Vol. 5: *General Health Perceptions.* R-1987/5-HEW. Santa Monica, Calif.: Rand Corporation, 1978.
Ware, J. E., Johnston, S. A., Davies-Avery, A., & Brook, R. H. *Conceptualization and Measurement of Health for Adults in the Health Insurance Study.* Vol. 3: *Mental Health.* R-1987/3-HEW. Santa Monica, Calif.: Rand Corporation, 1979.
Ware, J. E., Jr., Wright, W. R., & Snyder, M. K. *Development and Validation of Scales to Measure Patient Satisfaction.* Prepared for the National Center for Health Services Research, U.S. Department of Health, Education, and Welfare. Carbondale: Department of Health Care Planning, Southern Illinois University, 1976.
Ware, J. E., Jr., Wright, W. R., Snyder, M. K., & Chu, G. C. Consumer perception of health care services: Implications for academic medicine. *Journal of Medical Education* 50(11):839–848, 1975.
Warheit, G. J., Bell, R. A., & Schwab, J. J. *Needs Assessment Approaches: Concepts and Methods.* Superintendent of Documents, No. 017-024-00705-6. Washington, D.C.: U.S. Government Printing Office, 1977.
Webb, E. J., Campbell, D. T., Schwartz, R. D., Sechrist, L., & Grove, J. B. *Nonreactive Measures in the Social Sciences* (2nd ed.). Chicago: Rand McNally, 1981.
Weber, M. The meaning of "ethical neutrality" in sociology and economics. In E. A. Shils & H. A. Finch (Eds. and Translators), *The Methodology of the Social Sciences.* New York: Free Press, 1949.
Weber, M. Objectivity in social science. In E. A. Shils & H. A. Finch (Eds. and Translators), *The Methodology of the Social Sciences.* New York: Free Press,

1949. Reprinted in M. Brodbeck (Ed.), *Readings in the Philosophy of the Social Sciences.* London: Macmillan, 1982. Originally published 1949.

Weinstein, M.C., & Stasson, W. B. (Eds.). *Hypertension: A Policy Perspective.* Cambridge, Mass.: Harvard University Press, 1976.

Weise, F. O. *Health Statistics: A Guide to Information Sources.* Detroit: Gale Research Company, 1980.

Weiss, C. H. *Evaluation Research: Methods for Assessing Program Effectiveness.* Englewood Cliffs, N.J.: Prentice-Hall, 1972.

Weiss, R. S., & Rein, M. The evaluation of broad-aim programs: Difficulties in experimental design and an alternative. In C. H. Weiss (Ed.), *Evaluating Action Programs: Readings in Social Action and Education.* Boston: Allyn & Bacon, 1972.

Westoff, C. F., Potter, R. G., & Sagi, P. C. Some estimates of the reliability of survey data on family planning. *Population Studies* 15:52–69, July 1961.

Wholey, J. S. Evaluability assessment. In L. Rutman (Ed.), *Evaluation Research Methods: A Basic Guide,* pp. 41–56. Beverly Hills, Calif.: Sage, 1977.

Wilkinson, G. S., Mirand, E. A., & Graham, S. Measuring response to a cancer information telephone facility: Can-Dial. *American Journal of Public Health* 66(4):367–371, April 1976.

Wilkinson, G. S., Mirand, E. A., & Graham, S. Cancer information by telephone: A two-year evaluation. *Health Education Monographs* 5(3):251–263, 1977.

Williamson, J. W., Aronovich, S., & Simonson, L. Health accounting: An outcome-based system of quality assurance. *Bulletin New York Academy of Medicine* 51:727, 1975.

Wilner, S., Winickoff, R. N., Schoenbaun, S. C., & Coltin, K. L. The role of patient interventions in ambulatory quality assurance programs. *Health Education Quarterly* 9(1):42–54, 1982.

Wilson, H. S. *Deinstitutionalized Residential Care for the Mentally Disordered. The Soteria House Approach.* New York: Grune & Stratton, 1982.

Wilson, R. W., & Elinson, J. National Survey of Personal Health Practices and Consequences: Background, conceptual issues and selected findings. *Public Health Reports* 96:218–225, 1981.

Wilson, R. W., & Iverson, D. C. Federal data bases for health education research. *Health Education* 13(3):30–34, 1982.

Windsor, R. A., Baranowski, T., Clark, N., & Cutter, G., *Evaluation of Health Promotion and Education Programs.* Palo Alto, Calif.: Mayfield, 1984.

Windsor, R. A., Kronenfeld, J. J., Ory, M. G., & Kilgo, J. S. Method and design issues in evaluation of community health education programs: A case study in breast and cervical cancer. *Health Education Quarterly* 7(3):203–218, Fall 1980.

Winer, B. J. *Statistical Principles in Experimental Design.* New York: McGraw-Hill, 1971.

Wolle, J. Activities of the APHA Advisory Committee on Community Health Education Accreditation. *Health Education Monographs* 4:276–277, Fall 1976.

World Health Organization. *Expert Committee on Health Education of the Public.* First Report. Technical Report Series, No. 89. Geneva: World Health Organization, 1954.

World Health Organization. *Expert Committee on Training Health Personnel in Health Education of the Public: Report.* Technical Report Series, No. 156. Geneva: World Health Organization, 1958.

World Health Organization. *PAHO/WHO Inter-Regional Conference on the Postgraduate Preparation of Health Workers for Health Education.* Technical Report Series, No. 278. Geneva: World Health Organization, 1962.

World Health Organization. *Planning and Evaluation of Health Education Services.* Technical Report Series, No. 409. Geneva: World Health Organization, 1969a.

World Health Organization. *Research in Health Education.* Technical Report Series, No. 432. Geneva: World Health Organization, 1969b.

World Health Organization. *Handbook of Resolutions and Decisions of the World Health Assembly and the Executive Board* (Vol. 2. 5th ed.). Geneva: World Health Organization, 1983.

Wright, S. Path coefficients and path regressions: Alternative or complementary concepts? *Biometrics* 16(2):189–202, June 1960.

Yaukey, D. *Fertility in a Modernizing Country: A Survey of Lebanese Couples.* Princeton, N.J.: Princeton University Press, 1961.

Yaukey, D. W., Roberts, B. J., & Griffiths, W. Husbands' vs. wives' responses to a fertility survey. *Population Studies* 19:29–43, July 1965.

Yin, R. K. *Case Study Research.* Beverly Hills, Calif.: Sage, 1984.

Young, M. A. C. Review of research and studies related to health education. *Health Education Monographs* Nos. 23–25, 1967a.

Young, M. A. C. Review of research and studies related to health education practice (1961–66). *Health Education Monographs* Nos. 23–38, 1967b.

Young, M. A. C. Review of research and studies related to health education aspects of family planning (1967–1971). *Health Education Monographs* Nos. 33–35, 1973.

Young, M. A. C., Buckley, P. H., Wechsler, H., & Demone, H. W. A demonstration of automated instructions for diabetic self care. *American Journal of Public Health* 59:110–122, January 1969.

Zander, K., Bower, K. A., Foster, S. D., Towson, M. D., Wermuth, M. R., & Waldum, K. M. *Practical Manual for Patient Teaching.* St. Louis: Mosby, 1978.

Zapka, J. G., & Averill, B. W. Self-care for colds: A cost-effective alternative to upper respiratory infection management. *American Journal of Public Health* 69(8):814–816, August 1979.

Zapka, J. G., & Dorfman, S. L. Consumer participation: Case study of the college health setting. *Journal of the American College Health Association* 30:197–203, February 1982.

Zapka, J. G., & Estabrook, B. Self-care programs in medical settings. *Health Services Management Review* 1:75–81, 1976.

Zapka, J. G., & Mamon, J. A. Integration of theory, practitioner standards, literature findings, and baseline data: A case study in planning breast self-examination education. *Health Education Quarterly* 9:330–356, Winter 1982.

Index

CREDITS (continued from the copyright page)

Green and N. P. Gordon, Productive research and sampling methods, *Health Education* 13(3):4–10, May–June 1982, with permission of the Association for the Advancement of Health Education.

Chapter 11 is adapted from L. W. Green and F. M. Lewis, Issues in relating evaluation to theory, policy, and practice in continuing education and health education, *Mobius* 1:46–58, April 1981, with permission of *Mobius*, Institute for Health Policy Studies, University of California Medical School, San Francisco.

Various sections of other chapters are adapted from articles by Green and Lewis in *Health Education Monographs* and *Health Education Quarterly*, some reprinted in the *Heritage Collection of Health Education Monographs*. Permission to use these copyrighted materials has been kindly granted by the Society for Public Health Education, Inc., and Third Party Publishing Company.

Additional credits appear within the text.